'A GUID CAUSE

THE WOMEN'S SUFFRAGE MOVEMENT IN SCOTLAND

Scottish Women's Studies Series

BAJANELLAS AND SEMILINAS
Aberdeen University and the Education of Women 1860–1920
Lindy Moore

KATHARINE ATHOLL 1874–1960
S J Hetherington

STRATEGIC WOMEN
how do they manage in Scotland?
E Gerver and L Hart

UPSTAIRS TO DOWNSTAIRS
Advice to Servant Girls and Weary Mothers
edited by J Drummond

MARRIAGE & PROPERTY
edited by Elizabeth M Craik

SCOTTISH WOMEN'S · STUDIES SERIES

A Guid Cause

— The Women's — Suffrage Movement — in Scotland —

Leah Leneman

ABERDEEN UNIVERSITY PRESS

First Published 1991
Aberdeen University Press

© Leah Leneman 1991

British Library Cataloguing in Publication Data

A catalogue record for this book is available from the British Library

ISBN 0 08 041201 7

Typeset by MS Filmsetting Ltd
Printed by Athenaeum Press Ltd

'A guid cause maks a strong arm'

Old Scots proverb used on suffrage banners

Contents

List of Illustrations and Tables

Acknowledgements

One of the most rewarding aspects of this study has been the tremendous help and encouragement I have received from so many people, of whom I can name only a few.

The ESRC generously funded the research which made this book possible.

David Rubinstein, Christopher Smout, Rosalind Mitchison, and Graham Sutton read earlier drafts of all the chapters; their suggestions and comments have made this a much better book than it would otherwise have been.

The staff of the Scottish Record Office and National Library in Edinburgh, and of Strathclyde Regional Archives, the Department of Rare Books and Manuscripts, and Glasgow Room, Mitchell Library, Glasgow were unfailingly helpful. Ishbel Barnes, at the SRO, provided the initial inspiration for the book.

At the Fawcett Library, mecca for anyone working on women's history, David Doughan and Susan Cross provided expert knowledge and great kindness. Christine Rew of Aberdeen Art Gallery and Museum, Maureen Lochrie of Paisley Museum, and Nichola Johnston of the London Museum also gave time and help. Brian Smith of Shetland Archive sent me information I could not otherwise have acquired.

The memories of those who so kindly contacted me in response to my appeals in Scottish newspapers (named in text and footnotes) helped to bring the story to life.

Elspeth King, depute keeper of local history at the People's Palace in Glasgow deserves acknowledgement as pioneer in the study of the women's suffrage movement in Scotland although she cannot be blamed for anything that appears in this book as she would not agree to meet me.

Introduction

Why Study the Women's Suffrage Movement in Scotland?

The women's suffrage movement is one of those subjects which are considered to have been practically exhausted but which in fact are nothing of the kind. So far the story of the fight for the vote in Britain has been told almost exclusively from the point of view of the metropolitan leadership. Of course the struggle for the vote was a parliamentary one, so the headquarters of the campaigning organisations were all in London, but this emphasis ignores an important dimension of the subject. Women were active the length and breadth of the British Isles, and without the commitment of women far from London the movement would never have achieved the impact it did.

Read any book about the early women's movement in Britain and the names which crop up are all English (e.g. Mary Wollstonecroft, William Thompson and Anna Wheeler, Barbara Bodichon). The fact that one of the first three women's suffrage societies formed in 1867 was in Edinburgh may be generally known, but as the president of that society was the sister of Jacob Bright, the assumption is likely to be that the impetus came from England. Emily Davies and the struggle for women's higher education in England has received attention; the parallel, but totally separate, struggle to open Scottish universities to women has hardly been touched on. The reality – as will be seen – is that there existed a strong base of crusading zeal for women's rights in nineteenth-century Scotland which has been forgotten.

When we come to the key years in the struggle for the vote – 1906 to 1914 – the distortion becomes even greater. In any modern book on the subject, if Scotland is mentioned at all, it is as part of the 'provinces', a mistake no one ever made at the beginning of the century, when the idea of Home Rule was in the air. The popular idea of suffragettes as women who chained themselves to railings envisages everything as having taken place in London, while scholarly books on the subject have largely concentrated on the struggle within Parliament or on the leaders of the movement who were based in London. Even the most cursory look at contemporary sources, whether suffrage journals or the Scottish press, reveals what a distorted picture of the movement this gives.

Scotland featured prominently in the suffrage campaign. The Prime Minister, Asquith, and prominent members of government like Richard Haldane and Winston Churchill held Scottish seats, as did some leading opposition MPs like Arthur Balfour. Scotland was the great stronghold of Liberalism in the United Kingdom, which meant that Scottish by-elections were particularly closely monitored by suffrage organisations.

Within each of the main suffrage societies (as well as the Anti-Suffrage League) some kind of autonomous federation was set up within Scotland, maintaining strong links with the central body but operating with a degree of independence. The relationship between these semi-autonomous bodies and organisational headquarters was never an easy one; on the contrary, the stresses and strains caused by distance and differing viewpoints are particularly interesting features of the story. An additional dimension is provided by the existence of suffrage societies in Orkney and Shetland, which were further from the centres of suffrage activity in Scotland than those centres were from London.

As will be seen, the leaders certainly did not ignore Scotland. Emmeline Pankhurst spoke regularly in the major Scottish cities and travelled as far north as Thurso and Wick while Charlotte Despard, president of the Women's Freedom League, and Millicent Fawcett, president of the National Union of Women's Suffrage Societies, also appeared frequently in Edinburgh and Glasgow and occasionally further north. The extent to which the movement in Scotland relied on leaders from England and the extent to which it developed its own leadership is fruitful matter for enquiry. An enormous amount has been written about the Pankhursts; to write about the Scottish women who devoted themselves to the struggle for the vote is, for the most part, to rescue them from oblivion.

The marches and pageants, as well as the open-air rallies, the window-smashing, attacks on government ministers, and arson, so extensively written about in connection with London and the south of England, were all features of the Scottish movement. Nor were they mere imitations: the women represented in the grand procession were Scottish historical figures, and 'Scots wha hae' was the rousing song of the militants. Scottish churches and town councils were also drawn into the struggle.

The Scottish movement was never separate from the national movement; Appendix 1 provides a calendar of events at national level to enable readers to see how Scottish activity fitted into the whole picture. But what happened at local level? A typical town – in England or Wales or Scotland

– might contain a branch of the militant Women's Social & Political Union, and a branch of the militant but non-violent Women's Freedom League, plus a non-militant society affiliated to the National Union of Women's Suffrage Societies, and perhaps a branch of the Anti-Suffrage League as well. Because so many authors have concentrated on only one of the suffrage organisations the relationship between them at local level, the ways in which members of one regarded the others, and the extent to which they moved from one to the other has never been investigated. Scotland may have been unique in its sense of identity, but if this account of the movement in Scotland were to encourage historians to examine the situation in Wales or in different English regions, then that alone would justify its existence.

Thus the story which follows illuminates an aspect of Scottish history which few know about while at the same time looking at the women's suffrage movement in Britain as a whole from a new angle.

Author's Note

To refer to a woman by her surname would be out of keeping with the period. Using her Christian name alone would be equally inappropriate. (The only exception is Christabel Pankhurst who was regularly referred to in that way by her followers.) The title 'Ms' had not yet been invented. Therefore, women in this book are referred to by their full names or as they were styled at the time.

Prologue

Before 1867

Votes for women could never have been an issue before 1832 because so few men possessed the parliamentary franchise. The Reform Act (Scotland) of that year enlarged the electorate from 4,500 to over 65,000, but the majority of men were still not eligible to vote.[1] The agitation surrounding the passing of the Acts forced many to think about the issues surrounding the parliamentary franchise, and women, too, became involved.

In 1833 the *Edinburgh Review* discussed two books written by women on political economy (one by a Mrs Marcet and the other by Harriet Martineau). The reviewer did not disapprove; indeed he felt that the science of political economy could be recommended to women 'from its intimate connexion with the protection and comfort of the poor.' However, for women to think of venturing further into politics was a different matter. In words which could as easily have appeared three-quarters of a century later he wrote

> The less women usually meddle with any thing which can be called public life out of their village, we are sure the better for all parties. A deep sympathy with the precarious situation of their poorer neighbours, and an active benevolence in relieving the distressed, and in encouraging the virtuous, furnish them with a circle wide enough.[2]

The movement which at this time most radically challenged traditional ideas of the relationship between men and women was Owenite socialism. The followers of Robert Owen believed that a complete restructuring of society was necessary, with equality of the sexes an essential component. In her fascinating book on feminism in that movement, *Eve and the New Jerusalem*, Barbara Taylor noted that two of the main centres of Owenite activity after 1834 were Glasgow and Edinburgh.[3] The subject of women

and Owenite socialism in Scotland deserves further study, but it did not
feed into the later movement for women's enfranchisement. Indeed, as
Barbara Taylor convincingly argues, it was only after the Owenite
movement died that the middle-class women who were to lead the
women's movement in the later nineteenth century could campaign
without being accused of attempting to subvert society.[4]

Another movement in which the question of women's place in politics
arose was Chartism. Only two historians – Dorothy Thompson and
David Jones – have examined the part which women played in that
movement, but neither attempted to distinguish Scotland from England.[5]
Conversely, the two historians who revealed the distinctiveness of
Scottish Chartism – Alexander Wilson and L.G. Wright – did not ask
where women fitted in. There are enough scattered references in both
their books to show that women were very active in the Scottish Chartist
movement[6], but a study focusing specifically on the female component is
badly needed.

Within the movement as a whole, some of the leaders believed that
women should be enfranchised while others did not, for there were
widespread fears that asking for women to have the vote would jeopardise
the chances of a wider male franchise. Interestingly, one of the only cases
which Dorothy Thompson found of a working woman demanding the
vote was addressed to the women of Scotland[7], but there is no reason to
suppose that most Scottish women who belonged to Chartist groups saw
their role any differently from their English counterparts, which was to
support their menfolk in what was seen essentially as a class issue.

In his book *Women and Popular Struggles*, James D. Young argues that
Scottish Chartists 'were unquestionably more sympathetic to the agitation
for women's suffrage than the English'.[8] He produces no evidence for this
assertion, and even a cursory look at Scottish journals contradicts it. On
the front page of an issue of the Chartist Circular (published in Glasgow),
there was a series of questions and answers for those new to Chartism.
One question was 'Do you mean by Universal Suffrage, that men,
women and children should vote?' 'No', was the emphatic reply, followed
by the explanation that Universal Male Suffrage was really the correct
term, for what was meant was that 'every man twenty-one years of age,
unconvicted of crime, and of sound mind, should have a vote in the
election of the Representatives who are to make the laws he is called upon
to obey, and who lay on the taxes he is required to pay.'[9]

The Edinburgh Chartist paper, the *True Scotsman*, went into a fuller
discussion of the reasons why men alone should have the vote, using an
argument which surfaces again and again in later decades.

> The fair sex will not, we trust, accuse us of treating them with the slightest
> disrespect, when we state it as our opinion, that nature has not, in general

bestowed upon them those mental and physical attributes which qualify for the discharge of political duties. In every age, nature has borne testimony that the 'weaker vessels' are not qualified to enter the arena of political strife – and that they are out of their proper element the moment they attempt to subjugate man to their sway by any other weapons that those of persuasion and the bright example of virtuous conduct.

The article concluded that 'women are bound to "comfort" and encourage their husbands, sons, and brothers, in the prosecution of their claims for the possession of civil rights. The women of Birmingham, and other large towns, have done so; and we would recommend their example to the wives, daughters, and sisters of the working classes generally.'[10]

Far from being offended by this, a fortnight later the Women of the Political Union of Dunfermline sent a message of support to the Women of the Political Union of Birmingham and a cry to others to stand firm as the wives and daughters of working men in their struggle against the propertied classes.[11] Given this attitude, it is not surprising that the Chartist movement in Scotland did not apparently feed into the women's movement of the 1860s onwards.[12] The same could not be said about the next movement to be considered: the anti-slavery campaign in Scotland.

In the 1830s the east of Scotland had the Edinburgh Ladies Emancipation Society while the west had the Glasgow Ladies Auxiliary Society. Although the women's societies were affiliated to the men's, and played a crucial part in raising funds for them, women did not participate in the men's gatherings, whether public or private (nor apparently think of doing so), though men did play an active part in the women's societies.[13] Before 1840 British anti-slavery societies were unaware of the bitter schisms which divided the movement in America. In that year the British and Foreign Anti-Slavery Society organised the World's Anti-Slavery Convention in London, an event which sparked off the women's movement in America. The radical section of the American movement, followers of Lloyd Garrison, had appointed women delegates to the conference as a deliberate challenge to the denial of public platforms to women. The British and Foreign Society allied itself with the American group opposing the admission of the American women to the floor of the convention, and the women adjourned to the gallery, joined by Garrison and other male supporters.[14]

After the convention the question of women's rights surfaced in anti-slavery societies in many parts of Britain, with both those in favour and opponents of women's equal involvement touring the country. In Glasgow the Ladies Auxiliary Association remained in the hands of the moderates, but its position was seriously weakened by a breakaway group, the Glasgow Female Anti-Slavery Society, which was radical. In

Edinburgh the male society was conservative, but the women's society was radical.[15]

The leaders of the Edinburgh and Glasgow societies were Quaker families, the Smeals and the Wighams, both immigrants to Scotland from the north of England in the 1780s. William Smeal, a Glasgow merchant, was a leading figure in the Garrisonian section of the Glasgow men's societies. His sister Jane (the second wife of John Wigham in Edinburgh) together with her step-daughter, Eliza Wigham, led the radical Edinburgh women's society.[16] Eliza Wigham will appear in later chapters as an activist in the women's movement.

In the summer of 1854 the old Edinburgh emancipation society was replaced by the New Edinburgh Anti-Slavery Association. Its president was Duncan McLaren, who had been chairman of the Central Board of Scottish Dissenters. He was at that time Lord Provost of Edinburgh, and later represented Edinburgh in Parliament. Duncan McLaren has been called 'the living voice of Scottish middle-class dissenting radicalism'. His third wife, Priscilla, was the sister of the well-known Anti-Corn Law campaigner, Jacob Bright. She had been brought up a Quaker but was disowned for her marriage in 1848.[17] The McLarens would later become another focal point for the women's movement in Scotland.

Researching the subject of women in the anti-slavery movement Louis and Rosamund Billington found that feminism surfaced only amongst a minority of radical women, and furthermore that during the 1840s the energies of such women were diverted into other political reform movements, such as the Anti-Corn Law League.[18] Nevertheless, they concluded that 'feminism did draw upon the more radical elements of abolitionist ideology, and the experience of a network of women working within the reform milieu. In this sense, as later feminists recognised, the activities of their mothers, grandmothers and aunts in the anti-slavery movement laid the foundations of feminism.'[19] One woman who was at the World's Anti-Slavery Convention, and who shortly thereafter wrote an influential work calling for women's enfranchisement, was Marion Reid.

Unfortunately, that is one of the only things known about the author of *A Plea for Woman*. She was born Marion Kirkland, the eldest daughter of a Glasgow merchant, married Hugo Reid in 1839 and went to live in Edinburgh. She survived her husband who died in London in 1872.[20] In his autobiography a leader of the temperance movement in Edinburgh, John Dunlop, mentioned a meeting with Hugo Reid in 1846 and their agreement on women's suffrage[21], but neither Reid nor his wife appear to have played any active part in the women's movement.

However, her book arguing the case for women's suffrage was influential, though perhaps more so in the United States than in Britain. It was first published in Edinburgh in 1843 (the author's name being given as Mrs H. Reid) with simultaneous distribution in London and Dublin. It went into a second edition in 1845 and a London distributor produced a cheap edition in 1845. The first American edition appeared in 1845, and it was reprinted in 1847, 1848, 1851 and 1852.[22]   At the end of the 1830s many books appeared by women exploring their sex's rights, duties and needs. Most of those women believed as strongly as any man in the idea of separate spheres for men and women. They were progressive in calling for greater educational opportunities for women, and more equitable laws, but they did not believe that women were fitted to concern themselves with politics. It was the appearance of such books, and the review article on six of them – entitled 'Rights and Condition of Women' – in the Whig journal, the *Edinburgh Review*, in 1841 that sparked off Marion Reid's work, which aimed to show by reasoned argument why women should have the vote.[23]

She began her book by exploring ideas about women's influence and women's sphere. She believed that there were basically three classes of opinions.

1. Those who think that woman's sphere really and truly comprises only her domestic duties, and that her mind ought never to stir beyond these.
2. Those who think her mind ought to be enlarged, and her condition improved in some respects; but that she ought not to be equally privileged with man.
3. Those who think she has a just claim to equal rights with man.

She was not addressing those who fell in the first category, 'their prejudices being usually too obstinate and deep-seated for eradication', and while she herself fell into the third category she was particularly concerned with women in the second who had 'escaped in a great measure from the thraldom of old prejudices with regard to woman' but who seemed to have 'almost a nervous apprehension of being thought to step out of woman's proper place themselves, or of trying to induce others to do so.'[24]

An entire book devoted to showing the reasons why women needed to be able to elect their representatives to Parliament and why there was no justifiable cause for withholding this privilege from them cannot easily be summarised; with a paperback reissue readily available it is also unnecessary. *A Plea for Woman* was not mentioned in the *Edinburgh Review* so there is no way of knowing if any of Marion Reid's arguments had an effect on the reviewer who helped to spark them off. The original article in the *Edinburgh Review* concluded:

If those deviations from justice towards women, which at present deform
the law of England [sic], were effectually corrected, we do not doubt that
the demands for participation in political power, now made in their behalf,
would cease; and their most zealous defenders would recognize the
impolicy of attempting to remove them from that sphere, in which their
influence may be exerted most beneficially for themselves and others.'[25]

Doubtless there were women who agreed with this. There would always
be such women – right up to the time they were enfranchised – who
would work to improve the lot of their sex in various ways while at the
same time opposing the idea of female suffrage. However, more and more
women, while directing their energies primarily to one specific aim, came
to believe that the parliamentary franchise was a necessary corollary to
every other women's right.

It was in the 1860s that the women's movement in Scotland came to
fruition. Its focal point was Edinburgh, and a significant date was 1865
when the Edinburgh Essay Society (from 1869 the Ladies' Edinburgh
Debating Society) was founded.[26] The founder-president was a 19-year-
old woman, Sarah Elizabeth Siddons Mair (a great-grand-daughter of
Sarah Siddons) who would become a leader in the women's movement
over the next half century. The new Society provided a forum for
women's views and for the expansion of their minds and horizons.

The First Phase – 1867–84

According to James D. Young, in *Women and Popular Struggles*, 'a middle-class Women's Movement (apart from a few scattered individuals) simply did not exist in mid-Victorian Scotland.'[1] This must be one of the most ill-informed comments to appear in a book about Scotland, for the Victorian women's movement in Scotland was very effective indeed and has not begun to receive the coverage it deserves. Even here it cannot do so, since the subject of this book is the struggle for the vote, while the Victorian movement encompassed many other aspects of women's lives as well, such as education, entry to the professions, and married women's legal rights. At that time the vote was desired – as a historian put it –'primarily as a means of political pressure towards a better society.'[2] Although these broader aspects of the women's movement cannot be ignored – if only because the women involved in them tended also to support the suffrage cause – the Victorian women's movement in Scotland deserves an entire book.

Three Edinburgh households were pivotal in the women's movement in Scotland (although, as will be seen, other individuals also played important roles). Two of these were encountered in the prologue: the McLarens and Miss S.E.S. Mair (Miss Mair's mother was also involved). The third household was that of the Stevenson sisters: Eliza was one of the earliest members of the Edinburgh National Society for Women's Suffrage while Flora and Louisa were in the vanguard of virtually every feminist campaign in Victorian Scotland.[3]

One obvious question is how distinct the Scottish movement was from the English one. Certainly there were strong links. The Scottish leaders, who corresponded with their English counterparts, were always very much aware of all the developments in England, and it worked both ways, for English feminist and suffrage journals gave full coverage to every significant event in Scotland. Jenni Calder, writing about women novelists in Victorian Scotland suggests that a more rigorous and uncompromising attitude to social change in Scotland than in England led both to more constraint and to more vigour in Scottish women.[4] This type of qualitative judgment is difficult to prove, but the existence of different education and legal systems, and the fact that separate legislation was nearly always passed for Scotland, meant that the Scottish movement had to be independent of the English one.

Agitation over parliamentary reform was common to England and Scotland in the 1860s. (The English Reform Act of 1867 did not apply to Scotland, where the relevant statute was the Representation of the People (Scotland) Act 1868.) As in the 1832 Reform Acts, the Bills restricted voting to 'male' persons, but John Stuart Mill put forward a women's suffrage amendment. Duncan McLaren's biographer noted that McLaren, as MP, gave Mill's amendment unhesitating support and influenced others to do so.

> At the close of the debate a distinguished statesman turned to him and said, 'McLaren, how are you going to vote?' 'I shall vote for it, and I don't see how a man who had a good mother can do otherwise,' was the reply. 'I had a good and noble mother also,' was the rejoinder; and the two went into the lobby together and voted for the amendment.[5]

The defeat of Mill's amendment led to the formation of women's suffrage societies in London, Manchester and Edinburgh. They considered themselves as 'parts of one National Society – united yet independent.'[6] The Edinburgh Society was formally constituted in November 1867 (at that stage styling itself the Edinburgh Branch of the National Society for Women's Suffrage). Priscilla McLaren was president, Eliza Wigham and Agnes McLaren (Duncan McLaren's daughter by a previous marriage) were joint secretaries. Before the 1832 Reform Acts voting had never been restricted to 'male persons', so the object of the Society was 'To obtain for Women the ancient right of voting for Members of Parliament on a par with Men'. The obvious means of forcing Parliament to accept the women's claim seemed at that time to be petitions, and in 1867 some 2000 signatures were collected in Edinburgh alone. By the end of 1868 a further 55 petitions had been sent from Scotland with a total of 14,000 signatures. Between 1867 and 1876 some two million signatures were collected in Scotland.[7]

Another tactic – used in both England and Scotland – was to challenge the legality of the exclusion of women as voters. The basis of their argument was that an Act of 1850, commonly known as Lord Romilly's Act, provided that in all statutes previous or subsequent the word 'male' included females unless the contrary was expressly provided (which it was not in the Reform Acts of 1867 and 1868). A number of women therefore sent in claims to be registered as voters. In Edinburgh, 'Miss Burton

1 Priscilla McLaren — from J.B. Mackie, *Life and Work of Duncan McLaren*
(London 1888)

appeared personally in defence of her claim for the county, but it was
disallowed, and this decided the fate of the other claims'.[8]

The legal decision that women did not have the right to vote was made
in England at the Court of Appeal in the case of *Chorlton* v. *Lings*. In
Scotland the case was *Brown* v. *Ingram* which was heard in the Court of
Session on 30 October 1868.

> Their Lordships rested their decision upon the fact that there was a long and
> uninterrupted custom in Scotland limiting the franchise to males. That
> being so, section 56 of the Reform Act of 1868, which saved not only all
> existing laws relating to the franchise, but also all existing customs, was
> directly applicable, and was decisive against the claim.[9]

The *Aberdeen Journal* of 23 September 1868 sympathised with the claims of
women. The writer could not see why 'the principle of representation
accompanying taxation should be limited to males'. He went on, 'Why
should not womankind have equal rights with their fathers and brothers?
They have a thousand good reasons for what they are doing, which ought
to weigh with reformers. They are as intelligent, as a rule, as the great
body of the males for whose enfranchisement a fight has been kept up for
some years ... Every argument on behalf of reform is an argument in
favour of extending the suffrage to women.'

An article in the *Scotsman* of 13 November 1868 was similarly
favourable. The basis of this writer's argument was Lord Romilly's Act;
the lack of any clause in the Reform Acts exempting women, if looked at
'through the spectacles of logic and grammar and not through the twisted
coloured glasses of prejudice' meant that women should have been
included. He poured ridicule on the reasons put forward for denying
women the vote and concluded

> In this country the highest political rights are held by that one of the female
> sex who wears the honoured name of Queen Victoria, and these political
> rights have seldom been so well exercised in the history of the world, and
> there are many rights of property affecting the happiness and interests of
> thousands – such, for example, as the patronage of churches – habitually
> exercised by women. A vote in a Parliamentary election is about the lowest
> of all political rights. It is within the reach of every man who has property
> qualification a grade or two removed from beggary, although he can
> neither read nor write, and although he be as ignorant of political questions
> as a horse. And yet that small common political right is denied to women,
> however rich and however intelligent, and that too in a country in which

the legislative performances of M.P.'s and of noble Lords are of no effect until they have received the royal assent of a woman.[10]

While all this agitation for the franchise was going on, a new organisation dedicated to the higher education of women was being formed. The guiding spirit of the Edinburgh Ladies' Educational Association (later called the Edinburgh Association for the Higher Education of Women) was Mary Crudelius, the 28-year-old wife of a German in Leith. She had only a decade in which to see her work unfold, for she died at the age of 38, but the Association was well established long before then. One of the founder members (aged 22) was Sarah Elizabeth Siddons Mair.

There was no hope at that stage of the admission of women to Edinburgh University. As one writer has put it, 'Scottish universities were too introspective and backward-looking, fearing that any reform would introduce English ways and threaten their cherished traditions.' Therefore the scheme was to set up separate courses for women to be taught by professors at university level. Although the classes were not officially connected with the university, they had distinguished academics teaching them, and a high standard of examination, and thus demonstrated women's scholarly abilities.[11]

A major contributor to this venture – and in the years to come a strong supporter of women's suffrage – was Professor Masson. An Aberdonian by birth, the author of many distinguished works of history and literary criticism, David Masson was Professor of English Literature at Edinburgh University for thirty years and was later Historiographer Royal for Scotland.[12] His first course in English Literature for the Edinburgh Association attracted 265 women; 95 of them took the examination.

Glasgow also initiated classes of university standard at this time, though later it followed a different path by creating (in 1883) a separate college for women, Queen Margaret's, while the Edinburgh Association held out for full and equal admission to the university. St Andrews never attracted sufficient numbers for a course of lectures, but in 1877 it began an external examination, the L.L.A. (Lady Literate in Arts).[13] There was, of course, a similar movement in England at the time, but because of differences in the educational system, the English Boards were made up of schoolmistresses rather than being connected with universities.[14]

The agitation for medical education for women was quite separate, and one writer believes that women would have gained admission to universities much sooner if not for the medical controversy, as arts academics were, on the whole, favourably disposed toward the admission of women.[15] The story of Sophia Jex-Blake's attempts to gain admission to medical school at Edinburgh has been related too often to require retelling.[16] Agnes McLaren, who later qualified as a doctor, was involved in both the medical controversy and the suffrage struggle.

Mrs Crudelius withdrew herself from active work for the suffrage cause while setting up the Edinburgh Association, but, as she wrote to Agnes McLaren:

> I have every right to be numbered amongst the firm friends of all true progress; I was one of the first fifteen hundred women who sent a petition to parliament, have signed and got what signatures I could since, and quietly working, shall be glad to help you as far as I can. My *real* work and energy are however dedicated to the advancement of education.[17]

Mary Crudelius had received enthusiastic support for her ideas about women's higher education when the subject was discussed at the Ladies' Edinburgh Debating Society. In 1866 the Debating Society had been the first in Scotland (and probably in all Britain) to debate the question of women's suffrage, although the motion was defeated by 15 votes to 5.[18] In 1869 the Society's magazine, *The Attempt*, carried a favourable review of Josephine Butler's book of essays, *Woman's Work and Woman's Culture*; the review commended the essay in favour of women's suffrage.[19] The author of the review - under the *nom de plume* 'des Eaux' – was none other than Miss S.E.S. Mair.

The year 1870 saw the creation and election of the first school boards in Britain, and the women elected were generally at the forefront of the women's suffrage campaign. In Edinburgh this was Flora Stevenson, and so successful was she that she was re-elected for 33 years until her death in 1905, and in 1900 was unanimously elected chairman.[20] But in the 1860s the idea of women being elected to public bodies was revolutionary. Elizabeth Haldane remembered it happening when she was a child.

> One of the lady candidates (the word 'woman' was never, of course, used) was a Miss Flora Stevenson much respected by all Edinburgh society despite her being considered somewhat 'advanced' in her views. Now it struck me, could I help this lady's candidature? It seemed difficult, but I had an idea, for I knew that each householder had as many votes as there were candidates and even if I could secure one it would be a brave deed. At that time my father was suffering from headache and he liked me to sit by him and stroke his hair to set him to sleep. I waited till he was not quite asleep but, as I thought, in a peaceful state of mind, and then I screwed up my courage and said, 'Papa, do you think you would mind giving *one* of your votes to Miss Stevenson?' I can still remember the start of the peaceful papa, right out of his chair. 'What is the child speaking of?' he exclaimed in amazement. The world to him was evidently turning upside down, and so in fact it was.[21]

In Paisley Jane Glen Arthur was the first woman to stand in a school board election (in 1873). Mrs Arthur, a member of a prominent local family, was a typical activist in the women's movement of the time. (She was atypical only in being the mother of five children.) She was vice-president of the Paisley Ladies Sanitary Association (her sister was president) which in 1866 initiated a public bath scheme, and treasurer of Paisley Infirmary Dorcas Society which provided clothing and blankets for people in need upon their discharge from Paisley Infirmary. On 25 June 1873 the Glasgow satirical magazine, *The Bailie*, accorded her the honour of making her the first woman to be profiled as 'MEN YOU KNOW'. In view of the esteem in which Mrs Arthur was held the author was not at all surprised that she had come head of the poll in the school board elections. Becoming a member of a school board could still be considered 'womanly', but he expressed some concern over her 'inclination to espouse the cause of the "shrieking sisterhood," who rave about "woman's rights".' She was certainly active in the suffrage movement, chairing public meetings and holding her own drawing-room meetings, and she had the full support of her husband and other male members of the family.[22]

In 1870 Lydia Becker, president of the Manchester Women's Suffrage Society and a leading figure in the women's suffrage movement in Britain, established the *Women's Suffrage Journal*. Through her influence a women's suffrage bill was debated in Parliament every year in the next decade except 1874. The conspicuous name among the champions of women's suffrage in the House of Commons in 1870 was Jacob Bright, brother of Priscilla McLaren. In that year he appeared at the first public meeting in favour of women's suffrage to be held in Edinburgh.

The meeting was held on 17 January at the Queen Street Hall, which was filled to overflowing. Duncan McLaren presided, and the platform party also included the Principal of Edinburgh University, Sir Alexander Grant, and Professors Kelland, Masson and Calderwood, several MPs, half a dozen councillors, an advocate and other professional men. Resolutions in favour of women's suffrage were put forward by Jacob Bright and by Sir David Wedderburn, MP for South Ayrshire, both of which were carried by acclamation.[23]

By this time lectures on women's suffrage were being given the length and breadth of Scotland by Miss Jane Taylour of Belmont, Stranraer. A leaflet issued by the Edinburgh Society in 1868 mentioned an agent being employed by the committee 'to devote her whole time to the cause in visiting other parts of Scotland, in order to promote the objects of the Society'.[24] Apart from her purely honorary office of secretary of the Galloway branch of the National Society for Women's Suffrage from November 1870 no mention is made anywhere of Jane Taylour's position in the movement. Given the scope of her travels the obvious conclusion would be that she was that paid agent, but that it was not considered 'genteel' to say so. However, as will be seen, that was not so.

A lecture she gave at Barrhead provoked controversy in the *North British Daily Mail*.[25] On 17 March 1870 there was a brief report of the lecture, which had concluded with a motion in support of Jacob Bright's Bill for conferring the franchise on all women ratepayers: 'about a score of hands at most were held up in favour of the motion, but the greater number present declined to commit themselves.' On the 18th an indignant correspondent calling himself VERITAS complained about the biased report, insisting that the enthusiastic response to the speaker proved that the audience agreed with her and that the show of hands was not a true guide. This provoked the following response on 19 March from a correspondent signing himself ONE WHO WAS THERE.

> If a show of hands were no indication of the test of a meeting, I would ask *Veritas* what is? ... If *Veritas* could not account for the disinclination of the meeting to hold up their hands, perhaps I may enlighten him. Did he never consider that not above one man out of every eight or ten present were voters in the county; and that the men had sense enough to come to the conclusion that perhaps it would be more in accordance with justice, that they themselves should first be given their political rights, before they voted for their aunts and other female friends to be endowed with the franchise?

However, in that same month, Robert Cochrane, who in earlier decades had been a working-class leader of the Chartist movement in the west of Scotland, pronounced himself a recent convert to the women's suffrage cause, saying that 'when he saw men like John Stuart Mill leading in this movement, it was time to ask ourselves why we are in opposition.'[26]

The attitude of women involved in the suffrage movement toward unenfranchised males may be illustrated by a remark made in a report of the creation of a new branch of the National Society in Glasgow in March 1870. The committee were pleased to say that they had already obtained some 3000 signatures on petitions: 'These have been gathered mainly from the working classes who, if their convictions are not always formed, are at least free from narrow prejudice.'[27] (Such a note of condescension by middle-class women toward the working classes is a feature of the Victorian ethos which jars on the modern reader). Dorothy Thompson, commenting on the failure of Chartism to make inroads on middle-class opinion, makes a point which is relevant to the suffrage movement:

> The middle classes had been an articulate presence in British political life since the seventeenth century. The working people had appeared only as a

mob, or at the tail of middle-class movements – often, indeed, as an embarrassment to such movements. The working-class dissenters or the crowd supporting political demands had been used by the establishment to discredit the more respectable elements, and the taunt of rabble-rousing had been used against middle-class politicians as recently as 1832.[28]

Such fears were undoubtedly present in the Victorian women's suffrage movement and help to explain the persistent emphasis on respectability and the appearance of the 'best people' on women's suffrage platforms.

It was still a great innovation for a woman to lecture publicly so remarks like the following, in connection with Jane Taylour's lecture at Wigton, are important: 'Miss Taylour has all the requisites of a public lecturer. Her composition is chaste and elegant, her voice distinct and agreeable, and her manner attractive and graceful.'[29]

In January 1871 another public meeting was held in Edinburgh on the women's suffrage question, and this one had John Stuart Mill as a speaker – the only meeting out of London that he ever addressed on the subject.[30] In his opening remarks the chairman, Duncan McLaren, stated that the city and county of Edinburgh, and the burghs around it, deserved special notice for the way in which their representatives in Parliament had given the movement their support. The MPs for the city, county and university of Edinburgh, as well as the MPs for the burghs of Leith, Portobello and Musselburgh, had all voted in favour of the women's suffrage Bill in Parliament, while Edinburgh Town Council was the first public body to petition for it. With eloquent speeches by Mill and by Professor Masson, the meeting seems to have been a lively and inspiring one, and both their resolutions in favour of women's suffrage were adopted unanimously. According to Mill, 'the cause owes an immense debt to Scotland and in Scotland to Edinburgh'.[31]

By this time there were committees of the National Society in Aberdeen, Glasgow, St Andrews, and Galloway. On 3 April a public meeting supporting the claim of women householders to the franchise was held in Aberdeen. As it had been widely advertised that the principal speaker would be Dr Elizabeth Garrett Anderson, the crowd was so great that long before the start the Mechanics' Hall was so overcrowded that the meeting had to be moved to a much larger venue, the Music Hall, 'which was speedily well filled both in the area and galleries, the orchestra having also been stormed by the audience at an early stage.' The Lord Provost chaired the meeting. Dr Garrett Anderson said

I have been asked what good such an innovation would produce. I do not think it is at all necessary to show what good would come from this change. It is quite enough to show that the injustice exists ... It is in the faith that all

injustices are wrong that I would appeal to every person who cares for
justice, right, and fairness, to put aside this great injustice as between men
and women, and allow women to develop not only socially but politically,
as citizens, in the way that you develop – to give them a fair field and no
favour.

Three resolutions were carried unanimously, the third being that a
petition should be transmitted from the meeting to the Prime Minister,
the Lord Advocate and the MPs for the city and county of Aberdeen.[32]

Later that month Priscilla McLaren addressed a women's suffrage
conference in London and said: 'While many other earnest workers might
be named it would be unpardonable not to mention the extraordinary
exertions of one lady, who not only got up seven meetings herself but had
addressed forty-one public meetings with the greatest success – viz., Miss
Taylour of Belmont.' She went on to point out that all those meetings
'had been presided over by chief magistrates of burghs, sheriffs of
counties, and other influential gentlemen connected with the different
localities, and from each of them petitions had been sent to Parliament in
favour of women's suffrage.' She thought that these facts indicated 'that
the question had taken deep root in Scotland, and that the agitation would
go on until crowned with complete success. Wherever the deputations of
lady lecturers had gone, they had found the hearts and understandings of
the people most ready to receive them, and the more so that the society
has no paid agents – all this great work had been done from pure devotion
to the cause.'[33] This comment reveals that Jane Taylour subsidised her
campaigning herself and that, in contrast to the Edwardian period, the
nineteenth-century women's suffrage movement in Scotland employed
no paid agents.

In the autumn Jane Taylour travelled even further afield (often
accompanied by Agnes McLaren), giving lectures at Inveraray, Oban,
Inverness, Thurso, Wick, Tain, Dingwall, Forres and Elgin, and in
Kirkwall and Stromness in Orkney. The *Women's Suffrage Journal* published comments extracted from press reports of all those meetings, and
the *Orkney Herald* provided reports of the Kirkwall and Stromness
meetings.[34] The *Herald* of 11 October gave the former almost a complete
page, reporting her speech in full, which allows us an insight into how a
mid-Victorian Scottish speaker on the subject addressed her audience.

The first point of interest is that the Misses Taylour and McLaren were
accompanied on to the platform by ministers of the Established Church,
Congregational Church, United Presbyterian Church and the Free
Church. The second point is that the chairman, Provost Bain, stated at the
outset that he himself did *not* believe that women should be enfranchised,
as he was convinced that Parliament was always ready to look after

women's rights. But, while holding those views, he had lived long enough to know that 'we must often modify, alter, or even entirely change our most cherished opinions, to meet the case of altered circumstances, and the facts which further enquiry and knowledge often bring to our consideration.'

Jane Taylour began by pointing out the anomaly that the franchise was based on property, yet women were property owners without being able to vote. She then went on to the disadvantages women laboured under by not having direct representation in Parliament. She had often been told that women's well-being received as much attention under the present arrangement as it would if they were directly represented. In reply she asked: 'Was not this the substance of the answer given by those who opposed the demand for a Reform Bill? Did it satisfy those who then claimed the franchise? No, it did not; nor will it be one whit more satisfactory to us, for we share with them the conviction that to secure fair representation we must first secure direct representation.' She then discussed some of the unjust laws 'that press so barbarously upon those women who have had the misfortune to unite themselves to wicked and unprincipled men.'

From her speech it is obvious – and not unexpected – that the strong conviction that men and women were fundamentally different in their natures was as much a part of Victorian suffragist thinking as it was of anti-suffragism.

> Those err greatly who aver that woman becomes masculine by thus fulfilling the duties for which she was created. No! she does not. She is never more a woman than when so employed. It is not the kind of work done that makes or mars womanliness – it is the manner in which it is done, the spirit that enshrines it. We do not want to usurp anything, or to do anything unseemly or out of order, but to do our proper part in helping on the world's reform – helping on with a woman's power, and in a woman's way, all that is wise, elevating, humane, and holy.

She must have been persuasive, for the chairman closed the meeting by praising the 'tact, eloquence, and singularly lucid manner in which she has advanced the claims of her sex', confessing that 'after listening to her address, my former opinions on the subject which she has so well treated, have been considerably shaken.' Some indication of the importance which the British women's suffrage movement as a whole placed on Scotland may be gathered from the fact that its leading figure, Lydia Becker, travelled up from Manchester to address a public meeting on the subject in Dumfries on 15 December.[35] There was by this time a fundamental difference between England and Scotland. Although in both countries women were denied the parliamentary vote, English women ratepayers won the municipal franchise in 1867 while Scotswomen did not, as under Scottish law the municipal vote carried with it the parliamentary franchise. There is no evidence that Scottish women tried to do anything about this anomaly; it took an Englishwoman to urge them that if they could not get the length of a parliamentary vote they should at least ask for the same rights as English women had.

In the first few months of 1872 Jane Taylour continued to lecture in various parts of Scotland. However, when the Ladies' Edinburgh Debating Society debated the question 'Should Women be admitted to the Parliamentary Franchise?' in that year, the motion was again defeated, although this time by only three votes.[36] On 13 April a rather unusual event for this period – a large open-air women's suffrage meeting – was held on Glasgow Green. The crowd was said to number about a thousand, 'chiefly working men of the most intelligent type'. Not more than 50 of them left in the course of the two-hour meeting, which was dispersed at the end 'with some little difficulty, for the people wanted to hear more.' The speaker was Jessie Craigen, the daughter of an Italian actress and a Scottish sailor, and she later spoke – usually out of doors – all over the north of England, collecting workers' signatures on petitions. She was not employed by the movement but collected minimum expenses to keep her going.[37]

On 2 September 1872 Scotland featured in Lydia Becker's editorial on the front page of the *Women's Suffrage Journal*. The subject was the right of women to vote in school board elections. In England, where women already voted in local elections, this followed as a matter of course, but in Scotland it was unclear whether the electoral conditions would follow the precedent of the English Act and admit women, or that of other kinds of representative government in Scotland and exclude them. In fact it *did* admit them, which Miss Becker hailed as a 'distinct and substantial gain': 'We have always understood the Scotch to be a very logical people; and we think that it is much easier for them to rest in the position of affirming that women ought not to vote at all, than in that of affirming that they ought to vote sometimes, or on some questions which concern them along with the rest of the community; but not in all elections, nor in all such questions.'

In Ayr in December of that year a deputation of 'gentlemen favourable to women's suffrage' met with their MP, Mr Crawfurd, to put the case to him. Mr Crawfurd said he was always glad to meet with constituents but he did not agree with women's enfranchisement and thought that relying on men to speak for them was no way for women to win the vote. (Although of course he thought it fine for women to rely on men to speak for them in Parliament. And whether he would have consented to see a deputation of women must remain open to question.) He insisted that in his experience 'the majority of the females of the country were opposed to the movement, and did not thank those who were acting for them.' It is interesting to find a group of men making this gesture on behalf of women; apart from the rector of Ayr Academy their status is unknown, but the MP referred to the deputation as 'influential'.[38]

In January 1873 it was reported at the annual meeting of the Edinburgh branch of the National Society for Women's Suffrage that 95 public meetings had been held in Scotland the previous year 'which had mostly been presided over by the chief magistrate or other influential person in the town or district in which they had been held.'[39] This was the heyday of the Victorian women's suffrage movement, with meetings being held in every part of England and Scotland.

Jessie Craigen and Jane Taylour were still the indefatigable campaigners in the more remote parts of Scotland. In the autumn of 1873 Jane Taylour was back in Orkney, and both she and Jessie Craigen addressed meetings at Lerwick and Scalloway in Shetland. Jessie Craigen also addressed a meeting in Stornoway where the United Presbyterian minister was in the chair and nearly all the local gentry were present.[40]

By 1874 there were local women's suffrage societies or committees in Edinburgh, Haddington, Burntisland, Dollar, Cupar, St Andrews, Perth, Dundee, Laurencekirk, Aberdeen, Dumfries, Ayr, Glasgow, Alloa, Paisley, Helensburgh, Stirling, Inveraray, Tain, Wick, Kirkwall, Stromness, Lerwick and Dingwall.[41] However, at the end of 1873 Jane Taylour left for England. Although Jessie Craigen continued to address some meetings in Scotland for another two or three years, no other woman came forward who had the time and inclination to to travel to the less accessible parts of Scotland.[42]

Nevertheless, in spite of the decrease in public meetings, progress was still being made. The *Women's Suffrage Journal* of 1 August 1874 reported that a memorial from 10,127 Scottish women had been presented to the Prime Minister, Disraeli, acknowledging his past services in the cause of women's suffrage, and asking him to use his influence in favour of the current Bill before Parliament. Furthermore, some 340 petitions, with a total of about 54,000 signatures, had that session been presented from Scotland to Parliament in favour of the Bill. This was considerably more than in any previous year, 'and this great proportion of work done in Scotland is the more remarkable when it is borne in mind that the whole country does not contain a population larger than that of London alone.' Fourteen of the petitions came from Town Councils (although three other Town Councils – Linlithgow, Elgin and Dundee – had petitioned against the Bill).

Reports of Jessie Craigen's meetings strike a different note from those of Jane Taylour. For example, on 26 December 1874, at Kilbarchan, Renfrew, she had an audience 'almost entirely composed of working weavers' and the working man in the chair said that 'this was a working-class question, for the bad laws by which women were oppressed would never be got rid of till they gave women a fair share of representation, and these bad laws came keenest on working women.' On 12 May 1875 her large open-air meeting at Stenhousemuir Cross near Stirling was attended mostly by iron-workers and colliers.[43] On 9 February 1876 she held a meeting in the parish school at Limerigg, Stirling, described as 'a little cluster of cottages, not more than twenty, standing on a hill overlooking a country colliery district.'

> Though the snow was thick on the ground the workmen came from nearly all the collieries round . . . One old woman, with a shawl over her head, had walked many miles to the meeting. She came after it was over to sign the petition, declaring that she had suffered enough from bad laws, and would do anything to get them mended.[44]

Do these reports contradict the assertion made earlier, that working-class involvement was not desired? The answer is that it was *only* Jessie Craigen who addressed the working classes in Scotland, which makes such meetings an exception to the general rule. The reports themselves rarely failed to emphasise the 'respectability' of her working-class audiences. And during the same period a series of drawing-room meetings was being held in Edinburgh.[45]

Though in their debates the vote might go against it, the Ladies' Edinburgh Debating Society did not neglect the subject of the franchise in their magazine. In 1876 Flora Masson, daughter of Professor Masson, wrote an article explaining why women should have the parliamentary franchise. She considered first the justice of the claim, which she felt was self evident, and then the desirability of granting it. On the latter point she brought up the special needs of women and the near impossibility of obtaining fair laws for them while women could not vote for their representatives. As for fears that voting in elections would make women less 'womanly' she observed:

> Women in England do vote at present at municipal elections . . . They are allowed to vote in both England and Scotland at School Board elections; and in none of these cases have evil results been seen. No ugly transformation has occurred among the women of Edinburgh since three years ago, when they went up in large numbers to the polling-booths and voted for members of the School Board.

She went on to say that a large number of women sincerely wanted the franchise, and concluded with a brief history of the movement.[46]

In the *Women's Suffrage Journal* of 2 July 1877 Ella Burton, an active member of the Edinburgh Society, reported on the situation in Scotland. Over a thousand signatures on petitions to Parliament had been collected from women householders in Edinburgh, 300 of them from Newington, 'the wealthiest district, where many ladies of position, having begun to think over the matter, now take a warm interest therein.' She pointed out that petitions from female heads of households were very important, and that 'by the status of the women who sign them, the progress of thought on this subject can easily be estimated.' That session she had received 1,752 signatures from women householders in Scotland, of which 600 came from Aberdeen, 'where the enfranchisement of women meets with great support.' She felt this showed that 'although the Bill is *talked out* in Parliament this year, it is slowly and steadily in another sense being *thought out* by all classes of women.' The Society's success in attracting better off women she attributed mainly to a series of 19 drawing-room meetings held in Scotland 'which those ladies for whom public meetings have little interest have been easily persuaded to attend.' Miss Burton added that there had also been petitions sent from Edinburgh signed by specific groups: one by 35 ministers of different denominations, one by 52 medical men, and one by 205 rectors, headmasters, schoolmistresses, and teachers. A number of town councils had also petitioned Parliament that year, including Edinburgh, Forfar, Montrose, Aberdeen, Wick, Kirkcaldy, Dumbarton, Girvan, Selkirk, Jedburgh and Wigton.[47]

A brief (and very general) report of progress in Scotland was also given in the *Women's Suffrage Journal* of 1 February 1878. As proof of women's increasing participation in public affairs it mentioned that 'the other day during the contested elections for Leith one of the candidates was accompanied to the platform by several ladies'. The Edinburgh Women's Suffrage Society was at this time asking town councils to petition Parliament in favour of the women's suffrage Bill. Kirkcaldy Town Council agreed to do so by a majority of 13 to 5. Hawick Town Council did not, and a brief report of their discussion is revealing.

Mr Blaine: Let them remain in the kitchen, their proper place. (Laughter.) – The Provost, though approving of the movement, did not think a Council meeting a proper place to discuss a question of the kind – Mr Blaine moved that it lie on the table. (Hear.hear.) – Mr Ferguson moved that it be laid on the fire. (Laughter.) – Mr Watson protested against such a cavalier dismissal of the matter. The letter was very respectful, and ought at least to be acknowledged, whatever might be their opinion on the merits of the question. – The Provost, the Town Clerk, and Bailie Milligan pointed out that women had votes on School Board and other matters, and there was no reason why they should be excluded from the franchise. – Mr Eckford:

> Will they go to fight the Turks or the Russians? (Laughter.) – The Provost:
> Will you do it? (Great laughter.)[48]

Similarly revealing was the Conservative candidate's address in a by-election campaign for the constituency of Argyllshire.

> He must confess that he thought the ladies had got power enough already.
> (Laughter.) But somehow or other, although he spoke as a married man –
> (Laughter) – the ladies generally managed to get their own way.
> (Laughter.) He had not much experience of canvassing in Argyleshire, but
> from his experience elsewhere he found that if he got the good word of the
> wife he was very well satisfied. (Laughter.) But, joking apart, he honestly
> thought that ladies should not descend to the rough and tumble of an
> election. They had enormous powers as it was, and he should be very sorry
> to see them brought into the excitement consequent on an election, and
> thereby made to step down from the high regard in which they were
> presently held.[49]

In view of such attitudes it is not surprising that the author of an article in the Ladies' Edinburgh Debating Society's magazine in 1880, entitled 'Women and the Parliamentary Franchise' should write: 'It is the fashion among many people to laugh at this movement, to turn it into ridicule, and to sneer at its advocates as strong-minded, unfeminine, etc.' However, the writer clearly knew that many of the women she was addressing still had not been convinced that they should be enfranchised.[50]

The most significant event in Scotland in 1881 and 1882 was the granting of the municipal franchise to women ratepayers.[51] The Edinburgh women's suffrage society immediately seized on the illogicality of women being considered competent to vote for town councillors but not for parliamentary representatives, and urged town councils to petition Parliament. The discussion in Edinburgh Town Council revealed a spectrum of opinion from the most rabidly anti-suffrage ('Ladies were very useful and ornamental, but they should be kept in their own place') to the most heartily pro-suffrage. The motion to petition Parliament was carried by 19 votes to 16.[52]

The Convention of Royal and Parliamentary Burghs petitioned Parliament to extend the parliamentary franchise to the women who had been granted the municipal franchise and 12 town councils followed suit.[53] During 1882 the Edinburgh Society arranged meetings in various burghs 'for the purpose of arousing the newly-created electors to a sense of the duties and responsibilities of the municipal vote.' Jessie Craigen held meetings in Aberdeen, Dundee and elsewhere. Ladies connected with the temperance movement were said to be particularly active in this work.[54]

During the previous seven years a demonstration of women in favour of women's suffrage had been held annually in an English city. The winning of the municipal franchise by Scottish women was celebrated by holding it in Scotland for the first time in 1882. It took place in the St Andrews Hall, Glasgow, on 3 November. Rain had fallen heavily all day, so there were fears of a sparse turnout, but in the event the hall (which seated 5,000 according to one source and 7,000 according to another) was filled to capacity with women (only a few men were allowed in the gallery). Priscilla McLaren began her speech by saying, 'Scotland has witnessed many a noble gathering in the cause of liberty, but never one nobler than the one I look upon to-night, over which I have the honour to preside.' The *Glasgow Herald* gave the occasion good coverage with a full report of all the speeches.[55]

Two years later it was Edinburgh's turn to hold the meeting, or 'Scottish National Demonstration of Women' on 24 March 1884. The women's press waxed ecstatic over the event. It was the 'most magnificent meeting that has ever been held in Edinburgh', with the Synod Hall, the largest hall in the city, as venue. 'The hall keeper reported that he had never seen such a sea of faces as met his view when he opened the doors.' Both the great hall and the overflow meeting were filled, and up to a thousand people were turned away. The meeting was exclusively for women, with only a small number of men admitted to a portion of the gallery, and this too 'was soon crowded to excess'. 'The resolutions were carried with unanimity and enthusiasm.'[56]

The *Scotsman* had a different reaction. (Admittedly, his opening remarks did have a certain logic to them.)

> Viscountess Harberton of Carbery, County Kildare; Miss Tod, of Belfast; Mrs Scratcherd, of Leeds; Miss Balgarnie, of Scarborough; and Mrs Ormiston Chant, of London, came to Edinburgh on Saturday, and with the assistance of a few ladies resident in Scotland, some of whom are believed to be actually Scotswomen born, conducted a 'great Scottish National Demonstration,' to prove that the women of Scotland are pining under the galling slavery of the stronger sex, who deny to them the joy dearest to the female breast of becoming active politicians.

He suggested that Scottish women 'might have been trusted to be their own spokeswomen about their own grievances; these audible and voluble promptings arouse the suspicion that the grievances have been largely imported from without.'

The leader writer particularly resented the fact that men were confined to the gallery, 'and made to pay half-a-crown for the privilege of hearing themselves abused'. Such a blow to masculine *amour propre* was hard to

"THE LADIES' BATTLE."

(*The Women's Suffrage Demonstration in the St. Andrew's Halls, 3rd November, 1882.*)

2 Reproduced by permission of the People's Palace (Glasgow Museums)

3 Reproduced by permission of Paisley Art Gallery and Museum

stomach. The rest of his diatribe was the fairly standard 'separate spheres' argument about the unfitness of women to take part in politics. The very fact that the editor thought it worth devoting a lengthy leader to the event was, of course, an unintentional tribute, for there would have been no need to pour such vitriol on a movement that posed no threat. He concluded

> When they have learned to ask for what is practical, and have made it more plain that they are not taking undue liberties with the name and reputation of the women of Scotland, Parliament will be ready to lend a more favourable ear to their petitions, though, except in a moment of fatal weakness, it will never give them what they so unwisely ask for.[57]

The *Scotsman* also ran a letter written by a woman signing herself EDINA who stated that she had not attended the meeting 'from any sympathy or agreement with the mistaken and unwise theories propounded from the platform, but simply to hear and see the proceedings.' She insisted that she had visited various parts of the hall 'and everywhere heard many and frequent quiet marks of dissent.' The remainder of the letter was a lengthy anti-suffrage statement. In reply a woman signing herself STEWARDESS pointed out that all those in the hall were invited to hold up their hands if they disagreed, yet not one hand was raised. However, the editor gave EDINA the last word.

> It is quite true ... that there were no dissentient hands held up. Perhaps the 'dissent' of the silent ones may in some measure account for their being led by a strong sense of the fitness of things to abstain from taking any active part whatever in proceedings that were utterly wrong in principle, in clear and direct contradiction to natural and Divine law.

The correspondence was then declared closed.[58]

In 1884 the Third Reform Act enfranchised many more of the men of Great Britain – but no women. A women's suffrage amendment was moved to the Bill, but the anti-suffrage prime minister, William Gladstone, made certain it did not pass. Some 26 years after that a woman involved in the later struggle insisted that the suffragists should have revolted then and realised that new tactics were needed.

> There can be no doubt but that at this period very general support of the suffrage demand existed in the country. The records reveal a series of great meetings, extraordinary for that period, branches and committees even in the smallest towns of Scotland ... and resolutions in favour from municipal authorities and other responsible administrative bodies. The failure of the suffragists of that day to strike when the blow was necessary, and their

further failure to develop a new policy to meet the conditions which Mr Gladstone's action revealed, threw them back into impotence. They were in a blind alley.[59]

With hindsight one sees that she may have had a point, but certainly no one at the time saw it in such a light. For those involved in the movement it was simply another setback; the fight would go on. And in that year of 1884, when the Ladies' Edinburgh Debating Society debated the question, 'Is the Enfranchisement of Women desirable?', for the first time the Affirmative won, by a majority of five.[60]

The Politicising of Scottish Women –
1885–1905

Many historians take the view that the period after 1884 marked a low ebb in the women's suffrage movement, in contrast to the vigour of the 1860s and 70s when there was a parliamentary debate on the subject nearly every year. However, as David Rubinstein has put it, the comparison is 'between the novelty of the initial campaign and the realism of the long march.'[1] There were only three parliamentary debates in the next twenty years, but without the growth in women's political consciousness during that period the later militant phase is difficult to envisage.

In November 1886 Millicent Garrett Fawcett, a leading figure in the movement, told the annual meeting of the Edinburgh National Society for Women's Suffrage how she had met a Scottish woman of nearly 90 who remembered when no woman was allowed a vote in church affairs. She found it was very satisfactory to look back on the lifetime of one individual and see how much had been accomplished. Now there were women acting as poor-law guardians, sitting on school boards and taking part in many other types of public work, and women realised the close connection between parliamentary enfranchisement and other aspects of the women's movement. On the same page as the report of this meeting was an apposite note of a testimonial presented to Eliza Wigham (still joint secretary of the suffrage society) from her many friends in Scotland, England and elsewhere, in appreciation of her lifelong philanthropic work.[2]

The annual conference of the Convention of Royal and Parliamentary Burghs in April 1887 agreed, without discussion, to petition Parliament to extend the parliamentary franchise to women. That decision represented, collectively, all 82 town councils of Scotland, and in addition some 20 individual town councils sent petitions on their own accord.[3]

Throughout the Victorian period the usual demand was for the vote to be given to women householders who would have been eligible had they been men. As eligibility was based on property this meant only spinsters and widows would qualify, and anti-suffragists made much of the fact that a prostitute might have the vote, which she would lose if she became respectable and married. Some women felt strongly that it was wrong to deny married women the vote, but since even the very limited claim for unmarried women was opposed, they never went so far as to split the movement on the issue. There was, in fact, a schism in the national suffrage organisation in England, which lasted from 1888 to 1897, but it was over the question of whether societies which had other aims besides the attainment of the parliamentary franchise could affiliate. During that period there were two 'central' organisations, but the Edinburgh National Society for Women's Suffrage went on as before.[4]

Around this time the cause gained an influential Scottish member in Lady Frances Balfour. In her autobiography Lady Frances wrote that she could not remember 'any date, in which I was not a passive believer in the rights of women to be recognised as full citizens of this country.' Passive belief was one thing, active involvement another, for she was a daughter of the Duke of Argyll, and amongst the aristocracy, 'I can truly say that no one in my social class had the least feeling for, or wish to know more about these unwomanly women.' But as time passed she became convinced that 'it was a Cause which would make the world a place of more equal justice'.[5]

For some 25 years Lady Frances Balfour was very actively involved in the suffrage movement. Her formal position was as president of the London Society, and she lectured as frequently in England as in Scotland, but her Scottish roots went deep; indeed, the *Bailie* published an article lauding her championing of a wide range of Scottish causes without mentioning anything she did in England.[6]

In 1887, 1890 and 1892 the annual conferences of the Conservative Associations of Scotland urged the government to enfranchise women.[7] The discussions are not recorded, so we do not know what prompted those resolutions (within the Conservative party some of the leaders were nominally pro-suffrage while the rank and file was against it, while in the Liberal party more of the rank and file were nominally in favour while the leaders tended to be anti-suffrage). It may have been a ploy against the growing Labour movement, in hopes that giving a small number of propertied women the vote would hold back full adult suffrage. This view appears in a letter from a young member of the Parker Smith family of Jordanhill, Glasgow to her mother in 1891.

> We are steadily tending towards Manhood suffrage. This would be a dangerous and bad state of affairs considering their ignorance. The women householders whom it is intended should have votes are about a tenth of women. If they had this vote it would put off the day of manhood suffrage for a long time.[8]

By the early 1890s the most important development in the movement was women's growing involvement in political organisations. After the passage of the Corrupt Practices Act of 1883 the unpaid assistance of women was invaluable to both political parties and to the emerging Labour movement.

Women's Liberal Associations first appeared in England in about 1880 and the Women's Liberal Federation was formed in 1887. The Conservatives had the Primrose League which created a Ladies' Grand Council in 1884. At local level men and women worked together; nevertheless, unlike the feminist independent Liberal women, the Conservative women were subservient and content to remain in the background.[9] However, Frances Balfour noted that the Primrose League was responsible for women (presumably meaning Conservative women) becoming interested in politics for the first time and added that 'With all its absurdities, the Women's Cause gained much from the existence and the teapot life of the "P.L." '[10]

An English suffragist, Helen Blackburn, commented (in 1902) that those organisations, and particularly the Women's Liberal Associations, 'have brought on themselves the frequent reproach that they assist men to power, who afterwards use that power to deny them the simplest, quietest and most effective instrument for giving help to their principles. But', she went on, 'even those who stultify their own actions by their indifference – often more apparent than real – to the "pivot" question of the franchise, even they have contributed to throw down one of the chief bulwarks of the old resistance – the notion that "politics are unwomanly".'[11]

But what about the suffrage question? At the second annual meeting of the Edinburgh (The Scott) Habitation of the Primrose League on 6 December 1886 James Bruce, a solicitor, discussed female franchise. He thought that if the Conservative party were to make it a government measure it would add great lustre to the party and called for the enfranchisement of all unmarried women holding the necessary property qualifications. A motion agreeing was carried 'by a considerable majority'.[12]

From 1889 the Grand Council of the Primrose League attempted to forbid discussion of the women's suffrage question.[13] To not avail: the Grand Habitation (Scottish Branch) on 30 October 1891 unanimously resolved that the Grand Council should petition the government to bring in a women's suffrage Bill at the earliest opportunity. (The speaker said he did not 'advocate this so much from a political point of view as from the point of view of justice. This was simply an act of justice which must come, and great credit would reflect on the Government which carried it into effect.')[14]

The Primrose League's distaste for discussion of the suffrage question was partly because it had proved so divisive within the Women's Liberal

Federation, finally leading to a schism in 1892.[15] The Scottish Women's Liberal Federation had no such qualms. In fact Number 4 of the objects of the Federation was unequivocal: 'To secure just and equal legislation and representation for women especially with reference to the Parliamentary Franchise and the removal of all legal disabilities on account of sex and to protect the interests of children.'[16] Not being formed until 1892, its members had ample time to watch the long drawn out struggle within the English Federation and to start out with a clear idea of where they themselves stood on the matter.[17]

The Federation sent resolutions to leading members of the government as well as to all Scottish MPs during the summer of 1895, and not long after, when asked by the executive committee of the Edinburgh women's suffrage society for sympathy with the Society's intention of working to rouse women to take the opportunity of bringing women's suffrage forward, the Federation replied that 'they sympathised with the idea, and were themselves going to do what they could to further the cause.'[18]

Members of the Scottish Women's Liberal Federation were, of course, middle class, but support for women's suffrage was also growing amongst working-class women, as can be seen from the Women's Co-operative Guild. The Guild was established in England as an offshoot of the co-operative movement in 1883. The Scottish Guild was not established until November 1892; its president later wrote, 'possibly the proverbial caution had rather checked its growth, because the idea was not a new one at that date'. However, the English Guild's first resolution in favour of women's suffrage was not adopted until 1894, while the Scottish Guild sent a petition to the government for the extension of the parliamentary franchise to women in 1893. The Scottish Guild's position was that 'men cannot be free while women remain slaves'.[19]

Meanwhile the Edinburgh women's suffrage society continued its work much as before. In March 1893 several of its members helped the four women standing in the parochial board elections: the candidates were considered to have great odds against them but ultimately were all elected at the head of the poll. At the annual meeting in October of that year Priscilla McLaren – still going strong as president at the age of 78 – commented on the relief and blessing public work could be to a woman, citing examples of one woman who had lost a baby and another who had been widowed both finding a reason for living again in their public work. Many ladies had told her 'what suffering invalid lives they led until they engaged in public questions'.[20]

On 25 April 1895 women's suffrage was discussed in a leader in the *Glasgow Herald*: the Central Committee of the National Society for Women's Suffrage had just published the opinions of many religious leaders on the subject.[21] The Reverend Dr Lindsay of the Free Church College, Glasgow described the refusal of the franchise to women as 'a survival of theoretical Paganism'. To Dr Dowden, Bishop of Edinburgh, 'the sound reasons in favour of extending the franchise to qualified women householders seem enormously to outweigh all that can be alleged to the contrary.' The *Glasgow Herald* concluded: 'These opinions ... should do much to reassure those who imagine the movement to be out of harmony with the religious aspect of women's work and duty.'

A women's suffrage Bill was introduced in 1897 by a Conservative backbencher, Ferdinand Faithfull Begg. It passed its second reading in February by 230 votes to 159. Lady Frances Balfour was in the House of Commons and her letter to her daughter afterwards conveys something of the euphoria suffragists felt at that time. She had had a headache and fever and 'listened to the debate shivering, and was much bored by all the bad arguments I had to listen to.' When it came to the division for the Bill, 'the galleries packed with women held their breath. The crowd of friends coming back for the Aye lobby seemed to us so great, we thought it could not be, and the NO's had got mixed.' When they heard the numbers and a majority of 71 'we were left without words, "incredible" one woman said in my ear, then I was shaking hands with a dozen also being kissed, and I saw 2 sobbing!. ... No one had dreamt of such a success.' [22]

Press reports in both Scotland and England stressed the importance of such a parliamentary majority on this question. As David Rubinstein has said, that vote does not suggest that the women's suffrage movement was a declining force.[23] And whereas in 1895, when women's enfranchisement did not appear possible in the forseeable future, the *Glasgow Herald* was favourable to the cause, on 4 February 1897 it took a very different stance:

> Women are in a majority in the country ... and it cannot for a moment be held that they are on an equality with men in political education. Yet at a moment of grave crisis in the fortunes of the nation the votes of the women may decide a vital issue on the impulse of sentiment. Women cannot take part in warfare, yet by their votes they may forbid the nation to go to war when its very existence may depend on a resort to arms.

The note of panic is unmistakeable, and the leader plaintively asked, 'is not the power of women great enough already?'.

During the months before the Bill was scheduled for its committee stage the Scottish Women's Liberal Federation sent a circular to all the Women's Liberal Associations asking them to send up petitions from their constituencies.[24] However, when the Bill came before the House of Commons it was talked out. After that one might again have expected suffragists to consider a change in tactics, but they carried on much as before. The two separate 'central' organisations reunited as the National

Union of Women's Suffrage Societies (NUWSS) under the leadership of Millicent Garrett Fawcett (she became president in 1907). After the death of Lydia Becker in 1890, there was no journal devoted to women's suffrage until 1903, but the *Englishwoman's Review* covered all events concerning the movement, in Scotland as well as in England.

In 1899 and 1900 the Scottish Women's Liberal Federation devoted more of their energies to trying to get women eligible to sit on town councils than to the parliamentary franchise, but when the Town Councils (Scotland) Bill was passed in September 1900 it did not admit women as town councillors. For several years after that the Federation had a Women's Franchise and Local Government section, treating the two issues as closely related. Late in September 1900 the committee drew up a questionnaire to parliamentary candidates to elicit their views on women's suffrage and on the eligibility of women to town and county councils.[25] On 8 January 1901 the Federation reaffirmed its commitment to the parliamentary franchise for women.

April 1901 saw the launch in Glasgow of the *Lady's Review of Reviews*, an ambitious venture, aimed at women who wanted more from a journal than fashion and household hints. The first issue declared: 'Scottish women are not behind any more than Scottish men in everything that pertains to forward movements, and we think the time has come for a country that has its own social customs, its own law, and even its own religion, to have its own Ladies' Magazine.' By June the price of the magazine had been lowered from 3d. to one penny, and it fell from 60 to 24 pages, and after September it folded, with the comment, 'We have been mistaken in thinking the ladies of Scotland would support such a magazine, and we regret that their patriotism has not risen to the occasion.'[26] Scottish events received excellent coverage in journals like the *Englishwoman's Review*; perhaps it was the size of the Scottish population that was to blame rather than lack of patriotism.

There was certainly a new generation of Scotswomen whose horizons stretched beyond their mothers' and aunts'. An Act enabling Scottish universities to admit women to degree courses was passed in 1889, and in 1892 the first women were formally admitted. Eight of them were so far advanced in their informal studies that they graduated from Edinburgh University – in Arts subjects – in 1893. (By contrast, Oxford did not grant women full degrees until after World War I and Cambridge not until after World War II. Owens College, which became Manchester University, admitted women to some degree courses in 1888 and to all degree courses in 1899.)[27] Female medical practices were now being set up in Scotland as well.

A formidable recruit to the suffrage movement in the early years of the twentieth century was Dr Elsie Inglis. Known to posterity as the founder of the Scottish Women's Hospitals during the war, at an earlier date she was a very active worker for women's enfranchisement. As her biographer has said, many of the women in the movement were still leisured gentlewomen with little experience of the 'seamy side' of life. As a speaker Dr Inglis was able to describe a very different world and to campaign for the vote on the basis of the needs of women in the slums. She was a new kind of suffragist – a professional woman, emancipated, fulfilled, self-supporting, a positive thinker who stressed the need to win the vote in order to help women who were not so well off.[28]

In north-west England working-class women themselves were mobilising to obtain the franchise.[29] Priscilla McLaren strongly supported the 'Factory Women's Movement'. Mrs McLaren was by this time in her eighties and largely confined to bed in her Edinburgh home, but in 1901 she sent several hundred pounds raised from 'friends who profess an interest in the cause of woman suffrage' to the NUWSS secretary, Esther Roper. She was delighted by the new development, though she felt that 'in the old days women were much more earnestly anxious for the suffrage than they are now ... my time may be short but I have the old enthusiasm when we would have our cause discussed in the House of Commons and men were there in earnest to help us – they are simply playing with us now'.[30]

Priscilla McLaren's comments might indicate a movement at low ebb before the advent of militancy, but apart from events in Lancashire, and the 1897 House of Commons vote, a moribund movement does not sprout branches: in 1902 a new society was formed, the Glasgow and West of Scotland Association for Women's Suffrage.[31] The first meeting was held on 2 May 1902 at the home of a former president of the Glasgow Women's Liberal Association, Mrs Greig. Office-bearers were appointed, with Mrs Greig as president. Various associations were asked if they wished to appoint representatives to the executive committee; the Primrose League declined, but the Scottish Women's Liberal Federation, the Women's Liberal Unionist Association, and the Scottish Co-operative Women's Guild thereafter were so represented. (The Co-operative Guild also asked the Association to send it a speaker.)[32]

The Association's first public meeting on 13 December was accounted a great success, with over 200 ladies and gentlemen present. Flora Stevenson and Lady Frances Balfour addressed the meeting, and it was reported that the latter's speech 'was most helpful and encouraging, but she assured her audience that it is only by hard and persistent work on the part of women that the Franchise is to be gained, and that women must themselves insist on their desire to have this injustice removed.'[33]

The Glasgow Association liaised closely with the Edinburgh Society and in October 1903 affiliated to the NUWSS. There was also an

Aberdeen society with a membership of 60–70 which preferred to go its own way.[34] In 1903 the Women's Social and Political Union was formed in Manchester by Emmeline Pankhurst and her daughter Christabel, but at this time the new Union was unknown outside Manchester, while there was an unmistakeable upsurge in activities in both Scotland and England. A new magazine, the *Women's Suffrage Record*, was launched (in common with the previous *Women's Suffrage Journal* and all future women's suffrage journals, it covered Scottish events). The report of the annual meeting of the Edinburgh Society on 20 March 1903 was much fuller than in previous years. The work done in Lancashire amongst women textile workers had inspired the Scottish society to get up meetings in Dundee, Dunfermline, Kirkcaldy, Arbroath, Brechin and Forfar, towns with a large female factory population, and there resulted petitions to Parliament with some four thousand signatures.

In 1904 an election was in the air, and suffrage societies were forming committees in as many constituencies as possible. By June 1904 the Edinburgh Society had committees in Midlothian, Leith, Kirkcaldy, Dundee, the Borders, Perthshire and Stirlingshire. By January 1905 the Glasgow Association had committees in Castle Douglas, Dumfries, Motherwell, Paisley, Ayr and Greenock. Both societies employed full-time organising secretaries. In February 1905 the Aberdeen Society joined the NUWSS.[35]

The first act of militancy was in Manchester on 13 October 1905, when the Women's Social and Political Union disrupted a large Liberal meeting and Christabel Pankhurst spat in the face of a policeman in order to be arrested and gain maximum publicity for the women's suffrage cause, but this made no impact in Scotland. However, at the end of that year there was a General Election, and at the beginning of 1906 Great Britain had a new government, with an overwhelming Liberal majority. Scotland was the stronghold of Liberalism in Great Britain. If the new militant wing of the movement was determined to *force* the Liberal government to give votes to women, then Scotland was sure to receive plenty of attention.

The Movement in Scotland Revitalised – 1906–7

The traditional suffrage societies believed in working through the existing party structure and in supporting all individuals who professed themselves in favour of women's enfranchisement. The new militant organisation formed by the Pankhursts – the Women's Social and Political Union (WSPU) – favoured a different policy. The Liberal Prime Minister, Sir Henry Campbell-Bannerman – a Scot – agreed in principle with women's suffrage but refused to commit his government to formal support. Therefore, WSPU policy was to oppose all Liberal candidates in by-elections, regardless of their views on the suffrage question, and to heckle Liberal speakers by asking them if the Liberal government would give votes to women.[1] The militant women were dubbed 'suffragettes' to distinguish them from the constitutionalist 'suffragists'.

In January 1906 Flora Drummond – from Arran but now a leading member of the central committee of the WSPU in London – attended a meeting of the Prime Minister's in Glasgow. Sylvia Pankhurst described the occasion.

> Heckling is a regular institution in Scotland, and the Glasgow women declared that they would certainly receive courteous replies. On asking the usual question Mrs Drummond was at once flung out by the stewards and immediately afterwards one of her companions who had hitherto been a staunch Liberal approached her with hat awry and dishevelled clothing saying in bewilderment, 'Oh my, they pet me oot!'[2]

As can be seen from reports in any Scottish newspaper of the time, heckling was indeed an accepted activity at political meetings. Later chapters will reveal frequent brutal ejections of women who attempted to ask about votes; one might then argue a public opinion alienated by suffragette actions, but no such argument can apply to this first recorded ejection. Of course, politicians were open to challenge from the electorate, i.e. men, but such an explanation of differing behaviour toward the sexes is hardly sufficient. Somewhere deep in the male unconscious there must have existed a dividing line between acceptable and unacceptable behaviour on the part of women, with standing up and shouting out questions in public meetings on the wrong side of that line. The atavistic response of violent ejection was out of all proportion to the women's actions.

The women themselves realised that their actions put them beyond the pale.

> The woman who faces the crowd and stands up in a meeting to utter her protest against the subjection of women to men defies convention and throws aside that much-prized virtue – respectability. She gives up friendships that she values; often she renounces all her past life.[3]

At the end of April the WSPU created a disturbance in the women's gallery of the House of Commons which reverberated throughout the nation. The Scottish-born Labour MP, Keir Hardie, had tabled a resolution in favour of women's suffrage, and the women spectators found once again that it was being 'talked out'. A small group of them began shouting and disrupting the proceedings. The incident was widely condemned in the press; the National Union of Women's Suffrage Societies (NUWSS) dissociated itself from those women, as did affiliated societies like the Glasgow and West of Scotland Association for Women's Suffrage.[4] However, correspondence in the *Glasgow Herald* revealed support for women who had finally lost patience. A straw in the wind was that Miss J.C. Methven, secretary of the Edinburgh National Society for Women's Suffrage from the early 1890s and a very active worker for the cause in that decade, was one of those who wrote in support of the women.[5] Graham Moffat, a popular actor-manager, recorded in his autobiography a conversation which he overheard on a Scottish train between two passengers.

> 'It is an outrage!' angrily asserted one. 'Disgraceful that British women should behave like viragoes! I agree with the writer of the leader in this paper. They have put back their cause for, at least, half a century.'
> 'Have they?' queried the other. 'I am not so sure. I am as much against women getting votes as you seem to be, but would you and I be discussing their claims now if these women had not behaved outrageously? Would anything be done for them in the next half century if they keep quiet? I doubt it!'[6]

In May the Prime Minister received a deputation of suffragists. Louisa Stevenson went from Edinburgh, and the Scottish Women's Liberal

Federation also sent representatives.[7] However, all that Campbell-Bannerman told the women was that they should go on 'pestering'.

Meanwhile an independent initiative had been launched in Scotland by a group of women graduates who had formed a Scottish University Women's Suffrage Union. From 1868 onwards the four universities of Scotland had been entitled to return two members to Parliament. The electorate was the General Councils (including all graduates) of the universities; the word 'person' rather than 'male' was used in this section of the relevant statute. Women were first admitted to Scottish universities in 1892, and by 1906 more than nine hundred women had degrees from one of the Scottish universities. Their diplomas were identical to those issued to men, and they were admitted as full members of General Councils.

During the intervening years the elections were uncontested and therefore offered no opportunity for women to test the legislation. In 1906, when there was a contested election, a number of women graduates applied for voting papers and were unconditionally refused them. A group of Edinburgh graduates therefore formed a provisional committee to take legal action. They raised a sufficient sum to cover initial expenses and took the case to the Court of Session. The women (Margaret Nairn, Elsie Inglis, Frances Simson, Frances Melville, and Chrystal MacMillan) argued on two fronts: that the 1868 Act clearly specified 'person' rather than 'man' and that the universities had no legal right to withhold their voting papers.[8]

The case came before the Lord Ordinary in July 1906. Lord Salvesen ruled that 'person' in the 1868 act meant 'man' and that the Registrar was bound to issue voting papers only to those qualified to vote.[9] The women decided to appeal the case, though it would not be heard until the following year.

In the early autumn of 1906 the WSPU sent Teresa Billington to Scotland to gather members and form branches. A committed socialist (she was the first woman organiser in the Independent Labour Party) with a strong personality, Teresa Billington came from the north of England; in 1907 she married a Scot, Frederick Greig, and thereafter made her home in Glasgow (the couple adopted the name Billington-Greig). She was an inspiring speaker. After hearing her, one young woman – Helen Fraser – who had never taken any previous interest in women's suffrage was not only completely convinced of the justice of the cause but had agreed to chair Teresa Billington's next meeting.[10] Shortly after, Helen Fraser was appointed WSPU organiser for Scotland, and her life for the next few years was wholly committed to the cause of women's suffrage.

In October Margaret Irwin, secretary of the Scottish Council for Women's Trades and a member of the executive committee of the

Glasgow and West of Scotland Association for Women's Suffrage, wrote to the committee saying that she had listened with great pleasure to WSPU speakers and urged the committee to invite Teresa Billington to address a public meeting of the Association. This was the first intimation that the equanimity of this staid constitutional society was going to be shattered by the advent of the WSPU. After 'considerable discussion' the committee decided against issuing any such invitation.[11]

October saw the launch of a new weekly socialist journal in Glasgow. The *Forward* was a lively and refreshing paper, not least because its editor, Thomas Johnston, provided an open forum for differing views. The first issue (13 October) carried a moving and impassioned appeal for justice entitled 'Sex Bars and Prison Bars' by Teresa Billington. The following week Tom Johnston set out his own views: 'We can never have Socialism without complete democracy, and every privilege broken, every barrier burst, every sex and social hallucination swept aside makes clearer the road'. That same issue (20 October) also carried a pro-suffrage article by 'Lily Bell' – a pseudonym of Keir Hardie – and an interview with Emmeline Pankhurst, who addressed a meeting in Glasgow that month. Sylvia Pankhurst later commented that the socialist and suffrage movements were 'closely intermingled in Glasgow'.[12] Those close links continued long after Mrs Pankhurst and Christabel had moved far to the right of the Labour movement; Tom Johnston and *Forward* must take much of the credit.

At the opening of Parliament on 24 October a group of WSPU women created a disturbance in protest against the Prime Minister's refusal to hold out any hope of legislation for women's enfranchisement in the current or any future session. Eleven of them – including Teresa Billington – were arrested and imprisoned in Holloway. While she was in prison the *Forward* carried a series of feminist articles by 'Lily Bell'.

An approach was made by the WSPU to the Glasgow and West of Scotland Association: Helen Fraser asked the Association to give her and another Scottish WSPU member, Mrs Pearce, an opportunity of addressing a meeting and also to consider ways in which the two societies might work together. At an informal meeting Mrs Pearce made it clear that the WSPU was not connected with the ILP in any way, which may have reassured the committee (largely Liberal in its leanings), but she also insisted that the WSPU would continue 'to pursue the militant methods already adopted', whereupon the committee decided that there was no possibility of any kind of joint action at that time – another straw in the wind.[13]

The Scottish Women's Liberal Federation also continued its traditional methods of working for the vote, helped by certain Liberal men, particularly J.W. Gulland, MP for Dumfries Burghs. In February 1907 the

Scottish and English Women's Liberal Federations held a conference with
sympathetic Liberal MPs to forward the movement on constitutional
lines. Scottish Liberal MPs were asked to ballot for a place for a women's
suffrage Bill next session; two of them (Price and Dundas White) agreed
to give first place in their ballot to women's suffrage and four others (R.
Balfour, Findlay, McCallum, and Murray Macdonald) to give second
place. In the event, it was an English MP, W.H. Dickinson, whose
Women's Enfranchisement Bill was to receive a second reading, and the
Federation resolved to send whips in support of the Bill to Scottish Liberal
MPs.[14]

There was no breaking of ranks within the Scottish Women's Liberal
Federation, but the story within the Glasgow and West of Scotland
Association was a different one. On 17 January Grace Paterson told the
executive committee that she had been present at a meeting of the WSPU
in the Berkeley Hall and had 'been much struck with Miss Billington's
power as a speaker'. She therefore urged that Miss Billington be invited to
address meetings 'with a view to educating the women of Glasgow'.

> Miss Paterson said she felt very strongly that this Association was not
> successfully accomplishing this object and did not occupy the strong
> position it might and as a matter of fact that it is not nearly so strong as an
> old one which existed between 20 & 30 years ago.

Grace Paterson was not a young firebrand but a stalwart of the Victorian
women's movement. Born in 1843, she took part in the struggle for
women's admission to Glasgow university, in 1885 was one of the first
two women elected to Glasgow School Board, and was founder-principal
of the Glasgow School of Cookery that same year.[15] She was also a
founder member of the Glasgow and West of Scotland Association, and
her resolution was seconded by Margaret Irwin, by Glasgow's first
woman doctor, Marion Gilchrist, and by another founder member of the
Association, Janie Allan, a member of a wealthy shipping family who
were keen socialists. The committee came to no conclusions about what
action the Association should take in response to the dissatisfaction
expressed by some of its members.

Meanwhile the north east was experiencing its first onslaught of WSPU
activity, for an unexpected by-election in South Aberdeen brought the
WSPU out in force. Lindy Moore has researched this campaign thoroughly, through Aberdeen newspapers.[16] If Scotland was Britain's
Liberal stronghold then Aberdeen was Scotland's Liberal heartland, and
the local suffrage society membership overlapped with the women's
branch of the Aberdeen Liberal Association.

Teresa Billington-Greig (she married during this by-election) and Helen Fraser addressed meetings in Aberdeen in January, expounding the case for the vote and the rationale for the WSPU's opposition to all Liberal candidates irrespective of their views on women's enfranchisement. Some Liberal women were persuaded, but naturally the committee of the women's branch of the Aberdeen Liberal Association considered the policy utterly mistaken. At the beginning of February Emmeline Pankhurst was briefly in Aberdeen, and many meetings followed, including several in the open air. The WSPU meetings received extensive coverage – mostly favourable – in the local press, while the correspondence columns were full of the subject. The *Evening Express* gave Helen Fraser a particularly good write-up, and she herself later said that the best and 'most intellectual' audiences she ever spoke to in Britain were in Aberdeen: 'they appreciated really good speaking ... If you were logical, really full of matter, they loved it.'[17] The *Aberdeen Free Press* leader of 19 February called the women's campaign 'the most striking feature of the contest in South Aberdeen' and stated that the suffragists had 'shown that the movement is led by women of culture, of high character, and intense moral earnestness' and had caused many to think seriously about the question for the first time.

At the polls on 20 February the Liberal majority was slashed from over 4,000 to under 400. The WSPU claimed some of the credit, although the Liberal candidate (George Esslemont) had been unpopular. In any case, the WSPU presence had created great interest, and a local branch was established in the city, with a journalist, Caroline Phillips, as honorary secretary.[18]

Caroline Phillips wrote jubilantly to James Murray, MP for East Aberdeen and a staunch supporter of women's suffrage, after the first WSPU 'At Home'. It had been very successful and useful, 'because I got 23 new members; one cannot manage this in a big public meeting'. Although a 'scratch' affair, there were 'so many bright young accomplished people among our members' that putting together a programme had not been difficult: 'The remarkable feature of the meeting was that the question of Women's Suffrage was never lost sight of for a moment in the social gathering. Votes & politics are lively interesting subjects – not the dry dreary affairs that some of the older women ... make them.'[19]

At this stage it was still possible for militant and non-militant women to come together. In January a large public meeting in Edinburgh was chaired by Lady Frances Balfour with Teresa Billington on the platform. Miss S.E.S. Mair (president of the Edinburgh National Society for Women's Suffrage since 1906 when Priscilla McLaren died) said that 'she hoped that those ladies who gave their assistance on constitutional lines would give their support to other ladies who were working on different lines'.[20] Even in Glasgow Grace Paterson's motion that the Glasgow and West of Scotland Association join in a public meeting arranged by Janie Allan at which WSPU officials were to speak was passed by eight votes to six.[21]

A constitutionalist, Lady Steel, the widow of the former Provost of Edinburgh, created a stir in March by refusing to pay her taxes as a protest against the exclusion of women from the franchise. As a result some of her goods were sold at public auction at the Mercat Cross, Edinburgh.[22] She argued that non-payment of taxes was the best way of popularising women's suffrage: 'People attended suffrage meetings by the hundred. They would go to witness the sale of a suffragist's furniture by the thousand, as her own experience had proved.'[23] (The NUWSS eventually rejected tax-resistance because it was unlawful, but the militants took it up, and later a separate Tax Resistance League was formed.)

By now the first two Scottish women (both actresses) had been arrested in London and imprisoned in Holloway for taking part in an attempt to force an entry to the House of Commons, something that English WSPU members had already been imprisoned for. Annie Fraser, Helen's sister, was one of them. At the hearing when the magistrate said to her, 'you must admit you were obstructing the police', she replied, 'on the contrary, the police were obstructing me.' The other woman was Graham Moffat's wife, Maggie. The press called on him in Glasgow to find out how he took the news and were surprised to hear him say how proud he was of her.[24]

Early in 1907 a heated debate took place in the *Forward*. The nub of it concerned the relationship between the women's suffrage movement and the Labour movement, and between the demand for universal ('adult') suffrage and suffrage for women with property qualifications. Tom Johnston put the case for women's suffrage in a pamphlet published at that time; he felt that even a limited female franchise would remedy a long injustice and was worth campaigning for.[25] He did not object to the WSPU keeping free of party connections, but he did take exception to Teresa Billington's 'gratuitous slurring 'of the movement's 'best friend' when she claimed that Keir Hardie's lifelong support for women's suffrage was motivated by expediency rather than principle. Teresa Billington replied that Keir Hardie's support was both principled and expedient: 'Expediency is not always quite the vicious thing Mr Johnston appears to believe. Translated by Mr Keir Hardie, it would in this case probably read "for the best interests of his party and its objects." '[26]

Meanwhile, Tom Johnston opened his columns to J. O'Connor Kessack, an 'adult' suffragist whose dislike of the women's suffrage movement had not been mitigated 'either by reading the pamphlet by the Editor, or the articles of Miss Lily Bell.' All he really had to say (at inordinate length) was that the Bill before Parliament would enfranchise only propertied women and thereby delay the working-class vote. Teresa Billington was given the front page for her rejoinder, 'The Adult Suffrage Fraud'. She had been present when the Adult Suffrage Society was created, with the sole purpose of stopping the Women's Enfranchisement Bill. With only one exception 'the few branches of this society have either done nothing or devoted all their efforts to opposing the women's agitation. No single whisper of bona-fide propaganda for Adult Suffrage has been heard of.' (Others said the same, for though there were many sincere adult suffragists, the adult suffrage claim was largely a spoiling action against a women's suffrage bill.) She did not accept that only middle-class women would be enfranchised; most women lodgers who would receive the vote would be working class. In the same issue Tom Johnston himself refuted O'Connor Kessack's contention that mainly propertied women would be enfranchised ('The figures in my pamphlet stand to this minute uncontroverted, and I submit that until they are overturned Mr Kessack's whole premise and conclusions are unsound.')[27] The question of how many working-class women the Dickinson Bill would have enfranchised has remained in dispute. It did not become law so one will never know.

It was typical of Tom Johnston that in the very next issue he should again give an adult suffragist (who styled himself 'Ell Aitch') front page space for an attack on Teresa Billington's piece, while at the same time carrying a long letter from Flora Drummond on the importance of putting women's suffrage before adult suffrage. (It is of interest that a Glasgow socialist journal was read at WSPU headquarters in London and was considered important enough to warrant a long letter in reply.) A week later 'Lily Bell' responded to 'Ell Aitch', and then 'Ell Aitch' replied to that piece. By May O'Connor Kessack had been converted to the women's suffrage point of view, but Tom Johnston found another antagonist (Agnes Pettigrew, organiser of the Women Shop Assistants) to state the adult suffrage viewpoint and stir up the argument afresh.[28]

The Women's Enfranchisement Bill, popularly known as the Dickinson Bill, was talked out in the House of Commons before it could receive its Second Reading. On 9 March 1907 the *Scotsman* regretted that an open debate had not been held on the question. The paper came out firmly in favour of enfranchising women, but was to do an about-face in the years to come. The *Scotsman*'s support reflected Liberal fears that a majority of women would vote Conservative; for a virulently anti-Liberal newspaper like the *Scotsman* such an outcome was devoutly to be wished. Another Conservative paper, the *Aberdeen Daily Journal*, also devoted a leading article to the Bill on the same date but came out against women's enfranchisement, and held to that attitude in the years that followed.

Male support for women's suffrage was not confined to the socialists. After his wife's release from prison Graham Moffat 'succeeded in getting together a number of those poor brave things, the husbands and brothers of active suffragettes, and other male sympathisers, to form "The Glasgow Men's League for Women's Suffrage." '[29] Meanwhile, the WSPU was growing. Although the initial setting up of branches had been delegated to Teresa Billington, the Pankhursts were keen to stamp their own influence on Scotland, and in May Mrs Pankhurst addressed meetings in Aberdeen, in Glasgow and other west of Scotland towns (sometimes sharing a platform with Tom Johnston), and in Edinburgh. The *Edinburgh Evening Dispatch* called her 'a woman of charming personality', a comment which no popular newspaper would dare to make within a few years' time, no matter that it continued to be true.[30]

In June 1907 a central executive committee was formed to supervise the propaganda work in Scotland. A conference was held in Glasgow and attended by delegates from all the Scottish branches. The committee was constituted as the Scottish Council of the WSPU, with Teresa Billington-Greig as honorary secretary, Mrs Pearce honorary treasurer, and Helen Fraser continuing as Scottish organiser.[31]

In June a new suffrage journal, *Women's Franchise*, started in London, with reports of the activities of both the WSPU and the NUWSS in England and Scotland. Teresa Billington-Greig wrote the WSPU reports on Scotland, as much to rouse the enthusiasm of Scottish women as for information. Meetings were held in various parts of Scotland (apart from Edinburgh and Glasgow there were branches in Aberdeen, Dundee, Dunfermline, Kilmarnock and elsewhere), but during the summer the most intensive campaign was headed by Helen Fraser on the west coast. Places like Dunoon, Rothesay and Gourock attracted large numbers of holiday-makers and thus provided suffrage speakers with ready-made audiences.[32]

However, the current concern of the WSPU in Scotland was the planning of the country's first suffrage procession in Edinburgh on 5 October. (It was discovered only after the date had been fixed that the Prime Minister, Campbell-Bannerman, was to speak in the city the same day.) As the event was to be entirely peaceable the older suffrage societies in both Edinburgh and Glasgow agreed to take part in it. (The Scottish Women's Liberal Federation decided against doing so, but local Women's Liberal Associations, as well as Primrose League habitations, the British Women's Temperance Association, and Women's Unionist and Conservative Associations all joined in.) The Edinburgh Society was particularly pleased that not only would women be coming from all parts of Scotland, but Scotswomen living in England also planned to come up for the occasion. There was a formidable amount of planning to be done, not only in arranging the procession itself but in coordinating the efforts of the secretaries in the different towns, publicising the event all over Scotland, making arrangements for special trains and so on.[33]

Fortunately it all went right on the day. One woman who took part proclaimed it 'just one big triumphant, glorious success!'[34] The Edinburgh National Society's report for *Women's Franchise* was more sober. The procession had numbered between two and three thousand women, 'and in the very homeliness and simplicity of its appearance lay its strength and dignity'. The crowd watching it was 'a quiet, watchful, undemonstrative crowd, after the characteristic Edinburgh manner', numbering many thousands. 'There were cynical, amused, perplexed, or friendly smiles on the faces of the lookers-on' but no antagonism.[35] The *Scotsman* (7 October) also emphasised the crowd's demeanour but reported that the majority were 'evidently there merely from curiosity'; for the most part 'the spectators were impassive.'

The *Glasgow Herald* (7 October) compared the 'ladylike' methods of the Scottish campaign with the rowdy behaviour which had taken place in the south. The *Herald* reported favourably, if jocularly, on the procession, being particularly struck with the Glasgow Men's League (a group of men held a banner which read 'Scots wha hae votes – men' followed by women carrying a banner which read 'Scots wha haena votes – women') while noting that 'the Edinburgh male, fearful perhaps of the shafts of ridicule, was pretty conspicuous by his absence from the day's proceedings', the exceptions being members of the local Labour party who acted as stewards of the meeting which followed the procession.

The *Dundee Courier* (7 October) reported that some three hundred women travelled from Dundee for the occasion; the reporter recognised several amongst them, including two prospective candidates for the parish council, and noted that the Jute and Flax Workers' Union sent a large representation. His comments were favourable if condescending. The lengthy report by the *Dundee Advertiser's* 'Special Representative' (7 October), headed 'A CONVERT'S IMPRESSIONS' was wholeheartedly enthusiastic about the day, from the procession to the speeches which followed. The reporter had journeyed to Edinburgh 'not exactly an anti-suffragette [sic], but with views too hazy on the subject to bear repetition.' By the end of the day 'misconceptions had to be thrown to the winds, and in common with thousands of other Scotsmen I had to admit, big, brutal, burly, masculine wretch as I am, that not only have the women a case to state, but that they know exactly how to state it with the greatest possible margin of effect.'

The successful organisation of such an event might have fostered a greater solidarity amongst Scotswomen working for the cause, but in fact the autumn of 1907 was a period of schism. First of all, several women finally lost patience with the Glasgow and West of Scotland Association: Grace Paterson resigned entirely, while Dr Marion Gilchrist and Janie Allan resigned from the executive committee. The Association's paid organiser, Mary Phillips, also resigned.[36]

Although Mary Phillips's resignation was not recorded until October, she began writing the 'Woman's Point of View' column for the *Forward* in June and was involved in the WSPU's Clyde coast campaign during the summer. Her loyalties by then lay with the WSPU; as she was also a keen socialist she could never have fitted comfortably in the Glasgow Association. She claimed that her three years as organiser to a constitutional society had taught her the futility of such methods and the need for a militant policy.[37]

Once rid of dissident elements the Glasgow and West of Scotland could at least continue in its quiet, staid way without argument. A more serious rift had developed by then within the WSPU. Basically it was a disagreement between the concept of an organisation run on fairly autocratic lines from London and a democratic organisation with annual conferences to which branches would send delegates and decide policy. The first such conference was due to take place in October 1907 and, with the setting up of a Scottish Council which met regularly, Teresa Billington-Greig had set matters in train for this event. In the summer she wrote to Caroline Phillips in Aberdeen, 'What is vital is that as many as possible of the members should be elected by the branches and responsible to them.'[38]

Emmeline Pankhurst, her daughter Christabel, and Emmeline Pethick Lawrence, who controlled the WSPU in London, objected strongly to such a scenario. To Christabel the WSPU was involved in a 'war' and needed women who were willing to take orders. The conference was therefore cancelled and in place of a democratic constitution WSPU members were to sign a declaration of unquestioning loyalty to their leaders. It would be idle to pretend that only principles and not personalities were involved; from the time of the Aberdeen by-election the Pankhursts had been jealous of Teresa Billington-Greig's influence.[39] There was no way that Teresa Billington-Greig and others who felt as she did could remain within the WSPU so there was a complete rift. A breakaway group held the conference as planned, and most of the Scottish branches sent delegates. For a time it called itself the WSPU with the Pankhursts calling their organisation the NWSPU (National Women's Social and Political Union), but the breakaway organisation eventually became the Women's Freedom League.[40]

Partly perhaps because she was resident in Scotland Teresa Billington-Greig did not become president of the WFL although she was responsible for the work in Scotland. The WFL's leader, Charlotte Despard, was a remarkable character in her own right. An ardent socialist, she was born in Ireland in 1844 and went to school from 1857 in Edinburgh. Her biographer wrote that

> the years in Edinburgh left an ineradicable imprint. It could be detected in her speech, where, for example, she talked of the 'forenoon' rather than the morning and of a 'haar' rather than a sea-mist; but its most obvious result was a ferocious sense of duty and an unwavering belief in self-improvement, which were for ever in conflict with her undisciplined mind.

He also noted that during the suffrage campaign she found some of her most appreciative audience in Scotland 'where strong preaching had trained the palate.'[41]

The points of principle behind the breach were not aired in the suffrage press, but again the *Forward* provided a platform for differing views. Initially Mary Phillips commented that since Scottish affairs were managed by the Scottish Council and not by London the secession 'need not worry us', and that 'we owe the very existence of our Union, to the originality and courage of its founder, Mrs Pankhurst, whose untiring zeal in the cause of womanhood has led her to give herself wholly to it'. A few weeks later Amy Sanderson of Forfar responded with 'A Protest in the Name of Democracy'. Readers of the *Forward* knew there had been a split in the Union, 'and much as we all deplore it, there is no disguising the fact and writing as if people were ignorant of it. Better, it seems to me, to face it bravely and openly, and see exactly where we stand.' She set out the viewpoint of those who had, as she saw it, chosen democracy over autocracy.[42]

Mary Phillips responded the following week in her column, insisting that she had never sought to represent any faction 'but the truth, in a spirit as free from partisanship as possible'. She did not deny that Mrs Pankhurst's action was 'unconstitutional 'but felt that the 'spirit' rather than the 'letter' was what mattered: 'One of the first things that attracted me to the Union was the apparent disregard of its members for rigid and elaborate organisation' – an attitude which was doubtless shared by most, if not all, of the women who remained within the WSPU. Teresa Billington-Greig was then given front-page space for a strong attack on the Pankhurst actions, but thereafter Mary Phillips held out a conciliatory hand to the Freedom League, offering to publish news of all its Scottish activities.[43] In the years that followed – as will be seen – relations between Scottish branches of the WSPU and WFL were always amicable.

It is not known how many Scottish women remained in the WSPU and how many went with the WFL. Charlotte Despard's biographer wrote that 'almost half the League's membership was in Scotland', but he provided no source for this statement.[44] As will be seen in later chapters, the Freedom League maintained a strong presence in Scotland. Many Scotswomen were originally inspired by Teresa Billington-Greig rather than the Pankhursts so it is not surprising to find many personalities like Amy Sanderson in Forfar, Anna Munro in Dunfermline, and Maggie Moffat in Glasgow, following her lead. Yet the major Scottish WSPU branches remained intact, and at that time women like Caroline Phillips in Aberdeen and Helen Fraser in Glasgow remained loyal to the Pankhursts.

The differing development of the WSPU and WFL in Scotland must wait for later chapters, but one statement by a modern historian should be considered here. Les Garner has argued that the WSPU/WFL split in 1907 reflected the growing conservatism of Christabel and her mother and that the crisis was basically a simple left and right split within the WSPU.[45] In Scotland there were some socialist women in the WFL (notably Bessie Stewart Semple in Glasgow, Agnes Husband in Dundee, and Anna Munro), but many of the keenest socialists (e.g. Mary Phillips, Janie Allan, and, later, Jessie Stephen and Helen Crawfurd,) were members of the WSPU, which makes nonsense of this argument.

During the autumn of 1907 both militant organisations were busy in Scotland. Emmeline Pankhurst was in Edinburgh in November (presumably attempting to consolidate her position), while Helen Fraser addressed a meeting in the Town Hall, Inverness, with the Provost acting as chairman. Two or three hundred people were turned away at the doors, reported Miss Fraser, and by the end of the meeting the audience was enthusiastic: 'Inverness promises to be a "converted" city, and to give us a splendid branch.' (She added: 'It's the Fraser county, so it's specially pleasing to me to feel it is going to help well.')[46]

While in Scotland Mrs Pankhurst, along with Helen Fraser, made an in unpublicised visit to the executive committee of the Scottish Women's Liberal Federation to explain the WSPU's policy and to request that Liberal women refuse to work for the party unless the suffrage question was dealt with: 'Miss Falconer, in reply, thanked Mrs Pankhurst for explaining the position of her Union in endeavouring to promote the Enfranchisement of Women, and further stated that it was a question which the S.W.L.F. had always furthered in every way in their power.' However, the visit was unprofitable, for the Federation continued to work for suffrage as it always had done, through the Liberal party.[47]

While Emmeline Pankhurst was making her presence more generally known in Scotland, Teresa Billington-Greig was mainly concerned with organising the Women's Freedom League. Maggie Moffat became Scottish treasurer (the Scottish Council's treasurer, Mrs Pearce, having become joint honorary secretary, with Grace Paterson, of the Scottish WSPU). Teresa Billington-Greig spoke at suffrage meetings in the west of

Scotland, while Anna Munro spoke in the east. A primary concern was raising funds for Scottish headquarters.[48]

On the non-militant side, the most important happening in Scotland was the women graduates' appeal before the Extra Division of the Court of Session, which was heard on 22 October, with judgment passed on 16 November. Lord McLaren, in giving the judgment, said that 'it was an incontestable fact that women never had enjoyed the Parliamentary Franchise of the United Kingdom.' Therefore 'it was a principle of the unwritten constitutional law of the country that men only were entitled to take part in the election of representatives to Parliament' and that 'all ambiguous expressions in modern Acts of Parliament must be construed in the light of this general constitutional principle'. The court upheld the Lord Ordinary's decision and found the women liable for expenses.[49] However, there was still the avenue of appeal to the House of Lords, and by the following spring enough money had been raised for the case to go on.[50]

When not holding suffrage meetings themselves, members of both militant societies attended Liberal meetings and heckled the speakers. The *Forward* carried a front-page story (by Benjamin Roy) on such an incident at Kirkintilloch: 'There was only a small band of Suffragettes there – women, sitting among a crowd of "ladies" (that's the Liberal equivalent of a Primrose Dame)'. They sat quietly through the MP's speech, but when the Cabinet Minister, Captain John Sinclair, spoke about freedom for all he was immediately asked about freedom for women.

> Then there was a row.
> The lady wanted to ask a question, and because she did so, the chairman shouted 'Perlice,' 'Perlice,' while two local Liberal 'Pillars of Society' came up to the gallery and addressed the women (the 'ladies' of course were horrified) – and addressed the women as 'Hooligans'...

Eventually Captain Sinclair managed to finish his speech and beat a hasty retreat; when Helen Fraser queried his disappearance the police were again called for, and the women were removed from the hall.[51]

The most dramatic incident occurred in Aberdeen. A large Liberal meeting, with Asquith as the chief speaker, was planned for 19 December and Emmeline Pankhurst addressed suffrage meetings in the city before that date.[52] Her public meeting on 16 December was reported in the *Aberdeen Free Press* on the 17th while on the 18th the paper carried two letters about it. A number of young men had gone to the meeting specifically to interrupt the speaker with homemade 'musical' instruments, jeers and catcalls. Both correspondents took exception to this behaviour. The first one (signed A.C.G.) wrote:

Aberdeen has long been notorious for the rudeness of its young people, and I think the truth of this was never better exemplified than at Mrs Pankhurst's meeting last night. Whether one agreed with what the speaker said or not, she had at least a right to a quiet and courteous hearing.

And the second one (A.I.) wrote

Wishing to hear this lady's views at first hand, I was one of her audience last night. Any unprejudiced party will, I think, allow that she stated her case fairly and in a straightforward manner. Along with most of her hearers I was annoyed and ashamed at the rowdy element in the back settlements of the gallery.

Asquith's meeting took place on the 19th. That day a letter was published from the president, vice-president, and honorary secretary of the women's branch of the Aberdeen Liberal Association to Asquith stating that the Government's delay in introducing a Bill enfranchising women taxpayers placed a severe strain on their loyalty. The *Aberdeen Free Press*, a notable Liberal newspaper, devoted a lengthy leader to the letter: 'It is a portent of the difficulties in which the Liberal party will speedily be placed in the event of the continued refusal of the Government to bring forward a Bill conceding the Parliamentary vote to women taxpayers.' Liberal women had eschewed the policies of militants, and this was now being used to claim that Liberal women did not really want the vote. ('That is the reward which Liberal women have received for their party loyalty!') The editor could understand why they should be revolting and warned that if they were not heeded 'the field will be clear for militant action.'

Because there was so much unease in Aberdeen over the possibility of serious disruption, the WSPU decided that it would give Asquith an uninterrupted hearing if one question was put to him. As he might listen more cordially to a Liberal woman, Mrs Black, president of the women's branch of the Aberdeen Liberal Association, agreed to put the question. When she rose to do so, she was told that she was out of order and was greeted with loud calls so that she had to raise her voice. Her question was answered in a hostile manner, and then the Rev Alexander Webster – described by Sylvia Pankhurst as 'a Unitarian Minister and well known citizen of Aberdeen, a slender, elderly figure, with long grey hair and the face of a saint' – rose from the platform and attempted to move a women's suffrage rider to the official resolution. There was an uproar and three stewards rushed at him and attempted to eject him. Mr Webster defended himself vigorously until the MP, James Murray ('a strong man in physique and finance' as the *Forward* described him) ordered the stewards to withdraw. Mrs Pankhurst rose on her seat at the back of the hall and tried to protest against the proceedings on the platform but was dragged off by stewards.[53]

The incident had repercussions. The *Aberdeen Free Press* noted that 'many a Liberal left the meeting with the uneasy feeling that the suffragists had had the best of it. They had entered their protest constitutionally and respectfully, and yet they had been refused a hearing.' The *Aberdeen Evening Express* devoted a leading article to the subject under the title 'Methods of Barbarism' and also concluded that the suffragists had scored a triumph while the Liberals had come off badly. Christabel Pankhurst considered the affair 'a very great success'.[54]

And thus ended 1907, with the women's suffrage movement firmly established in Scotland, but with enormous potential for growth.

First Attempts to Rouse Scotland – 1908

'The movement in Scotland is very important. It is just now I believe at the point of taking a big new development', wrote Emmeline Pethick Lawrence to Caroline Phillips in January 1908.[1] She visited Scotland soon after and so did Emmeline and Christabel Pankhurst.

The Scottish Women's Liberal Federation continued to work with the Women's Liberal Federation (in England) and not with any suffrage society.[2] However, Mrs Black, president of the Aberdeen Women's Liberal Association, wrote to Lady Ramsay of the WSPU that

> the Liberal Women can do nothing *officially* in the way of cooperating with the members of the W.S.P.U. It would of course be directly opposed to our Constitution. We are however not bound as *individuals* and I shall be delighted to have a talk with you ... I shall invite a few of the more ardent reformers in our committee to meet you here.[3]

In Glasgow the War Secretary, Richard Haldane (a Scot and professedly pro-suffrage), addressed a meeting of Liberal women. The *Aberdeen Free Press* (10 January) was scathing:

> Women having no votes, it matters little to a party man like the War Secretary what he says. The smallest group of voters would in the circumstances have been treated with profound respect; they would have been flattered as typical of the highest intelligence and good sense. But women, because they cannot poll, can be put off with flippancy and persiflage. And Mr Haldane, though addressing an organisation of women Liberals, through whose zeal and activity many Liberal aspirants have been enabled to win seats, fell into a tone of cheap wit ... more suited to the music hall or the smoking concert than to a meeting of the Scottish Liberal Social Union.

But no matter how dismissively Liberal women were treated, the relationship between them and the WSPU, with its insistence on opposing all Liberal candidates, was never an easy one, and the public suffrage meeting in Aberdeen in February provoked controversy. Christabel Pankhurst spoke at the meeting. Elizabeth Somerville, one of the youngest members of the WSPU, recollected Christabel as 'almost like something from fairyland ... I always remembered her.' When asked about Mrs Pankhurst she replied, 'Oh, I thought she was wonderful. But Christabel was my love.'[4] Sylvia Pankhurst, who disagreed with her sister on many important issues, wrote that 'Christabel had the admiration of a multitude; hundreds, perhaps thousands of young women adored her to distraction.'[5] The obverse effect of a personality strong enough to inspire such worship was the capacity to antagonise those who did not fall under the spell.

On 5 February 1908 Annie F. Allan, secretary of the Aberdeen Women's Liberal Association, wrote to Caroline Phillips about the suffrage meeting there.

> I object strongly to Miss Pankhurst taking up the whole hour in a defence of the tactics pursued, we went to hear an educational address on Suffrage, not to hear the W.S.P.U. extolled all the time. It was not courteous. We ought to have had Mrs Pethick Lawrence. She would convert where Miss Pankhurst only irritates.

Caroline Phillips replied that Christabel had judged 'very rightly in the opinion of most people' that the audience she was addressing was composed chiefly of women who were well informed on the subject of women's suffrage, which justified her speaking along the lines she had.[6]

Scotswomen, both non-militant and militant, were also involved in events in London at this time. Lady Frances Balfour took part in a deputation to Asquith and wrote about its 'comic side' to her son, Frank, on 1 February. Asquith's secretary had demanded an assurance that no violence would be attempted: 'Our oldest member Miss [Emily] Davies, over 80, was with us, and we told her this was aimed at her.'[7] Lady Frances added that in the meantime 'our more violent sisters' were mobbing the ministers. Amongst the latter were two Scottish members of the Women's Freedom League, Anna Munro and Amy Sanderson, who had demonstrated at the houses of Cabinet Ministers and were sentenced to six weeks and a month respectively in Holloway for their 'crimes'.[8]

By this time the WFL had established Scottish headquarters in Glasgow. In February an Edinburgh Men's League for Women's Suffrage was formed.[9] Earlier that month Graham Moffat reported on an open-air meeting held in Glasgow to protest against the excessive sentences passed

on the women in London. O'Connor Kessack was the main speaker, but
Helen Fraser also got 'a splendid hearing, and any who tried their wits
against hers were sorry they spoke'. During her speech Moffat went round
the crowd with a copy of a petition to reduce the women's sentences, 'and
had an opportunity of hearing how her points were going home.'

> 'Will you sign this?' I asked one man.
> 'No' yet – haud on till I'm converted – I'm comin' roond.'
> 'Me tae,' said another. 'Come back wi' yer paper when she's dune.'[10]

Later in February Scotswomen were involved in another demonstration
in London. (While Parliament was sitting any demonstration in the
precincts, no matter how peaceful, was illegal.) On this occasion a group
of women travelled from Caxton Hall to the House of Commons in a
furniture van, causing immense surprise when they emerged; however,
the large body of policemen stationed around the House of Commons
(500 of them according to Lady Frances Balfour) quickly rallied and, as
Mary Phillips put it, 'the fray began in earnest'. Describing the incident to
her son Frank on 14 February, Frances Balfour wrote, 'I don't know
whether I like the policy, but I do admire the courage and resource of the
women.' Mary Phillips was one of the women involved, along with
another Scotswoman, Annot Robinson of Dundee, both of whom were
sentenced to five weeks in Holloway.[11]

In April 1908 there occurred one of the most important developments
in the history of the women's suffrage movement in Britain: Campbell-
Bannerman resigned as Prime Minister because of illness and was replaced
by Asquith. From having a premier who at least paid lip service to their
cause, suffragists were now faced with a man who as early as 1892 had
taken his first parliamentary stand as an implacable opponent to women's
suffrage. There is no doubt that Asquith's position – opposed by a
majority of his own Cabinet – was one of the main obstacles to women
obtaining the vote before the war. The Prime Minister's attitude would
cause increasing distress to Liberal women as the years went on; Lady
Frances Balfour, as a close family friend and erstwhile great admirer, was
particularly hurt and disillusioned by it. Although he was not a Scot,
Asquith's constituency was East Fife.[12]

April was also the month of the Kincardineshire by-election, the first
one since the new suffrage movement had become established in Scotland.
Both the WSPU and the WFL sent up organisers from England as well as
involving Scottish members. The WFL was first in the field, opening
committee rooms in Torry (a suburb of Aberdeen and the largest centre of
population in the constituency) and Stonehaven. The suffrage campaign
received plenty of press coverage, particularly in the Aberdeen papers.[13]

Amy Sanderson wrote of her visit, with Anna Munro, to Stonehaven, 'a hot bed of Liberalism'.

> Decidedly the most picturesque meeting I have ever attended. In the background the blue sea and the little harbour, where a fishing-boat rocked with a white sail unfurled on which were inscribed in black letters, 'Votes for Women.' We stood on a pile of herring-boxes, in front of us a crowd of fishermen and wives and young girls. The latter wore the Liberal candidate's colours, and vigorously opposed us. We had plenty of questions and good-humoured banter at the close, and marched back to the new town attended by troops of youngsters. That same evening we cycled back to Stonehaven from Newton Hill, after a fine meeting. It was a beautiful evening, a full moon shining on the water, and as clear as daylight. Miss Munro and I looked at each other as we pedalled along, and the same thought came into our heads at once. 'What a blessed change from Holloway Prison!'[14]

Reports in the suffrage press of by-election campaigns tended to be relentlessly upbeat, but in the *Forward* (2 May) Mary Phillips presented a different view.

> There are said to be three forms of baptism, through any of which one may pass in order to be dignified by the proud title ... of Suffragette. One is to be thrown out of a Cabinet Minister's meeting; another to go to prison; the third to fight in a bye-election. I have now passed through all these ordeals in turn, and I can unhesitatingly say that the last is by far the hardest of all.

In this by-election, as in so many to come, the Liberal candidate favoured women's suffrage while the Unionist did not, yet the WSPU campaigned for the latter. Partly because of this, 'we are made a target for jeers and insults such as I never expected to hear from the lips of Scottish men and women, and such as, I fear, have permanently lowered my opinion of my compatriots.'

The Liberal majority of 2,353 was cut to 1,698, a drop of 655 which was claimed as a 'victory' by both sides. Helen Fraser thought that 'considering the "touching faith" our Scotsmen have in Liberalism, and the persistence with which they stick to old opinions, it is a gratifying result.' She went on

> Many of them voted as one old man did, who said, 'Wha gaed me my vote? Gladstone; and I'm gawn to gie it to him.' Such loyalty much be extremely gratifying to Liberals, but it is rather trying for Suffragettes.[15]

4 Amy Sanderson. Reproduced by permission of the People's Palace (Glasgow
Museums)

Two more Scottish by-elections followed on the heels of Kincardineshire – Dundee and Montrose Burghs. Having lost in Manchester during this round of by-elections, Winston Churchill was selected for the safe seat of Dundee (where the Liberal majority at the General Election had been 5,000), which made it an important contest to the militant suffrage movement. Charlotte Despard and Emmeline and Christabel Pankhurst came up for the occasion and addressed public meetings. A large number of campaigners, both Scottish and English, were recruited.

The Women's Freedom League made the most impact in that campaign, albeit of a negative kind. A League member from the south, Miss Moloney, was determined to extract an apology from Churchill for some derogatory remarks he had made about suffragettes in connection with an English by-election, and her ploy was to ring a bell whenever he attempted to address a meeting to prevent him being heard. She was nicknamed La Belle Moloney by the press and, according to Eunice Murray, was 'the central figure of attraction.' But press comments were hardly favourable. The *Dundee Advertiser* commented that if a man had behaved in such a way, 'he would have got the clothes torn from his back, and he would have deserved it.'[16]

Though Dundee was such a safe Liberal seat, some suffragettes convinced themselves that having lost in Manchester Churchill could be defeated again.[17] Mary Phillips recorded:

> Seldom, say our English workers, have they met with a more encouraging reception than they have met from the people here, right through the campaign. All our best speakers have appealed to the electors day after day, eighteen or twenty daily meetings have been held, and always we have come in at night from our various 'pitches' with the same story – large and enthusiastic audiences, good sales of literature, substantial collections, and a general impression of sympathy and support from all sides.

Not only that, but on polling day Churchill was booed when he appeared.

> Yet – after four hours of tension, waiting for the result ... 2700 majority for the unscrupulous nominee of a false Government, for the man who was rejected of Manchester, but who has yet been received with acclamation by Dundee ... I repeat what I said after Kincardine – my opinion of my fellow-countrymen is permanently lowered. How we have reminded them of the traditions of Scotland, of the fights for freedom in which our forefathers led, and in which our foremothers were never found behind the men of England in striking a blow for justice for women! How we have sought to stir their pride and their patriotism in these matters, and by asking them never to allow it to be said that Scotland was a dumping ground for England's second-hand goods![18]

Such a dent in the Liberal majority might have been cause for rejoicing in most by-elections, but for someone like Mary Phillips who had believed he would be defeated, it was poor consolation. (Mary Phillips had an additional cause for bitterness as the socialists thought that the Labour candidate stood a good chance of coming second, whereas in fact he came a poor third after the Unionist candidate.) Helen Fraser showed more perception when she wrote that Churchill's victory had been a foregone conclusion: 'The mass of the Liberals believe in our claim, but their Liberalism is a religion to them, and to vote against their party for us they consider too much to ask. One must fight Scottish by-elections for their educative value.'[19]

The Montrose Burghs by-election took place two days later. The campaign was overshadowed by the Dundee election and only a few women were in the Montrose area beforehand, but they all rushed up (Emmeline Pankhurst included) for those last two hectic days. Amy Sanderson wrote of campaigning there with Anna Munro, and how the men, if impressed with the suffragettes' eloquence, would shout 'Ca awa, wifie, yer daein fine.'[20] The WSPU workers were involved in an unpleasant incident in the town of Montrose. The Provost there was the political agent for the Liberal candidate and used the police to attempt to move the women from the polling booth, though the women eventually won the day.[21] Emmeline Pankhurst argued that the result of the by-election – another reduced Liberal majority – showed that 'the stronghold of Liberalism is being shaken to its foundations', but Christabel was more honest when she later wrote of this period that the strength of party allegiance in Scotland 'meant a distinct setback to our work'.[22]

There was still another Scottish by-election to come, Stirling Burghs, the constituency of the late Prime Minister, Henry Campbell-Bannerman. The day after the Montrose Burghs polling day Mrs Pankhurst and all the Scottish and English WSPU and WFL campaigners moved to Dunfermline for the start of a 10-day campaign. As the constituency included not only Dunfermline but also Stirling, Inverkeithing, South Queensferry and Culross, all those towns had their first exposure to the new suffragette campaign methods, which included walking around with sandwich boards, ringing hand-bells, chalking pavements with notices of meetings, addressing passers-by from platforms on lorries and so on. On 11 May the *Glasgow Evening Times* applauded:

> The Suffragette makes many a dull contest lively. The heavy polls, the crowded meetings, are in no small degree the result of her presence. She is new and alive and fearless, humorous and pertinent and emphatic, unwearying and unconventional. The zest of the contest always hangs about her. She carries war into the enemy's camp. Her weapons are always

unsheathed. And as all true Scots love a fight, the interest and movement of the fray centre in her – the woman in rebellion, the woman who has at last arisen to fight for herself.

Helen Fraser regarded the Stirling Burghs as the only one of the four seats in which there was any hope of defeating the Government, but she was philosophical when the Liberal majority actually increased majority, stressing again the importance of educating public opinion.[23]

Scottish suffrage workers retired exhausted and attention shifted to London, where the NUWSS planned a procession in June. Their first procession in London, the previous year, was in such bad weather that it became known as the Mud March.[24] The National Union wrote to the Glasgow and West of Scotland Association hoping 75 members would go for the occasion, an impossible number for the Association to contemplate in view of the cost of travel. The Association also decided not to display posters for the event 'as we are at too great a distance from London for such an advertisement to be effective.' After the procession the Association member who did take part gave the committee an interesting account of it and of the display of banners, and the committee arranged an exhibition of suffrage banners.[25]

The WSPU procession was a week later (21 June), culminating in a monster demonstration in Hyde Park. The Scottish WSPU requested that all Scottish members taking part should meet at a fixed place and walk together as a Scottish contingent. (It had been hoped to arrange a special train to London, but sufficient numbers had not come forward.) The feeling expressed the week before the event was

> We in Scotland feel a little 'out of' the excitement which is felt in the South, but nevertheless, although our Scottish members cannot, on account of distance, be there in great numbers, yet those not present in body will be present in spirit.[26]

An Edinburgh WSPU office opened in June. In July the Edinburgh WSPU reported that the NUWSS had held its annual meeting in the city: 'As most of our members still belong to the National, we thought it best to help them in their meetings in every way we could – advertising, stewarding &c &c.'[27] Unlike the situation in Glasgow, the differing tactics of constitutional and militant suffrage societies had not yet divided the loyalties of women in Edinburgh who were working for the same end.

But the situation in Scotland was about to undergo a new twist. Because of the failure of the London procession and Hyde Park demonstration to have any impact on the Government, Emmeline and Christabel Pankhurst announced that greater militancy was the only answer. Stones had already been thrown at a Cabinet Minister's window, and nearly three-quarters of a century later Helen Fraser told Brian Harrison

> I was horrified, you know, I really was horrified ... And I said [to Mrs Pankhurst] 'you don't use violence, you use *reason* to get the vote' and she said 'you have to do what we tell you' and so on and I said 'I'll resign'.

Resigning 'was the best thing I ever did in my life'. It might seem that the obvious organisation for her to have gone to was the Women's Freedom League, but instead she went to the NUWSS. Millicent Garrett Fawcett, president of the NUWSS, wrote to her shortly after her resignation saying 'we regard you as a suffragist and we would like you to join us'; as Helen Fraser admired Mrs Fawcett she felt it was the right thing to do.[28]

Talking about her move from one society to the other such a long time after it happened, Helen Fraser made it appear relatively painless, but glimpses of how she felt at the time are provided by two letters. On 6 July 1908 she wrote to Isabel Seymour

> I have resigned my position here and am now out of it officially. It was utterly impossible to work with my Committee – I stood it as long as I could but I got to the stage when the thought of them made me feel hysterical – so I knew it was time to stop. I am still tired – very tired, in fact, just beginning to find out how tired I have been ... The members are very worried about my resignation and I am afraid it will spoil S.W.S.P.U. So many of them regard me as the movement that they can't believe it is true.[29]

On 20 August 1908 she wrote to Caroline Phillips

> I had a very worrying time before I resigned and felt very tired and ill when I did ... It doesn't seem true, even yet, that I am no longer connected with you all – I feel sure somehow we shall still work together for suffrage.[30]

Helen Fraser was right in thinking that her departure would mark the end of a separate Scottish WSPU, but she was not followed into the NUWSS by other Scottish women. Her remarks in the second letter help to explain why there were so few defections from one society to another. As will be seen later, not every Scottish WSPU member agreed with all of the Union's policies, but having bonded to a particular group of women it became almost unthinkable to leave them.

Helen Fraser was welcomed with open arms by the suffragists, although the president of the Aberdeen Suffrage Society, Louisa Innes Lumsden, had misgivings, and her letter to Helen Fraser was perceptive about one reason why some women joined militant societies.

5 Helen Fraser — from *The Common Cause* December 2, 1909.

I cannot but agree with you about the militant methods & perhaps your protest will do good – I hope so. But will your resignation open the way towards more violent methods in Scotland? This is the fear which seizes me. One has a *mean* feeling when one is quietly enjoying the good things of life & others are in prison for their convictions! And generous sympathy may hurry people into unwise action.[31]

Louisa Lumsden was born in Aberdeen in 1840; she joined the course of lectures given by university professors in Edinburgh in 1868, and later was one of the first three women to take the Honours Examination in Classics at Girton, Cambridge. From 1877-82 she was the first Headmistress of St Leonard's School for Girls in St Andrews, and some fifteen years later she returned to St Andrews as the warden of the first university hall of residence for women students there.[32] When the Aberdeen Suffrage Society asked her to become its president in 1908, she agreed, 'only stipulating that I should not require to give up much time to it; but I soon found that little time was left for anything else.'[33]

In her letter to Caroline Phillips quoted above, Miss Lumsden continued with a theme which will surface again in this book, as it surfaces in virtually every account of Scottish-English relations. She had received an appeal for funds from the NUWSS and wrote

> I think I *will* send them some trifling help – what I can afford. I would send it joyfully did I not wholly object to be addressed to as a woman 'of England'! That puts my back up thoroughly! I always feel that the little I can give I would rather give to Scotland. If I am told that this is narrow I reply that the narrowness & arrogance of English people begins the evil & a protest is most desirable.

Miss Lumsden contributed in another way to the suffrage work in Scotland by loaning Helen Fraser her horse-drawn caravan for a tour of the Borders during the summer.[34] This tour (which Helen Fraser described in the *Forward* 18 and 22 August) shows the extent to which the NUWSS was adopting new methods. For women to travel around in this way and speak in the open air would never have been contemplated before the advent of the WSPU.

The Glasgow and West of Scotland Association took umbrage at Helen Fraser's new position as organising secretary for Scotland. After all, as the Scottish WSPU organiser the year before she could be held partly responsible for persuading some important members of the Association to join the militants; now she had not only declared herself a constitutionalist, but was being thrust down their throats without prior consultation. The committee made it clear to the NUWSS that this was 'not an acceptable appointment'.[35]

The summer was a busy one for Scottish Women's Freedom League branches. On 25 June Winston Churchill addressed two meetings in Dundee, an afternoon one for women and an evening one from which women were excluded. In spite of attempts to keep suffragettes out of the afternoon meeting, many members of the WFL got in, three of them (plus two WSPU members) being thrown out of the hall for attempting to ask questions. Lila Clunas, the Dundee WFL secretary, regarded a 3.30 pm meeting as an insult to the women of the town; it may have been fine for ladies of leisure but excluded working women and those with homes and children to look after.[36] Anna Munro led a vigorous campaign in the Clyde holiday resorts and helped to inaugurate an east of Scotland campaign based at Carnoustie. Two sisters, Arabella and Muriel Scott, were particularly active in yet another WFL campaign, in East Fife.[37]

Mary Phillips spent her summer in Holloway. She had taken part in another illegal London demonstration and was sentenced to three months' imprisonment, making her the longest-serving suffragette prisoner. The WSPU arranged a 'rousing welcome' for her on her release from jail on 18 September: 'She is a Scotch lassie, and so we are having the pipers out in her honour.' It was a colourful occasion, with women decked in tartan, the skirl of four bagpipes, and a wagonette covered with purple heather and giant thistles. Her parents came down for the occasion, and Flora Drummond made a speech.[38]

Christabel Pankhurst wrote to Caroline Phillips of the 'fine Scottish welcome' they had given Mary Phillips and added, 'we think that other Scotswomen ought to follow her example.'[39] As usual when the WSPU arranged a show they did it well, and the London popular press, which thrived on such pictorial opportunities, gave it plenty of coverage.[40] It seems very much like modern, cynical press stunts, but Mary Phillips was moved.

> Of course I was very proud of the Scottish welcome, and as we sang 'Scots Wha Hae wi' Wallace Bled,' I thought of our national hero's defiant message before the Battle of Bannockburn to the English General who offered him terms of peace: '*We are not here for the purpose of treating for peace, but of abiding battle, and restoring freedom to our country.*' Shall not we, as Scottish women, make this an occasion for strengthening tenfold our determination to defy the Government in a similar spirit ... ?[41]

Scottish women had another focus for their suffrage campaign that summer and autumn, as the candidates for rector of Aberdeen University were Asquith and Sir Edward Carson.[42] Many female students faced a dilemma, being Liberal in belief but wishing to defeat the arch-opponent of women's suffrage even at the expense of electing a Unionist. There were enough women willing to campaign for Carson – or, more truthfully, to campaign against Asquith – for the contest to be a lively one.

In their journal, *The Premier*, the Asquith supporters insisted that they believed in the enfranchisement of women. They welcomed suffragists who appreciated the necessity for patience and they scorned suffragettes who negated all their political beliefs 'before one issue'. The Aberdeen University Women's Suffrage Association hit back in their journal, *The Suffragette*. Asquith – they recorded – had promised to withdraw his opposition if the movement had the undoubted support of the women of the country; let that support now be demonstrated. The university's student journal, *Alma Mater*, felt: 'Surely the new lady students must

6 The 'fine Scottish welcome' for Mary Phillips. Reproduced by permission
of the People's Palace (Glasgow Museums)

resent the down-your-throat methods of the exuberant Suffragettes. They
seem more like policemen arresting carters than civilised students canvass-
ing their fellows.' The journal also carried a wicked send-up of a
suffragette feminist harangue.[43]

Lady Frances Balfour was in Aberdeen in October and wrote to her
sister-in-law, Lady Betty Balfour, on the 15th.

> I had a crowded hour of glorious life yesterday! I was asked to stand as Lord
> Rector, the women-graduates candidate against Asquith and Carson –
> Object, not to put me in, but defeat Asquith, and show the Suffrage
> strength. The whole incident was full of excitement.

She consented providing she was assured of enough votes not to seem
ridiculous, but that same evening the women gave up the idea.[44] Her

candidacy was obviously only mooted in despair of ever defeating a Liberal candidate in Aberdeen.

Also in Aberdeen in October was the annual conference of Women Workers. Caroline Phillips had hoped that Mrs Pankhurst might have attended, but it was too soon after the Women's Parliament in London.[45] A Scottish WSPU member, Una Dugdale, reported on the conference on 'The Training and Practice of Citizenship'. This was so clearly relevant to the franchise question that many women must have been amazed that it was not on the agenda: 'it would therefore have have been far more logical to have called the subject of discourse "The Training and Practice of Non-Citizens (women) in doing that which has been left undone by the citizens (men)".' However, she was convinced that most of the delegates were supporters of the suffrage: 'the burning question was smouldering there, and broke out again and again in the rounds of cheers and applause when the most veiled reference was made to it.'[46]

Perhaps the most important suffrage event of the period was the Scottish women graduates' appeal before the House of Lords, which opened on 10 November. Much of the attention given to this case – and not just by suffrage supporters – was because Chrystal MacMillan herself pleaded it before the Lords. She stayed with a friend in London the week before who 'understudied the Lord Chancellor' enabling her to rehearse her arguments.[47]

The first day's hearing was comparatively brief, but when the case resumed on Thursday the 12th Chrystal MacMillan spoke for several hours without an interruption, going through all the legal arguments about why the term 'person' in the statute should be interpreted as including women.[48] Judgment was not given until mid-December, but in the interim Chrystal MacMillan was euphoric at how well the hearing had gone; many peers had called in during the day, and the press was very complimentary (she was called a modern Portia in some of the reports, while the *Daily Graphic* headed its story 'Miss MacMillan's Great Speech').[49]

Yet it came as little surprise when the Lords concluded that as only men had voted in the past, the term 'person' in a franchise act could never refer to a woman. Although defeated by the law, the women's perseverance must have caused many to ponder that the Lords were denying the vote to women while admitting them competent to plead a complex legal case before the highest court in the land. Chrystal MacMillan became a heroine to all three suffrage organisations in Scotland and was a guest of honour at several meetings in the new year.

The Scottish Women's Liberal Federation was also active that autumn. A suffrage week campaign was held in November with 75 meetings representing the activity of some 84 Women's Liberal Associations. A pamphlet by one of their members, Helen Waddel, entitled 'Liberal Women and the Parliamentary Vote', had been published and was popular with both Scottish and English Women's Liberal Associations.[50]

In December Emmeline Pethick Lawrence visited Edinburgh. At the reception the chair was taken by Miss S.E.S. Mair, and Dr Elsie Inglis took part in the debate on behalf of the constitutionalists, criticising militant tactics. It was reported that 'all shades of opinion were represented, several anti-suffragists being present.'[51] Apart from demonstrating again the closeness between militants and non-militants that still existed in Edinburgh, this was the first mention of anti-suffragists in Scotland.

Brian Harrison, in his definitive study of anti-suffragism in Britain, *Separate Spheres*, wrote that since *The Times* and other newspapers put forward the anti-suffrage case, articulating widely held views, the Antis (as they were popularly known) did not for a long time need a separate organisation.[52] However, by 1908 the suffragettes had had such an impact that an Anti-Suffrage League was formed in England with Lord Curzon as president, and in December an anti-suffrage article by a Scotswoman was published in the *National Review*.

The article – which was so enthusiastically received by anti-suffragists in England that it was subsequently reprinted as a pamphlet – was entitled 'What Every Woman Knows' and the author was Mrs Parker Smith of Jordanhill.[53] Brian Harrison noted that the political hostess enjoyed extensive influence without the vote and had no reason to support it.[54] Mrs Parker Smith certainly fell into that category. Indeed, the *Glasgow Evening News* (12 January 1909) specifically mentioned her unrivalled influence as a canvasser and the 'invaluable assistance' Mr Parker Smith, when he was MP for Partick, had received from his wife 'both as hostess and as President of the Partick Women's Liberal Unionist Association'. The gist of her argument in the article, (when translated from her coded language) was that menstruation, child-bearing and the menopause ensured that women could never play an equal part in public life with men. Dr Elizabeth Garrett Anderson poured ridicule on Mrs Parker Smith's claim, but it struck a chord in many readers, and there was talk for the first time of setting up a Scottish branch of the Anti-Suffrage League.[55]

Earlier that year Eunice Murray of the Women's Freedom League was asked by Teresa Billington-Greig to ascertain the views of her neighbours toward women's suffrage 'so that we may gauge the feeling in the country.' She received such discouraging responses that she concluded: 'If Cardross is an example 'twill be our great great great grandchildren that will vote.'[56] There was still a long way to go in persuading the Scottish people of the need for women's enfranchisement, but the mobilisation of the opposing forces shows how much progress the movement had made in Scotland by the end of 1908.

The Flowering of the Movement in Scotland – 1909

At the beginning of 1909 the WSPU leadership took firm measures to bring Scottish branches into line with the English. An article in *Votes for Women* on 7 January began 'Beautiful, haughty, dignified, stern Edinburgh, with your cautious steadfast people, you have not yet woken up to take part in our militant methods.' This anonymous individual had come up to Edinburgh to demonstrate how easy it was to don a sandwich board, sell copies of *Votes for Women* and hold open-air meetings, even in the winter.

Setting examples was not all that the WSPU came up to Scotland to do; as part of a major overhaul English organisers were installed in the Scottish branches. In Aberdeen the organiser was Ada Flatman, and Sylvia Pankhurst came to help. An office was opened, and *Votes for Women* painted a rosy picture.[1] The reality, as revealed in Caroline Phillips's correspondence, was a thoroughly messy bout of faction-fighting and mud-slinging.

It was by no means a straightforward England versus Scotland battle. Sylvia Pankhurst appears to have incurred the wrath of the 'faction' quite as much as Caroline Phillips did. A friend of Caroline's wrote to her about a meeting

> Yes, that *was* a field night. Our friends were out in full war paint. I was glad you were not present, and yet I regret that you missed the show. An atmosphere of virtuous indignation pervaded the front benches, and there was something irresistibly funny in the solemnity with which the enormities of our Secretary were reeled off from bulky MSS. After mauling you beyond all recognition, they lashed out against Helen Ogston, gave Constance Ogston a kick in passing, and as a grand finale, wiped up the floor with Sylvia Pankhurst.[2]

After Sylvia Pankhurst returned home Caroline Phillips wrote to her that the 'faction are re-established in full favour ... The same old lies about your coming & your sayings & doings when you did come have been repeated ad nauseam.' She added, 'I have got so used to the personal fault finding that I really don't mind it very much now.'[3]

In fact within a few months Caroline Phillips had been forced out entirely, and there is no record of any further involvement by her in the suffrage movement. The English organiser, Ada Flatman, cannot have made much impact, for two years later when Lilias Mitchell was sent up to start an Aberdeen branch of the WSPU she had no idea that one had ever existed. The final indication of how unpleasant this period was is that in neither of Sylvia Pankhurst's detailed accounts of her involvement in the movement (1911 and 1931) did she mention being in Aberdeen at this time.

Difficulties with English organisers will surface again in a later chapter, but for the most part Scottish WSPU branches did not object. The NUWSS imported English organisers too, usually without friction. The Women's Freedom League tended to use English organisers only for by-elections, otherwise relying on local secretaries, but the report of the WFL's fourth annual conference (9 January 1909) reveals some of the tensions inherent in an organisation with headquarters in London but a large Scottish membership.[4]

The conference began with Anna Munro complaining, with regard to press material, of 'the word "England" being used so often instead of "Britain" and "British". (Laughter and applause.)' And the central branch of Glasgow asked for a member of the Scottish Council to be on the executive committee since the former 'being so far from headquarters, do not get to know sufficiently of what is being done.' Anna Munro drew attention to the overlap between the work of the National Executive Council and the Scottish Council. Conversely, Middlesborough branch asked that an organising secretary be appointed for England, because that the present organising secretary (Teresa Billington-Greig) resided in Scotland, making it 'rather difficult for England to get the necessary attention'.

The Conference also discussed the relationship between the two militant societies. Edinburgh branch raised the question because one of its committee members belonged to both societies and sold *Votes for Women*, so that when someone said 'I wish to join your society' she had to ask *which* society. The Edinburgh representative was worried about the WFL losing its identity and asked some guidance from the Conference. Various delegates opposed the idea of hard and fast rules since cooperation with other societies was so helpful. Vague agreement was reached that anyone who was a member of another society should not be allowed to serve on a WFL committee.

What kind of woman became involved in the suffrage movement in Scotland, and what was her motivation for doing so? Discussion of social classes, jobs and marital status is reserved for a later chapter when the Scottish membership was much larger, but the account of one woman who became involved at this time undoubtedly reflects the experience of many others.

Lilias Mitchell belonged to a prosperous Edinburgh family. Her mother was keenly interested in the suffrage and they went to hear Mrs Pankhurst and Mrs Pethick Lawrence speak. 'Never shall I forget the blazing warmth of that meeting;' she wrote, 'we felt completely lifted out of ourselves, joined the society there and then and went home walking it seemed on air.'[5] She continued

> I was twenty-three at the time and was more than ready for an opening for work of this kind. In fact, after that meeting, the hockey, reading, music clubs, violin lessons, even dances, seemed sheer nonsense when the Vote had yet to be won.[6]

Helen Fraser described her life in similar terms, as consisting of balls and dances, amateur theatricals, and charitable work. A different road was taken by women like Anna Munro and Janie Allan. Their consciences were stirred by the socialist movement and they had been actively engaged in social work amongst the working classes before learning of the women's movement.[7]

The main thing all these women had in common was that once involved in the suffrage movement they committed themselves totally to it. Lilias Mitchell wrote of those years as 'a part of my life in which everything else was gradually swamped and I lived and moved and seemed to have my being in working for votes for women.' And Helen Fraser said of her suffrage work, 'You were giving your whole life to the thing ... your life was completely dedicated to that.' Helen Fraser was fortunate in having the support of her whole family. Lilias Mitchell had her mother's but wrote of 'the truly fierce discussion and furious fights we had at home ... my brothers were as strongly against as we were for.'

These women were 'pulled' into the movement, but others were 'pushed' into active involvement. Isabella Carrie, a Dundee schoolteacher, was sympathetic to the cause without feeling any need to play a part in it until she went to a meeting addressed by Winston Churchill. Before it started she noticed stewards going up to certain women, pulling them out of their seats, and hustling them roughly out of the hall. She had heard of

7 Lilias Mitchell (family photograph)

suffragettes being thrown out of meetings but had not seen it before, 'and it upset me very much.'

> It was a women's meeting and when Mr Churchill came in he made some sneering remark about women and the 'Liberal' women cheered him and I was so incensed that he would dare to talk like that to women that I stood up and shouted something at him. I don't remember what I said but not much as I was pounced on at once and, as I did not resist in any way, I did not think it was necessary to twist my arms nor push me down the Gilfillan steps, which they did. I stumbled on the steps and a policeman got a hold of me and held me kindly and gently till I had gained my composure and he patted me and said I was the gentlest Suffragette he had met. I said to him that I did not go to the meeting as a Suffragette but that I was one now.[8]

Some WSPU members outside invited her to join. She did so and though she did not have the temperament to become a public speaker or to take part in militant activities, she helped in the office and later provided a 'safe house' for visiting WSPU activists. She was 'very enthralled with Mrs Pankhurst's manner and address ... I found her a very cultured, clever, sympathetic and understanding lady, and an excellent speaker whose personality shone forth and she took her audience with her.'

To what extent did the Pankhurst personality cult exist in Scotland? Mary Phillips certainly subscribed to it. Her article in the *Forward* of 2 January 1909, after the release from prison of Mrs Pankhurst and Christabel, was a lengthy panegyric ('Dear, brave, noble women! As long as we live, we shall try to show, by every means in our power, the affection and the gratitude we bear you.' etc.). But later that year Mary Phillips moved to England, and no other Scottish woman wrote about the Pankhursts in quite such fulsome terms. Emmeline Pankhurst was certainly an inspirational figure to Scottish WSPU members, but on the whole it seems to have been the cause rather than individuals that inspired them.

On 6 February the *Forward* reported that Anna Munro of the Women's Freedom League addressed a meeting on 'Why Women are not Waiting for Adult Suffrage'. But most of the attention in Scotland at that time was focused on four by-elections: Forfarshire, Glasgow Central, South Edinburgh and Hawick Burghs. Scottish and English workers, including Adela Pankhurst (the only member of the family to work as a paid organiser), were active in all four constituencies, and *Votes for Women* regarded the by-elections as a 'godsend' because they generated so much interest and helped the recruitment of new members. But Mary Phillips wrote in *Votes for Women* (26 February) of the difficulties of working in a scattered rural constituency like Forfarshire: 'Not here, in isolated clachans amongst the hills and pine woods, do we find the wild joy and excitement of town electioneering'.

But there were also disadvantages to town electioneering. In Glasgow one WFL member had ribs broken as a result of the rowdyism there ('We are now afforded sufficient police protection to prevent any serious disturbances.') The report continued

> The University students add life and noise to some of the meetings, but their opposition is neither serious nor sensible, being evidently just an expression of the young male animal's irresponsible desire to express itself in inarticulate sounds, such as booing and crowing.[9]

The non-militant Glasgow and West of Scotland Association was unhappy about the NUWSS's handling of the Glasgow Central by-election. The Liberal opposed the enfranchisement of women, while the Unionist, Scott Dickson, professed support for women's suffrage but refused to commit himself to supporting it in Parliament. The Association therefore decided to do propaganda work only and sent a notice to *Women's Franchise* to this effect. The National Union then told the Association to work for Mr Dickson, and later queried on whose authority the report about doing propaganda work only had been sent to *Women's Franchise*. The argument dragged on for months afterward, with the National Union refusing to settle the Association's by-election accounts because it claimed that NUWSS policy had not been carried out.[10] The relationship between the NUWSS – the umbrella organisation for non-militant societies – and local societies was often difficult, though there was enough mutual respect for it to right itself eventually.

The Liberals held three of the four seats, with reduced majorities, but the Unionist took Glasgow Central. 'Let Glasgow flourish!', wrote Mary Phillips, 'She really deserves to do so, after the smashing blow she struck for Freedom last Tuesday!' Christabel Pankhurst later wrote that 'Glasgow led the way in finding the Government guilty. It was a magnificent message of support for the arrested and imprisoned women.'[11] This is absolute nonsense. Whether the suffrage issue swayed electors at all – newspaper analyses of the result did not even mention it – Glaswegian voters were hardly concerned with a group of women jailed in London. Sylvia Pankhurst was (again) more clear-sighted when, in discussing the difficulty of fighting by-elections in the Liberals' Scottish strongholds, she remarked, 'with the exception of Glasgow, which is not typically Scotch'.[12]

The NUWSS started its own paper, *The Common Cause*, in April 1909, which meant more space was available for coverage of Scottish activities. That spring and summer saw unprecedented attempts by both the militants and non-militants to spread the word all over Scotland. On 23 April *Votes for Women* reported on two successful meetings in Skye, and on 21 May the paper noted that Adela Pankhurst had opened a campaign in Inverness. As will be seen in later chapters, the WSPU did visit the north of Scotland, but only in Aberdeen did it establish any kind of local organisation. It was the NUWSS that mobilised local support wherever its members went. As early as June 1909 there were societies affiliated to the National Union in Aberdeen, Berwickshire, Dunfermline, Edinburgh (with satellite societies in Arbroath, Midlothian, Roxburghshire and Stirling), Glasgow (with satellite societies in Greenock and Kilmacolm), Inverness and Nairn. On 10 June the *Common Cause* reported that Helen Fraser was in Elgin.

> To judge by the local press, Elgin was amazed that Miss Fraser did not come on to the platform hoarsely shouting and brandishing an umbrella. It was virgin soil, however, and much must be forgiven to people who have never

heard a real Suffragist speak. The reasoning Scot was evidently impressed by Miss Fraser's eminently reasonable way of putting things ... Miss Fraser will return in September to complete the formation of a branch.

Meanwhile, the south was not neglected. Mrs Pankhurst was in Edinburgh in June, and the NUWSS held open-air meetings on the sands of Portobello, Musselburgh, and Joppa.[13]

In July there was a by-election in Dumfries Burghs (which included Kirkcudbright, Sanquhar, Lochmaben and Arran). By this time the NUWSS was also 'working' elections, and the different policies of the societies caused confusion. The Liberal candidate, J.W. Gulland, was one of the firmest supporters of women's suffrage in Parliament, so the NUWSS unhesitatingly supported him. To the WSPU, however, he was simply a member of the Liberal government and electors were therefore urged to vote against him. The WSPU campaign was English-run, though with Flora Drummond (who grew up in Arran) spearheading it; *Votes for Women* revealed how 'different' English suffragettes found Scotland. Helen Fraser ran the NUWSS campaign.[14] Both suffrage papers reported enthusiastic audiences. This was doubtless true, for the women speakers were lively and quick-witted, and provided better entertainment than most male campaigners. Once again the Liberal held the seat, which pleased the NUWSS, but with a reduced majority, which pleased the WSPU.[15]

On 17 July Winston Churchill addressed a meeting in Edinburgh on the Budget. In spite of all the precautions taken to exclude suffragettes, the meeting was frequently interrupted and he was accosted by suffragettes wherever he went. Outside the hall Adela Pankhurst addressed a protest meeting and then, accompanied by an Edinburgh woman, Bessie Brand (daughter of the late Sheriff Brand, Chairman of the Crofters' Commission), attempted to force a way into the hall. Both women were arrested, but charges were not pressed.[16]

In August and September the NUWSS undertook a Highland campaign, visiting Inverness, Fortrose and Rosemarkie, and south to Grantown on Spey, Boat-of-Garten, Aviemore, Kingussie, Newtonmore, Blair Atholl, Pitlochry and Perth.[17] Meanwhile Helen Fraser once again borrowed Louisa Lumsden's horse-drawn caravan to travel down the east coast from Aberdeen through Montrose, Brechin, Arbroath, Carnoustie, and Fife, then north again through Perth, Blairgowrie, Forfar, Edzell and Laurencekirk. Helen Fraser felt that the 300-mile tour had been worthwhile, but because of militant activities she had to 're-win' some sympathisers to the cause. More than ever she felt that 'our greatest friends are those who are brave and strong enough to go on plodding, quietly educating all the time.'[18]

And yet, without the advent of the WSPU, it is impossible to imagine such a caravan tour ever taking place.[19] Similarly, publicising meetings by chalking them on pavements – used throughout the caravan tour – had been pioneered by the WSPU. Eunice Murray of the WFL found it a 'beastly job' and only found the courage to continue because her companion, Chrystal Macmillan, remained so oblivious to the jeering crowd.[20] Lilias Mitchell described the chalking of Princes Street as a 'grisly business': 'One walked along like a normal individual then suddenly flopped on the pavement and wrote in big letters the announcement of a meeting at the Mound or the West End.' At Aberdeen 'someone thought I was ill and dashed forward to help me up!'[21]

During the Clyde Coast campaign by the Women's Freedom League that summer the women were told at Ayr that they would be arrested if they chalked the pavements, so they bought a bell and went through the town's principal streets 'crying' their meetings, with very satisfactory results.[22]

Earlier that summer some Scottish WFL members, including Arabella and Muriel Scott from Edinburgh and Lila Clunas from Dundee, took part in yet another 'Women's Parliament' in Caxton Hall, London, and march to the House of Commons; they were arrested and imprisoned in Holloway. This was also Lilias Mitchell's 'first real and horrid plunge into militancy'. She wrote of the 'terrible mêlée with the police'. She saw one grip a girl by the throat and push her against the crowd, which 'roused my indignation and undoubted fighting spirit for I knocked off his helmet, thus distracting him, but the next moment was firmly gripped and led off to the nearest police station'. She too ended up in Holloway.[23]

Lady Frances Balfour, although not a militant, was there with her sister-in-law (also a non-militant), Lady Betty, and described the occasion to Millicent Garrett Fawcett. The speeches at the Caxton Hall 'were of a very serious nature, almost like a service of dedication.' After the meeting a deputation of nine women, led by Mrs Pankhurst, left the hall; the remainder of the women were asked to remain seated in silent thought for three minutes before following.

The marchers were turned by the police into Victoria Street; they slowly battled their way to the west side of Parliament Square and up to Whitehall where 'we saw several arrests, the women all showing extraordinary courage in the rough rushes of the crowd round them.' At one point Lady Frances and Lady Betty were knocked over and feared the crowd would fall on top of them, but they were picked up by police and kept moving. Seeing 'one tall girl driven like a leaf up and down Whitehall' and others like her, Lady Frances attested to her admiration for 'the courage that dares this handling.' But while admitting that there was 'a fine spirit' she wondered 'whether it is not rather thrown away on these tactics.'[24]

The reporter who attended the WFL 'At Home' for Lila Clunas on her return to Dundee enjoyed the novelty of hearing someone discuss her prison experiences with pride rather than shame. Miss Clunas 'spoke with much naivete and a good deal of humour, both conscious and unconscious.' She was, of course, speaking to a Freedom League audience, who regarded her as a heroine.[25]

In August it was Glasgow's turn to experience militant methods and arrests. A Cabinet Minister was to speak on the Budget at the St Andrew's Hall, and a young suffragette, Alice Paul, spent the night before the meeting in the pouring rain on the roof of the hall in hopes of getting inside; when she was discovered and forced to leave she was cheered by a group of workmen for her pluck. That evening some women tried to force their way into the hall, and four of them – Alice Paul, Lucy Burns, Margaret Smith and Adela Pankhurst – were eventually arrested. (According to at least one press report, the crowd was in sympathy with the women.) Margaret Smith and, of course, Adela Pankhurst were English; Alice Paul and Lucy Burns were American students who had got caught up in the suffrage struggle, and who were later active in the American suffrage movement.[26]

A similar episode occurred in Dundee in September. This time a Miss Kelly, another London WSPU member, spent the night before a Budget meeting on the roof of the Kinnaird Hall, intending to lower herself by rope through the skylight during the meeting. She was not discovered on the roof, but the skylight window was locked so she had to let herself in by a window leading on to the stairs and was caught there. The *Dundee Advertiser* commented, 'We can admire the resource and courage, if not the sanity, of the young person who passed yesterday on the roof of the Kinnaird Hall'.

Once again a group of suffragettes, at the head of a crowd they had gathered, tried to force an entry into the hall. Three were arrested: Edith New, who was English, Alice Paul and Lucy Burns. The *Dundee Advertiser* found less to admire here:

> The attempt made by a small number of imported young women to induce a crowd to rush the meeting gave Dundee a good first-hand opportunity of estimating the nature of the movement in its degeneracy. The crowd was mainly lads and boys out for a lark. The excited young persons at the head of it were about as much like serious politicians with a grievance as their followers. They, too, were out for a lark, though perhaps they hardly knew it.[27]

The following day the court was packed, as it was the first time the 'cause' had figured in Dundee. The Dundee members of the Women's Freedom League passed a resolution 'admiring the ladies of the Women's Social and Political Union who displayed such courage and endurance'.[28]

A startling tactic had by this time been adopted by suffragette prisoners in England, the hunger strike. Initially such women were released before completing their sentences, but at Birmingham they had been forcibly fed. Dundee prison was reluctant to resort to this and found it difficult to deal with a totally new type of prisoner, 'ladies' who were not common criminals but who behaved in defiant ways. Edith New, Alice Paul and Lucy Burns refused to take any food or do any work and informed the prison governor that they intended to destroy as much prison property as possible (Lucy Burns broke the window in her cell). The prison commissioners advised the governor 'no punishment but simply defensive steps as far as possible, and the staff must be careful to retain their composure under irritating circumstances.'[29]

The suffragettes were released on 'medical' grounds after three days of fasting; the prison authorities were clearly anxious to get rid of them as quickly as possible. The *Dundee Advertiser* initially treated with levity the women's announcement that they would not eat: 'This is a pity; it is throwing away the chance of a lifetime. Unless rumour has been lying in a quite unnecessary way the Dundee skilly is the very finest of its kind, better – as skilly – than the far-famed Dundee shortbread is as shortbread. Not to taste it is to deny oneself indeed.'[30] However, in the days which followed, when the women proved that they were deadly serious, the tone changed, and by the time of their release, when they were weak and ill, it was entirely sympathetic. When Adela Pankhurst addressed an open-air meeting the crowd was estimated at 10,000, and she herself wrote movingly of how the suffragette prisoners were honoured by the people of Dundee. Emmeline Pankhurst came up to Dundee, was interviewed by the press, and addressed a crowded meeting at the Gilfillan Hall.[31] Since the MP, Winston Churchill, was a Cabinet Minister and the Prime Minister was MP for East Fife, Dundee inevitably became a focal point of the militant suffrage movement in Scotland.

However, on 9 October attention shifted to Edinburgh where a grand suffrage pageant and procession – far outstripping the modest effort of 1907 – was held. The main theme of the procession was what women 'have done and can do and will do'. All the arrangements were made by women (with Flora Drummond, nicknamed 'The General', in charge); banners were made and carried by women; even the bagpipes were played by women. Groups of women in professions and trades open to them – from fishwives to nurses – were dressed accordingly and carried their own banners. The most striking part of the procession was the pageant of

Scottish women who had played a part in the country's history (even if only a mythical one). Queen Margaret who brought the Roman form of Christianity to Scotland, the Countess of Buchan who crowned Robert the Bruce and was imprisoned in a cage outside Berwick Castle, Jenny Geddes, Grisel Baillie, women martyred in the Covenanting period, and, of course, Flora MacDonald. (But not Mary, Queen of Scots, presumably because she was regarded by suffragettes as a victim rather than a heroine.)

Many new recruits came forward during this period. One, who was alive to tell the tale in 1989, was nine years old at the time. Her family had recently undergone a tragedy, for the only other child, her young brother, had died of diphtheria. Passing the Edinburgh WSPU office on Queens-ferry Road, which was decked with publicity for the pageant, Bessie Watson and her mother went inside to investigate and emerged WSPU members; a grieving family (for Bessie's father fully supported them) had an absorbing new interest in life. Bessie had learned to play the bagpipes two years earlier (on a set specially made for her), and so she took part in the procession (on the float that carried the Countess of Buchan in her cage).[32]

The press unanimously praised the fine organisation and the gorgeous spectacle – and the sun shone! No one could count the spectators, though it was thought that most of the city's population lined the streets. The *Scotsman* (11 October) insisted that 'they were passive spectators, and nothing more', and the *Glasgow Herald* (11 October) thought the same. However, the *Edinburgh Evening Dispatch* (11 October) reacted differently.

> The imposing display achieved its object. It advertised to tens of thousands the aim and object of the suffragettes, and it made it abundantly apparent to all who had eyes to see, ears to hear, and minds to understand that behind this movement there is a solid phalanx of resolute and unflinching womanhood bent upon obtaining the vote, and fully determined that they will triumph over every obstacle.

But the *Evening Dispatch* felt that it would have been better for the suffrage cause if the programme had ended with the procession, for 'the speeches in the Waverley Market must have counteracted much of the good effect of the street spectacle.' The speeches – which were so badly disrupted by rowdyism that the police had to be called in to restore order – were said to be woefully lacking in sense and reason: 'It may be an exciting and congenial thing for the militant suffragettes to glory in violence, but we entirely mistake the temper of Scottish womanhood if it allows itself to be led astray by the foolish Pankhurst heroics of Saturday.'

While the WSPU gained publicity for the suffrage cause in the capital, the non-militants spread the word in other parts of Scotland. At the end of

8 Bessie Watson (photograph in private hands)

9 Women's suffrage procession, Edinburgh, October 1909. Courtesy of The
People's Story Museum, Edinburgh

September Helen Fraser spoke in the Borders, and a new society was
formed in Galashiels. The Scottish University Women's Suffrage Union
undertook major campaigns in the south-west and the north of Scotland.
The main speaker in the south was a graduate whose commitment to the
cause grew more militant in the years to come. Her name was Frances
Parker. During September she spoke in Ayr, Troon and Prestwick before
going on to Stranrar, Newton Stewart, Kirkcudbright, Castle Douglas,
Moffat and other Dumfries and Galloway towns. The main speaker in the
northern campaign was Chrystal MacMillan; she spoke in Caithness and
Sutherland, as well as in Orkney and Shetland. This was no easy trip, for
apart from the distances involved, steamers were irregular, making it
difficult to arrange meetings.[33]

In Shetland the nucleus of a women's suffrage society already existed.
Christina Jamieson – a woman with a fine mind whose brothers were
given all the educational opportunities while she was expected to remain
at home – was the secretary and guiding spirit. As a result of Chrystal

10 Christabel, Emmeline and Adela Pankhurst, and Emmeline Pethick-Lawrence in Edinburgh for the procession. From the suffrage collection of Miss Gorrie, by permission of the National Library of Scotland

11 Christina Jamieson (photograph courtesy of B. Smith; print by Ian Tait,
Shetland Museum)

MacMillan's visit to Orkney the Orcadian Women's Suffrage Association
was formed, 'making a good beginning with twelve members'.[34]

During the summer the secretary and chairman of the Glasgow and
West of Scotland Association proposed a Scottish Federation within the
NUWSS. They invited all the non-militant local Scottish societies to a
conference, which took place in the autumn. The conference agreed to
form a Scottish Federation, and the first Council meeting was held on 27
November.[35]

In October Winston Churchill was in his constituency, and both
militant societies were active. The Women's Freedom League did only
what constitutional societies had been doing all along by requesting an
interview with him. The *Dundee Courier* reported: 'The concession has
been wrung from the President of the Board of Trade at the point of a
bayonet. Swearing that he would ne'er consent in December last, he
veered round in a few weeks, and though later Mr Churchill endeavoured
to establish conditions he has now unconditionally surrendered.'[36] On
Monday the 18th he received the deputation and told the women that
their cause had 'marched backwards' over the past four years, that the
mass of people were still unconverted, and that he himself would render
no assistance to the cause unless militant tactics were discontinued.[37]

Before this, on the 16th, there was an unpleasant episode involving
WSPU members. Not surprisingly, there are different accounts by the
opposing Dundee newspapers, by the suffragettes, and by the police
constable.[38] Winston Churchill was addressing an open-air meeting in
Abernethy. According to Adela Pankhurst's contemporary statement and
Sylvia Pankhurst's later account, because of Churchill's promise to meet
the WFL deputation the WSPU had no intention of disrupting his
meeting but planned only to stage a separate protest nearby. The *Dundee
Advertiser* was convinced that the women believed their voices would
carry far enough to cause a disturbance. All accounts agreed that the four
women (Adela Pankhurst, Mrs Helen Archdale, Mrs Catherine Corbett,
and Miss C. Jolly) had no sooner arrived on the spot in a car (driven by a
male chauffeur) when they were surrounded by a crowd of hostile men
who gave them no chance to speak.

The men – led by stewards wearing Liberal rosettes – were clearly
geared up to the arrival of the women (as the *Courier* put it, 'the crowds
were evidently spoiling for an encounter with the Suffragettes'). The men
surrounding the car attempted to move it away and succeeded to some
extent, thereby damaging the tyres as the brake was still on. They grabbed
at the women's clothes and threw mud and divots at them; the women
defended themselves to the best of their ability before at last admitting
defeat and allowing the chauffeur to drive away. They held the stewards
responsible for the incident, for individuals in the crowd had attempted to

help them; the *Courier* carried a letter from a male eye-witness who expressed outrage at the stewards' conduct. Both Dundee newspapers claimed that a force of Perth county police had been present but did nothing. The superintendent who had been there insisted that he and his men had done all they could in the circumstances.

The superintendent also claimed that the *Courier* – a Unionist paper – had magnified matters to make political capital out of 'only a small – indeed almost a frivolous affair'. But his report, by laying the blame on the suffragettes, reveals his own hostility to them, and the incident was a foretaste of increasing male aggression toward suffragettes.[39]

On Tuesday the 19th – after Churchill's response to the WFL had been made public – there occurred what the *Dundee Advertiser* described as 'scenes of extraordinary rowdyism'. Three women – Mrs Archdale, Mrs Corbett, and another English suffragette, Maud Joachim – led a crowd to storm the doors of the Kinnaird Hall, where Churchill was to speak. At the same time Adela Pankhurst and another Englishwoman, Laura Evans, had concealed themselves in a room overlooking the hall and were throwing stones at the roof windows; it took the police three-quarters of an hour to extricate them. The *Courier* strongly condemned their actions ('A good cause ought to be promoted in a better manner'). However, the paper also carried a letter from Miss A.J. MacGregor, a local landowner, who had spoken with Churchill: 'On his assertion that the militants were a band of silly, neurotic, hysterical women I brought the interview to a close.' She held no brief for the WSPU but 'no Union could so hold together in loyalty, good organisation, and self-imposed discipline if its members could truthfully be so described.'[40]

The five women were arrested and sentenced to 10 days' imprisonment. They immediately went on hunger strike. The Scottish Office advised the prison commissioners that unless medically certified unfit the prisoners should be forcibly fed and to consult with the prison governor at Newcastle who had had recent experience. The medical officer found that the two married women and Adela Pankhurst to be unfit but thought the other two could be fed if necessary. He anticipated 'a good deal of difficulty in obtaining the services of nurses to assist'. On the third day the medical officer thought it advisable to prepare to feed Laura Evans and Maud Joachim, but after examining them with another doctor decided that a further delay would do no harm. Next day the doctors found only one of the women fit to be fed but decided to do so 'would expose her to a mental strain of an unjustifiable nature', a consideration that would not have been taken into account in any English prison. All five women were therefore released.[41]

Flora Drummond was on hand to greet them and to issue statements to the press. The women commented on how well they had been treated in prison, and Flora Drummond said it was a great triumph for Scotland that forcible feeding had not been resorted to. The press picked this up. Far from being pleased at the contrast being drawn between the policy of the Home Office and Scottish Office, the Secretary for Scotland was indignant. He demanded full information on forcible feeding (euphemistically termed 'artificial feeding') for future use by the Scottish prison service.[42]

Votes for Women speculated on why the Dundee prisoners had been released after four days, while women jailed in Birmingham, Newcastle and Manchester for comparable offences were still in prison. Dundee was the constituency of a Cabinet Minister and Churchill might fear the wrath of electors; Mrs Corbett was the sister of an MP and Mrs Archdale the daughter of the late editor of the *Scotsman*; or perhaps Lord Pentland, the Secretary for Scotland, did not wish to share the odium of his counterpart in the Home Office. Readers were left to make their own choice. The true reason, as revealed by prison records, was simply the great reluctance of the doctors at Dundee prison to undertake forcible feeding.

Scottish anti-suffragists made the point that none of the five women came from Dundee, and in fact only Helen Archdale was a Scot.[43] Why was this? Scots activists at this stage were generally in non-militant societies and in the Women's Freedom League rather than in the WSPU (Mary Phillips had by then gone to England). But Scottish WFL members had been imprisoned in Holloway, so there can be no denying their courage and determination. They may have felt that actions directed against the Houses of Parliament were more important than activism in Scotland. But the likeliest explanation is that at this stage Scottish women faced a psychological barrier when it came to committing acts of militancy on their home ground, preferring the comparative anonymity of large-scale London demonstrations.

Without any repetition of the dramatic events of September and October, there was plenty of suffrage activity in Scotland during November and December, especially after a General Election was called for the New Year. In November Lady Betty Balfour, president of the Edinburgh branch of the Conservative and Unionist Women's Franchise Association, said that if the women of their Association 'emulated the courage of the militant Suffragists without their lawlessness, and their cheerful devotion without their violence, they would do well. They had made people like her feel that the time had come when those in favour of women's enfranchisement could no longer sit with folded hands and let others fight the battle.'[44]

The WSPU held meetings in Glasgow, Paisley, Helensburgh, Stirling, Edinburgh and Dundee; at many of those meetings the Dundee hunger strikers related their prison experiences. Christabel Pankhurst held a public meeting at the King's Theatre in Edinburgh. At the St Andrew's

Hall, Glasgow, a large audience included many men and represented all shades of political opinion and 'every class of society'.[45]

Dundee was not ignored by the constitutionalists. The Gilfillan Hall, which seated 1,700, was full to overflowing with hundreds turned away for a public meeting with the Lord Provost in the chair, and with Chrystal MacMillan and Dr Elsie Inglis as speakers. The event was described as 'one of the best meetings we have had in Scotland'. Further north the Nairn society arranged its first public meeting, with Lady Frances Balfour as the speaker. The reporter noted that in the north there was a good deal of confusion about the different societies and methods, and the speech had clarified the situation for all the listeners.[46]

Lady Frances wrote a letter to Millicent Garrett Fawcett, the NUWSS president, on 16 December. Before speaking to a Scottish Emigration Society in Edinburgh she had lunched with four of the officials. They were intelligent, practical women, but they were anti-suffrage, having never thought about it and knowing only the militant side.

> After about ten minutes elementary talk I was constrained to say something in the following style. 'It would be impossible in England, to be asked to lunch with, & meet women engaged in such a work as yours, & to find all firm antis. It would also be impossible – may I suggest so quite civilly – to find such total ignorance both of the cause and its methods.' Loud laughter, & a promise to consider it 'from another point of view.'[47]

Millicent Garrett Fawcett herself spoke at public meetings at this time in Edinburgh, Glasgow and Kilmacolm.[48]

In November Edinburgh Town Council received simultaneous deputations from the NUWSS, the WFL and the WSPU, protesting against the giving of the Freedom of the City to Asquith. Their protests had no effect.[49]

In the north the Orcadian society numbered 42 members by mid-December.[49] The Shetland society was handicapped because none of its members were public speakers, and it did not have the money to bring up speakers from the south. The Society therefore concentrated on distributing suffrage literature. On 3 December the executive committee discussed a letter from the NUWSS which asked for a donation to the General Election Fund, and for a delegate to be sent to the National Union's special council meeting in London. It was impossible for the Society to afford to send a delegate, but £1 was sent to the election fund. Neither Cathcart Wason, the Liberal MP, nor the Unionist candidate, supported women's suffrage, so the Society could not support either and confined itself to propaganda work.[51]

The Scottish Women's Liberal Federation was also active as the election approached. Asquith was asked to receive a deputation. Circulars were sent to Women's Liberal Associations, asking them to approach their local men's Liberal Associations, and either jointly or separately to urge all Liberal candidates to include women's suffrage in their election addresses. The Scottish Women's Liberal Federation cooperated with the Women's Liberal Federation in England in approaching Scottish Liberal MPs known to be friendly to women's suffrage. Helen Waddel's pamphlet, 'Liberal Women and the Vote', was revised and reissued.[52]

The Women's Freedom League opened its Scottish Suffrage Centre on Sauchiehall Street in Glasgow at the beginning of December. There were offices, a shop, and a hall which served as a tea room, meeting place and art gallery, attracting many passers-by.[53]

By the end of 1909 there can have been few, if any, Scots unaware of the issue of 'Votes for Women'. The activities of the suffragettes in Dundee might have raised some hackles, but the press coverage the women received – especially as they were the first suffragettes imprisoned in Scotland – certainly brought them to the public's notice. The tours by non-militant speakers the length and breadth of Scotland spread the cause far beyond the cities of the south, and the establishment of local societies ensured that the work would continue.

The Years of Truce 1910–11

In the wake of the General Election, the Liberals still in power but with the loss of a hundred seats, an all-party parliamentary committee was formed to frame a women's suffrage bill. It became known as the Conciliation Committee and the bill as the Conciliation Bill. In view of this in February 1910 Christabel Pankhurst announced a truce on militancy by the WSPU. The Women's Freedom League followed suit.

The WFL's annual conference that January again raised the subject of women belonging to both militant societies. This time it was unambiguously resolved, by 20 votes to 2, that members of other militant suffrage societies should not be members of WFL committees; the Scottish Council had already found it 'absolutely necessary' to pass such a resolution.[1] But women were free to belong to more than one society, and the names of some activists crop up in both *The Vote* and *Votes for Women*.

During the early months of 1920 the WSPU in Scotland organised a bazaar, or 'Scottish Exhibition', to be held in Glasgow at the end of April. *Votes for Women* explained that it was now more necessary than ever to hold meetings and distribute literature, all of which took money; raising money was one reason for holding a Scottish Exhibition and Sale of Work. Besides:

> We are all familiar with the idea that the militant Suffragette is a person with rudimentary notions of cooking, who cannot sew, and is, in fact, not domesticated. This is her chance to demonstrate in Scotland, as she did in London last year, that the hands which know how to throw stones on occasion – and on principle – are, in truth, among the most skilful and adept in wielding the needle, the paint-brush, or the cooking-spoon![2]

The suffragettes' need to prove their femininity was integral to the ideology of the period. From Emmeline Pankhurst downwards, militant suffragettes sought to disprove their 'battleaxe' image and to show that in spite of stepping so far out of line they were still 'ladies' in every important way. Some exceptions to this rule will emerge in the course of the book, but it was true of the vast majority. Even three-quarters of a century later Elizabeth Somerville (who had been a child member of the WSPU) was concerned to stress how 'really ladylike' were the suffragettes she knew.[3]

Another rationale for the Scottish Exhibition was that to reach men and women hitherto untouched by the movement. It was the first suffrage exhibition held in Scotland and so was regarded as indicating the strength of the movement in Scotland.[4]

The WSPU rated the bazaar a great success. Stalls sold all manner of hand-made items, from hats to a quilt embroidered with the names of all the hunger strikers. Tableaux of Famous Women were greatly appreciated, as were the plays put on in the theatre, all of them touching on the suffrage question, thus combining education with entertainment. The *Glasgow Herald*'s reporter was particularly struck with the replicas of prison cells, showing the comparative luxury of the First Division cells allocated to 'political offenders' against those in the Second or Third Division allocated to suffragettes. The bazaar showed the world (according to Mrs Pankhurst, reported in the *Herald*) that no suffragette forgot 'to take a great interest and devote a great deal of her time to that kind of work which was considered essentially to be women's work.'[5]

It is difficult to gauge the success of the Scottish Exhibition. It was covered in Scotland only by Glasgow newspapers and was somewhat damned with faint praise. Yet it raised over £1,700, and many of the artists, needlewomen and general assistants who had originally helped out of love for their art or because a friend had asked them were converted to the cause.

All of the suffrage societies vigorously campaigned in Scotland in early 1910. The WFL learned that the truce was not respected by all parties when some Glasgow members held their first meeting in the Ibrox district. They were surrounded by a howling mob of boys, were pelted with 'potatoes, stones, herrings, clods of earth, manure', and their temporary platform was assailed – 'yet the police officers stood far back gazing complacently into vacancy over the heads of the crowd'. The crowd was ugly at the close of the meeting, but then one gentleman came to their assistance 'and let the hooligan element perceive that we were not quite without a champion'. The women resolved to be back the following week, 'and we shall continue to return until perfect order and sympathy are given us.'[6]

Lady Frances Balfour spoke at three drawing-room meetings organised by the non-militant Glasgow and West of Scotland Association for Women's Suffrage, resulting in about a hundred new members for the

Association. There was a *contretemps* when the NUWSS initially refused to recognise the Scottish Federation on the lines proposed by Scotland. However, not long after, the National Union passed new rules recognising federations of local societies, as long as all the societies were affiliated to the NUWSS. The Scottish Federation established an office in St Andrew's Square, Edinburgh; Miss S.E.S. Mair was elected president and Dr Elsie Inglis was secretary.[7]

During the past year membership of the Edinburgh Society had risen from 384 to 854 and income from £231 to £858. And at the end of its first year's existence, the Inverness Society had 188 members. A new society was formed in Perth at this time, with some 80 members. Cooperation between suffrage organisations was easier during the period of truce, and Florence Hilliard, the NUWSS organiser responsible for the formation of the Perth society, thanked the members of the Women's Freedom League 'who had given her so much help'.[8]

In Shetland Christina Jamieson based her arguments on the island economy and social structure. From spring through autumn most of the men were away at the fishing while the women worked the crofts.

> It is quite true that many of the menfolk, in the self-complacency fostered by the uncritical adoration of these same women, take the work of the women for granted and quite overlook its value. Still the general feeling of equality is such that Shetland men as [a] rule "don't see why women soodna vot'."

The men of Norway had given their women the vote without a fight: 'Will not the men of Shetland show themselves worthy of their kinship to these free descendants of the old Norse Vikings whom they yearly unite in commemorating?'[9]

It was a different story in the cities, and in early May an NUWSS organiser in Edinburgh remarked, 'To the man in the street all those working for the Suffrage appear to be rich women or women of the leisured classes. They find it difficult to believe that we want the vote for the benefit of our country and in order to help our poorer sisters.' Siân Reynolds has noted that historically, 'the cause of skilled women workers was championed only by middle-class reformers ... in particular by women in the suffrage and rights movements. This reinforced the notion that women's rights were essentially a middle-class cause foisted on to working women from outside'.[10]

It is difficult to measure the extent of working-class involvement in the women's suffrage movement in Scotland. (The Labour movement's connection with the suffrage movement is a separate question which will be discussed in a later chapter.) That the movement was *largely* middle class is undeniable. Middle-class women had the time and money to spearhead the movement, and it is their names that appear as presidents and secretaries of local branches and societies, as organisers and as speakers. However, for England Olive Banks found that while most prominent activists were middle class, no less than 20 per cent of the older generation and 23 per cent of the younger generation were working class. These women did not remain in the background but worked as organisers in the movement, and their lives were well documented.[11]

Such women were not to be found amongst Scottish organisers, but they were active in other ways. Jessie Stephen, a working-class woman who joined the WSPU in 1909 at the age of 16, insisted in an interview that the picture of the movement as solely middle class was a 'distortion'. There were, she said, 'a tremendous number of working-class women'. Elizabeth Somerville's parents were working class (her father was a bookbinder), and she too knew of other working-class women in the WSPU. A Dunfermline factory worker, Jenny McCallum, a member of the Women's Freedom League, was arrested in the 1908 disturbance outside the House of Commons and imprisoned for a month in Holloway. Not one of these women's names can be found in any suffrage literature of the period, and it is only historical accident that has rescued them from obscurity. (Jessie Stephen remained an activist throughout her life which is why she came to be interviewed; Elizabeth Somerville contacted me in response to a letter in the *Scotsman*; and the story of Jenny McCallum comes from a 1968 issue of the *Dunfermline Press*.[12]) How many Scottish working-class supporters have remained in obscurity can never be known.

Writing of England, R.S. Neale found that radical middle-class suffrage campaigners began to influence organisations of women workers but captured the enthusiastic support only of a small minority. He believed the only genuine working-class pressure for the vote was from the Women's Co-operative Guild. Similar pressure came from the Scottish Co-operative Women's Guild, though a history of the Guild published in 1913 emphasised that members had nothing to do with the militants.[13] No evidence has so far emerged of any working-class involvement in Scottish societies affiliated to the NUWSS.

By 1910 anti-suffragists in Scotland were sufficiently rattled to unite their various committees into a Scottish National Anti-Suffrage League. The president was the Duchess of Montrose, who in many ways epitomised the type of woman who opposed the suffrage. She was rich and titled; she held the honorary degree of LL.D. from Glasgow University; and she was active in numerous charities, being president of the Scottish Council of the British Red Cross Society and other such organisations. She believed that reforms could be achieved by means other than granting the vote to women, and that to do so would pose a threat to the State.[14]

In June and August 1910 the NUWSS concentrated on spreading the word well beyond the cities. One organiser, Florence Hilliard, worked in the south-east, while another, W.H. Lamond, spent the time in Orkney and Shetland, taking in some of the smaller islands that Chrystal MacMillan had not managed to get to the previous year. She ended up in Caithness, and a John O'Groats Society was formed. Helen Fraser helped to form four new societies around Inverness which, joined together with the existing ones, constituted the North of Scotland Federation. Meanwhile, the Women's Freedom League ran its usual summer Clyde campaign.[15]

The WSPU staged another Hyde Park demonstration on 23 July. Rather than try to chivvy Scottish women to find the fare to London again (especially as many had done so to take part in a suffrage procession in June), there was a simultaneous mass meeting on the Calton Hill in Edinburgh. Lucy Burns, the American student who was now Edinburgh WSPU organiser, wrote: 'Face to face with the revered monuments of their own rebellious history, Scottish men and women cannot fail to see that the fight for freedom is a continuous one, and that women are carrying on to-day the old battle of Scotland, the glory of the race.' The WFL united with the WSPU for this event, and the Edinburgh National Society for Women's Suffrage, the Scottish University Women's Suffrage Union, the Conservative and Unionist Women's Franchise Association, and the Men's League for Women's Suffrage also took part.[16]

The weather was less kind than in past years, for 23 July was a day of heavy rainfall, but the *Edinburgh Evening Dispatch* reported that 'the ardour of the demonstrationists was not to be dampened'. The reporter further noted, 'Of rowdies there were none. All had come to be enlightened or else to express their sympathy.'[17]

Earlier in July the Conciliation Bill had received its Second Reading in the House of Commons. The bill enfranchised only unmarried women who already possessed the municipal franchise on the basis of property qualifications. It was supported by suffragists because it at least established the principle of women voting for Members of Parliament.

In common with their English counterparts, Scottish newspapers devoted leading articles to the debate. After the first day the *Edinburgh Evening Dispatch* commented that 'the House of Commons paid the greatest compliment to the fair sex that could possibly have been paid – it gave us a first-class debate, with a minimum of froth and noise.' The Unionist newspaper, the *Scotsman*, recorded that the suffragists had 'succeeded in impressing upon the mind of Parliament the conviction that their movement is not to be treated lightly.' But were the sexes to be considered equal or was a much more restricted proposition acceptable? 'The suffragists have at last discovered the way of discretion; they do not ask support for a measure founded on the equality principle ... They submit a plain, business-like proposition'. The *Scotsman* could accept this only if it were a final and not an interim measure and warned against socialist schemes to 'bring about adult suffrage, and thus to hand over the supreme direction of the Empire to women': 'A nation governed by women would not live long – it would end as quickly as a State run by Socialists.'[18]

The non-party *Glasgow Herald* (12, 13, 14 July) devoted leading articles to all three days of the debate. Previous debates had been 'largely *pour rire*. But now it is realised that women have claims to very serious consideration'. Yet the *Herald* feared the Bill as the thin end of the wedge. 'If the vote is given to one, it is given to all.' For 'the demand of the Suffragists is one that it becomes increasingly difficult to resist if the claim is made ... in the name of reason and justice. In point of intellectual ability and culture a growing proportion of women are quite equal to the exercise of the franchise.' Though the *Herald* refuted some anti-suffrage arguments, nevertheless 'the possibilities and probabilities suggested by the opposing arguments are so numerous and perplexing that the political intelligence of the country must be given fuller opportunities than it has yet enjoyed of considering a momentous question in all its bearings.'

The *Glasgow Herald* changed tack after the Bill passed its Second Reading by a majority of 109 votes, split right across party lines. Now the measure was 'undemocratic'. And the militants were warned against resuming their old tactics, for 'the country requires to be convinced that reform is wise and necessary, and the country will not be bullied.'

At this stage, while the future of the bill lay in the balance, there was no danger of the militants breaking their truce. In September Emmeline Pankhurst toured the Highlands, speaking at Lossiemouth, Elgin, Inverness, Craigellachie, Grantown-on-Spey, Newtonmore, Wick, Thurso, Dornoch and Lochinver. This was the first time many of those towns had heard the militant point of view, and *Votes for Women* reported enthusiastic audiences.[19]

The NUWSS leader, Millicent Garrett Fawcett, also toured Scotland in September. She, too, spoke at Newtonmore, where her sister, Elizabeth Garrett Anderson, had a holiday home. She addressed four meetings in Dundee, the largest of which was presided over by the Lord Provost, and in addition she spoke at St Andrews, West Calder, Haddington and Coldstream. The leader of the Women's Freedom League, Charlotte Despard, was in Scotland in November, speaking in Edinburgh and Glasgow. In Edinburgh she 'held her audience in a spell, broken at frequent intervals by rounds of applause'. And Louisa Lumsden's horse-drawn caravan again plodded down the non-militant road, this time with the Scottish University Women's Suffrage Union, who spent 11 weeks travelling through Aberdeenshire and Banffshire. Frances Parker was in charge; fifty different places were visited and 58 meetings held.[20]

The Scottish Federation of the NUWSS asked all town councils in Scotland to petition Parliament in favour of the Conciliation Bill. Glasgow resolved to do so unanimously. (Councillor Pratt, who brought the motion, was a member of the executive committee of the Glasgow and West of Scotland Association for Women's Suffrage.)[21] Edinburgh Town Council resolved to take no action, but North Berwick, Hawick and Fraserburgh town councils followed Glasgow in petitioning in favour of the bill, as did Kirkwall.[22]

The Glasgow and West of Scotland Association worked for the Conciliation Bill by organising a petition from women municipal voters and forming deputations to wait on MPs. The Scottish Women's Liberal Federation was also active in traditional ways.[23]

Suffragist optimism at this time can be seen in the title of a series of articles by Tom Johnston in the *Forward* – 'What Will Happen When Women Get the Vote'. In the first article, 'If I Were a Woman', he insisted that the 'present agitation is not so much a struggle for a vote as a great sex awakening'. He attempted to imagine what it would be like to be an upper-class woman, a middle-class woman and a working class woman after 1912 when the vote would be won, with minds stretched far beyond the confines of domesticity. The second piece was entitled 'What Women Will Do!' and the third 'The Woman of the Future'. He envisaged great changes. Newly-thinking women would see the advantages of co-operative housekeeping, and families would in consequence club together and have common dining halls and the cooking done by professionals. Tenements and cottages would disappear and life would become more 'social'. Marriages would contain equal partners, and 'all the stupid paraphernalia of rings, jewels, ornaments, and cosmetics, not being necessary to attract admiration, will vanish like a dream.'[24]

The Conciliation Bill ran out of time and did not receive a Third Reading that session, but many expected that the next session would see a revived Conciliation Bill passed into law. (Sylvia Pankhurst wrote a history of the women's suffrage movement which was published in 1911 in the expectation that the movement was about to end, having achieved what it set out to do.) Meanwhile, the Prime Minister had called another General Election in order to to obtain a mandate for the reform of the House of Lords.

For suffrage campaigners Dundee was again a particular focus of attention. Winston Churchill – now Home Secretary – received deputations from Liberal women, constitutional suffragists, and the WFL.

According to the WFL report, he spoke mildly to the first of these, more strongly to the second, 'culminating in a battle-royal – to quote a local paper – when Mr Churchill and the Women's Freedom League met face to face'. 'To judge from his remarks on our opposing him', continued the report, 'Mr Churchill evidently considered that his condescension in receiving us ought to have turned the scale. All left him feeling that the Suffrage will be won in spite of Mr Churchill, who is holding it back while desirous of claiming credit when victory was won.'[25] A different kind of protest, by a WSPU member, took place at a women's meeting.

> Mr Churchill was speaking of the gallant Liberal Party when Miss Moorhead rose and reminded him that the said gallant party was forcibly feeding women in prison, and in order to express her indignation she threw an egg at the Home Secretary, who had ordered this brutal treatment. She was ejected with great violence.[26]

This is the first mention of Ethel Moorhead who in the years to come emerged as the most forceful character in the women's suffrage movement in Scotland. As may be gathered, Ethel Moorhead was not content to be 'ladylike'.

Vigorous campaigning was also carried out in Glasgow and Edinburgh. The Glasgow and West of Scotland Association received resignations in the wake of the election because it had operated on a strictly non-party basis, which meant, in some cases, opposing Liberal candidates if they were not in favour of the Conciliation Bill.[27] In Edinburgh the WFL did most of its election work in the East Division where the Liberal candidate, though nominally in favour of women's suffrage, did not reply to the League's questions. Freedom League members, therefore, waited by the polling booths with postcards that stated 'I have this day recorded my vote, and urge you as my representative to support the demand for the immediate enfranchisement of duly qualified women.' They ended up with 1,734 signed cards to deluge the MP with on his return to Westminster.[28]

The NUWSS held its first large public meeting in Glasgow in mid-December, with Millicent Garrett Fawcett, its president, as speaker. They had worried how much support a constitutionalist meeting would attract, but the St Andrew's Hall was packed, and the audience was enthusiastic.[29] Asquith was to be presented with the Freedom of the City of Edinburgh on 20 December, and the WFL, in conjunction with the WSPU and the Men's League, launched a protest – to no avail, of course, except in focusing attention on the suffragettes.[30]

The balance of power was broadly unchanged by the General Election. At the beginning of 1911 the Scottish Women's Liberal Federation noted that in the new Parliament there were 43 Scottish Liberal MPs favourable to women's enfranchisement of whom 12 had referred to it in their election addresses (six unsuccessful candidates had also done so). The Federation thanked all Liberal candidates who included the question in their election addresses and invited new Liberal MPs favourable to suffrage to become members of the Liberal Parliamentary Suffrage Committee.[31]

The Women's Freedom League suffered a trauma early in 1911 when Teresa Billington-Greig left it and lashed out publicly against the whole militant suffrage movement. (It was the fact that she did so in such a public way that most angered suffragettes, for naturally the anti-suffragists reacted with glee.) The failure of the Conciliation Bill to receive a Third Reading had led the WSPU into briefly breaking the truce in November 1910, culminating in a particularly nasty clash in London, known ever after as Black Friday. It was the breaking of the truce that caused Teresa Billington-Greig to examine where the movement had got to. In articles and a book she argued that the 'emancipation-in-a-hurry spirit' had narrowed the focus of the movement into concentrating entirely on the vote, forgetting the wider issues of sex equality. A letter in *The Vote* signed AN OLD EDINBURGH MEMBER was one of many that took issue with her views: 'To obtain laws needs machinery other than to alter customs, and I took it that the object of the Freedom League was to alter the law, to obtain the vote first, as a sound foundation on which women may work as they please for their own wider emancipation.'[32] But some of Teresa Billington-Greig's observations were shrewd.

> Daring to advertise in an unconventional way the movement has dared nothing more ... It pays for one breach of decorum with additional circumspection in all other directions. 'I do interrupt meetings, but I am a perfect lady,' expresses the present poverty of spirit. 'I knocked off a policeman's helmet, but I only want a little thing, a quite respectable little thing – a vote.' This is banal.[33]

Teresa Billington-Greig attacked not only the militant movement in general but also the Women's Freedom League in particular, claiming that it had 'dropped steadily to a position of mediocrity ... The Freedom League had its opportunity and lost it.' The League had never explained or defended its course of action because of a self-denying ordinance passed early on which forbade members to criticise the WSPU: 'We were committed to submit to all criticism and to utter none'.[34] WFL members must have been deeply hurt by her remarks, but there was no breaking of ranks, and not only did the Freedom League continue its suffrage work up to and through the war, it also (unlike the WSPU) survived for decades afterwards as a key organisation fighting for women's rights. And in spite of all she said in 1911, after the war Teresa Billington-Greig became actively involved again with the Freedom League.[35]

In any case, during the early months of 1911 suffrage workers were primarily concerned with the Conciliation Bill. In March Emmeline Pankhurst spoke in Edinburgh, Glasgow and Ayr. By the end of April many town councils had carried resolutions in favour of the Bill: Arbroath, Brechin, Broughty Ferry, Cumnock, Dundee, Forfar, Fraserburgh, Glasgow, Haddington, Hamilton, Hawick, Inverness, Inverurie, Kilmarnock, Kilwinning, Kirkwall, Lerwick, North Berwick, Perth, Saltcoats, Stromness, Thurso, and Tranent.[36] And this time when Edinburgh Town Council voted on a motion to petition Parliament it was carried by 24 votes to two.[37]

In view of all this the Scottish Anti-Suffrage League mobilised itself. The Glasgow branch was already active in January, with meetings held in Hillhead, Camlachie, Kingston, Partick and Ballahouston. Two English executive committee members, Gladys Pott and Mrs Greatbatch, toured Scotland at the end of February, visiting Edinburgh, Dundee, Glasgow, Paisley, St Andrews, Peebles, Galashiels and Gullane, holding both public and drawing-room meetings. By this time men and women antis had combined their societies into one, and St Andrews University provided some stalwarts for the anti-suffrage cause. Professor McIntosh presided over two meetings, and William Knight, Emeritus Professor of Philosophy, contributed a lengthy two-part article entitled 'Woman Suffrage: A National Peril'.

> Woman and man are not alike, but constitutionally different ... Man has the creative, the devising, the directive, the compelling, legislative power; woman has the enduring, the consoling, and the restoring power ... To grant the Parliamentary vote to women would be to inflict on them a burden too grievous to be borne.[38]

Suffragists and suffragettes regarded the antis with humorous contempt. 'They were late in the field', wrote Lady Frances Balfour, 'badly organised and full of class distinction; in argument the Suffragists were veterans, and rode through the Antis like standing corn, they were always defeated, horse and foot, bag and baggage ... we whetted our swords, on their silly and easily refuted sayings.'[39] What these women failed to realise was what Brian Harrison has brought out so convincingly in his book, that the Anti-Suffrage League 'was a mere superstructure upon a widespread anti-suffragism which it only partially controlled.'[40]

By the spring of 1911 the militant societies must have been chafing for 'real action', for an idea of the Women's Freedom League for a symbolic gesture was seized on so avidly that although the Pankhursts initially stood aloof the WSPU ended up playing an equal part in the operation. The census took place on 3 April, and the militants announced that as they were not considered full citizens they would not allow themselves to be counted. Elaborate arrangements were made for women to be absent from their homes overnight. Individuals with large houses offered accommodation to census evaders. A large cafe was hired by Lucy Burns in Edinburgh for WSPU members and others who did not want to be counted; the WFL headquarters in Glasgow served the same purpose for both local members and those in outlying districts, as did the WSPU office in Dundee. Games, music and 'waxwork caricatures elaborately prepared and rehearsed for the occasion' were planned to make the night pass enjoyably.

Lucy Burns told the press that the object of the census boycott 'was simply to bring the women's movement before the public'. In this it succeeded brilliantly, while exposing the schizoid nature of the popular press. The *Dundee Courier* attacked the boycott as 'foolish', 'fatuous' and 'silly', while at the same time carrying a splendid picture of some Dundee census-evaders. In the *Edinburgh Evening Dispatch* a leading article denounced the women as 'foolish and misguided' and deprecated their lack of moral sense, while on the same page were jolly reports of how the census-evaders spent the night, how much interest they attracted, and how greatly they enjoyed themselves (a reporter spent the night outside the cafe just to question them on this when they emerged). The *Scotsman* did not devote a leader to the event but gave it full coverage, with accounts of how the census-evaders occupied themselves, why they had taken the action they had, and how satisfied they were with the result.[41]

The Women's Freedom League considered the census protest one of its most successful events 'because of the opportunity it gave the ordinary members to take part'. (But Anna Munro, organiser of the Glasgow protest, was much more satisfied than was Marguerite Sidley who was responsible for Edinburgh where 'people were cautious and timid'.) Only one census-resister was harassed by police, a Mrs Halley of Dundee. Her daughter remembered her mother saying she had had 20 people in the house during the census evasion.[42] Mrs Halley was one of many 'ordinary members' whose names did not feature in suffrage journals.

All suffrage societies continued to work for the second Conciliation Bill which was to be introduced on 5 May 1911. Shetland Women's Suffrage Society wrote to their town, county and parish councils asking them to petition the MP to support the bill. (The county council did so; the letter was received too late for the town council's monthly meeting; Lerwick Parish Council deferred consideration, but Dunrossness Parish Council petitioned.) The Glasgow and West of Scotland Association held a series

12 Census night in Edinburgh. From the suffrage collection of Miss Gorrie, by
permission of the National Library of Scotland

of meetings in support of the bill in St Rollox, Govan and Partick,
resulting in eight new societies being formed with 250 members.[43]

Lady Frances Balfour was in the House of Commons for the debate on
5 May when the Bill passed its Second Reading by a majority of 167.
Many of the old campaigners were profoundly moved and believed their
time had come at last, but Lady Frances found the sight of the militants
demonstrating outside 'dreadfully upsetting', though 'the police were
very sympathetic and did no "moving on".' She did not linger: 'I was
upset by the old memories. I have seen so many scenes and the change in
our prospects and the style of debate are so great.'[44]

On the 19th of June there was a by-election in Ross and Cromarty. By-
elections were held for many more reasons at that time than they are at
present; for example a new appointment within the Cabinet would
require a by-election. In the days before opinion polls, by-elections were
important indicators of swings. Apart from the president of the Inverness
Women's Suffrage Society, Mrs Hunter, who spoke at some meetings, in

this instance all the campaigning was done by one NUWSS organiser, Alice Crompton. During her first six days she addressed 21 meetings, but the arduous work was compensated for by the response she got, for everywhere she found that 'the Highlandmen are in great sympathy with our cause'. Both the Unionist candidate, who professed himself in favour of women's suffrage, and the Liberal candidate, a firm believer in adult suffrage, invited her to address the electors from their platforms after their own speeches were over. She got as far as Lewis and addressed three meetings in Stornoway, resulting in the founding of a new society there ('the most westerly in Great Britain') with an initial membership of 25. The Liberals held the seat with a reduced majority, and Alice Crompton could see why he was popular, since at all times he represented the interests of the crofters in Parliament, no matter being too small for him to bring forward at Westminster: 'Accustomed to real representation, these Northern men are quick to see how hard is the lot of unrepresented women.'[45]

Not all English English suffragists were as attuned to Scottish sensibilities. The *Common Cause* of 15 June, looking forward to the procession in London on the 17th, had a front page drawing headed 'The March of England's Women'. Not surprisingly, this drew irate letters, and the editor apologised.[46]

The march in London was a special occasion as it was held in honour of the Coronation of King George V. Fifty Scottish WSPU members took part, and ten-year-old Bessie Watson played her pipes in the procession. The Scottish Federation of the NUWSS sponsored Christina Jamieson to go as the Shetland Women's Suffrage Society's delegate. The Women's Freedom League gathered a Scottish contingent from Edinburgh, Glasgow, Aberdeen, Perth, Dundee, Dunfermline, and Alloa, all 'wearing our tartan, heather and thistle'.[47]

The Freedom League tried but failed to persuade Glasgow Town Council to send a representative However, the Council did agree to the NUWSS request to join a deputation in support of the Conciliation Bill; Councillor Pratt was the representative. The Glasgow branch of the Scottish Anti-Suffrage League protested.[48]

The WFL carried on its usual summer Clyde campaign and reported nothing but kindness, helpfulness and interest on the part of both locals and visitors. ('One of the institutions of Rothesay is the heather seller, "Heather Jack", who, with quaint courtesy, presents a sprig of white heather to our leader, Miss Munro, whenever she is taking boat to some of the other Clyde resorts.') The speakers were surprised that they frequently encountered members of the public who had never before heard anyone speak on women's suffrage.[49] This kind of educative propaganda is easily overlooked in accounts of the movement which concentrate on clashes with police and so on, but it formed the core of the work of all the suffrage societies. And at this time, after more than a year of truce, women's open-air meetings did not attract hostility.

The same warmth and friendliness attended Emmeline Pankhurst's tour of Scotland in August and September. She started in Largs, Dundee and other southern towns but concentrated on the north-east, including Turiff, Fraserburgh, Peterhead, Ballater and Nairn. Lady Betty Balfour came up specially to Nairn to chair the meeting there, and meetings throughout were notable for the influential (often titled) individuals who chaired and attended them and the multi-party representation on the platforms. The highlight of the tour was Lady Cowdray's At Home at Dunecht House, near Aberdeen, for which over a thousand invitations were sent. The theme of Mrs Pankhurst's speeches was the need to support the Conciliation Bill (because it was the only one capable of being passed by the current Parliament).[50]

Later in September there was a by-election at Kilmarnock Burghs, another Liberal stronghold. All three suffrage societies campaigned. The constituency covered five towns – Rutherglen and Renfrew on the outskirts of Glasgow, Dumbarton to the north and Port Glasgow to the south, and, of course, Kilmarnock. It was a three-cornered contest. The Unionist candidate not only opposed women's suffrage, but the WFL reported (and was echoed by the other societies) 'his views on women in general are such that we have a double reason for not wishing him to be returned to any constituency'. The Liberal candidate was also anti-suffrage, but the Labour candidate, Mr T. McKerrell, was wholeheartedly in favour of enfranchising women and pledged himself to support the Conciliation Bill.

The WFL remained strictly non-party, but both the WSPU and the NUWSS campaigned vigorously with and for McKerrell. Alice Crompton commented that the WSPU's adoption of the same by-election policy as the NUWSS greatly eased the work. All three societies combined for two large meetings, with Labour MP George Lansbury as speaker. Helpers came from Edinburgh and the north of England, and the Scottish University Women's Suffrage Society also helped out. Anti-suffrage women also addressed the public, which the suffragists thought was a great help to their own campaign. All in all it was a lively by-election, attracting much attention, even from English papers. Although the Liberal got in the Labour candidate polled nearly 3,000 votes, transferred from both Liberals and Unionists.[51] The exceptional feature of the campaign was the degree of cooperation between the different suffrage societies, something possible only during this period of truce.

On 4 October a large audience in Oban heard Lady Frances Balfour speak on women's suffrage. The chair was taken by the MP for

13 Anna Munro. Reproduced by permission of the People's Palace (Glasgow Museums)

Argyllshire, Mr J.S. Ainsworth. His vote of thanks was seconded by the Bishop of Argyll and the Isles, who 'came "with an open mind," but his splendid speech told of a mind favourably impressed.' The newly-formed Oban Women's Suffrage Society had forty members, and a society was also formed in Gourock. In November Alice Crompton reported on new societies formed at Selkirk and Hawick, bringing the total of societies in the Scottish Federation to 39.[52]

The work done – and difficulties faced – by one such society may be gleaned from the minutes of the Shetland Society. Their MP (Cathcart Wason) was resolutely anti-suffrage, and in October the Society wrote to the Chairman of the Liberal Association requesting him to ask the MP to abandon his opposition to the Conciliation Bill. Distributing literature was still the most useful thing the Society felt it could do with its time and money; as none of the pamphlets they had seemed entirely suitable, Christina Jamieson agreed to write one 'to meet the requirements of the district'. The Society hired 'Cinematograph films' of the suffrage procession in London for local showing, and sent handmade Shetland goods to help Scottish Federation funds.[53]

In October 1911 a Scottish anti-suffragist caused an uproar at the National Union of Women Workers conference in Glasgow. Lady Griselda Cheape was at that time president of the St Andrews branch of the Scottish Anti-Suffrage League. (The *Anti-Suffrage Review* featured her on the front page of one of its issues as a prominent anti-suffragist.) Her particular interest was in the nursing of sick children, and before her marriage she had worked as a nurse. She was intensely religious and based her opposition to women's involvement in politics on biblical injunctions concerning woman's sphere in relation to man's.[54]

Lady Griselda told the conference that a girl coming out of prison had been met by a suffragette and offered a guinea a week if she would hit a policeman and go to jail. This allegation provoked an angry response from the audience, but she insisted she had heard it from a friend who had seen the letter from the girl. Further voluble protests followed, but she claimed that there was the gravest moral danger in sending young girls out into the streets at night to work for the suffrage cause. ' "It was from the standpoint of morality, and not of politics," she added, "that I object to women's suffrage" – a remark which drew a hurricane of hisses and shouts of "Shame!" during which Lady Griselda retired.'[55]

Ten days later she stated that she had discovered that her friend only *heard* of the alleged letter from someone else and had not actually seen it; she would not have made the allegation if she had realised this. 'At the same time', she continued, 'what I have seen with my own eyes – girls selling papers at street-corners by the gutter – is, simply, to my mind, most undesirable and a grave danger.'[56]

Lady Griselda's pronouncements suggest a woman of small intellect and much eccentricity. Her grand-nephew, Hugh Cheape, grew up hearing tales about her. She was remembered as a formidable woman with a dreadful temper and unusual ideas on bringing up children. It was family lore that her sons 'were often tied to the tail of the dog cart and driven into St Andrews by Lady Griselda as sufficient punishment for some mis-demeanour or other, the young criminals having to canter, run or gallop behind the cart.'[57] It is difficult to imagine that a spokeswoman of this calibre did the anti-suffrage cause much good in Scotland.

Jessie Stephen remembered the reactions of women like Lady Griselda Cheape to her selling *Votes for Women* when Brian Harrison interviewed her over 50 years later. 'It was women who were the bitchy ones', she told him, 'because they thought we were "lowering their standards" [said in a posh accent]'. They would say:

> Oh – 'you get back into your proper place, coming out in public and making an exhibition of yourself' – that sort of thing. Of course that never worried me because I'm a fighter by nature.[58]

Jessie Stephen was another exception to the 'always be ladylike' rule. She was working class, but 'respectability' was every bit as important to working-class women as it was to the middle classes; she simply happened to be a particularly strong, pugnacious character. It is clear from the exhortations in *Votes for Women* that many women found hawking suffrage papers a terrible ordeal and only did it because the cause meant so much to them. It 'required courage and determination for it left one feeling desperately cast down', recorded Lilias Mitchell, 'though that was soon thrown off by the warmth of companionship at "the Shop"'.[59]

Emmeline Pethick Lawrence of the WSPU spoke in Edinburgh, Aberdeen, Dundee, Stirling and Glasgow at the end of October, while Charlotte Despard, president of the WFL, spoke in Edinburgh and Glasgow at the end of November.[60] But between those two dates the consensus was shattered, for the Prime Minister announced that no further time would be given to the Conciliation Bill that session. A Reform Bill would be introduced in the next session to enlarge the male vote, with the possibility of a women's suffrage amendment to it. His announcement effectively 'torpedoed' (to use Lloyd George's oft-repeated word) the Conciliation Bill.

The WSPU immediately announced a renewal of militancy. The WFL decided to wait and see. The NUWSS publicly condemned the militants' decision (the Shetland Society sent the NUWSS circular letter to local newspapers.[61]) The constitutionalists publicly affirmed their faith that the Government would do the right thing, but in private many must have felt betrayed. Lady Frances Balfour wrote to Lady Betty on 28 November, 'I think this is my last year of suffrage. If we get it it ends itself – If we don't I think younger hands must bear the brunt of the fray.'[62] Her mood did not last – she was back in harness soon after – but it was a low ebb for many.

With the ending of the truce came the end of any real hope for the enfranchisement of women before the war. But of course no one knew that at the time, and in Scotland, as elsewhere, the women's suffrage movement continued to grow – and grow – and grow.

Coming to the Boil – 1912

The end of the truce affected all three suffrage organisations. Campaigning was carried on for a series of Scottish by-elections in January and
February 1912, but increasingly the WSPU (and the attention of the
media) concentrated on dramatic gestures in their 'war' against the
Government.

On 9 February Winston Churchill visited Glasgow. A woman
attempted to enter the car she thought he was in and broke its window.
Annie Rhoda Craig was the wife of a stevedore, a member of the ILP, and
secretary of the Dumbarton branch of the WSPU.[1] At the hearing before
the Central Police Court the chief witness for the defence was Frances
Mary Parker, who gave her address as 502 Sauchiehall Street, the premises
of the WSPU. Frances Parker was earlier encountered as secretary of the
non-militant Scottish University Women's Suffrage Union, and her
appearance at this time as a WSPU member is significant. The view of the
historian of the WSPU, Andrew Rosen (which will be discussed again in
a later chapter), is that escalating violence drove many women out of the
organisation.[2] In Scotland, at least, there were individuals whose frustra-
tion at the apparent uselessness of non-militant methods led them in
precisely the opposite direction.

When asked in court why she had been in the crowd when the car was
attacked Miss Parker replied that 'she "wished to do the same as this lady,
if she got the opportunity – (laughter) – because she wished to bring to Mr
Churchill's notice the fact that women were not being treated fairly in the
matter of votes."' This statement 'was received with applause by a
number of ladies in court'. Miss Parker continued 'I merely wish to point
out that I did not see Mrs Craig guilty of any disorderly conduct
whatever, because I think that by precedent it is a quite constitutional
form of agitation.'[3]

Mrs Craig was sentenced to 10 days' imprisonment (in accordance with
WSPU policy she refused the alternative of paying a fine). The governor
of Duke Street prison allowed her to wear her own clothes and to be

excused a bath on admission, privileges which English suffragette prisoners had successfully agitated for.[4]

Later that month in London there occurred the most dramatic militant
protest so far, and a number of Scotswomen took part. This was a
concerted window-smashing raid, spread over three days, which resulted
in more than 200 arrests and imprisonments.[5] Lilias Mitchell travelled
down from Aberdeen where she was now the WSPU organiser. Lucy
Burns, the Edinburgh organiser, stayed at the same London hotel, and
Lilias wrote, 'How thankful I was for her company – the thought of
breaking big shop windows scared me!' The smashing of windows on
Regent Street began on the Saturday; 'Scotland had Kensington High
Street to do and . . . the thought of tackling it made me shake from head to
foot.' But after attending a service at Westminster Abbey on the Sunday
and joining in the singing of 'Christian Seek not yet Repose', she was
'somehow cheered immensely.'

On Monday morning in the Underground, with a hammer up her
sleeve, she 'had another fit of abject fear and positively crawled out at
Kensington High Street.'

> There I stood at Barkers' windows waiting for eleven to strike when
> suddenly I saw a well-known Glasgow member being marched along
> between two policemen. Feeling now quite sick, I banged a window with
> my hammer, people stared and I stared, and then I banged another window
> breaking it thoroughly. People now fled but a commissionaire – a very nice
> man – seized hold of me and without saying a word marched me through
> the shop, passing the buyers who made nasty remarks and landed me in a
> small room . . . I was trembling with fatigue and the general beastliness of it
> all. Fortunately a policeman arrived very soon who cheered me up. 'Never
> you mind miss' he said . . . 'we had to do something just the same before we
> got the vote'. The kind comfort in his voice made me able to face the room
> full of prisoners like myself.[6]

Most of the women received prison sentences. One who did not was
Elizabeth Finlayson Gauld of Edinburgh. She was the matron of a
children's home ('the mother-guardian of forty-two orphan girls') which
she was loth to abandon by going to prison, so she agreed to give the
undertaking required by the court that she would not break the law again.
She made it clear that she would agitate as much as she pleased, by
speaking or writing, in any lawful way, and she emphasised her belief that
the WSPU methods were the only ones left to women.[7] In fact she
proved far more useful to the movement than many women not so
constrained, for there were few Scottish suffrage events in which she did
not subsequently play a key role.

The sentences passed on the women bore no relation to the damage they had caused, but depended on when they appeared before the magistrates. As the hearings went on the sentences imposed became progressively harsher (except that women with previous convictions automatically got longer; Lilias Mitchell received a four-month sentence). Thus, Helen Crawfurd, who was sentenced on the first day, got one month, while an Edinburgh woman, Ellison Gibb, sentenced a few days later, got six months. A group of eight women had travelled down from Glasgow and were reunited in Holloway. Helen Crawfurd was the first to be sentenced, and each day after that when a fresh load of prisoners was brought in she would shout out, 'Are there any there from Scotland?' On about the third day she heard the reply (from one of the Glasgow contingent) 'Scotland for ever'.[8]

Helen Crawfurd was a comparatively recent convert to the suffrage cause. She was born in the working-class Gorbals district of Glasgow where her father was a baker, but she spent much of her childhood in England, and when the family returned to Glasgow it was to the middle-class West End. While she was still very young the local minister fell in love with her and asked her to marry him. She was astonished as he was a much older man, but he persevered and she eventually accepted him, having been persuaded that it must be God's plan for her to become a missionary. Religious and married to a man of the cloth, and coming from a Conservative family background, Helen Crawfurd was not an obvious candidate for the militant suffrage movement, but a WSPU meeting in Rutherglen persuaded her of the rightness of the cause. Unlike those who came to the women's movement via socialism, it was Helen Crawfurd's involvement in the women's movement that led her to socialism and later on to active participation in the Communist Party.

Lilias Mitchell's resolve had been stiffened by the service at Westminster Abbey; likewise Helen Crawfurd, the Sunday before the raid, heard her own husband preach a sermon on Christ making a whip of cords and chasing the money changers out of the temple: 'This I took as a warrant that my participation in the raid was right.' Most of the other Glasgow prisoners were socialists. Two sisters, Margaret and Frances McPhun, were graduates of Glasgow University and were active in the suffrage and socialist causes in the west of Scotland both before and after their incarceration in Holloway. For another Glasgow woman – Janet Barrow-man – it was a one-off act of militancy.

Janet Barrowman's brother was interviewed by Brian Harrison in the 1970s. He insisted that although the whole family believed in the suffrage, it was an older sister, Mary, who – fearful of losing her own job as a teacher – pushed Janet into this act. She was sacked from her job as a clerk in a Glasgow firm in consequence but found another job and was apparently content to have made the one gesture.[9] Helen Crawfurd remarked of her stay in Holloway:

> We were, of course, told that we must not speak to one another in the exercise yard, but to speak the truth, the women Suffrage prisoners were mostly women of the middle and upper classes, and the wardresses were women who might have been in domestic service. The wardresses could not discipline them; indeed, they were more afraid of the prisoners, than the prisoners were of them.

Serving a much longer sentence than Helen Crawfurd, Lilias Mitchell endured more. In the interim Emmeline and Christabel Pankhurst and Emmeline Pethick Lawrence had been tried for conspiracy and imprisoned in Holloway. The suffragette prisoners were instructed by the WSPU to go on hunger strike as a protest against the jailing of Mrs Pankhurst. Lilias wrote in her memoir that she was terrified of being forcibly fed and of fighting against it: 'My heart had something wrong with it from Scarlet Fever and I felt sure that I would die – which at that time was unthinkable and awful.' When the time came she was almost paralysed with fear and put up such a poor fight that 'they got some liquid over my throat without pumping it through my nose. It sounds a small thing now but it was not really for there was a big principle at stake.' Mrs Pankhurst was released the next day so the hunger strike was over, but Lilias 'struggled on with this devastating misery of having failed. I was a coward.'

Shortly after this Lilias Mitchell wrote a long letter to her sister, Kirsty. In it she expressed her disappointment in herself and described Holloway on the night when the prisoners were forcibly fed as 'a sort of hell for two hours'. As for the other Scottish women, Edith Hudson, an Edinburgh WSPU activist, 'fought splendidly – knocked down all the six wardresses & told the doctor what she thought of him! Miss Janie Allan barricaded her door & they were about 20 mins [sic] before they managed to force the door open!' She went on to express her desperate desire to get out, with a *cri de coeur* that she would never have uttered publicly: 'How I wish there need be no more militancy.'[10]

At the time she wrote that letter Lilias Mitchell hoped for an early release, but it was not to be, and some three months later the prisoners heard that Mrs Pankhurst (always referred to by Lilias as 'our Leader') was coming again and they were all to go on hunger strike for her and until everyone was out. Lilias was glad to have another chance 'and determined to fight to the end.' She won her first battle and did not have to fight again for she was released the next day. She felt 'awful at leaving everyone behind but burstingly glad at being "out".' After a brief holiday with her mother, whose support buoyed her up enormously, she returned to her post in Aberdeen.

All of the released prisoners were presented with a personally inscribed 'illuminated address', designed by Sylvia Pankhurst and signed by Emmeline Pankhurst, commending their bravery.[11] Reactions to the London raid varied greatly. The Cabinet Minister Richard Haldane wrote to his sister Elizabeth on 5 March, 'The suffragettes are behaving like mad women. They are spoiling the chance of the Conciliation Bill.'[12] The *Forward*, on the other hand, carried a front-page article supporting the women's action and claiming that they were 'now being punished by the Government-instructed magistrates with a callous and vicious savagery that probably the men of no other country on earth would stand by and tolerate.'[13]

The police feared a Glasgow 'raid' when a middle-aged woman who gave the name of Emily Hickson or Green smashed six plate glass windows on Sauchiehall Street. She was a member of the Glasgow branch of the WSPU and the matron of a home for women in reduced circumstances, the patron of which was Janie Allan (her gesture was thought to be prompted partly by indignation at the treatment endured by Janie Allan in London). But WSPU officials were as surprised as anyone else at the incident and told the press that they deplored such isolated forms of protest as futile.[14] This was not an attitude adopted by the WSPU with any consistency, but the name of Emily Green or Hickson does not crop up at any other time, and it is possible that isolated protests were acceptable when committed by an inner circle of activists but not by outsiders.

Whatever the public thought of window-smashing as a means of getting the vote, the extensive press coverage of the raid and subsequent conspiracy trial focused attention on women's enfranchisement, which could only benefit non-militant supporters of the suffrage. On 11 March a meeting was held in Edinburgh to consider forming a Scottish Churches League for Woman Suffrage. Such church leagues already existed in England, and indeed it was the secretary of one of them who had written to several Scottish ministers suggesting a league for Scotland. One Scottish minister, who moved that such a league be formed, remarked that it would 'lift the question out of the quagmire of politics into a far higher region altogether.'[15]

The League was established, with Lady Frances Balfour as president. It encompassed all the Scottish churches and was active until the outbreak of the war. Many members believed as strongly as did the anti-suffragists that women were higher and purer beings than men but concluded that far from this being a reason to exclude women from politics, it was a reason to let them play a beneficial part in the affairs of the nation.

The growth of non-militant societies continued apace. By the end of March 1912 the number of societies within the Scottish Federation had gone up to 44. Over 500 meetings had been held during the previous year, many of them in large halls. The secretary wrote in the *Common Cause* that it was 'quite impossible to do justice to the Scottish Federation's work in March – it is already far beyond the limits of space permitted, though some reports are not yet to hand.' Those to hand included Hawick, Tayside, Peebles, Dundee, St Andrews, Kilmacolm, Perth, Innerleithen, Lenzie, Gourock, Crieff, Ardrossan, and Edinburgh.[16]

However, the end of hope for the Conciliation Bill led the NUWSS to adopt a new election policy. As only the Labour party put the enfranchisement of women on its manifesto, the NUWSS no longer claimed to be non-party but actively supported Labour candidates, with a separate Election Fighting Fund raised for the purpose. As will be seen in Chapter 11, the Scottish Federation was seriously divided over this policy, with the Edinburgh Society wholeheartedly in favour and the Glasgow Association opposed.

Militant window-smashing in London, and the Glasgow incident, had repercussions when a mob of 200 men and boys marched on the WSPU shop in Sauchiehall Street, flinging iron bolts and weights through the windows. No arrests were made. The Women's Freedom League office in Edinburgh was also smashed up, but the League was pleased at the resultant local press coverage of WFL policy.[17]

However, WFL policy had to be reconsidered when the Conciliation Bill was defeated at its Second Reading in March. A special conference was held, and a stormy session it proved to be. Most National Executive Committee members severed their connection with the WFL, though this actually had less to do with policy than with the way the League was run, which in turn came down to the personality of Charlotte Despard. Although a firm believer in democracy, Charlotte Despard was a strong personality. She tended, moreover, to forget the committee structure from time to time and make statements on behalf of the WFL which no one else had heard about. Disaffected members of the National Executive Committee challenged her leadership and were defeated.[18]

The Scottish branches remained loyal to Charlotte Despard. Alexia B. Jack, the Edinburgh WFL secretary, said at the special conference, 'she knows perfectly well what we think of her in Scotland; we love her and respect her; nay more, we think there is no personality in the League equal to hers.' The Edinburgh branch supported the new National Executive Committee (which now included Anna Munro), and the existing representatives from Scotland – Agnes Husband, Alexia Jack, and Eunice Murray – were all re-nominated.[19]

The Freedom League continued to call itself a militant society and indulged in mild forms of law-breaking like tax-resistance but eschewed violence. However, as argued earlier, its most important role was in educating public opinion and this it continued to do with vigour. Unlike NUWSS members, who condemned WSPU violence as counter-productive, WFL members supported those in their 'sister society' who committed acts which they themselves would not consider. One reason for the continuing survival of the WFL may have been that it offered a home to young women who found the idea of being a 'constitutionalist' stuffy but did not want to get involved in violence. But even more important was the bonding between the women in the Scottish WFL branches.

Subsequently, the WFL followed the NUWSS lead and supported Labour candidates in three-cornered contests, though initially this was strongly resisted by the Glasgow branch. In July successful joint demonst-rations of the WFL, NUWSS and ILP in support of women's inclusion in the Reform Bill took place in Dundee and Edinburgh (in Edinburgh the National Federation of Women Workers, the Women's Labour League and the Men's League for Women's Suffrage also took part).[20]

The NUWSS and WFL also carried out separate summer campaigns. The NUWSS mounted one in Sutherland and founded a new society at Dornoch. At Bonar Bridge the suffragists had arranged a meeting in the library 'but at 8.15 only seven people had arrived, most of the rest of the village being outside urging one another to come in! We decided to go out to them, and finding a wagonette, held a delightful open-air meeting. About 100 adults listened to us.' They sold about thirty copies of the *Common Cause*, gained nine members and thought that 'we shall look back on this as one of the most pleasant meetings in Sutherland.' Later in the summer they campaigned in the Elgin burghs, taking advantage of the Banff Agricultural Show.[21]

An encouraging sign for Women's Freedom League campaigners that summer was the increasing interest of women in the crowds, 'or perhaps rather the fact that they are expressing it more freely.'

> At Kirkcaldy a man tried to explain the discrepancies in the Insurance Act by the statement that women's expenses are less heavy. It was good to hear the sarcastic rejoinder of a working woman. 'Oh! ay! they can eat gress!'[22]

In July and August the west coast campaign, based at Rothesay and with Anna Munro again in charge, was in full swing. She found the crowds more sympathetic and interested than ever before, and over a hundred meetings were held without rowdyism. Women joined the League in large numbers; a branch was established at Rothesay and 140 dozen copies of *The Vote* were sold, so the campaign paid for itself.[23]

While the NUWSS and WFL did most of the serious campaigning at this time, the WSPU got most of the attention of the press. One September night two suffragettes replaced all the marker flags at Balmoral Golf Course with new flags painted in the purple, white and green colours of the WSPU, with messages attached about the forcible feeding of suffragettes and 'Votes for Women'; a similar message was painted on a wayside memorial fountain. As the Royal family was in residence at the time this created a furore in the London press, though the *Glasgow Herald*, more relaxed, remarked that 'there was much amusement on Saturday when it was found that during the night suffragists had eluded the vigilance of the police guards at Balmoral Castle'.[24]

The perpetrators were unknown and would have remained so but for Lilias Mitchell's unpublished memoir for she happened to be one of them (the other she called simply 'a prominent suffragette'). She described it as 'the sort of adventure that is tremendous fun once it is over; the walk there was lengthy and seemed unendingly so when we got within the private grounds.'

Votes for Women emphasised that the gesture was not meant to show disrespect to Royalty but was carried out because Cabinet Ministers were in the area. In fact both Asquith and the Home Secretary, Reginald McKenna, were pounced upon by two suffragettes while they were playing golf at Dornoch. Once again this was Lilias Mitchell and her colleague. The incident appears to have been kept from the press, nor is there any evidence of the women being charged with assault, presumably because the Prime Minister had no wish to appear in court in such a case (see Chapter 9 for a similar ocurrence which did reach the papers).

One incident which received press coverage at this time was the smashing of a glass case at the Wallace Monument near Stirling by a suffragette calling herself Edith Johnston but who was in fact Ethel Moorhead, encountered in the last chapter throwing an egg at Winston Churchill. In the interim her father had died and she had moved from Dundee to Edinburgh where she was making a name for herself an an artist. (She took part in the window smashing raid in London but was released 'owing to failure of the evidence'.[25]) Brian Harrison claims that suffragettes gave false names when they were arrested to save their families distress.[26] Ethel Moorhead's last family link apparently died with her father, yet she came up with different names nearly every time she was arrested; judging by all her other actions her motive was to make life as difficult as possible for officialdom.

The attack on the Wallace Monument was loaded with symbolism; as has already been seen in an article by Mary Phillips, Wallace's fight for the liberty of Scotland was a favourite theme in Scottish suffragette propaganda, and 'Scots Wha Hae' was a popular song. To make this clear to the public an open-air meeting was held at which Elizabeth Finlayson Gauld and Muriel Scott explained that the glass had been smashed 'in order to draw the attention of the people to the fact that their liberty was won by fighting.' Mrs Finlayson Gauld concluded by saying that the woman who smashed the glass was the daughter and granddaughter of a soldier (the Moorhead family had returned to Scotland from India only in 1905), and that it was a great pity that the daughter of a soldier should have to fight herself for liberty.[27]

'Edith Johnston' spent one night in a police cell in Stirling prison and made a fuss about conditions there after her release. (In response the Chief Constable wrote to the prison commissioners, 'I have no doubt that Miss Johnston's complaint is made for the sole purpose of carrying out the avowed policy of the Suffragists to cause trouble.') At Perth, where she was sentenced to seven days, according to the governor, she 'refused to give any information regarding her previous history, but she appears to be respectable, and I would say well brought up.' After she left and lodged various complaints with the prison commissioners, he described her as 'insolent and defiant' and sent them a note from the matron stating that the prisoner 'behaved very badly. She defied all authority and refused to conform to any of the Prison Rules'.[28]

Coming to the WSPU at a comparatively late date, Ethel Moorhead is unlikely to have suffered the traumas faced by many women during the leadership crisis of autumn 1912. Christabel Pankhurst had decided that the WSPU could not be conducted by someone who was in and out of prison, so she escaped to Paris where she remained until the outbreak of the war (her mother, Emmeline, stayed in Britain and endured repeated periods of imprisonment and hunger strikes). Then, because the Pethick Lawrences could not go along with the extent of the violence planned by Christabel, they were informed that their services were no longer required. Although they expressed no bitter feelings in public (and they continued to edit *Votes for Women* while Christabel started her own paper, *The Suffragette*) WSPU members found it all rather hard to take.

Lilias Mitchell confessed that Christabel being in Paris 'made me angry' and that the split between the Pankhursts and Pethick Lawrences 'was felt by us all badly'. However, she stuck by the Pankhursts and was sent to Newcastle to replace the WSPU organiser who joined the other faction. Later she was WSPU organiser in Birmingham. She was not active in the suffrage movement in Scotland again, but she continued to carry out militant acts and to suffer imprisonment. She was a model WSPU organiser, always doing what was considered necessary, no matter how much she disliked it, even placing a small bomb at a railway station. (In

her memoir she merely wrote that 'suburban stations were set on fire', but
the leader of the bomb-planting expedition, Mary Richardson, wrote of
being accompanied by 'Lilian' Mitchell, mentioning her Scottish accent;
as it happened near Birmingham it was undoubtedly Lilias.[29])

In September 1912 came a test of the NUWSS's new policy of
supporting Labour candidates, for there was a three-cornered contest at
the Midlothian by-election. The Scottish Federation protested against the
NUWSS supporting the Labour candidate, Provost Brown, because he
had not pledged himself to vote against the Third Reading of the Reform
Bill if women were not included. But the NUWSS campaign organiser
told the Scottish Federation that any other course 'would stultify the
policy of the Union'. The Scottish Federation was still not satisfied, but as
Provost Brown promised to follow whatever line was taken by the
Labour Party on the Reform Bill, the joint Election Fighting Fund
committee and by-election committee supported him. Some of the
executive committee contested this decision (including the Scottish
member, Chrystal MacMillan), but the majority voted in favour of it.[30]

Scottish Federation members played some part in the by-election
campaign, but the most prominent Scotswoman in it was Annot Robinson who, as Annot Wilkie, had been arrested on one of the first WFL
deputations in London and had gone to the north of England after her
marriage. The NUWSS brought up many of its strongest Labour and
working-class campaigners from England and waged a lively campaign
which received attention in both the national and local press. The
Edinburgh Evening Dispatch (6 September 1912) commended the NUWSS
campaign: 'Their work is thorough, orderly and methodical, yet it goes
with such a swing, and is carried out with such enthusiasm and devotion
that it has entirely caught the appreciation and approval of the electorate.'

The NUWSS paper, the *Common Cause*, gave the by-election a great
deal of coverage. A particularly interesting piece, by an English working-
class organiser, Ada Nield Chew, was entitled 'Women and the Scottish
Labour Movement'. She had experience of the labour movement in both
countries and this campaign bore out her previous impression that 'the
Scottish working man has lacked that necessary grounding which the
progressive English working man so often gets. The Scotchman is a little
backward in appreciating the importance of the woman's cause because
his own women are a little backward, too – not backward in native
intelligence; but are tradition-bound and home-bound.' On a Saturday
night she would always find women in the ILP rooms of any large English
town, but on visiting the Edinburgh rooms she found many friendly men
but not a single woman (she asked the caretaker's wife whether she might
meet some if she stayed longer and was assured she would not). 'Our view
of the inevitability of the alliance of woman and labour is new to men and

14 Midlothian By-Election. Dalkeith Committee Room. From *The Common Cause* 5 September 1912

women alike here', she continued, 'but it is a very special joy to see the dawn of its intelligence pierce their minds.'[31] The result of the by-election was that a safe Liberal seat fell to the Unionists with Labour recording 2,413 votes. The NUWSS considered this a success for the new policy.[32]

Later in September the honorary political secretary of the Men's League for Women's Suffrage, J. Malcolm Mitchell, held a successful series of open-air meetings around Inverness under the auspices of the North of Scotland Federation. This was the first time a speaker from the Men's League had ventured so far north, and he attracted large audiences of working men. A branch of the Men's League was formed under the leadership of a prominent supporter of women's suffrage, Bailie MacEwan.[33]

The NUWSS was careful about the extent to which it criticised the WSPU, but controversy was created by a report from Largs by an NUWSS organiser, Mildred Watson, which appeared in the *Common Cause* on 12 September. She found the work there exceedingly difficult as the WSPU were holding meetings in the town, and she was told by a number of people that everyone was disgusted with the tactics of the militants. The WSPU organiser at Largs wrote to the *Common Cause* questioning the accuracy of Miss Watson's statement. On the 26th two letters appeared in reply. Mildred Watson regretted having hurt the feelings of the WSPU, 'knowing how self-sacrificing' the members were, but she stood by her statement, not only for Largs but elsewhere on the west coast too. And Elsie Inglis wanted readers of the *Common Cause* to know that as secretary of the Scottish Federation she received reports every week from secretaries and organisers in every part of Scotland about the public's difficulties in distinguishing the constitutional suffrage movement from the unpopular militants.

Scottish militancy was in the news again in early October. A Liberal meeting was held in Edinburgh with Sir Rufus Isaacs (prosecutor for the Crown in the conspiracy trial against Emmeline Pankhurst and the Pethick Lawrences) as principal speaker. The WSPU organised a series of interruptions, with some nine women rising at intervals to ask about votes; all of them were brutally ejected, as was a man who protested that this 'was not like Scotland'. The chairman of the meeting later claimed that the interrupters did not belong to Edinburgh but had come up from London. In the *Scotsman* (5 October) Muriel Scott retorted that she had been to London only twice in her life, once as a child and again in 1909 'when I experienced His Majesty's hospitality in Holloway'. The other interrupters, she insisted, were also Edinburgh residents.

An eye-witness wrote in *Votes for Women*, 'I was amazed and ashamed that such treatment should be meted out to women in the heart of my beloved Scotland, the land of so-called religious and political liberty'. That the brutality of the ejections was not exaggerated by the suffrage press is clear from three days' worth of correspondence in the *Edinburgh Evening Dispatch*, with the editor himself weighing in. The first day's column was headed MAULING SUFFRAGETTES and began with a long letter by a woman from the Transvaal who had watched the scene in disbelief. What struck her most was the 'brutal joy' of the men watching the women being thrown out. No sooner did a woman move to ask a question than men rushed at them 'and even struck them as they might some wild animal', while the crowd cheered: 'I was sick with horror, and what was worse than seeing the women ill-treated was the sight of the gloating faces of the men'.[34]

The letters over the next two days conveyed a wide spectrum of reactions, from those who thought the women were quite 'leniently' treated and 'had only themselves to blame' to further expressions of horror and outrage at what had happened. The paper's editor came down firmly on the side of the latter. He considered the militants' conduct to be 'foolish and entirely indefensible' but did not see that this justified such violent behaviour by the men.[35]

The incident had a dramatic sequel several weeks later. One of the interrupters, Ethel Moorhead, had been hit in the ribs by the man sitting next to her (her letter describing this was published in the *Evening Dispatch* on 5 October). The man was Peter Ross, a maths teacher at Broughton School. On 25 October she marched into his classroom with a whip, shouted that he had struck her at Sir Rufus Isaacs's meeting and raised her whip. He grabbed her hand and led her to the headmaster's room, where she hit him with her fist. When she was taken into custody she fought against being searched and against being put under the measuring gauge; she then broke the window in the cell because 'she thought she had been treated with undue violence.'[36]

At her trial on 2 November the court was crowded. When she entered she was greeted with applause by the suffragettes in the gallery. When being cross-examined she was asked

> Where did you get this whip? She replied – Bought it.
> Was it for the purpose of assaulting Mr Ross? – I have a dog. (Laughter)
> Then it was for a dog you bought it? – Both of them. (Laughter)[37]

The Women's Freedom League thought that Ethel Moorhead had been treated with 'gross indignity' as an untried prisoner and unfairly in Court where she had not been allowed to describe the assault on her which provoked her own attack. Ethel Moorhead paid a fine of £1 under protest and later appealed unsuccessfully on the grounds that she had not been allowed to speak in mitigation of the sentence.[38] Ethel Moorhead was fast becoming a heroine of the militant suffrage movement in Scotland.

It is not surprising that the popular press should report such incidents. Open-air meetings had lost their novelty value, and processions had been given up as useless. However, that autumn of 1912 a new gesture captured the imagination of the press without incurring anyone's disapproval. This was a women's march from Edinburgh to London. (Initially it was to have been from London to Edinburgh, but the WFL pointed out to the instigator, Mrs de Fonblanque, how much more publicity there would be for a march to the capital.[39])

The WFL played the most prominent part in the march, but the WSPU supported it, as did the NUWSS (after initial fears of militant action were allayed[40]). The idea was that the women would gather signatures for a petition which would be presented to Asquith in London. Most of the women walked small sections, handing on the petition at strategic points, but six walked the entire length of the route.

On 12 October the march commenced from Charlotte Square at a rally addressed by Alexia Jack (the Edinburgh WFL secretary), Elizabeth Finlayson Gauld, Ethel Moorhead, Anna Munro, and Charlotte Despard. The marchers – plainly dressed in brown, with green cockades in their hats – attracted enormous crowds all along Princes Street. The *Daily Mail* reckoned there were ten thousand spectators, while the *Edinburgh Evening Dispatch* remarked that the crowds were from 10–20 feet deep in many places and that 'a large force of police had difficulty in clearing the way, but as no hostility was shown at any time towards the women the procession along the city's principal street was accomplished in safety.' The *Scotsman* commented that the suffragettes had 'succeeded in attracting the largest crowd of people they have ever managed to get together in Edinburgh.' Rousing open-air meetings were held at Portobello and Musselburgh, and people clamoured to sign the petition.[41]

The women received good publicity all along their route (the only hostility encountered was in Peterborough) and a rousing welcome on their arrival in London on 16 November. Nannie Brown, an Edinburgh Women's Freedom League member, started with the intention of returning home after a few days, but 'found the march was so intensely enjoyable' that she went all the way to London. She was one of the six women presented with a silver badge for completing the full 400 miles, and on her return entertained Scottish WFL branches with her recollections of 'humorous incidents' on the march.[42] The following extract conveys something of the flavour of her talk.

> One day after toiling up a long hill, very muddy and very steep, the most welcome sight met our eyes – a large white flag, made of an old pole and a sheet, and printed on it in huge black letters the strange device – 'Votes for Women'. It was waving gaily from the most tumbledown looking house; the owner of which, a little woman, received us with enthusiasm, and rushed us into her quaint little parlour, where a huge teapot and large plates filled with bread and butter met our delighted gaze. She assured us she had been looking out for us all day, and had had everything ready, so that no time might be lost. A neighbour contributed a great basket of apples from her garden, so we set off again rejoicing, ready for anything.[43]

Although the WSPU supported the march militancy was not suspended meanwhile. An unusual incident occurred at Ladybank in October during

Asquith's visit. When Ellison Gibb, a WSPU member from Glasgow, attempted to interrupt the Prime Minister, a young man placed a hand over her mouth and effectively gagged her. ('All the witnesses laughed heartily', reported the *Dundee Advertiser*.) She in turn entered a charge of assault against the man, and the trial was on 19 November.[44]

The *Dundee Advertiser* of 20 November reported proceedings in full, as well as giving a short leader to what was seen as something of a test case. Cupar Sheriff Court was crowded for the occasion. Sheriff Armour-Hannay held that an assault had been committed but a technical and trivial one which the complainer had called upon herself 'by her unjustifiable conduct'; he fined the man a token five shillings. The suffragettes complained about the lenient penalty, but the *Advertiser* thought the Sheriff's decision was 'only tenable on the basis, which every ardent Suffragette would repudiate, that women are entitled to preferential treatment as being physically the weaker sex. ... Despite the Sheriff's decision, we think he acted like a good citizen.'

Between bringing the charge and the trial Ellison Gibb spent some of her time in Dundee prison. At about half past midnight on 29/30 October a Dundee constable saw a hammer lying on the pavement and discovered that a window in the savings bank on Euclid Street had been smashed. To deaden the sound, the glass had first been smeared with treacle over which was spread brown paper bearing the words 'Votes for Women'. The police were on the alert for further incidents and at about 3 a.m. they noticed two women 'perambulating the streets'. The policemen hid themselves while the women pasted treacled brown paper on a window of the Inland Revenue offices, then threw 'two pieces of iron' toward it. The policemen sprang up and arrested the women, who were Ellison Gibb and Fanny Parker (now no longer content merely to commend others' militant acts).[45]

At the trial the women admitted having committed the offence 'as part of a campaign that was being committed throughout the country'. They were sentenced to three days' imprisonment and went on hunger strike; relief was expressed within the Scottish prison system at the short sentence as forcible feeding was not required.[46]

The Scottish Anti-Suffrage League took advantage of the ill will engendered by the militants' actions by staging a grand anti-suffrage demonstration at the St Andrew's Hall, Glasgow, on 1 November. The principal speakers were Lord Curzon and the Marchioness of Tullibardine. The Marchioness was of a very different stature from the Scottish anti-suffrage spokeswomen so far encountered. The reporter from the *Forward* (2 November) remarked that she claimed for women nearly everything that the suffragists claimed, apart from the vote, and that her speech in many ways 'breathed the spirit of the new woman.'

15 Nannie Brown. Courtesy of The People's Story Museum, Edinburgh

16 Nannie Brown's silver badge. Courtesy of Scottish National
Ethnographical Archive, National Museums of Scotland

I know that many earnest-minded women have joined the Suffrage
movement out of the very reality of their care for the individual. Facts have
come to their knowledge with regard to social evils which are a terrible
stain upon our civilization and our Christianity ... I admit that though in
the past women have tried to hold up ideals of chivalry and purity, we have
sometimes not achieved as much as we might, because we have shirked
knowledge of these evils. I agree with our Suffragist opponents that our
ignorance has contributed something towards their existence; and ... I
regard it as an obligation laid on married women and women of mature
age, leading sheltered lives, to know something of the main facts of those
evils, in order that they may be able to bring more definite influence to bear
on the men of their own families on these matters, and that whenever there
is necessity for legislation dealing with these subjects they may be able to
put the woman's point of view before them.[47]

In a letter published in the Glasgow Herald Ellison Gibb called Lady
Tullibardine's speech 'in essence a pro-suffrage one', and commented that
it was impossible not to be impressed with a speech 'conceived in so
beautiful a spirit and delivered with so much earnestness and sincerity',
while the speech itself constituted 'the finest and most convincing
refutation we could have had of the purport of the meeting.' As Brian
Harrison put it, she 'spoke so well for anti-suffragism that her audiences
could not understand why, whatever she might say, such a woman should
not vote.' And in fact when women not only had the vote but could stand
for Parliament, as Duchess of Atholl she became one of the earliest and
most distinguished female MPs.[48]

As a counterblast to the anti-suffrage meeting Lady Betty Balfour
instigated a large suffrage demonstration in Glasgow. The Scottish
Federation, the Conservative and Unionist Women's Franchise Association, and the Glasgow and West of Scotland Association worked
together to make the event a success. It was held at the St Andrew's Hall
on 9 December, with Lady Frances Balfour presiding and the Earl of
Lytton as principal speaker. The event was given good coverage in the
Glasgow Herald.[49]

Both militant excesses and anti-suffragists' meetings kept women's
suffrage constantly in the public mind. The main beneficiaries were the
constitutional societies. Reports to the Scottish Federation of meetings in
October and November came from societies in Aberdeen, Dunfermline,
Kilmarnock, Tayside, Cupar, Leven, Falkirk, Alloa, Lenzie, Stirlingshire,
St Andrews, Hawick, Crieff, Haddington, Orkney, Perth, Kilmacolm,
and Oban. The Women's Freedom League organised a meeting in
Edinburgh in November, with Charlotte Despard as speaker, and the
Edinburgh National Society for Women's Suffrage sold tickets and

provided stewards, an example of continuing cooperation at local level between two different suffrage organisations.[50]

However, in late November the militants again hogged the headlines. The Chancellor of the Exchequer, Lloyd George, was to speak at a public meeting in the Music Hall, Aberdeen, and police were on the alert for suffragette activity. At the end of a Liberal women's meeting in the afternoon a woman was found near the platform who could give no good reason for being there. After a further search the police discovered 'what appeared to be a bundle of clothing in one of the pay boxes ... On close inspection the "bundle" proved to be two women, who, in the descriptive phrase of one of the officials "were huddled up like buckies."' The women refused to come out, and forcible ejection from such a confined space proved difficult. Explosive caps of the kind used for toy pistols were found in their possession but no pistol; presumably they had some other way of detonating the caps.[51]

Next day (30 November) most of the Scottish papers devoted leading articles to the incident. The *Scotsman* thought that firing the caps might have caused a panic in the hall and referred to the militants' 'reign of terror'. The *Aberdeen Daily Journal* insisted that 'a panic would inevitably have taken place, and in all probability many lives would have been lost. The militant Suffragist campaign has, therefore, developed into one which amounts to murder.' This seems like a ridiculous over-reaction to something that did not happen, but in the previous weeks an attempt had been made to burn down a Cabinet Minister's house in England and a theatre in Dublin, and nobody knew what the suffragettes would do next.

WSPU members in Aberdeen expressed delight at the publicity achieved by their efforts to annoy the Chancellor of the Exchequer. The three women arrested in the Music Hall gave their names as Joyce Locke, a student from London, Fanny Parker, who was said to speak 'with a Glasgow accent', and Marian Pollock, who refused to divulge anything about herself. In addition, two women were arrested for other offences. An English suffragette, Emily Wilding Davison, used a whip to attack a church minister whom she mistook for Lloyd George. And a woman calling herself Mary Humphreys, but who was in fact Ethel Moorhead, threw a stone at the window of a car which she thought contained the Chancellor.

When the women appeared in court the magistrate adjourned the case for two days and Joyce Locke threw her shoes at him. 'SUFFRAGETTES RUN RIOT AT ABERDEEN' screamed the headline of the *Dundee Courier*. When the court re-convened the women involved in the Music Hall incident were incensed that the charge against them was breach of the peace, since all they had done was struggle against their captors. They were found guilty and sentenced to five days' imprisonment (naturally the alternative of paying the fine was spurned). 'As the three were removed from the Court', reported the *Aberdeen Free press*, 'some of their friends shouted after them, "No Surrender!" and the three lustily shouted back also "No Surrender".' 'Mary Humphreys' was found guilty of malicious mischief and sentenced to ten days' imprisonment; she refused to leave the dock and was forcibly removed 'amid cries of "Shame!" from the gallery of the Court.'[52]

The women did not make life easy for the staff at Craiginches Prison. 'Prisoner Humphreys' had only been in her cell a few hours when she broke several panes of glass in her window. 'This form of "protest",' reported the governor, 'I subsequently ascertained from her comrades, is quite the right thing to do, and has the authority and approval of the party as helping to illustrate in a practical manner their refusal to recognise the law as it stands in regard to their voting disabilities.' During the next four days all of the prisoners smashed their windows at one time or another, and carried out further protests by refusing to quit the exercise yard and struggling against being carried off. Prisoner 'Humphreys' then smashed the gas-box and mantle in her cell and threw shards of glass at anyone who passed along the corridor; she was removed – 'kicking, fighting and struggling desperately' – to the only strong cell.[53]

The women went on hunger strike, but forcible feeding was not considered. Three of them served only five days, and the other two were released early on part payment of their fines by sympathisers without their knowledge. Emily Wilding Davison and 'Mary Humphreys' subsequently wrote to the *Scotsman* denying that their fines had been paid and calling this a 'trumped-up excuse to hide a fine reality', the supposed reality being that 'Bonnie Scotland will not adopt the barbarity of forcible feeding!'. As the prison governor stated clearly in an internal Scottish Office file that the fines had been paid, the women appear to have deluded themselves.[54]

In the wake of the affair the Aberdeen newspapers were inundated with letters. An Aberdeen non-militant observed in the *Free Press* (6 December) that the paper's editor had condemned the tactics and proceedings of the militants, but it was 'in the power of yourself and your brother-editors to remedy the evil to a very large extent.' Militant suffragism could flourish only in the 'sunshine of continuous newspaper advertisement' so if editors would make a 'self-sacrificing resolution' not to report their actions, the militant movement 'would probably collapse'.

Such a self-sacrificing resolution was never on the cards, and the fascination which the suffragettes continued to exert on the press is manifest in the story of 'Marian Pollock'. The *Dundee Advertiser* (12 and 13 December) discovered that on her release from prison this suffragette had taken a train to Dundee and that she belonged to the city. The reporter learned her real name but told readers that he had promised not to divulge it until she consented. On the 18th the paper reported that 'considerable interest' had been aroused by the announcement that the 'mysterious Dundee suffragette' was to address a meeting at the Foresters' Hall, (where Fanny Parker, now Dundee WSPU organiser, also spoke) and that a large number of the public attended the meeting 'to satisfy their curiosity'. No doubt they did, but it was the *Advertiser* which had created that curiosity. The paper reported that she had revealed herself as May Grant.

> Some of her hearers, she thought, had known her since she was a little girl, as the daughter of a clergyman, and as having taken part in mission work. Now she appeared on the platform as a gaol-bird! Perhaps some of them had not heard the call of the oppressed, sweated, betrayed women. Nothing but political power would give their sisters the help they needed in the struggle for existence.

This period marks a decisive change in the movement in Scotland. In earlier years Scottish women had been arrested for militant activities in London, while women arrested in Dundee were English, presumably because Scottish women found it hard to face the glare of publicity where they had families and were known. But the government's continuing prevarication had hardened attitudes. No longer did the Scottish movement rely on English activists; there was a solid core of Scottish women prepared to act and to stand up in public and affirm their commitment to militancy.

This seems an appropriate place to pause and assess the composition of the movement in Scotland since by now all the women listed in Appendix 2 were actively involved. Nearly all the women about whom anything is known were of independent means. Those who had occupations comprised: one factory worker (Jenny MacCallum), one domestic servant (Jessie Stephen), one warden of a university hall of residence, one matron of a children's home and one matron of a private hospital, eight teachers, three clerks/shorthand typists, five doctors, three actresses, two writers, and three artists.

As divorce was possible only for the wealthy, marital status may be inferred from styles of address. These have been broken down for the different organisations in Table 1. (N.B. Only women alive and active in the Edwardian movement are included.) Of course, a woman listed as 'Mrs' could conceivably have been a widow, but only two of the women, one in the WSPU and one in the NUWSS, are *known* to have been widows. In view of Elizabeth Finlayson Gauld's position as matron of an orphanage it might seem logical to assume that she too fell into that category, but a woman who knew her, and who kept a collection of suffrage material, scrawled on a letter of hers, 'Husband a chronic drunkard who has bashed up his wife's life!'.[55] As can be seen, the

TABLE 1

STYLES OF ADDRESS OF SCOTTISH WOMEN ACTIVE IN THE MOVEMENT

	WSPU		WFL		NUWSS	
	N	%	N	%	N	%
MISS	48	73	18	69	15	71
MRS	18	27	8	31	6	29
TOTAL	66		26		21	

composition of the three organisations is very similar.[56]

Married women involved in the movement usually had the active support of their husbands. As Olive Banks has written, this was not simply a happy accident, for women with some commitment to feminism gravitated toward men who shared their views.[57] One example of marital support is given in a letter to me from Dr Mary Tod. Her mother, Margaret Simpson Barnett, was a member of the Edinburgh National Society for Women's Suffrage, and regularly attended meetings while her husband looked after the children. 'I was brought up in a happy feminist home', she wrote, 'and look back on those days with much pleasure.' Another emerged in an interview with Dr Elizabeth Baxendine whose mother was an Edinburgh WSPU member; although Mr Baxendine was a registrar of births and deaths, he nevertheless supported his wife's census-resistance in 1911.[58]

In the closing months of 1912 militancy was on the increase and so too was the reaction against it. On 5 December, after suffragettes interrupted Augustine Birrell's rectorial address to the students of Glasgow University, a group of students marched on the WSPU office in Sauchiehall Street and wrecked the premises.[59] At this time a new form of militant protest spread from England to Scotland. Bottles of corrosive fluid (or sometimes a thick black liquid) were dropped into pillar-boxes, damaging or destroying letters. An English suffragette speaking at a WSPU meeting in Edinburgh described it as 'guerilla warfare of a type which embarrassed a Government, and at the same time resulted in no arrests being made'.[60] Women may have escaped arrest, but if anything was needed to show that WSPU members were beginning to live in a world of their own, it was the attacks on pillar-boxes. The government was not the least bit embarrassed by it while thousands of letter-writers suffered and were alienated from the women's cause.

Increasingly the WSPU convinced itself that it was pitted against a host of unbelievers and enemies, and the Scottish Federation of the NUWSS was forced to spend as much time repudiating militancy as promoting the cause. The belief that arson was the only way to achieve the vote had not yet spread from England to Scotland, but it was soon to come.

Action and Reaction – January–June 1913

'A Record of Betrayal': that was Miss J.C. Methven's verdict on the struggle for women's enfranchisement, in the *Suffragette* of 17 January 1913. Miss Methven had been secretary of the Edinburgh National Society for Women's Suffrage in the 1890s, and had joined the earliest Scottish Women's Liberal Association. But what were the results of all their constitutional work in the years up to 1905, the demonstrations and meetings they had held, the petitions, letters, and resolutions? 'It had been of no avail', she recorded. Militancy was the only way.

Yet hopes remained for a women's suffrage amendment to the Reform Bill, and the WSPU sent a deputation of working-class women from all over the country to see Lloyd George. It was headed by Flora Drummond; two women went from Dundee and eight from Edinburgh, including four members of the Women's Co-operative Guild and three Newhaven fishwives, who wore their 'picturesque costumes'.[1] The *Dundee Courier*'s London correspondent reported that one of them made the best speech of the day at a WSPU meeting 'because it was so entirely artless and unpremeditated'. She said that like Jeanie Deans they had come from Edinburgh to London to plead for their sisters. 'Then, adopting the fisherfolk's phraseology, she said – "We hae a guid cause and a guid captain, splendid officers, and a willin' crew".' She said that she was not used to making speeches, but that she and her friends at least made a good advertisement for the WSPU 'if they might judge by the crowds that watched them in the streets. "You wad think," she said "that we were a new kind of animal or freaks."'

> Proceeding in the same frank style, which was hugely enjoyed by the audience, the speaker said that the people of Scotland were not so enthusiastic about woman suffrage as most of them seemed to be in London. 'They were not so easily converted in Scotland,' she said, 'and they are very conservative in their Liberalism.' There was great laughter at this.[2]

The debate on the Reform Bill opened on 24 January and was marked by a high level of oratory and seriousness. However, the Speaker of the House then dropped a bombshell: a women's suffrage amendment to that bill would so alter its nature that it would have to be withdrawn and a new statute drawn up to await consideration in a future session of Parliament. The uproar was tremendous throughout Britain. The militants were convinced that Asquith had known this beforehand and deliberately deceived them, though the *Scotsman* – one of the most anti-Liberal newspapers in the country – thought 'no Minister can be imagined as deliberately planning to get himself and his Government into the exceedingly disagreeable and embarrassing situation of to-day.'[3]

The *Glasgow Herald* (27 January) began its leader on the subject by stating that 'the outstanding lesson taught by the troubles which the present Government has created for itself in regard to woman franchise is that no Government, under existing conditions, can make this question part of its official policy.' The editor went on to say that the present Cabinet was sharply divided on the issue, that a Unionist government would be equally divided, and that a private member's bill would never pass into law. No measure of woman suffrage could be passed without the consent of the electors, and the *Herald*'s editor therefore advised suffragists to concentrate on convincing the electorate that their cause was just. He claimed that women had never seriously tackled this and that the movement had gone steadily backwards.

Not surprisingly, letters in the correspondence column (29 January) challenged these conclusions. Margaret Gibb pointed out that the electors in general had never been in favour of any extension of the franchise, but that had not stopped three Reform Acts being passed. Eunice Murray denied that the suffragists had failed to win public support or had gone backwards: 'Can a cause have gone back in which over £100,000 was raised last year and in which the general public supports five weekly suffrage papers? . . . Can you point out any question before the electors, even Home Rule, which has raised the same amount of attention, which in the course of a year has so often filled the largest halls in the country as votes for women?'

The response of the WSPU to the Reform Bill 'betrayal' was predictable. Guerilla warfare and secret arson were publicly proclaimed by the Pankhursts. The *Glasgow Herald* shed crocodile tears of sympathy for the effect this would have on the constitutionalists' work, while in the *Forward* George Barnes suggested that the best policy for suffragists was 'to "ca' canny'.'[4] Sylvia Pankhurst later wrote that she regarded the new policy of secret arson 'with grief and regret, believing it wholly mistaken and unnecessary', although she would not publicly repudiate it. As far as she was concerned, 'the old, defiant, symbolic militancy performed in the sight of all, punished with a severity out of all proportion to its damage, if damage there were, had roused an enormous volume of support'.[5] But for women who had suffered violence at the hands of men while carrying out those open acts of militancy, and had undergone imprisonment and perhaps forcible feeding for such acts, the attraction of 'guerilla warfare' was obvious.

As Table 2* shows, the new kind of militancy was largely successful in avoiding arrests. At this time arson attacks in England were already under way, but they took considerably longer to manifest themselves in Scotland, where the favoured policy at the beginning of 1913 was still pillar-box attacks.

The press was aware that pillar-box attacks were not random but were part of a concerted campaign, and Jessie Stephen, who took part in that campaign, told Brian Harrison that it was organised 'with a military precision'. They met at a specified time and venue, were handed their bottles of acid and told the precise time and place they were to drop them in. Being dressed in the muslin apron, black dress and cap and cuffs of a domestic servant she was never suspected of any kind of nefarious activity.[6]

The acid, she explained to Harrison, was obtained by one of their members who was a chemist, for professional women 'were able to help us in a thousand different ways'. Asked if any members objected to doing it she replied, 'in that case they refused to take on the job, but they would never give us away.' She confirmed that members could choose what tasks they were prepared to undertake, pillar-box attacks, arson, or interrupting political meetings. Dr Elizabeth Baxendine recalled that her mother, an Edinburgh WSPU member, strongly disapproved of the pillar-box attacks.[7] All of this contradicts a view of the WSPU as a centralised autocracy whose members had to obey orders. It also supports the earlier contention that women remained within a particular suffrage organisation not because they always believed wholeheartedly in its policies, but because of a strong bond of loyalty which developed between its members.

Not all of the militancy in Scotland at this time was of the secret kind. Heckling – which was, of course, militancy only when carried out by women – continued. Asquith visited his constituency at the end of January and, not surprisingly, suffragettes were awaiting him. On the 30th he was presented with the Freedom of the City of Dundee. Precautions were taken to exclude suffragettes from the public meeting at the Kinnaird Hall, but they proved futile, and a concerted series of interruptions and

* See p 274.

ejections punctuated the Prime Minister's address. Before the meeting one of the interrupters, May Grant, overheard someone ask another, 'Why are you going?' and the reply 'Oh, to see the Suffragettes'. ('Shades of the old gladiators', commented May Grant.) It was not only women who interrupted, for when Asquith said that it was an honour to be made a burgess of Dundee, a young man seated in the back gallery called out, 'You are not worthy of it'. Soon after his violent ejection May Grant shouted, 'How dare you come to Dundee? How dare you, you traitor to women?'.[8]

The Dundee branch of the Women's Freedom League and other suffrage societies organised a series of open-air protests against the granting to the Freedom of the City to the Premier. The *Dundee Courier* reported that 'the crowds gave the speakers an attentive hearing, but were in no way raised to any enthusiasm.'[9]

The day before the Dundee incident Asquith addressed a meeting in Leven. A determined effort was made by suffragettes to rush the hall. One of them, who gave her name as Margaret Morrison and was said to speak with an English accent, threw cayenne pepper into the face of a policeman and was arrested. She was taken to Methil police office where she broke all the panes of glass in the cells. After that she turned the water on in one of the privies, flooding the passage, and when the officers finally forced their way in she poured a bucket of water over them.[10] From all this it should not be too difficult to work out that 'Margaret Morrison' was Ethel Moorhead. And, knowing something by now of Ethel Moorhead it is also easy to guess that this was not going to be the end of the story.

From Methil she was removed to Dundee prison. When she arrived the medical officer reported that she was 'good tempered and reasonable' and 'in a fairly sound mental condition'. However, the following day, after a visit from her friends, she turned, in the words of the prison governor, 'from a lamb to a lion' and smashed eight panes of glass in spite of having given him her word that she would not break or destroy anything. The medical officer then decided that she was a 'weak minded person of defective self-control'. The next day she went on hunger strike. Plans were made to transport her to Perth prison after her trial where she could be forcibly fed.[11]

Her trial at Cupar sheriff court certainly received all the press coverage any suffragette could have wished for. In the first place she refused to stand. When asked by Sheriff Armour-Hannay if she was in poor health she replied that she was perfectly able to stand, and when he said, 'It is very disrespectful to the Court', she responded, 'Yes, I mean it to be.' She also refused to plead because she denied the 'justice of the proceedings'. When the constable who had pepper thrown into his face was asked to identify the accused she would not lift her veil – 'a constable on her left attempted to lift the veil, but only succeeded in tearing it, and she struggled away from him. The attempt to unveil her was abandoned.' She was found guilty and sentenced to £20 or 30 days' imprisonment; naturally she chose the latter.[12]

The day after the trial both of the Dundee newspapers devoted leading articles to the case. The *Courier*'s editor wrote, 'Miss Morrison's enthusiasm for the cause is probably sincere. Her sense of the injustices under which women labour is possibly strong and deep. But the actions which spring from these quite legitimate foundations fail lamentably to impress'. And the *Advertiser*'s editor considered that 'her processes of thought would discredit even the nursery'; he found it impossible to divine 'what possible correspondence there can be between her aim and her methods'. The *Suffragette*, on the other hand, commended her 'fine spirited speech'.[13]

The non-militant Leven Women's Suffrage Society saw Asquith's presence at Leven as a favourable opportunity for suffrage propaganda and spent a week quietly distributing pamphlets. The society was annoyed that the press covered all the militant activity without even mentioning their own methods, 'which have been gently educating the district during the last two years up to its present friendly attitude.'[14] It is difficult to blame the press for concentrating on the sensational, but in fact Scottish newspapers regularly reported local non-militant meetings, often very fully.[15]

Meanwhile Ethel Moorhead alias Margaret Morrison was taken to prison on 4 February. She refused to allow herself to be examined, struggling against the medical officer when he attempted to do so. He told the prison governor that he could not examine her by force and could not conscientiously feed her without an examination after a 4-day fast. He felt it would be safer leaving her to starve for a few days than to attempt to feed her: 'He had examined her in Septr. She was fairly sound but a frail creature and up to all the tricks about feeding resisting.' The governor told him not to feed her meantime and that he would ask instructions from the Scottish Office. The Secretary for Scotland granted authority to discharge the prisoner if and when necessary, and she was discharged on the night of the 6th.[16]

Forcible feeding was being carried out in England, and a heated debate on the subject took place in the correspondence columns of many newspapers. The *Dundee Advertiser* devoted a leading article of 22 February to a condemnation of the militants and another one on 24 February to a defence of forcible feeding. Some correspondents disagreed but suggested that the women should be left to starve. This provoked letters in response, the most eloquent of which was by May Grant. The 'let them starve' policy had been tried in Scotland, she suggested, 'where, to the honour of our country, forcible feeding has never been resorted to'. Miss 'Morrison', for instance, had recently been released from Perth prison 'in a state which showed she could only have been detained longer at the risk of her life.' The woman had been allowed to starve but her resolution had not been overcome. Miss Grant, recalling her own hunger strike, assured the editor that if a prisoner did not break down during the second day, the day of irresistible craving ('which has never yet been "irresistible" in the case of a Suffragette'), she would not break down at all. 'Besides, you entirely under-estimate the determination of women who know they are in the right, and you greatly over-estimate their fear of death'.[17]

The *Dundee Advertiser* believed that women should not be enfranchised, its leaders condemned the militants in the most forthright and unequivo-cal manner, and yet throughout the years of the militant suffrage campaign the correspondence columns were filled with letters from May Grant and other militants – far more so than any other Scottish paper. And when the editorials were savaged, as they often were, the editor sometimes added a note to the bottom of a letter to try and justify himself. (Naturally he also carried anti-suffrage and anti-militant letters, but they were certainly outnumbered by the others.) He seems to have had almost a love-hate relationship with the militants.

The editor of a very different Scottish paper, the *Forward*, remained constant in his support for the women. On 1 March Tom Johnston expressed his dismay that not only were papers like the *Dundee Advertiser* and *Glasgow Herald* attacking the militants but that even the *Daily Citizen*, a Labour newspaper, joined in the chorus of condemnation. He did not suggest that 'we must willy nilly attempt a justification for every act done by half maddened women driven to frenzy by cool, calculated, mocking sleight-of-hand politics', but he did think that 'Reformers of every brand and hue should pause before attempting to damp out the few remaining embers of human spirit left in the people'.

> There is no argument, no case, no justifiable ground for riot or rebellion inside a pure political democracy. There a minority must either convert the majority, submit, or leave the country. But here the women are not persons within the political meaning of the word: they have no votes: they are forbidden access to the ballot boxes: they have tried reason, argument, and pleading without success: and now they are convinced that they will not be treated as persons until they make themselves a nuisance and a terror.

But even now there were WSPU members who tried non-violent tactics. Many Women's Freedom League members had resisted paying taxes, but now it was the turn of Janie Allan, a wealthy WSPU member who refused to pay her supertax, and appeared before the Court of Session. Her argument (which she pleaded in person) was that the Finance Act of 1911 which imposed this tax referred to 'persons' and she maintained that 'if I am not a person for the purposes of the Franchise Acts, I ought not to be considered a person within the meaning of the Finance Acts.' She held that the legal position of a woman was 'thoroughly illogical and unjust' and thought it was 'the duty of every woman to protest against a continuance of this injustice'. Naturally the the Court decided against her, and she had to pay, but she had made her point.[18]

Non-militant campaigning also continued in Scotland. In February a public meeting was held in the Town Hall, Inverness, on 'The Religious Aspect of the Women's Movement'; the chief speaker was Dr R.J. Drummond, a vice-president of the Scottish Churches League for Woman Suffrage, and he was supported on the platform 'by clergymen representing all the different religious denominations in the town'. A meeting on the same lines was held under the auspices of the Scottish Churches League in St Cuthberts Hall, Edinburgh, in March.[19]

In the wake of the Reform Bill shock the NUWSS sought to affirm the solidarity of the non-militant movement, and all societies within the Union were asked if they would send messages of support for the president, Millicent Garrett Fawcett, and a small contribution towards the cost of a badge to be presented to her. The Shetland Society wired a message and sent two shillings.[20] The Edinburgh and Glasgow societies which, being more accessible, had had a good deal of contact with Mrs Fawcett over the years, sent warm and personal messages. The Inverness Society sent a fulsome one in Gaelic (with an English translation). Some 49 Scottish societies sent notes of appreciation.[21]

On 14 March the annual Council meeting of the Scottish Women's Liberal Federation was held in Glasgow, with no fewer than 350 delegates present. The press noted that 'the leading subject discussed in the course of the day was that relating to the enfranchisement of women, which was strongly advocated'. Miss H.E. Waddel (a member of the Glasgow and West of Scotland Association for Women's Suffrage) presided, and during her address 'spoke almost entirely on the Suffrage'. This was by no means approved of by every woman within the Federation. Elizabeth Sophia Watson of the Dundee Women's Liberal Association, wrote to the *Advertiser* that the 'suffrage-before-party group in the S.W.L.F.' had never yet been a majority of the delegates and were only 37 in number at this particular Council meeting.[22]

An even sharper division occurred during the meeting of the Scottish Christian Union of the British Women's Temperance Union in Dundee. The delegate from St Andrews branch moved that women's suffrage be no longer a national department of the British Women's Temperance

Union, in order to avoid 'shipwreck on this rock'. That pillar of the Scottish anti-suffrage movement, Lady Griselda Cheape, naturally agreed, as did over thirty other women, but the motion was defeated by a large majority.[23]

The most controversial event of this period was the meeting held at the St Andrew's Hall, Glasgow, on 13 March, when Emmeline Pankhurst was the principal speaker. The *Glasgow Herald* (14 March) noted that unusual public interest was taken in the proceedings because she was on bail on a charge of incitement to violence, a condition of her bail being that she had to refrain from remarks calculated to lead to a breach of the law. She did so, and the *Herald* gave a straightforward account of her speech and of the disturbance at the beginning of the meeting, which was sensationalised by the evening papers.

The WSPU knew that a group of university students planned to break up the meeting so some 300 male stewards were recruited, including fifty dockers and twenty carters. When Janie Allan opened the meeting, a number of the students loudly interrupted her, but they were no match for the stewards, and though fighting broke out, once the troublemakers were ejected there was no further disturbance. Jessie Stephen told Brian Harrison that it was she who recruited the dockers ('being in the trades union socialist movement I was able to speak to them') who were such big men that one of them could lift two students out of their seats. The whole thing, she said, was over in ten minutes.[24]

The *Glasgow Herald* listed the names of the platform party, which included clergymen of nearly every denomination with their wives. This sparked off a lively correspondence. The first letter commenced, 'I think it is a very distressing thing that so many of our clergymen openly countenance the militant suffragists', while the second began, 'The vast majority of the citizens of Glasgow have been waiting to hear what explanation the ministers of the Gospel who were present on the platform of Mrs Pankhurst's meeting have to offer for their extraordinary conduct.' On subsequent days women (not just WSPU members; Eunice Murray of the Women's Freedom League was one) wrote in to thank the ministers for appearing on the platform. Mary Aitkin, in a long letter defending militancy, thought that their presence was 'one of the most hopeful signs of the times. At last the Church is waking up to the fact that the roots of the women's movement are deeply intertwined with all that is purest and most spiritual in life and religion'. And a member of the platform party (James Gray, minister of Berkeley Street United Free Church, Glasgow) defended his conduct: 'We are men and citizens as well as ministers and must be allowed to think and act for ourselves.[25]

Emmeline Pankhurst addressed a public meeting in Edinburgh the day after her Glasgow one. Prior to it letters appeared in the press from those who felt strongly that the Town Council should not have let the Synod Hall for such a meeting. However, on the night, 'contrary to general expectation', the event passed off without any disturbance.[26]

But militant suffragettes in Scotland were now experiencing a backlash. On Monday 24 March the *Edinburgh Evening Dispatch* reported – under the headline 'SUFFRAGETTES MOBBED IN EDINBURGH' – that on the previous Saturday evening two suffragettes took up a stand in an open cab in North St David Street; the first had hardly begun to speak before she was booed and hissed, and 'several of the bolder spirits in the crowd commenced to clamber on to the carriage with the view of removing the speaker.' She resisted, and eventually a police inspector forced his way through and ordered the women to drive off, 'which they did accompanied by the jeers and booing of the crowd'. Both suffragettes wrote to the paper (25 March), claiming that the report was exaggerated and inaccurate, the real cause for the disturbance being a particularly drunk man. One of the women, E.H. McDonald, suggested that 'Suffragettes Mobbed by Drunks and Hooligans' would have been a more accurate headline, and that the so-called bolder spirits in the crowd 'might more truthfully have been referred to as "bottled spirits".'

There was disagreement over a report of another such incident in the *Evening Dispatch* on 7 April, but the opening paragraph of the article echoes reports from other parts of Britain at this time.

> A decided change has come over the temper of the crowds who are in the habit of attending the open-air meetings in Edinburgh. Instead of being accorded a patient hearing as on former occasions, the speakers find, that since outrages on public property have become part of the suffragist campaign, this courtesy is denied to them.

According to the report, the previous evening a speaker had taken up a position on the Mound and had been listened to patiently by a fairly large crowd until questions were invited, at which point the crowd became very disorderly and 'rudely jostled' the speaker until some police constables escorted her to a car awaiting her. Ethel Moorhead wrote in (8 April) to deny that the police came to the rescue: the police had been conspicuous by their absence until the speaker, 'protected from the hooligan element and conducted to the car by a band of supporters', was safely inside. An anonymous witness (signed EQUALITY) also found the report misleading in some ways, but no one denied that there had been some unpleasantness.

In early April, following the sentencing of Emmeline Pankhurst to three years' penal servitude for criminal conspiracy, the arson campaign spread from England to Scotland. Only a handful of those responsible were caught, but it is worth emphasising that nearly all of them were Scottish, not English. On 5 April the Western Meeting Club at Ayr Racecourse was destroyed, the damage being estimated at £3500. An unsuccessful attempt was also made to burn down the stand at Kelso racecourse.[27]

Five arrests were made in connection with the Kelso attempt. One of them was a man, Donald MacEwan, who had ordered the taxi which took the women to Kelso and accompanied them there. The others were all Edinburgh WSPU members. Agnes and Elizabeth Thomson were sisters aged 67 and 65 years (hardly the stereotype young WSPU militants). Edith Hudson was encountered in an earlier chapter as a prisoner at Holloway who fiercely resisted forcible feeding. She was remembered by Elizabeth Somerville as being 'about the most gentle person I knew'.[28] And finally there was Arabella Scott, a university graduate and a teacher who, along with her sister, Muriel, had been arrested at an early date for taking part in an attempted Women's Freedom League deputation in London. The prisoners were released on bail, and the trial was fixed for 19 May.

In his history of the WSPU Andrew Rosen wrote that the repeated schisms and the increasing violence of the WSPU gradually drove the women of greatest stature from the organisation, leaving behind the more mediocre types who were willing to obey blindly.[29] This may have been true of national leadership, but it is manifestly untrue for Scotland. Fanny Parker and Arabella Scott were women of courage and intellect who had been involved in the movement from the beginning of its revival in Scotland in 1905; neither were WSPU members before 1912, when the apparent futility of all their work up to then led them to embrace the extreme militancy of the WSPU. And far from the new policy putting off potential recruits, in the short period between 1 April and 17 May 1913 the Glasgow branch of the WSPU acquired 108 new members. The only recorded defection of a Scottish WSPU member to the NUWSS at this time is a Pencaitland woman, Miss J.C. Howden.[30]

On 8 April suffragettes turned their attention to Aberdeen, though with a minor offence, that of cutting out in large prominent letters in the turf of Duthie Park the words 'Release Mrs Pankhurst'. But a fire broke out in the early hours of 3 May at an Aberdeen school; the latest issue of the *Suffragette* and postcards with militant messages were found nearby so that no one was in any doubt about who was responsible. The *Aberdeen Free Press* (5 May) noted the absence of an expected mob attack on the local WSPU office in Bon-Accord Street: 'Current opinion attributes the outrage to militants who have come up north for the purpose'. This was probably true, for there is no evidence of any Aberdonians being WSPU activists.

In the interim various historic houses in the Borders, like Floors Castle and Mellerstain, had double police guards, and their grounds were closed to the public. Since the Kelso incident rumours had been rife of suffragettes 'equipped for walking tours' being seen in the Borders.[31] At this time the WSPU campaign created more panic than damage.

On 27 April the pavilion of Perthshire Cricket Pavilion was destroyed by fire. The *Glasgow Herald* (28 April) did not leap to conclusions: 'the fire may have been the work of militant suffragists, but there is no evidence to prove that this was the case'. The *Edinburgh Evening Dispatch* (28 April) knew 'nothing to account for the origin of the outbreak but the impression is strong in the city that it is the work of suffragists'. But the Dundee papers harboured no doubts about who was responsible, and on the 29th the *Courier* revealed that the secretary of the cricket club had received a message from suffragettes claiming responsibility for the fire. Its grief-stricken leading article – 'Forfarshire, Perthshire's nearest neighbour and dearest rival, will give ready sympathy to the Big County in its loss' – must have caused many women to shake their heads at men's priorities.

Under the circumstances it was either brave or foolhardy for two Dundee suffragettes – Miss Parker and Miss Christie – to stage an open-air meeting in Perth the day after the fire. 'Scenes of intense excitement, probably unequalled within the memory of the oldest inhabitants of the town, were witnessed in Perth last night', reported the *Advertiser*. The meeting had been chalked on the pavements, and a crowd of over a thousand (according to the *Courier*) awaited the suffragettes' arrival. The women were never given the chance to speak, for they were howled down and pelted with missiles. The reporters agreed that the women remained cool in the midst of very real danger; even after the police drew batons to protect the women, the mob continued to press on. The *Courier*'s headline, 'FRENZIED CROWD AT PERTH' appears justified.[32]

Perhaps to emphasise that its opposition was to militancy rather than to women's suffrage, under the headline 'NON-MILITANT SUFFRA-GETTES VISIT FIFE', the *Dundee Courier* of 6 May reported, 'The Women's Suffrage campaign in East Fife is being vigorously prosecuted by a number of capable female exponents of the cause.' On the same date a leading article discussed the women's suffrage bill presented by W.H. Dickinson which was just then before Parliament.

The Dickinson Bill went further than the Conciliation Bill for it proposed to enfranchise not only women with household qualifications but also the wives of existing voters. The *Glasgow Herald* (7 April) estimated that this would add some six million voters to the register, increasing it by 75 per cent. The editor of the *Herald* revealed that however much 'sympathy' he might have expressed with suffragist aspirations in the past, at heart he feared women as much as the more honest anti-suffragists did. He argued (as did many anti-suffragists) that in domestic affairs there would be no problem (which was why women's suffrage had proved satisfactory in Australia and New Zealand), but that with the responsibility for an Empire, and at a time when Europe was 'waging a bloodless war of armaments, which may for us at any moment turn into a real sanguinary war for the defence of the Empire and our own homes', women with votes could not be relied upon to support the government in waging a war that would cost the lives of many of those whom they held dear.

At its Second Reading on 6 May the Dickinson Bill was defeated by 267 votes to 221. The newspapers blamed the militants. The *Aberdeen Free Press* (7 May) was surprised that the Bill received as many votes as it did, in view of its scope and the prevailing militancy. The House of Commons had rightly interpreted the feelings of the country: 'The public has been exasperated beyond measure by the senseless outrages which have been committed by the militant suffragists, and would at this juncture have condemned as a surrender to terrorism and an affront to the community any step taken towards the enfranchisement of women.'

The Scottish Women's Liberal Federation sent a resolution to Scottish Liberal MPs recording its 'profound disappointment and indignation' at the rejection of the Dickinson Bill. The executive acknowledged 'with satisfaction and gratitude the support of those Scottish Members who voted for the Bill', but could not ignore 'the deep discouragement to all political effort and work on the part of the Liberal Women of Scotland who have for so many years laboured consistently and persistently in the furtherance of Liberal principles'.[33] A socialist and WSPU member, Janie Allan, wrote simply: 'The Dickinson Bill was defeated. Scarcely anyone expected otherwise, least of all the Suffragists.'[34]

Another private member's bill which received some attention from suffragists was the Scottish Home Rule Bill. Although women were included as electors in the first draft, they were excluded from the bill as presented to Parliament. The Scottish Women's Liberal Federation, the Scottish Federation of the NUWSS, and the Scottish Council of the Women's Freedom League all organised strong protests to this; the WFL headed its report 'THE LATEST INSULT TO SCOTSWOMEN'.[35]

The WSPU had gone well beyond making such peaceful protests, and on 11 May Farington Hall in Dundee was burnt down, with damage estimated at £10,000. The *Dundee Advertiser's* recorded: 'The public will learn with intense indignation, but without the faintest surprise that the destruction of Faringdon Hall is regarded by the authorities as due beyond question to the Suffragettes. A more wanton and purposeless outrage could hardly be conceived.'[36]

In the wake of such acts, suffragettes attempting to hold open-air meetings were increasingly met with shouting, boos, hisses, and flying missiles, making it impossible for them to speak, and needing the assistance of the police to escape. Press reports of incidents in Edinburgh and in Broughty Ferry both mentioned the coolness with which the women faced their attackers and continued their attempts to speak.[37]

On 19 May the four women and one man charged with the attempt to set fire to the stand at Kelso racecourse were tried in Jedburgh. The jury found the charge against Agnes Thomson not proven and recommended Elizabeth Thomson (who was 65) to the leniency of the Court. The judge sentenced her to three months' and the rest to nine months' imprisonment.[38] Janie Allan wrote with particular bitterness about the sentence imposed on Donald MacEwan who took no active part in the attempt: 'The only thing clearly brought out at the trial was that he appeared to be in sympathy with the aims and methods of the militant women'. She compared his sentence with sentences imposed on men who had committed indecent assaults on children, nearly all of whom had got considerably less than nine months.[39]

Once inside Calton Jail the prisoners went on hunger strike.[40] In the interim between the charge being brought and their conviction a new statute had been rushed through Parliament, the Prisoners (Temporary Discharge for Ill Health) Act, known from the first as the Cat and Mouse Act. Releasing women sentenced to long periods of imprisonment after only a few days because they refused to eat made a mockery of the law, while forcible feeding received such a bad press, with many leading members of the medical profession opposing it, that the government was reluctant to continue sanctioning it as a means of keeping women in prison. The new Act, therefore, allowed prisons to release hunger-striking women when their health had reached a critical stage, but under a licence which required them to return on a specified date when they were fit again, and to go on releasing them and re-imprisoning them until their sentence was served. The main flaw in the Act was that suffragettes never willingly presented themselves at prison gates after their licences had expired, which meant that the police had to attempt – with varying degrees of success – to keep them under surveillance after they had been released on licence.

Elizabeth Thomson was released under the Cat and Mouse Act on 23 May and Arabella Scott on 24 May. The *Edinburgh Evening Dispatch* reporter had no luck with Miss Thomson, but at Collesdene House, Joppa, 'the delightfully situated mansion of Mrs Grieve, a prominent sympathiser with the movement', Arabella Scott was happy to be interviewed. He described her as a 'sweet-faced young lady' though 'obviously weak and ill'. She told him that the prison authorities 'were most kind and humane' and that in this respect the treatment was 'better in Scotland than in England'.[41]

Edith Hudson was released soon after. The *Evening Dispatch* reporter found her at the home of Dr Grace Cadell and informed readers that she was 'a woman of fine physique' who 'should soon be as fit as a fiddle and ready to go back to the Calton for further "martyrdom".' Dr Cadell would say little of Miss Hudson's condition, other than that she had been very weak on her arrival, but 'There was sufficient cheerfulness in the tone to indicate that all was well'.[42]

Grace Cadell was born in 1855 and became one of the first students of Sophia Jex-Blake's Edinburgh School of Medicine in 1887. She led a rebellion against Dr Jex-Blake, was expelled, and sued for damages. Later she was appointed co-equal consultant at the Bruntsfield Hospital with Elsie Inglis.[43] When the WSPU started up in Scotland she became president of Leith branch, but at the time of the split she adhered to the Women's Freedom League. She was a tax-resister, and her furniture was sold at public auction. Edith Hudson was only the first released prisoner sheltered by her (on 9 May 1914 she described her home to the *Edinburgh Evening Dispatch* as 'a house of refuge for the suffragettes').

None of the three women returned to prison when their licences expired. Elizabeth Thomson and Edith Hudson vanished, and though the police watched out for them at WSPU meetings they were never found. Arabella Scott, however, remained at large and was even interviewed by the press on 10 June, after her licence had expired. She had given a promise to Leith School Board, her employers for the past five years, that she would commit no further acts of militancy, and the Board therefore kept her on its waiting list of teachers.[44] On 12 June she was rearrested, again went on hunger strike, and was released on the 16th. When her licence expired on the 27th she did not return, and the police briefly lost sight of her.[45]

Suffragettes continued to undergo rough treatment. On 3 June Fanny Parker and May Grant went from Dundee to Perth to address an open-air meeting and were pelted with vegetables and rotten eggs. The *Dundee Courier* reported the general belief that the women would not risk returning after the hostile reception of their previous visit. The paper reluctantly admitted that the crowd was not as hostile as on that other occasion, while the *Edinburgh Evening Dispatch* stated that the women received an excellent reception from the 'adult portion of the audience', although suffering 'considerable abuse' from the younger members. They managed to speak for about an hour. The *Evening Dispatch* noted that some of their answers to questions from the audience were greeted with sympathetic laughter. At the end of the meeting they were surrounded by a strong cordon of police; missiles of all kinds were thrown, but the police bore the brunt of them.[46]

On 16 June the *Scotsman* published a letter from the president of an Edinburgh Church Guild complaining that 'the popular hostility to the movement contains an element of danger for women who have no connection with the suffragists, militant or otherwise'. A party of young women connected with the Church Guild had set out one evening for a ramble on Arthur's Seat and some children set up a cry that they were suffragettes; a crowd of youngsters, incited and encouraged by adults, speedily gathered and started throwing gravel at the women until the police intervened.

One evening, genuine suffragettes were chased all over Edinburgh by a crowd of university students. Three WSPU members attempted to speak in front of the Student Union; they were driven away by a volley of missiles, and when they moved on to another site the students followed them and continued to make trouble until the women took refuge at a police station. A male witness (who signed himself JUSTICE) wrote to the *Evening Dispatch* to protest against the students' behaviour.[47]

The *Evening Dispatch* subsequently asked the students for their side of the story. They insisted there was no organised opposition to the suffragettes: 'They were far too busy to worry themselves about such matters and only interfered with the suffragettes when they came and annoyed them by shouting and yelling outside the Union'. Since suffragettes did not shout or yell, and students were rarely too 'busy' for a bit of a lark, this fails to convince. Brian Harrison asked Jessie Stephen why the students were so hostile to women's suffrage. She replied that they couldn't have cared less about women's suffrage, 'it was just that they were out for mischief, and women were easy targets as they saw it.'[49]

Militancy was now in full flood. As a bastion of anti-suffragism St Andrews was an obvious target. There were threats to damage the golf links prior to the Amateur Championship but, reported the *Glasgow Herald*, it came to nothing 'owing to the vigilance of the watchers'. T.G. Jarrett remembered that the Green Committee of the Royal and Ancient Golf Club, St Andrews Town Council Links Committee and the local Ratepayers Association organised a round-the-clock watch involving 300 volunteers.[50] It was not usual WSPU tactics to give warning of militant intentions, so perhaps their sole aim was to cause all that trouble without actually intending to act.

The real St Andrews attack took place at the university, where a wing of the Gatty Marine Laboratory was destroyed by fire (a full report appeared in the Scottish newspapers on 23 June). The university archive has retained the letters sent to Professor McIntosh at the time, expressing

All that remains of the refreshment room at Leuchars Station after the disastrous fire which broke out there in the early hours of yesterday morning.

17 *Edinburgh Evening Dispatch* 1 July 1913

sympathy and rage at the act of destruction, letters from as far afield as Canada, Australia and India. Mr D. Mackay of St Andrews wrote that he understood that the professor had been singled out for punishment because he had acted as Chairman at an anti-suffrage meeting ('Once I was asked to do so & was not free to accept: I fear you may have taken my place, therefore I regret your injury the more.')[51] Given a choice of targets, an anti-suffrage connection had obvious appeal but, as can be seen in Table 2, the range of buildings attacked was too haphazard to argue any such link.

How many such fires were really the work of suffragettes? Militancy provided good cover for arsonists of all kinds, and the WSPU was happy to be associated with any such act (simply by reporting it in the *Suffragette*). Even when suffrage literature was found near the spot it could have been left by anyone wanting to implicate the WSPU. The truth can never be known. In the case of two attacks on the last day of June – the burning down of Leuchars railway station and of Ballinkinrain Castle, Killearn (with an estimated damage of £70,000) – no suffrage literature was found, but everyone 'knew' that suffragettes were responsible.

Before that date, however, the most shocking event of the whole of the militant suffrage campaign had occurred, one which had surprising repercussions in Scotland. On 4 June Emily Wilding Davison threw herself in front of the King's horse at the Derby. She never regained consciousness and died on 9 June.[52]

The prominent Scottish constitutionalist, Lady Frances Balfour, wrote to her son, Frank, on 6 June.

> The militants have certainly the power of doing things undreamt of in the philosophy of other people ... Arson not unknown, but to try and make the Derby a failure was certainly the unforeseen. I admire the courage that can face a cataract of galloping horses, and meet with a violent and painful death. She must have known if she escaped the horse, she would be probably torn in pieces by the crowd. Suppose it had been done to save the King's Life, or for some religious cause, as the world see religion, how she would be lauded!! I said a word as to her courage at one of my meetings, which made people say I agreed with the militants. I don't, but I think they teach us the old story that what people will die for has behind it ultimate success.[53]

It was not easy for Scottish women to attend the funeral in London, but a memorial service was held in the Albert Square, Dundee. The proceedings opened with a hymn, and the *Dundee Advertiser* reported that 'the crowd was very orderly and attentive, and seemed greatly impressed by the women, who were in mourning attire.' Many WFL members were present, 'not only to show their sympathy with a sister society, but to pay their meed of admiration to this splendid heroine.'[54]

Emily Wilding Davison was buried in Morpeth, which was accessible from Edinburgh and was therefore attended by some Scottish sympathisers. Some men who believed in women's suffrage but had played no part in the campaign were deeply moved by the death of this young woman. A gardener at Morpeth said that she had 'given us something to hitch on to, and, by God, we will do it.'[55]

'Ye Mauna Tramp on the Scottish Thistle'
July–December 1913

One of the women present at the burial of Emily Wilding Davison in Morpeth was Maud Arncliffe-Sennett, a member of the Actresses' Franchise League who had at various times been on the WSPU and WFL executive committees but fell out with each in turn.[1] Before her marriage she had appeared on the stage in Edinburgh, and though she had no other Scottish connections she was a charismatic character. A 77-year old businessman from Edinburgh, Alexander Orr, was also present at the burial, and he suggested that in view of the strong feelings expressed by many of the men there she should form a deputation of men from Scotland and the north of England to wait on Asquith in London.[2] He offered his assistance, and she also had the enthusiastic support of WFL member Nannie Brown (who had completed the Edinburgh to London march the previous year) and her sister, Jessie.

A sizeable faction of the Women's Freedom League had always wanted to admit men as members. (The subject was debated at nearly every annual Council meeting, and it occasionally surfaced in *The Vote* as well. In the issue of 27 June 1913 the Edinburgh WFL branch described an open-air meeting at which two male supporters had spoken, concluding with the words 'We owe a debt of gratitude to men who thus openly champion our Cause.') Such women were ready to help in any way they could, and they mustered more than thirty men, including councillors, bailies, ex-provosts, J.P.s, ministers, barristers and solicitors, and teachers. They called themselves 'northern', and there were a few from the north of England, but the great majority came from either Edinburgh or Glasgow.

In view of Glasgow Town Council's support of women's suffrage in the past it is not surprising that such a deputation should have attracted Glaswegians, but the response of Edinburgh is more unexpected. Jessie Brown gave the credit to Maud Arncliffe-Sennett. In a letter to Harry Arncliffe-Sennett on 7 July Miss Brown wrote that what his wife had accomplished was 'miraculous': 'It has been remarked in the past, that if

18 The Scottish Men's Deputation at No.10 Downing Street. *Edinburgh Evening Dispatch* 19 July 1913

you can move Edinburgh people, you can succeed anywhere. This Mrs Sennett has done.'[3] ('Ye mauna tramp on the Scottish thistle' became the motto of the Edinburgh branch.)

Asquith refused to receive the Scottish deputation, but the men went to London regardless and presented themselves at Downing Street at 11 am on Friday 18 July. The resultant publicity was everything they could have hoped for. 'The prospect of seeing staid and grave bailies and councillors from Glasgow and Edinburgh acting in a manner which to the man in the street seemed suspiciously like defiance of authority drew a good many spectators to Downing Street this morning, and caused a diversion in Whitehall for an hour or more', reported the *Glasgow Herald*'s London correspondent. The story appeared in the London evening papers on the 18th and in the rest – as well as in the *Manchester Guardian* and the Scottish press – on the 19th, in some cases on the front page with pictures.

The deputation was received by the Scottish Government Whip and the Prime Minister's Secretary, the Prime Minister himself being point-edly absent, but the men refused to speak to 'underlings'. Instead they

addressed the crowd who had gathered to see them, and having had the
foresight to print pamphlets containing the speeches they had planned to
deliver to Asquith they sold those to the public at a penny apiece.

In the afternoon the deputation went to the House of Commons to
speak to the small group of Scottish MPs who had consented to see them.
It was a stormy session, with the deputation accusing the MPs of
misrepresentation, and it became even stormier when 'hon. members –
forgetting that they were not in the House – began giggling over the
descriptions of the operations under the Cat and Mouse Act.' Eventually
one man 'rose abruptly, and clapping his hat on his head, said "You're not
honest – you're a lot of Parliamentary frauds," and with that walked out.
His fellow-deputationists cheered and thumped the desks.' The Scotsmen
did at least have a pleasant evening, for a reception was held for them by
the Actresses' Franchise League and the Men's League for Women's
Suffrage, at which the Scots were lauded, and rousing speeches were
made. ('Mrs Finlayson-Gauld, a Scotswoman, said a few words in a
splendid, inspiriting way that made her audience feel that they must be up
and doing.')[4]

'As the deputation was connected with the question of the Women's
Suffrage', wrote Janie Allan, 'the references to it in the Press were
generally in the amused contemptuous strain, which, for some curious
reason, seems to be thought appropriate to a subject vitally affecting the
interests of the larger half of the population.'[5] The *Glasgow Herald* (22
July) wrote of the deputation as provoking a 'hearty and spontaneous
laugh'. The *Dundee Advertiser* (19 July) remarked that the 'Glasgow
Magistrate' considered himself 'one of the most stupendously dignified
personages on earth', while 'in his secret heart the Edinburgh Magistrate
knows himself to be more dignified still. Together these Magistrates
schemed to overawe the Prime Minister with the awful dignity of their
persons ... The "insult" lies not in a refusal to know what they had to say,
but in the refusal to look upon themselves in their "unruffled dignity".'

Lila Clunas, May Grant and other Dundee suffragettes reacted with
rage to this article, in fact May Grant wrote that the leader provided 'a
very strong justification of militancy in connection with the agitation for
women's suffrage.' The tone of it was 'a further proof of the utter futility
of constitutional methods in the prosecution of our agitation; they are
invariably treated as a huge joke.' (The editor felt obliged to justify
himself and added a note after the letter: 'It was the deputation itself and
its pretentious officiousness that struck us as ridiculous rather than the
pretext of its jaunt to London. Of course, Miss Grant can see reasons for
militancy in anything.')[6] Meanwhile the Women's Freedom League
commented bitterly on press reports of the 'courtesy' and 'good nature' of

the police who allowed Bailie Alston to address the crowd from the steps
of Number 10 Downing Street, since only a few weeks earlier two WFL
members – one of them a Glasgow woman, Janet Bunten – had been
sentenced to 14 days' imprisonment in Holloway for similarly addressing
people from Downing Street.[7]

On the Sunday the Scottish 'male suffragists' held a demonstration in
Hyde Park in conjunction with the Men's League and the Actresses'
Franchise League. The *Edinburgh Evening Dispatch* (21 July) reported that
the Scotsmen were listened to with 'sympathetic attention'.

> At one point, when a Scot was waxing more indignant than usual, a native
> of Edinburgh, which city he confessed he had not seen for fourteen years,
> called out, 'Eh, but these Scots are grand!'

The London *Standard* (21 July) enjoyed the 'red-hot vitriol poured out by
Councillor Crawford'.

> He spoke for thirteen minutes and a-half, and in that time he referred to Mr
> Asquith as a 'flea', as 'pig-headed,' as a 'humbug,' and an 'ass', and
> mentioned his opinion that the Prime Minister's colleagues in the 'West-
> minster Gas Works' are 'foolish piffling pigmies'.

The Hyde Park demonstration may have had longer-term repercussions
in London, for an English suffragette wrote to Maud Arncliffe-Sennett
about the 'wonderful change' which had come over the London public.
She had been listened to quietly and attentively the day before by a crowd
of men, whereas a few months earlier there had been hooting and insults
and a rush to get away to safety: 'undoubtedly our Scotch friends have
had a good share in bringing this about when they spoke so frankly and
cleverly in the Park'.[8]

On the Monday some of the Scotsmen made another attempt to see the
Prime Minister while the rest tried to see the Home Secretary. In the
evening they had an unsatisfactory interview with the Secretary for
Scotland (Mackinnon Wood). The *Edinburgh Evening Dispatch* (22 July)
reported on the return of the Edinburgh deputationists next morning:
'The greeting of the suffragettes to the men, who like the knights errant of
old had gone forth to do battle for their cause, was warm and sincere. It
reminded one oddly of Stanley and Livingstone.' The rebuff which the
men had received from Asquith, and their unsatisfactory meeting with the
Scottish MPs, had a powerful effect on them, and they returned with the
intention of forming a new organisation, the Northern Men's Federation
for Women's Suffrage.

In the interim, visitors to Hyde Park had seen more Scots. Expanding on the Edinburgh to London march the previous year, the NUWSS organised a 'suffrage pilgrimage' from all corners of the kingdom, converging in London on Saturday 26 July. Twenty platforms were set up, with two of them allocated to the Scots. The *Dundee Advertiser* called the event a 'uniquely impressive demonstration'.[9] Chrystal Macmillan was the Scottish chairman, and Alice Low and Louisa Lumsden spoke. Miss Lumsden remembered, when she stepped down from the platform, people coming up to congratulate her, 'one man saying he came from Perth, another from Aberdeen and so on.'[10]

In Scotland, as in England, that summer, many churches and public buildings – including Holyrood Palace – were closed to the public for fear of attacks by suffragettes, much to the dismay of tourists who had travelled long distances to see them. J.D. Allan Gray remembers his mother taking him into St John's Episcopal Church to show him the fan-vaulting and being 'turfed out (very politely) by a verger who explained that he had instructions to protect the church from arson by suffragettes.'[11]

The Women's Freedom League launched its usual Clyde campaign as well as an east coast campaign based at Montrose. Anna Munro had by this time gone down to England, where she married and settled, but Alison Neilans proved an effective organiser for the west coast campaign. On 17 July the *Glasgow Herald* carried a letter from a gentleman, John Hunter, who wrote from Rothesay that he had listened to Miss Neilans every day 'with extreme interest' and had felt disappointed that evening when he learned that Eunice Murray would be the speaker

> but once I had heard her convincing, eloquent and logical speech I was quite delighted, and feel persuaded if people had the opportunity of hearing her, and if Cabinet Ministers had that privilege, the vote would be won without delay ... Miss Murray made one feel it was a great thing to be born a woman and to be a Suffragist, and when she smilingly assured us her Cause was the greatest of the age, and asked us all to help her in the struggle, we felt, who heard her, that we must do our share to help this great movement forward.

Eunice Murray was a member of the Freedom League and secretary for 'Scottish Scattered Members' from the beginning, but it was in those latter years that she emerged as a particularly fine speaker and also as the writer of some of the Freedom League's most popular pamphlets.

The only complaints which the organisers of both the west coast and east coast campaigns had throughout the summer was of occasional spells of bad weather. The crowds – usually between 500 and a thousand – were orderly and attentive. Drunks were usually put out of meetings by members of the audience, often women. Some women came every night; one, who attended every evening for a month, said to Miss Neilans, 'I just weary for eight o'clock and the meeting.'[12]

This warm response to the Freedom Leaguers is in contrast to the scenes reported in the last chapter. The likeliest explanation of the difference in treatment is that in Scotland, at least, overt hostility to suffragettes was almost entirely an urban phenomenon. The women always made clear that the WFL did not advocate or commit acts of violence, but if they had been in say Edinburgh or Perth they might not have had the chance even to explain where they stood on the matter.

Meanwhile the WSPU arson campaign continued. On 24 July at 2 am a Glasgow police constable passing along Park Gardens discovered a woman inside Number 6, along with firelighters and paraffin, and suffrage literature. A few hours later a second woman, covered in soot, was captured attempting to escape from the house. She said she was 'Margaret Morrison'; the woman found in the house refused to give her name. They were taken to Duke Street prison and immediately went on hunger strike. 'Margaret Morrison' smashed the glass in her cell and was removed to a strong cell. She demanded her rights as an unconvicted prisoner and knocked the prison governor's hat off because he 'dared to stand in the presence of a lady with it on.' He was certain that 'Prisoner Morrison' was an old offender and the second woman a first offender.[13]

He was quite right, for Margaret Morrison was, of course, Ethel Moorhead, as the press soon discovered. The other woman was Elizabeth Dorothea Chalmers Smith, a medical graduate, the wife of the minister of Glasgow's Calton Parish Church, and mother of five (again, not the stereotype young, single militant). After a day or two Ethel Moorhead agreed to take some food, but Mrs Chalmers Smith continued to fast, so that on the 28th the prison medical officer certified her unfit to appear in court. When Ethel Moorhead appeared at Western Police Court Bailie Campbell said it was too serious a matter for him to deal with and remitted her to the sheriff court where, after telling the Bailie that he was evading his responsibility, she was conveyed by cab. The *Edinburgh Evening Dispatch* (29 July) reported that 'as she alighted she was greeted by about a dozen other suffragists, from whom she received a bouquet of roses.' When she emerged from court and an officer attempted to prevent her speaking to the women, 'she exclaimed, "Don't push me. If you put your hands on me again I'll have you in for assault."' (The article was headlined 'MISS MOORHEAD'S AUDACITY'.)

Dorothea Smith was released under the Cat and Mouse Act; she did not return to prison when her licence expired on 5 August. When the prison

19 The Edinburgh WSPU caravan. *Edinburgh Evening Dispatch* 8 August 1913

governor asked the chief constable of Glasgow to apprehend her 'he declined to take any action', saying he had no knowledge of the Act and would have to look into the matter. However, she was apprehended at Tighnabruaich and taken to court. Both women were indicted and released on bail, to be tried before the High Court in Glasgow on 15 October.[14]

The WSPU in Scotland never entirely gave up other methods of campaigning, and in August 1913 Jean Lambie organised and took part in a caravan tour of the Borders, where the women addressed a series of open-air meetings. (Launching the tour, Elizabeth Finlayson Gauld called it 'purely a constitutional means of bringing the claims of women before the people.') The touring women received a warm reception wherever they went.[15]

Meanwhile the NUWSS held a Suffrage Summer School in St Andrews, attended by women from all over Britain. The NUWSS president, Millicent Garrett Fawcett, addressed them on 20 August, while the second session was inaugurated by Louisa Lumsden, first warden of the university hall in which the students attending the summer school were meeting. Her address was 'a stirring call to service'.[16]

On 24 August Arabella Scott was found taking part in a WSPU protest in London and was rearrested under the Cat and Mouse Act and returned to Calton Jail. Instead of a simple hunger strike the new WSPU policy was for women to go on hunger and thirst strike, a far harder thing to endure and far more damaging to the health. Agnes Thomson and Ethel Moorhead wrote to James Devon, the medical member of the Scottish Prison Commission, asking him to intercede on Arabella Scott's behalf. She herself said she would not leave voluntarily under licence, and when the order came for her release on the 29th she 'behaved in an uproarious manner and had to be ejected by force.' (The physical vigour of someone liberated on medical grounds puzzled at least one of the prison commissioners.)[17] When her licence expired and the police sought her at Ethel Moorhead's residence, where she had gone after her release, she was not to be found. In fact she went to the south of England where, under an assumed name, she worked as a WSPU organiser; but this did not come to light until many months later.

At the end of August a 'sensational' attack was made by two suffragettes on the Prime Minister while he was playing golf at Lossiemouth. Men and women often relaxed by the side of the golf course to enjoy the sea breezes, so no particular notice was taken of two women sitting arm-in-arm. But when Asquith and his daughter passed near them they leapt up, grabbed his arms, shouted at him, knocked his hat off and pulled his hair. Policemen quickly appeared and, after a struggle, arrested the assailants. Onlookers hissed and shouted, 'Duck them in the sea!', but the women were safely conveyed to Elgin Police Office and put in custody. 'Mr Asquith showed his contempt at the outrage and demonstrated his self-control and sangfroid by holing out his ball and continuing the round.'[18]

The following day was market day in Elgin, and many farmers and visitors heard the news for the first time; it was 'the sole topic of conversation' and 'the excitement was intense'. On the Sunday the suffragettes, out on bail, somehow learned that Asquith would be attending Duffus Church. They sat directly opposite him and stared at him throughout the service. When it was over the congregation waited at the door 'in anticipation of a "scene." On Mr Asquith coming out the suffragettes, it is stated, contented themselves with calling him a "Hypocrite" and other such epithets.'[19]

The arrested women initially refused to give their names or addresses, but when warned that bail would be refused, one of them said she was Flora Ellen Smith and gave the WSPU's Edinburgh address while the other gave the name of Winnie Wallace with the WSPU's Dundee address. The *Dundee Advertiser* knew there was no local suffragette of that name and rushed round to the WSPU office to try and solve the mystery. The reporter got no information out of May Grant, temporary organising secretary, and he wondered if *she* was Winnie Wallace, but he soon found out that she was not, for she went north to provide bail for the prisoners. After the case was dropped because it would have meant the Prime Minister appearing in court, the reporter went to the WSPU office again and was chagrined when May Grant still refused to divulge Winnie Wallace's identity.[20] The press clearly regarded suffragettes in the light of show business celebrities who belonged to the public domain.

The north-east saw non-militant methods as well at this time. In order to raise funds the Aberdeen Association for Women's Suffrage organised a 'flower day': ten 'enthusiastic young women' sold flowers at the corners of the principal streets adjoining Union Street. The *Aberdeen Daily Journal* (10 September) reported that 'the quiet methods and pleasant solicitations of the flower sellers elicited the sympathy of the public, and flowers were purchased by all classes of the community'. (The article commented on the influential support which the non-militant suffrage movement enjoyed in Aberdeen city and district.)

In Edinburgh and Glasgow the Northern Men's Federation was getting under way. An open-air meeting was held by Berwick branch in August, followed by two in Edinburgh early in September. At the core of the Federation were the men who took part in the deputation. They were joined by other men who, as *The Vote* put it, were willing to do more than merely affirm their support for women's suffrage, but were 'prepared to sacrifice time and money.' The inaugural meeting of the Northern Men's Federation in Glasgow was held on 11 September, the keynote of which was 'its striking unanimity and enthusiasm.' By the middle of September *The Vote* was able to state that the Northern Men's Federation was 'an established fact', with centres in Midlothian, Glasgow and Berwick-on-Tweed. Later in September, with Maud Arncliffe-Sennett in Scotland, many more meetings were held in Edinburgh and Glasgow. (May Grant wrote her an enthusiastic letter about her forthcoming visit to Dundee, but the Federation never caught on there.) At an Edinburgh WFL meeting Councillor Crawford said that the Premier's refusal to receive the deputation had been a blessing in disguise because 'it had roused in the men indignation against the autocratic behaviour of the Government'.[21]

At the end of September the Scottish Federation of the NUWSS also decided to enlist male support, with a monster deputation to the Prime Minister from men's organisations in Scotland. The Glasgow and West of Scotland Association for Women's Suffrage approached the Conservative and Unionist Association, the Liberal Association, the Labour Party, the

Trades Council, and all the branches of the trade unions, asking them to send representatives.[22]

All three of the women's organisations were campaigning in their own ways in the autumn. Charlotte Despard, president of the Women's Freedom League, spoke at meetings held by the Edinburgh, Glasgow, and Dundee branches; her visits were always said to inspire the Scottish members, while she herself wrote enthusiastically about Scotland. The League also continued to cooperate with the other organisations: at the end of October the Dundee branch took part in demonstrations arranged by the local WSPU branch to protest against forcible feeding.[23]

The Scottish Federation of the NUWSS launched its winter campaign in October. Dingwall witnessed its largest ever suffrage meeting – an assembly of 500 – with Lady Frances Balfour as the speaker. Lady Betty Balfour, Millicent Fawcett and Louisa Lumsden also addressed Scottish Federation meetings in the autumn. In November meetings were reported at Castle Douglas, Crieff, Cupar, Dunfermline, Hawick, Kilmarnock, Kirkcaldy, Lenzie, Leven, North Berwick, Orkney, Oban, Paisley, Perth, Scone, and Wick. In contrast to the frequent complaints made by constitutionalists in England about the way in which the press wrote only about the militants, the Scottish Federation was gratified by 'the local papers being eloquent in praise of "non-militant methods" and the "high level of the speeches".'[24]

Some of the difficulties facing the more 'remote' societies may once again be seen in the Shetland Society's minutes. The Society's new president was Mrs Mackinnon Wood, wife of no less a personage than the Secretary for Scotland. But Christina Jamieson, the secretary, did not break this news because a speaker from the Scottish Federation had been promised, and she wanted to announce the arrival of that speaker at the same time. Having twice written to the Federation about the speaker without receiving a reply, she now read in the latest issue of the *Common Cause* an account of the speaker's northern tour, which included Kirkwall, and which was already over. The committee was furious over the this treatment, and considered withdrawing from the Scottish Federation.[25] Fortunately matters were smoothed over, with a promise of a speaker in November. Because of the distances involved, communications between a society like the Shetland one and the Scottish Federation in Edinburgh were even more difficult than between the Scottish Federation and the NUWSS in London. The women in such circumstances who carried on campaigning for the suffrage without the constant stimulus of events in the urban centres deserve particular credit for their perseverance.

On 15 October Ethel Moorhead (as 'Margaret Morrison') and Dorothea Smith were tried at the High Court of Justiciary. The court in Glasgow was crowded, 'well-dressed ladies constituting a considerable proportion of the total'. Both defendants 'seemed remarkably self-possessed'. They advised the judge, Lord Salvesen, that they intended to defend themselves. He asked them if they would not be better with a legal adviser, and Ethel Moorhead replied, 'We usually find they made a muddle of it.' The charge was housebreaking with intent to set fire, and the defence was that no 'breaking' had taken place (the women had entered during the day, by pretending to view the house with intent to purchase, then hid themselves), so there was no case to answer. However, Lord Salvesen directed the jury that if they thought entry had been secured fraudulently with the intention of setting fire to the house then a verdict of Guilty should be returned, and twenty minutes later the jury returned such a verdict.[26]

When the Advocate-General moved for a sentence Ethel Moorhead vehemently protested, telling Lord Salvesen that he had misdirected the jury but that he could still behave justly by declining to sentence them. He paid no attention but tried to impress on them the gravity of their situation. Ethel Moorhead interrupted: 'Now just give us your sentence. We don't want to hear any more. We refuse to listen. Please sentence us.' Lord Salvesen had her removed to the cells below for contempt of court; Dorothea Smith added her own protest, but the judge ignored her.

When he pronounced sentence of eight months' imprisonment what the *Glasgow Herald* called 'a scene of indescribable disorder and confusion' broke out with 'startling suddenness'. The women in the court rose from their seats and shouted in chorus 'Shame, shame' and began to throw apples and other missiles; a bundle of legal papers was hurled at the Bench and came apart in the process. An unusually large number of policemen had been stationed in the court, but even they had difficulty coping with the disturbance, though ultimately three women were arrested. (One of them, Jane Lynas, was Dorothea Smith's younger sister.)[27]

'Margaret Morrison' and Dorothea Smith were taken to Duke Street prison and immediately went on hunger strike. James Devon of the Prison Commission discussed their treatment with the Secretary for Scotland. In England, where there were many suffragette prisoners, the Home Office took the view that if a prisoner discharged under the Cat and Mouse Act was sure to immediately commit another act of violence then she should be forcibly fed. No such 'moral certainty' existed in this case ('though one would not be surprised if Morrison broke out again before long'), but as their crime was attempted arson any discharge under the Act should not exceed seven days and the police should keep a special watch on them.[28]

On 19 October prisoner 'Morrison' fainted, but she refused any stimulants, and when a doctor came she 'treated him with the utmost impertinence, stoutly refusing examination'; he, however, satisfied himself that she was 'in a somewhat enfeebled condition'. Dorothea Smith allowed herself to be examined and was also 'showing some degree of weakness'. Both women were discharged under licence on the 20th; Ethel Moorhead was taken to a nursing home and Dorothea Smith to her Glasgow residence. They were due back in prison on the 27th, but on the 28th and 29th the *Edinburgh Evening Dispatch* and *Glasgow Herald* reported that the prison commissioners had told the chief constable that they had not returned. (The prison commissioners asked the chief constable how their confidential letter to him had got in the hands of the press, but he had no explanation.) 'Margaret Morrison' had in fact left the nursing home some time before the 27th; it was thought that she had gone to England. Dorothea Smith was believed to be still in her home in Glasgow, where the police kept a 24-hour watch.[29]

On 11 November the chief constable advised the prison commissioners that Dorothea Smith apparently had no intention of leaving her house, so that the watch would have to be kept up indefinitely unless authority was obtained to enter. The Rev William Chalmers Smith asked the prison commissioners if a letter from him concerning his wife's health would 'deliver me from the infliction of detectives posted round by house'. On 19 November Dorothea Smith escaped by changing clothes with a friend visiting her for tea; one of the detectives had his suspicions aroused as the car was driving off, but he was too late to stop it.[30]

Dorothea Smith was never apprehended, but what did her husband think of it all? He was in the High Court for her trial, but that did not mean that he approved of her activities, for their daughter asserted many years later that 'he was a real Victorian husband, who believed that his wife's place was in the home.' In a study of English feminists Olive Banks found that marriages did not survive the active opposition of a husband to his wife's bid for independence. That proved to be the case in this marriage, for she eventually left him, taking her four daughters with her (the two sons remained with their father, who forbade them to visit their mother, though he reserved the right to see his daughters).[31] As a medical practitioner Dorothea Chalmers Smith was well loved and long remembered; several women wrote to me about her in response to my letter in the *Sunday Post* and article in the *Glasgow Herald*. A piquant note comes from a letter written by a woman who remembered 'seeing the Rev Smith letting his purchase of whiskey slither from his hands, as he came out of the corner of the street where I lived. It was well known he was often "tipsy", I don't know how he ever held his charge in a church'.[32]

At the beginning of November Asquith unveiled a memorial to the late Sir Henry Campbell-Bannerman at Stirling. As his car was approaching Bannockburn four women stood in the road and signalled for it to stop. When it showed no signs of doing so one of the women placed herself in its way, 'deliberately facing the chance of being killed.' The chauffeur

20 Dorothea Chalmers Smith. Reproduced by permission of the People's Palace (Glasgow Museums)

managed to stop the car in time whereupon the other three leapt onto the steps of the car, one brandishing a dogwhip and the others sprinkling the occupants with red pepper. A car filled with detectives followed the Prime Minister's car, and the women were seized and conveyed to the police office in Stirling.[33]

A large crowd assembled in front of the sheriff court for the appearance of the women on the following Monday. They gave fictitious names – Violet Asquith, Maud Allan, Margot Tennant and Catherine Douglas – though the police were said to be aware of their real identities (one was 'a prominent Edinburgh woman' and the other three came from Glasgow). *Votes for Women* stated that the women 'treated the whole proceedings with scorn'. While each made her declaration alone the others were accommodated in one of the witnesses' waiting rooms. The *Scotsman* reported that several of their friends were present, 'and, judging from the sounds of mirth which emanated from the room, they did not appear to be regarding their position with seriousness.' They were released on bail and nothing further was heard about the case as the Prime Minister had no wish to prosecute.[34]

That autumn was the heyday for suffragette interruptions of public meetings and the brutal ejection of the interrupters. Not that the women expected anything else: Elizabeth Somerville remembered her mother going to such meetings 'packed with corrugated paper'.[35] However, the incidents invariably caused controversy.

Dundee was the first city to experience this. On 9 October Churchill addressed a meeting of women Liberals. Tickets were carefully scrutinised as each woman entered; nevertheless, even before the meeting began the organiser ordered stewards to eject eight women by force (a correspondent later learned that 'a lady' had pointed out potential interrupters), while more women interrupted Churchill after the meeting started and were also thrown out.[36]

The report of the incident in the *Dundee Advertiser* was followed by a letter defending the stewards' actions, and this in turn provoked three letters disagreeing. One woman asked, 'What magic can there be in the simple phrase, "Votes for women" that it turns some who once were men into wild beasts?'. A.J. MacGregor felt so strongly that she asked the women who had been ejected to get in touch with her in order to take some kind of action. She was contacted by three members of the Women's Liberal Association who had been treated in this way but they had received sufficient apologies from the organiser of the meeting, while the WSPU did not, as a matter of policy, bring charges in such cases. Therefore, all Miss MacGregor could do was to 'appeal to the respectable citizens of Dundee to see to it that no more of such disgraceful scenes shall occur at any future meeting. Women have every right to bring forward their demand, one of the pressing political questions of the day'.[37]

On 3 November it was Glasgow's turn, when a number of women were ejected from a British Women's Temperance Association meeting addressed by the Secretary for Scotland. Again the incident sparked off correspondence in the press. One member of the B.W.T.A. was greatly distressed at the behaviour of the stewards: 'Granted that it was their duty to remove the offenders, was it necessary to twist their arms, thump them viciously between the shoulders, and otherwise maltreat them?' 'ANOTHER MEMBER OF THE B.W.T.A.' thought that 'the women deserved all they got. How could you remove a woman without violence who lay down and fought? ... Why did they not go out quietly after making their protest? There was not a few of us who think they disgraced their womanhood in this fashion.' This was responded to by 'A SUFFRA-GIST MEMBER OF THE B.W.T.A.' who had risen to make a protest and was 'violently hurled' from the meeting. She had been prepared to leave quietly but was not permitted to say so; a hand was clamped over her mouth and she was dragged from her seat.[38]

Aberdeen was the next city to experience something similar, when an Irish Home Ruler, T.P. O'Conner, addressed a public meeting. The first woman to interrupt clung to the railings and some half dozen stewards had great difficulty in extricating her. The woman was May Grant, and the following day she said at an open-air meeting that she did not think much of the argument that men should have the vote on the basis of their physical superiority, as it had taken six or eight of them to remove her the previous evening. Other interruptions and ejections had followed hers, amid 'general uproar'.[39]

Three nights later O'Conner spoke at Perth City Hall, and a similar scene took place. At one point May Grant and another woman 'were bundled out screaming and struggling, the audience standing in a state of much excitement.'[40] Jane Mitchell, a Liberal, who had often read descriptions of the ejection of suffragettes from public meetings, first experienced it at Perth. Her shame at the Liberal attitude to suffrage was strengthened 'by the unjust and illiberal treatment meted out to offenders.'

> Had all interruptions been followed by summary ejection, one might have questioned the wisdom, but not the justice, of the procedure. But when a scarcely audible 'Votes for Women' was the signal for something like pandemonium, while other interruptions equally irrelevant and more noisy, were allowed to pass unnoticed or treated as matters for laughter or jocular remark, one could not help wondering if our boasted British love of 'fairplay' had vanished?[41]

The attitude of individual speakers toward the question of women's suffrage had no effect on the policy of interruptions. One 21 November an anti-suffrage M.P., William Young, addressed a meeting at Longforgan which was disrupted by interruptions and ejections, while on the same night this also occurred at a meeting addressed by Keir Hardie in Dundee. Keir Hardie's meetings in Aberdeen and Edinburgh were also targets for suffragette interruptions.[42] As Keir Hardie was one of the best friends the suffrage movement had, some explanation was due. Mrs Lyons explained to Aberdonians that the militants knew perfectly well that he was personally a loyal supporter of the women's movement, but they interrupted him because he was a member of the Labour party which helped to keep the Liberal government in power. Lila Clunas used more or less the same words in her letter to the *Dundee Advertiser*.[43]

In Edinburgh the WSPU and WFL premises were wrecked after suffragette interruptions of a meeting of university students addressed by Lord Haldane. Two students were arrested and tried for the offence. (They apologised to the WFL for mistakenly thinking that it was a militant society; the Edinburgh secretary, Alexia B. Jack, insisted that the WFL *was* a militant society, 'but our militancy does not include plans to attack private property'.)[44] At the trial, 'in spite of evidence sufficient to convict a dozen Suffragettes', the students were dismissed with a verdict of Not Proven.[45]

The following month William Smith, organising secretary of the Dundee Liberal Association, was brutally attacked at Wormit. He received a letter signed 'Suffragette' stating that the thrashing he had received 'was given you in part-payment of the way you have again and again assaulted men and women Suffragists at Liberal meetings this autumn.' The *Dundee Advertiser* hoped that in their own interests militant women would be able to clear themselves of responsibility for this act. The following day a long letter from S.F. Jolly justified such revenge attacks (she even cited Moses slaying Egyptians), and asked why women attending meetings could be 'brutally assaulted with impunity, but when some one ventures to thrash one of the bullies there must be a great effort to "bring the criminal to justice." ' The editor added: 'This singular product of the fanatical mind needs no comment.'[46] It is undeniable that the WSPU's policy of interrupting meetings brought out the worst elements in men.

Between October and December 1913 both non-militants and militants turned their attention to the Scottish churches (not to the issue of women's place in the church, but merely to the church's attitude to women's enfranchisement). Their approaches were very different. The non-militants – led by the Northern Men's Federation – wrote to presbyteries (both Church of Scotland and United Free Church) asking them to pass a resolution in favour of women' suffrage and to overture the General Assembly to do the same. (When Dorothea Chalmers Smith was housebound in October she wrote enthusiastically to Maud Arncliffe-Sennett about the best ways of approaching Glasgow presbytery.[47])

Dundee presbytery discussed the Federation's letter on 3 December and voted in favour of a motion by the anti-suffrage Rev Harcourt Davidson that the presbytery take no action in the matter. He offended many by suggesting that women were better off not having to bother themselves with something so meaningless as a vote. The *Dundee Advertiser* wondered how Mr Davidson would answer women who asked 'if the vote is useless, why not give it to us?.' May Grant reminded the presbytery that it was women who filled the churches, ran Sunday Schools, raised church funds, and visited the poor and sick. 'As one who is deeply, passionately, attached to the Auld Reformed Kirk o' the Realm', she wrote, 'and who has served her for ten years at home and for four and a half years abroad, I protest against the attitude of her ministers – an attitude as banal as it is insulting.'[48]

Glasgow presbytery did affirm support for women's suffrage, an action which so alarmed the anti-suffragists that the Scottish League for Opposing Woman Suffrage put out a circular letter signed by two of its presidents, the Duchess of Montrose and Sir John Stirling Maxwell, addressed to all Church of Scotland ministers, imploring them to keep the Church free of 'such disruptive influences.'[49]

While individual WSPU members involved in the church, like Dorothea Chalmers Smith and May Grant, supported the approach to the presbyteries, WSPU policy with regard to churches (in both England and Scotland) was very different. On 6 October the *Edinburgh Evening Dispatch* reported 'extraordinary scenes' in South Leith United Free Church the previous evening, when the Solicitor-General gave an address there. He had only spoken a few words when a woman interrupted by saying that she protested against the Solicitor-General speaking, because he belonged to a government that denied votes to women. According to the *Evening Dispatch* reporter, 'the congregation listened aghast', not realising at first that this was a militant suffrage demonstration. 'So unlooked for was the scene that quite a sensation was caused among the congregation, most of whom got on their feet.' More interruptions then occurred, the most dramatic being by 'a smartly-dressed dame of middle-age, who had the appearance of a typical militant'. When self-appointed stewards tried to remove her she clung tenaciously to the pew and had to be dragged by force into the aisle, resisting every inch of the way to the door. She brandished an umbrella and managed to land a few blows on the heads of her captors. 'So vigorous was her attack that she had to be temporarily deprived of her umbrella until she was ejected.'

The shocking thing to observers of this scene was that it took place in church, while to suffragettes the only relevant fact was that the speaker was a member of the Liberal government; in other words, the suffragettes behaved as they did at any other public meeting. A more usual ploy in the following months was for suffragettes to interrupt a service with a prayer of their own and then leave quietly. This occurred for the first time in Edinburgh, at St Giles' Cathedral, on 19 October. Just after the intercessory prayer had been recited about a dozen women rose and chanted: 'God save Annie Kenney, Margaret Morrison, and Dorothea Smith. Their enemies torture them, for they know their cause is righteous.' The *Suffragette* claimed this as the first militant protest against injustice and oppression in St Giles' Cathedral 'since that of brave Jenny Geddes.'[50]

During that autumn there was a by-election at South Lanark. It was a three-cornered contest, in which the Labour candidate (a local miner, Tom Gibb) gave full support to women's suffrage. Therefore, the Election Fighting Fund – formed by the NUWSS to support Labour candidates in such contests – took over.[51] The NUWSS brought up its heavyweight socialist campaigners from England – Margaret Robertson and Ada Nield Chew, who were English, and Annot Robinson who was a Scot; two more Scots, the Gordon sisters who were organisers for Edinburgh and Newcastle, were also active. The *Common Cause* covered the election campaigning in depth, and the *Forward* gave Margaret Robertson front-page space three weeks running.

It was a difficult constituency to cover, being 30 miles long and 25 miles broad, with no large towns in it (Lanark, NUWSS headquarters, did not belong to the constituency but to Falkirk Burghs). A motor car was essential, and the weather was so dreadful that open-air meetings were impossible. But the response the women received was remarkable: in one particular week they held 28 meetings and sold 1,258 copies of the *Common Cause* and 462 badges. Wherever they went they found their audiences courteous, friendly and sympathetic to the cause of women's suffrage. Even in some of the remote farming villages, where no propaganda work had ever been done, the people 'seemed to require no conversion at all'. And the campaign had its lighter moments – 'Blow up the school and gie us a holiday!' the children in Lanark would shout cheerfully.[52]

What comes across strongly in the *Forward* articles is the suffragists' sympathy with the hard life which women endured in those mining and farming villages, where housing and sanitation were atrocious, and women slaved on the land for a pittance. These particular campaigners did not offer the vote as a panacea for women's wrongs; they were fighting this campaign as socialists as much as suffragists and preached both messages simultaneously. The women of South Lanark approached the meetings with trepidation and left them with pride in their sex 'as they heard their menfolk say that the women were the finest speakers of them all'.[53]

James Young claims that the major, and perhaps only, aim of the suffragettes in Scotland was to win the suffrage for women of property, which they regarded as an end in itself, in contrast to the English who supposedly had a wider outlook and saw the vote 'as a means of improving the legal and social status of women as a whole'. The 'middle-class outlook' of Scottish suffragettes, argues Young, led socialists like John Maclean to criticise them.[54] This is nonsense. Of course some women had a more limited vision than others, but to distinguish between Scottish and English women in this way is not justified by the evidence. The women's suffrage movement was largely middle class, but the socialist movement needed middle-class members as well as the working classes. A campaign like South Lanark (which involved English and Scots working closely together), and the continuing support given to the suffrage movement by that socialist – and indigenously Scottish – journal, the *Forward*, shows how wrong he is.

Before concluding this chapter, it is time to turn back to the 'male suffragists'. On 8 November the *Forward* reported a public meeting in Glasgow's Bridgeton Division under the auspices of the Northern Men's Federation. The chief speaker was Henry Harben JP; other speakers were Bailie Alston, Maud Arncliffe-Sennett, and Helen Crawfurd, who 'welcomed the Northern Men's Federation as a new order of chivalry: it came to fight for the oppressed and for the sweated woman worker.'

On 14 November a mass meeting was held under the auspices of the Northern Men's Federation in the Synod Hall, Edinburgh. The *Evening Dispatch* gave it splendid advance publicity, with pictures of the principal speakers – Maud Arncliffe-Sennett (costumed for her role as Joan of Arc), Mrs Cavendish Bentinck, and Sir John Cockburn K.C.M.G., a Scot by birth who had been Prime Minister of South Australia. A reporter was also there for the event and provided a summary of the speeches. The WFL considered the meeting 'a brilliant termination of the autumn campaign in Scotland'.[55]

The Women's Freedom League and the Votes for Women Fellowship (formed by the Pethick-Lawrences after their dismissal from the WSPU) fully supported the Northern Men's Federation, but some WSPU members had mixed feelings. Kathleen E. Roy Rothwell wrote a long letter to the *East of Fife Record* (20 November) explaining her motives in working for the Federation. Her adherence to the WSPU and her belief in

21 Maud Arncliffe-Sennett as Joan of Arc. *Edinburgh Evening Dispatch* 12 November 1913.

its policies were as strong as ever, she wrote, but at the same time she was anxious to put an end to militancy and felt that the only way to do this was to get the men to vote for women's suffrage and against the Liberal government. She found it very difficult 'to make men who have a vote understand that they have a responsibility towards the women who have none': 'Every man who has said to me "I will do nothing till you stop militancy" makes me so militant that I hardly know how I may be able to resist this incitement.'

Men in town councils all over Scotland were being forced to think about the issue of women's suffrage for they were being approached and asked to petition Parliament. Edinburgh Town Council considered a motion put forward by Councillors Crawford and Bruce Lindsay that the Lord Provost, Magistrates and Council petition Parliament in favour of granting the parliamentary franchise to women on the same terms as men. On 2 December the motion was carried by 29 votes to 14. (The Lord Provost voted against it.) The *Scotsman's* leader on the following day rebuked the Council for involving itself in matters outwith its local government remit. Letters – some agreeing, some disagreeing – followed. An article in the *Forward* criticised the Council for quite a different reason – the 'considerable element of levity' in the debate.[56]

The Glasgow and West of Scotland Association for Women's Suffrage asked Glasgow Town Council to appoint two of its members to represent it on a deputation to the Prime Minister. The Council appointed no less than the Senior Magistrate and Lord Provost to go, though not before the Scottish League for Opposing Woman Suffrage had argued against any involvement.[57]

Ironically, while there was all this fuss going on Dollar Town Council unanimously elected a woman as its Provost. Mrs Louisa Malcolm had been the first woman to be elected councillor in Scotland and now became the first woman provost.[58]

The Heather on Fire – January–March 1914

Approaches by suffragists to town councils and presbyteries in the opening months of 1914 seemed to anger the press almost as much as militancy. Edinburgh presbytery was the first to receive the full blast of press disapproval. On 7 January the presbytery discussed three letters. The Northern Men's Federation asked it to overture the General Assembly in favour of granting the parliamentary franchise to women; the Edinburgh National Society for Women's Suffrage requested that it receive a deputation, while the Scottish League for Opposing Women's Suffrage protested against the presbytery having anything to do with the question. There followed what the *Glasgow Herald* called a 'somewhat lively discussion'.[1]

The Rev Dr Burns moved that the presbytery take no action. He said that although he himself was a supporter of women's suffrage he believed that it was not within the presbytery's 'spiritual jurisdiction'. Professor W.P. Paterson, on the other hand, had grave doubts about the wisdom of granting women the vote but nevertheless moved that the deputation be heard. As for the argument that the Church should have nothing to do with political matters, 'Shades of John Knox!' he exclaimed. In the end the presbytery decided that to overture the General Assembly was not within its province, but by a vote of 32 to 25 it agreed to receive the deputation.

The *Scotsman* next day criticised the presbytery's lack of logic. If its members had dismissed both requests they would have acted consistently (and, in the view of the editor, correctly), while if they had deferred the decision on the overture to the General Assembly until they had seen the deputation that would also have been correct. But the choice they had actually made was 'ridiculous and absurd': 'What is the sense in receiving a deputation after the case which the deputation are going to argue has already been decided against them?'[2]

A member of the presbytery, A.J. Findlay, wrote in to say that the

editor had missed the point: the requests concerning the overture to the
General Assembly and the reception of a deputation came from two
different sources, and therefore there was no inconsistency in the presbytery's position. The editor added his own note to the bottom of the letter,
insisting that the communications had been discussed in tandem.

> Besides, what sort of courtesy or policy is it to say to a woman that you are
> willing to listen to her but not before deliberately arranging that you shall
> do nothing to assist her? Presumably the women's deputation do not desire
> a tea-party talk with the Presbytery; they desire effective support, and they
> cannot now get it from the Presbytery. Mr Findlay and those who voted
> with them are not unlike the Irish Judge who sentenced his prisoners before
> trial, and after declaring the sentence was courteous enough to say that he
> would hear what the unfortunates had to say.[3]

Other presbyteries also refused to commit themselves one way or the
other. The only exception, apart from Glasgow, was Irvine presbytery
which passed a resolution in favour of women's suffrage and agreed to
overture the General Assembly.[4] None of the United Free Church
presbyteries were willing to take any action.[5] On the whole, as the *Dundee
Advertiser* (6 February) put it, 'the spiritual power is coy and reluctant; it
stands aloof from worldly strife, and evidently regards this question as
strife.' The contrast was being made with town councils, although in fact
very few town councils went as far as Glasgow in sending representatives
to join the men's deputation.

On 13 January Edinburgh Town Council was thanked by the Edinburgh National Society for Women's Suffrage for renewing its resolution
in favour of women's suffrage and was asked to appoint representatives to
take part in the deputation. The motion to do so was defeated by 21 votes
to 22. The *Edinburgh Evening Dispatch* was scathing. It was wrong for the
Council even to have expressed an opinion on the subject, but that had
been 'a comparatively menial offence, for nobody cared very much
whether Bailie This or Councillor That favoured women's suffrage or
not.' However, for a Corporation supposedly representing the people of
Edinburgh to even consider sending representatives on the deputation was
a different matter entirely. Edinburgh Town Councillors were elected 'to
keep Edinburgh going as a good business proposition', not to become
involved in matters that were none of their concern, unless they did so as
private individuals.[6]

The *Dundee Advertiser* (3 February) expressed similar views. Dundee
Town Council had expressed 'moral support' for women's suffrage while
Aberdeen Town Council, which had originally copied Dundee, later
amended its resolution to express 'unqualified support'. At Inverness the

Council had decided to send a delegate to join the suffrage deputation. The proper course, the editor thought, was that of St Andrews Town Council which had voted to take no action. Town councillors had no mandate to speak for the public in this matter: 'It is a sheer piece of audacity for the Suffragists to try and manufacture public opinion in their favour in this artificial way, and it is astonishing to find responsible public authorities lending their support to carry out such manuoeuvres.'

The next day's correspondence columns carried a riposte from the secretary of the Dundee Women's Suffrage Society, Mary J.H. Henderson. She asked whose opinions, if not those of the municipal electors, the municipal bodies were supposed to represent. In October 1910 the Town Council of Dundee had passed a unanimous vote in favour of women's suffrage and the municipal electorate had had ample opportunity of challenging the stance of their representatives since then. 'Let me assure you, sir', she continued, 'that in Dundee the Suffragists do not need to "try and manufacture public opinion," which has never been disregardful of the part which women play in the commercial prosperity of the city, nor slow to respond to the efforts of those women who strive to discharge faithfully the duties of their citizenship.' The editor still had the last word for he added a note to the bottom of the letter contending that 'a vote of a Municipal Council on this subject is of no more representative effect than a vote passed by it on the Westminster Confession. The municipal representatives are chosen to administer the business of the town, and not to serve as mouthpieces for the opinions of the electors on politics.' Which must have come as a surprise to councillors elected on party platforms.

At this time the WSPU attempted a new tactic: to address theatre audiences in the interval of a play (which must have taken considerable nerve). Glasgow's Royalty Theatre was the first Scottish example of this, on 3 February. Immediately after the curtain fell on the first act of 'The Little Damozel' a woman arose and addressed the audience. Banners were unfurled over the front of her box with the words 'He who permits oppression furthers the crime' and 'Let Scotland protest against torture in English prisons'. The forcible feeding of English suffragettes formed the theme of her appeal to the audience. Her voice carried clearly throughout the house, and the other four women in the box held the door against interference from the outside. 'The incident caused considerable excitement in all parts of the theatre', reported the *Glasgow Herald* (4 February), 'which was intensified by a number of ladies in different sections of the auditorium distributing bills and throwing about quantities of suffrage literature.' Eventually the door to the box was forced open and the speaker agreed to desist and leave the theatre with her companions.

According to the *Suffragette* (13 February) the women were cheered by the 'great bulk of the audience'. The *Herald* did not report the audience's reaction but carried letters on that subject. One on 5 February signed 'SPECTATOR' stated that the women were 'treated so abominably by the commissionaires and others who were ejecting them' that she felt it her duty as a woman to protest; as a result she was 'roughly seized by a commissionaire and pulled up the steps of the circle, and was only released when several ladies in the auditorium interfered.' On 7 February Eleanor Walker, 'a reluctant spectator of the pathetic farce which served the playgoers of the Royalty Theatre as an entr'acte last Tuesday night', insisted that this was pure fiction and that the women had suffered no indignities whatsoever. She felt that 'though devotion and self-immolation to a cause may be ethically beautiful, a sense of proportion and of the ludicrous might be more efficacious where that cause is concerned.'

Suffragette demonstrations also took place at His Majesty's Theatre in Aberdeen and the King's Theatre, Dundee; in its report of each the *Suffragette* claimed that the women had been applauded and that the response of the audiences had been 'distinctly friendly'.[7]

A similar tactic was to address diners at a restaurant. Glasgow had its first such protest in January at 'the Fruitarian Restaurant of Messrs Stuart Cranston, Limited'. A woman who had been quietly lunching with three companions rose and addressed the customers on the subject of women's suffrage while the others distributed leaflets. The *Suffragette* claimed that diners' interest was keenly aroused; but in an Edinburgh restaurant (according to the *Glasgow Herald*) 'the diners did not take kindly to the innovation, and there was a volley of sarcastic remarks, the shuffling of feet, and the tinkling of cutlery and crockery.' When the suffragette refused the manager's request to stop, 'the good humoured patience of the diners began to give out. A piece of banana skin thrown by a young man narrowly missed the speaker, but the next missile, the remainder of a bun, struck her on the head.' At which point she stopped and paid her bill.[8]

The Church was not ignored by the militants either in this period. On Saturday 22 February two WSPU members asked Dr Wallace Williamson of St Giles' Cathedral if he would pray for suffragette prisoners enduring hunger and thirst strikes for consciences' sake; he declined as such a duty 'lay rather with the prison chaplain'. The next day. Sunday, a number of women, as well as three men, went to St Giles' and chanted their own prayer after the intercessory prayer. On being requested to leave, all but two of them did so. Those two chanted another prayer after the hymn; they were arrested on leaving the church and taken to the police station but were discharged after a short detention.[9]

Those were all open forms of protest, but the WSPU's 'secret' campaign also continued. Toward the end of January home-made bombs were placed inside the glass winter garden, the Kibble Palace, in the

Botanic Gardens in Glasgow. Only one bomb exploded, shattering the glass on the north side of the Palace. No suffrage literature was found (the *Glasgow Herald* did not mention a suffrage connection), but the hiding place of the women was said to have been discovered, and the incident was attributed to suffragettes.[10]

Miss W.K. Bowie, whose mother was a keen suffragist, lived on the north side of the river across from the Botanic Gardens. After 76 years she still remembers being awakened by a loud explosion in the early hours of one morning and being taken in daylight to see the damage done to the Kibble Palace by the suffragettes.[11]

Not long after this the most spectacular of Scottish arson attacks took place: three mansions in the Upper Strathearn district of Perthshire were set ablaze on the same night, and two were completely destroyed. Suffrage literature was found near them all. One of the houses, Allt-an-Phionn, St Fillans, was the property of Mr G. Stirling Boyd, whose wife was a leading anti-suffragist; it was conjectured that the suffragettes were wreaking revenge. However, the second mansion-house which was destroyed, the House of Ross, built only four years earlier, belonged to Mrs D. Maclagan of Edinburgh who had never displayed any antagonism to the movement; in fact, she told the *Dundee Courier*'s reporter, her daughter was a suffragist.[12]

Although the third mansion-house, Aberuchill Castle, was the least damaged it attracted the most publicity. 'SERVANTS AT PERTH-SHIRE CASTLE NARROWLY ESCAPE AWFUL DEATH WHEN BUILDING IS FIRED BY SUFFRAGETTES' screamed the *Dundee Courier*, whose headlines always sought to convey the full story. The *Suffragette* denied that there had been any risk to human life, claiming that the servants slept in a separate block.[13] However, Mrs Isobel Cartwright's letter to me supports the original reports. She was four years old at the time and remembers being wakened at about 4 am by her mother, who said 'Get up Isobel, the Castle is on fire.' Her father was chauffeur to the family who owned the estate; they were in Cheshire at the time, so Isobel and her mother were alone in the rooms above the garage. The male servants (gardeners, gamekeepers and foresters) also slept in detached accommodation, but three housemaids and three laundry maids slept in the attics of the main house. It was the head housemaid who awoke, smelled smoke, found a wing of the house on fire, and woke the others. The men succeeded in putting the fire out with hoses, though not before valuable furniture and paintings had been destroyed. Mrs Cartwright also remembers the 'great red glow in the sky' above the House of Ross that same night. 'If these acts were carried out by members of the Suffragette movement', she wrote, 'then one can only marvel at their clever organisation.'[14]

22 Annie Rhoda Craig

Two women who had been watched by Dunblane police because they were strangers to the district left for Glasgow by the morning train and were followed by a detective. In Glasgow they tried to shake him off by separating and hurrying off in different directions. He went after one of them and eventually succeeded in having her arrested by the Glasgow police.[15]

The woman gave her name as Rhoda Robinson, and she stuck to that name throughout, though she was later recognised as Annie Rhoda Craig (see Chapter 7). She was handed over to the Perthshire police, placed in custody at Dunblane and then transferred to Perth prison. She went on hunger strike but soon after was released on bail. Initially the sheriff-substitute at Perth refused to grant bail as she had given no address and he was not satisfied that she would appear for trial. Her counsel argued that that was not a ground for the refusal of bail. Bail was eventually fixed at £800 (the availability of such a sum may indicate the WSPU's financial position). Early in May the Crown dropped the charges against her for lack of evidence (and bail was refunded). However, as she was later charged with another act of fire-raising before Dumbarton Sheriff Court (her own part of the country), it seems likely that she really was one of the women responsible for the Strathearn fires.[16]

During that same month of February male suffragists travelled from Scotland to London. There were, in fact, two initiatives – one by the Scottish Federation of the NUWSS and one by the Northern Men's Federation – timed to coincide on the 14th. Each of the organisations asked Asquith to receive a deputation. The Northern Men's Federation organised an afternoon meeting in the Memorial Hall, Farringdon Street, and the NUWSS held one in the evening at the Albert Hall.

Forty-nine societies affiliated to the Scottish Federation approached various public bodies and they were astonishingly successful in recruiting male support for the deputation. No less than 76 Scottish men's organisations were prepared to send delegates, 59 from Glasgow alone. The Shetland Society approached the Town and County Councils and, in spite of the distance involved, each of them appointed a representative to the deputation. Glasgow was the only one to send its Lord Provost, and the Glasgow and West of Scotland Association complained that the *Common Cause* did not accord this fact the prominence they thought it deserved. Dealing with a lord provost did not prove easy as he was terribly anxious about the contents of the letter which was being sent to the Prime Minister. Katherine Lindsay, secretary of the Glasgow and West of Scotland Association, had to write to Millicent Fawcett, president of the NUWSS, for help on this point ('He said that if it was meant to demand a Government Measure he could not go on the deputation, as this was asking an impossibility, & might bring on a General Election'). She had then to write a second time to ask Mrs Fawcett to send him a copy of the letter 'as he wishes to be quite certain what he is committing himself to' ('He is really most troublesome', she added).[17]

The Lord Provost need not have worried, for Asquith refused to meet the Scottish Federation's deputation. Most of the men nevertheless travelled down from Scotland to take part in the Albert Hall demonstration, and a reception was held for them before the meeting, with Miss S.E.S. Mair acting as hostess.[18] However, as this was a meeting of men from all over Britain, it received considerably less coverage in the Scottish press than the Northern Men's Federation. (And, of course, the Women's Freedom League and the Votes for Women Fellowship gave the Northern Men full coverage in their journals.)

The Northern Men were similarly rebuffed by Asquith, but thirty of them marched to Downing Street anyway; only ten were allowed into the street, which 'aroused the indignation of the rejected ones'. In any case Mr Asquith was 'not at home'. The London correspondent of the *Glasgow Herald* thought their visit to the capital was 'better stage managed than on the former occasion.'

23 Support for the Scottish men in London

The public were evidently more disposed to give these earnest crusaders
from the North a patient hearing, and the cordial character of the
interviews with the Scottish members of Parliament was in strong contrast
to the encounter of last year, when the exchange of views between the
parties was more forcible than polite. The Scotsmen were made much of by
the great ladies of the suffrage movement, which is reckoned to have
obtained a fillip from the imposing spectacle of 100 hard-headed and logical
Scottish minor public men ranged on the platform at the week-end protest
meetings.[19]

At the meeting in the Memorial Hall a member of the deputation said that
their object was 'to convince Mr Asquith that on the women's suffrage
question the heather was on fire', and that the Prime Minister would be

deserted by many in the ranks of his followers at the next election. Councillor Crawford said that Mr Asquith had 'insulted a proud and determined race'. At a demonstration by the men in Trafalgar Square the following day Bailie Alston described the refusal to meet the deputation as 'an insult which they would fling back in Mr Asquith's face'. According to *The Vote*, the large crowd in Trafalgar Square 'thoroughly enjoyed the determination, the fighting speeches, the vigour, and the humour of the Scotsmen.'[20]

Votes for Women told readers about some of the men who took part. From Edinburgh Councillor Crawford had moved the resolution in the Town Council to petition Parliament for women's suffrage, and his seconder, Councillor Bruce Lindsay, was also present, as was the senior member of the Town Council, Bailie Murray J.P. The honorary secretary of the demonstration, Mr J. Wilson McLaren, had been joint secretary of the Edinburgh Central Division Advanced Liberal Association but severed his connection with that Association because of the government's attitude toward women's suffrage. From Glasgow came Bailie Alston among others; he was the parliamentary Labour candidate for Camlachie and was said to be a 'veritable guardian of the poor.'[21]

The men stressed as they had done on the previous occasion that Asquith's refusal to see the deputation had been a blessing in disguise. They returned to Scotland full of fighting spirit and held a successful meeting on the Mound in Edinburgh on 14 March. One of the participants, John McMichael, wrote to Maud Arncliffe-Sennett, 'A couple of years or so since such a meeting by men, would never have been thought of.'[22]

Just after the men's return from London the redoubtable Ethel Moorhead was back in the news. On 17 February two women were looking around the exterior of Traquair House in the Borders. The housekeeper came out and asked them what they wanted; they said they were interested in the old house and asked to see the interior. The housekeeper 'said "we are not allowed to let any one in because of the suffragettes." On hearing this they turned their faces away for a moment and one said "you are quite right, its [sic] horrible what the women will do"!' After the women left, the estate office phoned the police.[23]

When interviewed by the police at a hotel in Innerleithen the women gave their names as Mrs Marshall and Miss Stewart, tourists residing at a hotel in Peebles; they would give no further information about themselves. They walked back to their Peebles hotel the following day, and when the hotelkeeper was shown a picture of Ethel Moorhead in the Police Gazette he recognised her as 'Mrs Marshall'. She was therefore arrested under the Cat and Mouse Act. 'Miss Stewart' was not known and was therefore released. (According to the Traquair estate office only three hours after she had 'stupidly' been released Peebles police received a telegram from Crieff that she was wanted there in connection with the burning of the three Perthshire mansions.) Ethel Moorhead was taken to Calton jail.[24]

The Traquair estate office thought of Ethel Moorhead as 'the head of the movement in Scotland' and the *Glasgow Herald* (19 February) referred to her as 'the leader of the suffragists in Scotland'. The suffragettes in Scotland never had a 'leader', but it says much about Ethel Moorhead's personality that she was regarded as such. Immediately she was arrested she went on hunger strike.

On 19 February the prison governor wired the Secretary for Scotland for authorisation to feed Ethel Moorhead 'artificially' (the euphemism generally used for forcible feeding by prison officials at the time). He stated that she was suspected of having taken part in fire-raising in Perthshire and Renfrewshire since her previous release. The Scottish Secretary gave his sanction and forcible feeding commenced on 21 February. Word got out and suffragettes gathered round the prison late at night, attempting to send messages of cheer by means of a megaphone. 'Keep the flag flying', 'No surrender', 'Your friends are thinking of you' were some of them, until a police constable moved the women on.[25]

This was the first time forcible feeding was carried out in Scotland, and it came as a shock. Janie Allan wrote in the *Forward*: 'It had been fondly believed that this barbarity was to be left to England'.[26] The man who took responsibility for the decision was the medical member of the Prison Commission, Dr James Devon. Dr Devon had written a well-regarded book, *The Criminal and the Community*, published two years earlier, in which he expressed the opinion that forcible feeding was not a good idea.[27] However, when Elizabeth Finlayson Gauld and Janie Allan called on him he informed them that no matter what the risks were he considered them justified to 'protect the public from the operations of Miss Moorhead'. Janie Allan said to him 'this meant that we were prepared to injure permanently a woman's health, to which I replied that for my part I was of opinion that if a woman's health could only be preserved by allowing her to set fire to other people's houses, we must with regret risk her health.'[28]

Initially the feeding was carried out by medical officers from the Morningside Asylum, but the directors of the asylum objected, and Dr Devon therefore recruited a man who had had plenty of practice in 'artificial feeding' at asylums, Dr H. Ferguson Watson. But on the evening of 25 February Ethel Moorhead was hurriedly released – under licence – into the custody of Dr Grace Cadell, for she was seriously ill with double pneumonia. A WSPU procession organised for that evening to demand her release was changed into a protest against forcible feeding.[29]

There were, from the first, two versions of what caused the pneumonia. The prison version was that on 21 February Ethel Moorhead broke her cell windows and tore her clothing, 'thus exposing herself to the danger of a chill.' These actions were not denied, but Dr Cadell stated categorically that it was food getting into her lungs in the course of the eighth feeding that was directly responsible for the pneumonia. Ethel Moorhead's own statement really stirred things up. It appeared in the *Suffragette* of 6 March under the headline 'SCOTLAND DISGRACED AND DIS-HONOURED!'. No one outside the suffrage movement paid much attention to that journal, but the same statement appeared in the *Edinburgh Evening Dispatch* of 5 March, and that could not be ignored.

It was a lurid tale of tubes and gags and torture and vomiting, and of being carried fighting to the operating room. On one particular day she felt as if a hot wire had been put in one ear, 'an excruciating pain, which made me give a piercing scream'. During the last feeding before her illness she compulsively choked and coughed; afterwards she had difficulty breathing and felt a pain in her side. That night two nurses sat up with her: 'I was asked if I wanted to send for any relatives, and the priest was sent to administer the sacraments.'

Dr Ferguson Watson indignantly denied Ethel Moorhead's allegations, insisting that 'she was not tortured in any way: neither was she hurt, in fact she made no attempt to struggle.' Even at the time of her discharge, he reckoned, 'she was quite fit to be fed.' The matter reached Parliament with a question tabled for the Scottish Secretary. A detailed list of queries arising from Ethel Moorhead's press statement was sent by the prison commissioners to the prison governor. The replies confirm at least some of her allegations: for example she was certainly carried from her cell fighting, and she did cry out 'someone has been putting hot irons in my ear', although it was denied that anyone had done such a thing. The priest's visit was downplayed as arising from a simple request from Ethel Moorhead to the medical officer: 'He replied of course you can I'll send him to you. No mention was made of the administering of the Sacrament.'[30]

The Commons statement naturally blamed Ethel Moorhead's pneumonia on her exposure to the cold and made much of the warrants issued for her arrest on suspicion of the other fire-raising charges. Ethel Moorhead replied that 'in order to account for the introduction of medieval torture into Scotland ... Mr MacKinnon Wood was trying to whitewash himself by vilifying me.'[31]

Ethel Moorhead was due back in prison on 9 March. Grace Cadell stated that her patient would not be fit to return by that date, and an extension was granted. A 24-hour police watch was kept on Dr Cadell's house, but all the policemen had to go on was a photo of Ethel Moorhead;

none of them had seen her in person, and some of the women who visited the house resembled her in appearance. On the night of the 10th a policeman saw one such woman leave the house with the doctor in a motor car. The following day a search warrant was obtained and the police looked inside the house for Ethel Moorhead but did not find her. Dr Cadell refused to say anything.[32]

Ethel Moorhead had escaped, but the repercussions were not yet over. From the date of her release with pneumonia James Devon had been bombarded by letters from suffragettes. Elizabeth Finlayson Gauld wrote bitterly that he had done his 'Duty'.

> So did those who drove in the nails on Calvary. So did those who let loose the lions in ancient Rome. So did those who lit the faggots round Joan of Arc so did those who tortured or slaughtered our Covenanting forefathers so did the tools and sycophants of every tyrant since the world began.[33]

On 16 March an Edinburgh suffragette, Jean Lambie, attacked Dr Devon with a dogwhip in Glasgow; she said she held him responsible for introducing forcible feeding into Scottish prisons. James Devon did indeed claim responsibility for the forcible feeding of Ethel Moorhead 'because I believed it would be an advantage to fix their [the militants'] attention on somebody. It does not increase the risk to me and it may diminish that of others ... My personal view is that the risk is very slight and I have been far too frequently threatened by lunatics in and out of prison to worry about this lot.' Dr Devon did not press charges against Miss Lambie.[34]

'Medieval' prison regimes evoked a symbolic militant response. In the early hours of the morning of 26 February the church of Whitekirk in East Lothian – one of Scotland's most beautiful medieval churches – was completely gutted by fire and militant suffrage messages were found nearby. Recently it has been suggested that the burning of the church was due to the refusal of Haddington Church of Scotland presbytery to receive an NUWSS deputation. But the WSPU was not concerned with deputations to presbyteries, and the timing of the act is significant – only a few hours after Ethel Moorhead's release from prison with pneumonia. The *Suffragette* headed its story of the burning 'SWIFT RETRIBUTION FOLLOWS SCOTLAND'S BETRAYAL', and several months later Janie Allan wrote to the chairman of the Prison Commission, 'I do not know if you are aware that the burning of White Kirk was the direct result of the forcible feeding of Miss Ethel Moorhead in Calton Prison.'[35] Indeed, one militant suffragette, Catherine Blair, actually put it in print:

Hitherto in Scotland the authorities had refused to torture political prisoners, but no sooner had they introduced this medieval barbarity into the Calton Jail, than a medieval church was burnt in protest.[36]

Catherine Blair was the wife of a farmer in East Lothian. She was a keen WSPU member, and though as a mother of four she did not take part in militant activities herself, she provided a safe haven for suffragettes released under the Cat and Mouse Act; she organised, chaired, and spoke at WSPU meetings; and she wrote innumerable letters to newspapers, defending militancy and calling for the enfranchisement of women. (Between July 1912 and February 1914 she had ten letters published in the *Haddingtonshire Courier* alone.) Her husband gave her his full support, in fact he resigned the vice-presidency of the local Liberal Party because of the party's treatment of the suffrage question and the militants.[37]

The destruction of Whitekirk caused anguish to those who had loved the old church, none more so than Lady Frances Balfour. She wrote to her son Frank that it had made her 'both ill and unhappy ... It has roused the deepest feeling that has yet been felt.' She and her sister-in-law, Lady Betty Balfour, helped to organise a fund for the restoration of the church 'as suffragists'.[38]

Yet Lady Frances was one of many who wrote letters to the *Scotsman* in the weeks that followed to argue that the cause of women's suffrage was no less just because of the criminal acts of some of those who supported it. As the east of Scotland's paper, the *Scotsman* naturally carried both a leading article and an enormous amount of correspondence on the burning of Whitekirk.[39] However, the debate on militancy which raged within its pages was also to be found in many other newspapers of this period.[40]

A typical leading article appeared in the *Aberdeen Free Press* on 11 March. 'Militant suffragism has passed from hysteria into stark madness', it began. The women who committed these acts were 'really lunatics who should be subjected to constant restraint and supervision, or who, if it could be managed, should be deported to some outlying part of the Empire'. The only result of the militants' strategy was to 'arouse deep and general public irritation and resentment and to excite ever-increasing prejudice against a movement which otherwise, instead of being set back, would have gathered way rapidly ... One of the most lamentable effects of the violence of the militant suffragists is the grave injustice which it does to the non-militant suffragists.'

The non-militants concurred with this view and reacted with particular anger to the charge that the consitutional suffrage movement benefited from militant acts. Elsie Inglis, as secretary of the Scottish Federation of

Women's Suffrage Societies, wrote to the *Scotsman* that 'exactly the opposite is the case'; after each outburst of militancy she received letters from a number of the Federation's societies saying that people would not come to suffrage meetings 'and that the spirit of antagonism aroused makes it almost impossible to carry on the work.'[41] However, the extent to which the constitutionalists were prepared to condemn the militants still varied greatly.

The Glasgow and West of Scotland Association put forward the following resolution for the Scottish Federation annual meeting:

> That we the members of the Scottish Federation W.S.S. while yielding to none in our conviction of the justice of our claim for equal suffrage protest against the methods of the militant suffragists & record our strong disapproval of, & deep regret at, the wanton destruction of Whitekirk church, one of our most notable National Monuments.[42]

At the Glasgow society's next meeting 'a letter was read from Dr Everett McLaren resigning from the Executive Committee on account of the Resolution against Militancy put on the Agenda for the S.F. Annual Meeting'. The Edinburgh Society wrote to the Glasgow one asking if it would be willing to leave the word 'wanton' out of the resolution, but 'it was agreed that the Resolution remain as it was.' At the same meeting one committee member moved that 'we ask leave of the Council to withdraw the Resolution'. The secretary recorded that 'after a good deal of discussion, a vote was taken, & it was agreed that the Resolution should stand, by 12 votes to 7.'[43]

The Women's Freedom League's attitude can best be seen from entries in Eunice Murray's diary: 'Every day brings some fresh conflict or burning or destruction from the WSPU ... I blame the Government never the women.' She felt the WSPU tactics brought awareness of the issues to everyone, and caused many to support the cause. Although 'my type of mind could never do the things they do', she could not blame them: 'No – I blame the Government.'[44]

The subject of militant suffragism continued to be discussed long after the campaign was over. In her autobiography Lady Frances Balfour wrote that militancy 'was very much like the position of anglers on a Scottish river, bent on having good sport, and constantly maddened by swarms of midges, no equipment saved the man from their stinging importunity, they were everywhere.' But this was arguably a description of militancy in its early stages, and Elizabeth Haldane, another non-militant, wrote: 'In the earlier years the attacks were termed pinpricks, in the later they were dagger thrusts, and done by women, noble in themselves, who were persuaded that they were serving their country by doing this.'[45]

Early 'militancy' consisted of nothing more than interrupting speakers at political meetings and attempting to march on the House of Commons. When this was fruitless it escalated to attacks on individuals and the destruction of letters, and finally into arson, by which time the aim was no longer to persuade the Government of the rightness of the cause, but to *force* it to concede the vote to women. Recently, writers have seen this as a reactive phenomenon, with each shift in militant tactics the response to ever more repressive treatment, which in turn produced a reactive leadership, having to respond to such developments and harness them in some way or else become irrelevant.[46] Brian Harrison saw the shift as a 'fourfold process, involving insulation from the surrounding society, growth in internal solidarity, repudiation of society's values, and escalation in the types of militancy that are considered necessary.'[47]

Harrison also noted that the WSPU was not capable of generating 'the continuous and coherent planning needed ... for militancy to be seriously disruptive ... Buildings were destroyed, letters were burned, windows were smashed, but on no systematic over-all plan, and with no hope of extracting governmental concession'. Andrew Rosen made a similar point in his history of the WSPU: Christabel's tactics 'were not bothersome enough to create a crisis of magnitude sufficient to bring about the passing of a women's suffrage measure.' He believed that if commercial and industrial targets had been chosen instead of mainly private houses, it might have been different. He also equated the final stages of the WSPU campaign with millenarian movements and wrote of the organisation's 'devotion to the politics of apocalypse'.[48]

It is difficult to imagine any Government conceding victory to a middle-class organisation of women who were causing havoc but who posed no real threat to the state and who lacked mass support. Thus far the arguments of Rosen and Harrison are convincing, but the impression they convey of hysterical women out of all touch with reality is given the lie by everything that we know of the Scottish arsonists, who were highly intelligent and deeply motivated, by no means unbalanced. This is not, however, to deny the apocalyptic fervour found in the movement at this time by Rosen, for it comes across strongly in a report in the *Edinburgh Evening Dispatch* (11 March) of a WSPU meeting in the Synod Hall. The reporter was horrified that 'an audience almost entirely composed of women, many of them mere girls, rapturously applauded speeches which for violence, lawlessness, and reckless incitement to crime, we have never heard matched in any public meeting.'

> From beginning to end the speeches ... were a monstrous slander on the human race. All male creatures were represented to be contemptible cowards and fools; Englishmen brutal bullies; Cabinet Ministers liars and

knaves; politicians of all parties beneath contempt, 'cheap as dirt'; clergy-men, doctors, newspaper men, and public officials self-seeking hirelings; and members of all other suffrage societies blacklegs and traitors.

However alienated the public might be, crass male officialdom was always capable of restoring sympathy to the militants, as occurred in Glasgow on 9 March. A public meeting was advertised in the St Andrew's Hall for that evening, with Emmeline Pankhurst as the chief speaker. Mrs Pankhurst had been in and out of jail – hunger-striking, being released under the Cat and Mouse Act, and being rearrested – throughout the previous year. After her last release she had not been found, and therefore it was to be expected that the police would attempt to rearrest her in Glasgow. However, one man later insisted that those not involved in the suffrage movement did not necessarily know this, and attended the meeting out of simple curiosity to hear her.[50]

The WSPU was geared up for a fight, Mrs Pankhurst writing to a friend, 'There is now a Scotch bodyguard and they are eager for the fray'.[51] The 'bodyguard' was on the platform, which was ringed with barbed wire concealed by flowers and bunting.

Unlike Christabel, who remained at a safe distance in Paris, Mrs Pankhurst 'was always *there*, always involved, and always willing to do herself what she asked other women to do'; Rebecca West aptly described her as a 'reed of steel'.[52] Because of this she inspired tremendous – indeed, fanatical – devotion amongst her followers. An eye-witness described the beginning of the scene at the St Andrew's Hall thus:

> A little woman, pale and fragile as a snowdrop, with deep luminous eyes, whose light twelve months of slow torture have not quenched though they have turned her hair to silvery whiteness – a sea of upturned human faces full of reverential awe and foreboding pity – a silence, almost painful in its intensity of sympathy, and then – with a sudden cry of 'danger' from one of the stewards and the heavy tramp of many feet, the doors were swung violently open and a stream of policemen and detectives poured into the hall with drawn batons.[53]

With police swarming within and around the building it was amazing that she managed to reach the platform. Jessie Stephen revealed to Brian Harrison that Mrs Pankhurst had been inside the hall all afternoon: she was smuggled in with 'a corporation basket of laundry.'[54]

She now beheld a hall filled with 3000–4000 spectators, while the platform full of women was being assailed by police. Battle broke out. Janie Allan shot blanks from a revolver into the faces of the oncoming policemen, other women flung flowerpots and chairs at them, and the policemen cut their hands on the hidden barbed wire. The women could not defend Mrs Pankhurst for long against such a large force, but in fact much of the violence took place after she had been captured and dragged off. A member of the platform party (Ellen Currie M.A., of Glasgow) wrote, 'The police behaved in a very hysterical brutal fashion. With baton in hand they struck at everyone who came within their reach: no mercy was meted out to perfectly non-offending persons.' Women were hurled from the platform into the hall; statements were taken afterwards from them and from women who had been struck from behind; many were painfully bruised.[55]

Not surprisingly, some policemen were injured, and the press emphasis on these infuriated suffragettes.[56] Concern for the police was seldom uppermost in the minds of the Glasgow public and was little evident in the correspondence columns of the *Glasgow Herald*. Many letters were from men, such as Robert L. Bremner: 'As a citizen of Glasgow I write to protest against the brutal, unmanly, and cowardly exhibition of Monday night.' Glasgow's 'shame' and 'disgrace' were phrases used more than once. The *Herald*'s editor noted that the letters offered 'the most copious evidence of the widespread feeling of disgust and indignation aroused by the mishandling by the Glasgow police authorities, in conjunction with Scotland Yard, of a task which ought to have been carried through in such a way as to avoid a riot in a public hall and the use of violent tactics.'[57]

The general feeling in the press was that if the police were going to arrest Mrs Pankhurst they should have waited until the end of the meeting. The police version was that, knowing resistance would be offered, they thought if they delayed they might lose her so they acted while they had her in full view. The press reaction to that was that having Mrs Pankhurst elude arrest would still have been preferable to the mêlée that ensued.[58]

On 12 March Janie Allan led a deputation of fourteen women to the magistrates of Glasgow, saying that they came not as suffragists but as citizens and ratepayers of Glasgow, urging a public inquiry. A few days later a deputation of men travelled to London to ask Scottish MPs for a parliamentary inquiry. (It was believed at that time that Scotland Yard had been partly responsible for what had occurred, which was not in fact true.) According to the *Suffragette* there was general agreement that an inquiry should be held; according to the *Scotsman* the deputationists were sent away with a flea in their ear. Both accounts agreed that the men were told that their proper course of action was to bring the matter before Glasgow Town Council. On their return to Scotland they therefore did so but were ruled out of order, as the Corporation had no jurisdiction over the police. After the deputation withdrew 'a strong scene occurred, when members of the Corporation shouted each other down'.[59]

The magistrates' report was issued on 30 March; in it many eye-witness accounts were denied, and the report was severely criticised in the Glasgow press.[60] It was remitted by the magistrates to a sub-committee for further consideration, and the story will be picked up again in the next chapter. But there were more immediate repercussions.

The first of these was that more than a hundred women joined the WSPU in Glasgow in the days following the incident (by 10 April Glasgow branch had 203 new members).[61] Christabel Pankhurst, writing to Janie Allan from Paris, felt that 'the Glasgow members and Glasgow citizens generally can do a very great deal to take advantage of the events of last Monday. The action the Government took there has given Glasgow this opportunity.' She 'rejoiced to hear that so many new members have joined the Union as a consequence' and hoped it would be possible 'to keep up the agitation on this issue for some time to come.'[62] The cold and calculating tone of this letter is in marked contrast to the emotions of those close to the scene. To Christabel they were nothing but grist to the anti-government mill, but to Janie Allan, who collected the statements of women involved and injured, they meant much more than that.[63]

Although the police at first tried to stop the St Andrew's Hall meeting taking place after the arrest of Mrs Pankhurst, there was nothing unlawful about it and it eventually went ahead, with Flora Drummond making a rousing militant speech. She did the same in Edinburgh the following night at a meeting which Mrs Pankhurst was to have addressed and then in Dundee the next night. At Dundee the *Advertiser* (12 March) said that without Mrs Pankhurst the meeting was 'robbed of much of its interest' and the hall was not even full.

One Dundee woman who had mixed feelings about Mrs Pankhurst's arrest was Isabella Carrie, the quiet schoolteacher who had joined the WSPU after being flung out of a Liberal women's meeting. She provided accommodation for WSPU members from afar, but they always arrived after she went to bed and departed after she left for work. Mrs Pankhurst was to have stayed there when she came to Dundee, and Miss Carrie was determined to stay up and talk to her. She was 'very excited and anxious about her visit and very much afraid she might be arrested in Dundee and perhaps in my house so my first reaction when I heard of her arrest ... was a feeling of relief but I was truly very sorry indeed that I had not met her.'[64]

The most dramatic response to Mrs Pankhurst's re-arrest was in London where Mary Richardson slashed a famous painting, the Rokeby Venus. In Scotland Helen Crawfurd broke two windows in the army recruiting office and was arrested. She wrote in her memoirs that she 'felt some protest should be made, and that if I took the lead, other women would follow.' None did, but she nevertheless felt that her protest 'was quite valuable from a women's suffrage point of view', especially as Janie Allan organised a picket outside Duke Street prison. Helen Crawfurd was on hunger strike for eight days before being released under the Cat and Mouse Act.[65]

On 15 March the WSPU arranged for church interruptions to take place all over Britain, and several Scottish churches were affected. In Glasgow Cathedral the women approached the Rev D. McAdam Muir before the service to ask that prayer be publicly offered for suffragettes in prison. He was willing to pray for all prisoners, but that was not good enough, and at the service a group of women chanted, 'Oh Lord, save Emmeline Pankhurst, Helen Crawfurd, and all brave women suffering for their faith. Amen.' No attempt was made to eject them, and afterwards they distributed a leaflet entitled 'The Appeal to God'. Similar incidents occurred at the Tron Kirk in Edinburgh, at St Paul's Cathedral Church, Dundee, and at the West Parish Church, Aberdeen.[66]

As this was the first such occurrence in Aberdeen the local press gave it full coverage. Three women stood up and chanted the following words from a book held between them:

> O Lord, open the ears of this congregation to our message.
> Lord, bless and save Mrs Pankhurst.
> Lord, bless and prosper our cause.

The *Daily Journal* noted that they 'began in rather weak and trembling voices, visibly affected by nervousness' but gained confidence as they went on so that the third intercession 'rang through the whole church.' According to the *Free Press*, 'indignation was freely expressed that the sanctity of the service should have been so disturbed, and strong disapproval of the occurrence was voiced by representative members of the congregation.'[67]

A week later seven women interrupted a service at St Giles' Cathedral by chanting 'God Save Emmeline Pankhurst'; on this occasion they were arrested and charged with breach of the peace. They were freed on bail and tried before Edinburgh City Police Court on 30 March. The principal witness for the prosecution was Sheriff Guy, an elder of St Giles', who had caused the women's arrest. The Rev G. Stott, Cramond, who had conducted the service, testified that the incident caused a 'wave of excitement'; witnesses for the defence insisted either that they had not even heard the chant or else that it had caused no disturbance. However, the women were found guilty. At a WSPU meeting in Edinburgh Elizabeth Finlayson Gauld called this 'an example of what the Church might be reduced to when it had lost the spirit of the Great Master.'[68]

Impasse – April–July 1914

By April 1914 the Scottish Federation of the NUWSS included 63 societies, with a membership of 7,370 (see map on p. 189). The Women's Freedom League had branches in Cowdenbeath, Dundee, Dunfermline, Edinburgh, Glasgow, Kilmarnock, Kirkintilloch, Lochgelly, Paisley, Perth, and Rothesay, plus a 'Scottish Scattered'. And there were branches of the Scottish League for Opposing Women's Suffrage in Ayr, Berwickshire, Burntisland, Cupar, Dollar, Dundee, Edinburgh, Glasgow (with two sub-branches, Camlachie & Dennistoun and Kilmacolm), Kirkcaldy, Largs, Nairn, Perth and St Andrews.[1] The WSPU had branches in Edinburgh, Dundee, Glasgow and Aberdeen, but membership records were no longer kept and no new branches were being formed.

On 3 April suffragettes tried to set fire to a mansion-house in Lanarkshire. The house was unoccupied except for a caretaker who was awakened by a noise at 2.30 am. When he went down to the parlour he was astonished to find a woman there. He fired two shots from a revolver to alert the constable on the beat; this also alerted the others with her who made their escape. He locked the frightened woman into the kitchen and telephoned the police who arrested her. Three quarter gallon flasks of paraffin oil were found nearby, plus matches, and suffrage literature.[2]

The suffragette was said to be a small woman of about 40 years of age with an English accent. She gave her name as Frances Gordon. Sylvia Pankhurst referred to her as 'Frances Gordon (Frances Graves)'; nothing further has emerged about her under either name. The lady owner of the house in fact declined to prosecute, but as the case was already in the hands of the police the action was taken by the public prosecutor, with the trial fixed for 22 June.[3]

A by-election now arose in the Prime Minister's constituency of East Fife. Asquith was about to take up the post of Minister of War and therefore had to stand for re-election under the old rule that required this. He stood unopposed but nevertheless had to appear before his constituents, and with press attention focused on Scotland this was obviously an excellent opportunity to forward the suffrage cause.

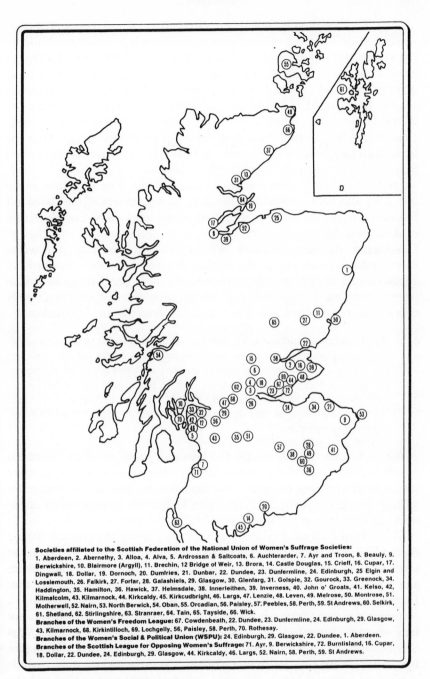

Societies affiliated to the Scottish Federation of the National Union of Women's Suffrage Societies:
1. Aberdeen, 2. Abernethy, 3. Alloa, 4. Alva, 5. Ardrossan & Saltcoats, 6. Auchterarder, 7. Ayr and Troon, 8. Beauly, 9. Berwickshire, 10. Blairmore (Argyll), 11. Brechin, 12 Bridge of Weir, 13. Brora, 14. Castle Douglas, 15. Crieff, 16. Cupar, 17. Dingwall, 18. Dollar, 19. Dornoch, 20. Dumfries, 21. Dunbar, 22. Dundee, 23. Dunfermline, 24. Edinburgh, 25 Elgin and Lossiemouth, 26. Falkirk, 27. Forfar, 28. Galashiels, 29. Glasgow, 30. Glenfarg, 31. Golspie, 32. Gourock, 33. Greenock, 34. Haddington, 35. Hamilton, 36. Hawick, 37. Helmsdale, 38. Innerleithen, 39. Inverness, 40. John o' Groats, 41. Kelso, 42. Kilmalcolm, 43. Kilmarnock, 44. Kirkcaldy, 45. Kirkcudbright, 46. Largs, 47. Lenzie, 48. Leven, 49. Melrose, 50. Montrose, 51. Motherwell, 52. Nairn, 53. North Berwick, 54. Oban, 55. Orcadian, 56. Paisley, 57. Peebles, 58. Perth, 59. St Andrews, 60. Selkirk, 61. Shetland, 62. Stirlingshire, 63. Stranraer, 64. Tain, 65. Tayside, 66. Wick.
Branches of the Women's Freedom League: 67. Cowdenbeath, 22. Dundee, 23. Dunfermline, 24. Edinburgh, 29. Glasgow, 43. Kilmarnock, 68. Kirkintilloch, 69. Lochgelly, 56. Paisley, 58. Perth, 70. Rothesay.
Branches of the Women's Social & Political Union (WSPU): 24. Edinburgh, 29. Glasgow, 22. Dundee, 1. Aberdeen.
Branches of the Scottish League for Opposing Women's Suffrage: 71. Ayr, 9. Berwickshire, 72. Burntisland, 16. Cupar, 18. Dollar, 22. Dundee, 24. Edinburgh, 29. Glasgow, 44. Kirkcaldy, 46. Largs, 52. Nairn, 58. Perth, 59. St Andrews.

24 Map showing suffrage (and anti-suffrage) societies in Scotland in 1914

Two English WSPU members, Olive Bartels and Leonora Tyson, waylaid Asquith at the railway station when he left Cupar for London. On market day in Ladybank they addressed a crowd but, according to the *Dundee Advertiser* (8 April), they 'had a pretty rough time.' First a piper marched by, 'and even the English ladies failed badly in the competition against the Scottish national music.' Then they were surrounded by schoolchildren who shouted them down and, according to the *Dundee Courier* (8 April) 'pelted them with pieces of crust and wood.' After the school bell rang peace was restored, 'and Miss Tyson thereafter had a good hearing.' (In the *Advertiser*'s version they were then 'undisturbed, but little interest was taken in their remarks.') At the same time members of the NUWSS also held an open-air meeting, and members of the Women's Freedom League distributed pamphlets protesting against the re-election of Asquith as MP for East Fife.

Margaret McPhun, a socialist WSPU member from Glasgow, wrote entertainingly about the events of that day and how they would have appeared to a visitor 'unacquainted with the little peculiarities of British Prime Ministers.' For one thing the visitor would have found that nearly every man in Ladybank was a policeman, a detective or a journalist.

> Above, all, he could not have failed to realise that the interest of the day's proceedings centred not in the little Masonic Hall where Mr. Asquith was delivering a speech rightly characterised by the *Herald* as one of 'deliberate, determined and incredible dullness,' but in the square outside where an ever-growing crowd seethed round the platform of the 'fighting women'. Above and beyond all, the impressive thing was the atmosphere of tense, nervous excitement...[4]

A few days later the Edinburgh and Glasgow branches of the Northern Men's Federation held a demonstration at Cupar and announced their intention of opposing Asquith at the next General Election because of his attitude toward women's suffrage. The Federation held further rousing open-air meetings in the weeks ahead.[5]

On 7 April Helen Crawfurd was rearrested under the Cat and Mouse Act and spent five days on hunger strike in Duke Street prison; this was so soon after her previous ordeal that she fainted the night before her release and was said to be in a state of collapse the morning they let her out. During the five days she was inside, WSPU members kept up a continuous picket (in two-hour shifts) outside the prison, which was not far from the constituency of the Secretary for Scotland. One of them, Mrs S.C. Wilson of Glasgow, wrote of those who came to watch: 'We learnt much of their life; they learnt much of us because the pickets were a visible symbol of a central Idea – the fight for ideal right and justice, and the courage of the Suffragette.' Participation in pickets also helped women hesitant about stepping out of 'their quiet home' to learn to 'become more fearless in what they do'.[6]

This was a period when the issue of Scottish Home Rule was watched intently by all the suffrage organisations except the WSPU. The annual meeting of the Convention of Royal and Parliamentary Burghs in Edinburgh on 7 April discussed the question of women and the vote in a Scottish Home Rule Bill. Two hundred burghs sent 400 representatives, including two women, Provost Louisa Malcolm, of Dollar, and Councillor Annie Barlaw, of Callander. The committee on Local Self-Government for Scotland had included women's votes in its draft report, but the Annual Committee had deleted that section. Mrs Barlaw moved for its reinsertion.

> She asked them not to be influenced by their dislike of militancy, and demanded that justice should be done to the women who had worked for the franchise quietly, steadily, and on constitutional lines. Was there any man present who would dare say that the women of Scotland had not as much intelligence as the women of the colonies or of Finland? (Applause and laughter)

After much discussion a motion granting the vote to women on the existing municipal basis (against a motion including women on the same basis as men) was carried.[7]

When the Bill came before parliament the NUWSS worked hard to secure a women's suffrage clause. Both English and Scottish executive committee members (the latter including Elsie Inglis, Mary J.H. Henderson, and Andrew Ballantyne) lobbied MPs. The Scottish Secretary, Mackinnon Wood, promised his support for the inclusion of women in the Bill. Some Scottish MPs favoured women's enfranchisement yet opposed the clause lest the Bill lose the support of English anti-suffrage MPs. The Scottish Women's Liberal Federation demanded 'the inclusion of the women as electors as in accordance with Liberal measures of local self-government'.[8]

At a specially convened meeting of the Scottish Liberal Members a women's suffrage clause was inserted in the Bill, by a majority of 16 to 12, some members not voting. Catherine Marshall of the NUWSS whipped up support among suffragist MPs of all parties: Scottish Liberals were thanked for including women in the Bill, Liberal suffragists and all Labour MPs were urged to support the Second Reading since the Bill 'offered to women an instalment of their demand for political representation', and Unionist suffragists were asked not to oppose a measure that would 'remove a large part of the political injustice under which women labour'.[9]

Votes for Women pointed out that the Scottish and Welsh Home Rule Bills, which gave women votes, were private ones while the Irish Home Rule Bill, a Liberal government measure, did not. Women should therefore 'remember that the present Scottish Bill is only in the nature of a "kite", and that it has not behind it, at present at any rate, the official backing of the Liberal Government and its Whips.' Nevertheless, the inclusion of a women's suffrage clause was 'a healthy sign of the times.'[10]

The Scottish Home Rule Bill came before the House of Commons for its Second Reading on 15 May. What most concerned the Women's Freedom League was that prominent anti-suffragists hailed the federal system embodied in the Scottish and Welsh Bills as the solution to the women's suffrage question: women could be allowed to vote on domestic issues while 'all questions of Imperial and foreign policy, of the control of the Army and Navy, will be entirely beyond their province.' The leading female anti-suffragist in England, Mrs Humphry Ward, wrote to *The Times* promoting this compromise, but the WFL made it clear that it was working 'for the complete political equality of women with men' and would not be content with anything less. The NUWSS president, Millicent Fawcett, welcomed Mrs Ward's endorsement of the enfranchisement of women in local parliaments but emphasised the National Union's own commitment to suffrage for the national (or 'Imperial') parliament as well.[11]

The women's suffrage clause dominated the debate. The *Glasgow Herald* thought the promoters of the Bill had handicapped it 'when they spatchcocked into a Scottish Home Rule Bill an instalment of Woman Suffrage.' In fact, the seconder of the Bill, the Liberal MP for East Perthshire, William Young, made it clear that he would vote against a Third Reading if the women's suffrage clause remained (attacking part of a Bill he was seconding struck MPs as curious). The Marquis of Tullibardine, Unionist MP for West Perthshire, was against granting the parliamentary franchise to women but said he would not object to women voting for a local parliament. Indeed, that was 'about the only part of the Bill which I might be in favour of.' *Votes for Women* commented that the debate 'became at moments a sort of wrangle over the women's claim to enfranchisement, and the Bill was finally talked out, largely, if not wholly, because this was the easiest way of disposing of the contentious clause.' Other press reports agreed with this view of the matter.[12]

Meanwhile, the sub-committee appointed by the Glasgow magistrates to consider the report on the actions of the police while arresting Mrs Pankhurst stated on 9 April that it saw no cause for complaint against the police. However, it recommended that the relevant documents be forwarded to the Secretary for Scotland, who could initiate a public inquiry if he saw fit. Janie Allan wrote to the Secretary for Scotland on the same date, pointing out that the magistrates' committee could not be said to be an independent tribunal with regard to police action. She offered to supply statements on oath concerning individual cases of assault, an offer which the magistrates had refused. The *Daily Record* thought that the Glasgow magistrates were wise to refer the question to the Secretary for Scotland, since some kind of inquiry seemed necessary in view of the conflicting evidence.[13]

On 12 May the Scottish Secretary replied that as the magistrates' committee was the authority charged with administration and control of the police it was up to them to decide if a further inquiry was necessary; if they did then he would appoint a commissioner for the purpose.[14] The magistrates were clearly not going to take the matter any further, but Janie Allan hired counsel to explore other means of bringing the facts before the public. He discouraged legal action against any particular policeman, as evidence about the wider scene would be thrown out as irrelevant. He recommended an unofficial inquiry. If Janie Allan could persuade a prominent citizen to act as a commissioner for such an inquiry, the evidence would all be brought out.[15]

He thought that if anything was to be done it should be done at once, but this was not possible as Janie Allan was determined to take part in a deputation to the King in London, which the WSPU knew very well would lead to the arrest and imprisonment of the women involved. Her counsel was dismayed at this decision and wrote to her solicitor

> What would be thought of a General in command of an army in the field who, just at the time when he had to lead his forces against the enemy suddenly announced he must leave them because a brother General, 400 miles away, was about to be beleaguered in a town and he must go and be shut up with him? C'est beau mais ce n'est pas la guerre. With the greatest respect I could not imagine anything more foolish or more futile than that Miss Allan should take the step she proposes at the present time.[16]

However, Janie Allan went to London and took part in the WSPU's attempt to present a petition to the King. It was a thoroughly nasty affair, with brutal attacks by plain-clothes policemen on many of the women. Janie Allan was amongst some 60 women arrested and imprisoned.[17] It says a great deal about the attitude of WSPU activists at this time that someone like Janie Allan should feel it so necessary to suffer – as if she was not genuinely committed unless she shared the pain and misery of other suffragettes.

The attempt to set up an unofficial inquiry went on – a letter from Janie Allan's counsel to a possible commissioner has survived – but it came to nothing.[18] Meanwhile, a prominent Scottish 'Mouse' was rearrested and conveyed back to Scotland.

Since the previous summer Arabella Scott had worked as a WSPU organiser in Brighton under the name of Catherine Reid. The police found out and arrested her on 2 May. The Detective-Inspector's account of the journey from Brighton to Edinburgh tallies closely with Arabella Scott's own. She resisted every inch of the way, refusing to walk so that she had to be carried, struggling, onto the train to London. Between Victoria and Kings Cross stations she kicked and broke a window in the taxi (telling the driver to send the bill to the Home Secretary), and at each possible stage in her journey she shouted out that women were being tortured under the Cat and Mouse Act. On the train north she tried to break the carriage windows and to pull the communication cord. Arriving at Waverley Station at 6 am, where a number of WSPU members were waiting for her (she stated that they were 'roughly pushed aside'), she 'again refused to walk and had to be carried to a Cab struggling violently, and bawling and shouting as previously described'. She claimed that she was very roughly handled on her arrival at the Calton jail; under the circumstances this was hardly surprising.[19]

Arabella Scott had gone on hunger and thirst strike the moment she was arrested on 2 May. On the 8th Dr James Dunlop found her in a state of such weakness that 'her further detention ... would be attended with considerable risk'. She was liberated that afternoon and was taken to Dr Grace Cadell's house, where 'she refused to leave the vehicle, asserting that she would not accept freedom until she was set free unconditionally.' She was then driven to her mother's house where the same thing happened. Eventually her sister Muriel persuaded her to go to Dr Cadell's house. Her pulse was said to be 'very weak'.[20]

Elizabeth Finlayson Gauld thanked Dr Dunlop for releasing Arabella Scott without forcibly feeding her, but asked him if it was not 'fatuous and cruel' to force a woman to endure hunger and thirst for several days for a cause she would die for if necessary.

> This is no idle statement. I have spoken to these brave women again and again, and believe me when I say I have cowered before the spirit of self sacrifice they have shown and the calmness with which they relate their experiences and their readiness to suffer the full penalty.'

'There is no whining from them', she continued, 'We lesser women do all that. It is a relief to our pent up feelings.'[21]

Arabella Scott was due back in jail in Edinburgh on 22 May. On the evening of 18 May a reception was held in her honour, and afterwards she was accompanied by a large number of suffragettes to Waverley Station where she caught the midnight train to London. Her aim in heading south again was to take part in WSPU campaigning against the Liberal candidate in a by-election in Ipswich. Her defiance of authority there seems quite remarkable, for she and other WSPU members carried notices like 'Here is the Mouse, Where is the Cat?', 'Will the Mouse be re-arrested before the poll?', and 'Due in prison yesterday – why not arrested?' The gamble paid off, for she was left alone. The outcome of the by-election was that the Liberal lost the seat. (The jubilant WSPU took the credit; political commentators did not agree.)[22]

Militant activity was still taking place in Scotland. On 23 May the *Evening Dispatch* reported: 'The suffragette picture-slashing craze has spread to Edinburgh, for this afternoon a suffragette attacked a valuable picture of His Majesty, King George, in the Royal Scottish Academy, Edinburgh, with a hatchet and damaged it considerably.' It happened at about 12.30 when there were many visitors; having attacked the picture the suffragette was immediately seized by an attendant and did not resist. She was said to be about 25 to 30 years of age and gave her name as Maud Edwards but would not reveal any more about herself. The police thought that she did not belong to Edinburgh. Later in the day she was released on bail.

One might have expected this to be a time of total solidarity between WSPU members, without the petty infighting and backbiting that took place earlier, e.g. in Aberdeen in 1909. A letter from Christabel Pankhurst to Janie Allan reveals that this was far from being the case.[23] 'There is in Edinburgh a small handful of people who are decidedly cantankerous', she wrote, 'and the person who is organising for the time being is made to feel the effect of this.'

> These people criticise Miss Mary Allen at the present time, but profess to have had a great admiration for a previous organiser, Miss Lucy Burns. As a matter of fact, Miss Lucy Burns was virtually driven away from Edinburgh, so unhappy was she because of the attitude of a few members.

Apparently some Edinburgh members wanted Jean Lambie to be the organiser, but Christabel considered the idea 'preposterous' and wrote that 'on no account should we agree to the appointment of Miss Lambie to an official post in the Union' (Christabel's reasons for this are unknown).

Christabel reassured Janie Allan that difficulties with organisers arose from time to time and were nothing to worry about; she was certain that Edinburgh would settle down. The letter continued

> As to the question of English organisers working in Scotland, when Englishwomen say they object to being organised by Scotswomen, it will be time for Scotswomen to say they object to being organised by Englishwomen. When Englishwomen say they will not accept Miss

Arabella Scott as an organiser, it will be time for Scottish members to say they will not have Miss Mary Allen or any other Englishwoman as an organiser. In my opinion, there is a very great deal that English women and Scottish women can learn from each other. Where W.S.P.U. organising is concerned, barriers between England and Scotland, England and Wales, England and Ireland, would, in my opinion, be a very great mistake, and in every way would have a narrowing effect. So far as the English W.S.P.U. members are concerned, we shall be only too glad to have any number of Scottish organisers. I do not see why Edinburgh members should not adopt the same broadminded and friendly attitude.

Christabel's mention of Ireland raises the question of how the situation there compared with Scotland. In fact, Christabel previously had some acrimonious correspondence with a suffrage leader in Ireland, Hanna Sheehy Skeffington. The movement in Ireland was quite distinct from that in Great Britain, and given Anglo/Irish relations at the time it is not surprising that Irish suffragists should resent any WSPU attempt to muscle in. Christabel wrote to Hanna Sheehy Skeffington: 'I know that there has been some feeling that only Irish women can appeal to the Irish. The same thing used to be said in Scotland but experience proved that it is not nationality but personality that counts.' Hanna Sheehy Skeffington did not accept the parallel: 'The position in Ireland is very different from that of Scotland – you know that as well as any Irishwoman – therefore your analogy with Scotland does not hold.'[24]

She was right in that, unlike Irishwomen, Scottish women were proud to be British; yet they were also proud to be Scottish and resented their national sensitivities being ignored. Given the preponderance of the English in the movement, Christabel was missing the point in contrasting the English acceptance of Arabella Scott as an organiser with Scottish women's desire to have Scottish organisers. (A comparison with the Welsh situation would be useful here, but so far no one has tackled the wealth of source material to publish anything on the women's suffrage movement in Wales.)

Internal tiffs were not confined solely to the WSPU. The Glasgow and West of Scotland Association for Women's Suffrage dismissed the organiser they had acquired from the NUWSS, telling the National Union that 'Miss Shakespeare was not suited to Glasgow and Glasgow was not suited to her.'[25] But the main bone of contention between the Scottish Federation and the National Union was the Election Fighting Fund (E.F.F.), the campaign for Labour by-election candidates.

The Scottish Federation formed its own E.F.F. committee, one member being Andrew Ballantyne, chairman of the Glasgow and West of Scotland Association and an ardent Liberal. The central E.F.F. committee objected to Ballantyne being on the committee. There was a general issue of whether the National Union had any right to interfere with Scottish Federation decisions, and a specific issue of Ballantyne as a member of a Scottish E.F.F. committee. The Edinburgh Society was at that time the only one carrying on E.F.F. work and wanted to remain under the wing of the central E.F.F. committee while the Scottish Federation wanted to control all E.F.F. work in Scotland. Chrystal Macmillan supported Ballantyne's membership on the grounds that 'it was necessary to have members of Committee not in sympathy with the policy or the minority would not be represented.'[26]

Three different attitudes can be found in Scotland on the policy of supporting Labour candidates. In Edinburgh (but not in Glasgow) some NUWSS members like Lisa Gordon were in sympathy with the Labour movement and therefore wholeheartedly in favour of the policy. Pragmatists like Elsie Inglis felt that the Labour party was the best hope for the women's suffrage movement but distinguished this expedient support from support for Labour for any other reason. And thirdly the staunch Liberals of the Glasgow committee opposed the policy but wanted to retain some control over the situation. The central committee in London decided against the Scottish Federation proposal for E.F.F. work in Scotland; a compromise was thrashed out, but the wrangling over the Scottish Federation's constitutional rights and Andrew Ballantyne's membership continued through June and July.[27]

The Women's Freedom League does not appear to have had any of these difficulties. In June it launched a Clydebank campaign. A series of meetings was held during the lunch break at the Singers' Works and the shipbuilding yards, and the speakers attracted hundreds of workers, both male and female. During that same month Ada Broughton addressed Women's Co-operative Guilds at Dalmuir and Kilbowie Hill. And when Eunice Murray addressed an evening meeting at Dunbarton, ILP members helped to sell suffrage literature. (Eunice Murray also spoke at Northern Men's Federation meetings.) During July the WFL ran its usual successful Clyde Coast campaign.[28]

Even the most distant women's suffrage societies benefited from the enormous interested generated in the issue. In May a visit to the Shetland Society by a speaker sent by the NUWSS led to the enrolment of 45 new members and 17 supporters. The annual meeting of the Scottish University Woman's Suffrage Union in Glasgow in June received excellent press coverage. The Edinburgh National Society held a 'suffrage flower day' (rather like the one previously held in Aberdeen) both to raise funds and attract members and to 'bring once more to the notice of the citizens the fact that there is a large body of men and women in the city who, while deploring the excesses of some sections of suffragettes, are not to be deterred in their struggle for political enfranchisement.' And the NUWSS was preparing for another suffrage summer school at St Andrews, this time for a full month instead of a fortnight.[29]

It is important to not to lose sight of all this non-militant activity, for the conflict between the WSPU and the government (in the form of the prison service) was now so great in Scotland that it will take up the remainder of this chapter.

Towards the end of May the Scottish Office and Prison Commission decided not to take any steps to rearrest Arabella Scott, but on 18 June, in the course of a police raid on a London house in search of another militant, she was discovered, rearrested, and brought back to Scotland. Once again she made the journey as difficult as possible. According to the police superintendent 'she would not walk a step and did all she could to impede the progress of those who carried her by placing her feet against doorways, catching hold of any fixture within reach, and holding on as long as she could. She even tried to bang her head against any hard substance.' Naturally she refused to eat or drink, and she would not speak either – until she realised that the train was not going to Edinburgh. After Larbert she asked the police officer their destination and was told it was Perth.[30]

The authorities, embarrassed by the failings of the Cat and Mouse Act, had resolved to send all suffragettes convicted in Scotland to Perth, and forcibly feed them. Dr Ferguson Watson, who had forcibly fed Ethel Moorhead at Calton jail, was now probationary medical officer at Perth prison, where Arabella Scott was forcibly fed for five weeks, until 26 July. This extraordinarily lengthy punishment will be described later in this chapter. Meanwhile, another suffragette had been convicted in a Scottish court.

On 22 June Frances Gordon was charged before the High Court in Glasgow with attempting to set fire to Springhall House in Lanarkshire. Her counsel unsuccessfully tried to have the case thrown out on the technicality that housebreaking with intent to set fire was a crime unknown in Scotland. Miss Gordon pleaded not guilty, but the jury returned a verdict of guilty. Before Lord Cullen passed sentence she made what the Glasgow Evening Times called 'Miss Gordon's Remarkable Speech', saying that her action had been premeditated. She had travelled a great deal and wanted to impress 'on all people in England [sic] the seriousness of the women's cause'. She was sentenced to one year's imprisonment and as she left the court she shouted to the gallery 'Trust in God, constant war and fight on.' The Evening Times made no mention of any disturbance in court, but the High Court records refer to three women who refused to give their names being charged with contempt of court 'in respect that they interrupted the proceedings of the Court by shouting and yelling (or by throwing missiles in the direction of the bench)'.[31]

When Arabella Scott was not quickly released from Perth prison, and when Frances Gordon was also sent there, the WSPU correctly inferred that the women were being forcibly fed. They organised a series of protest meetings in Perth.[32]

The King and Queen were to tour Scotland in mid-July. The Scottish Office and police department were ready for disturbances; Scotland Yard sent up men to look out for English militants while the Scottish Office asked the chief constables of Glasgow and Edinburgh for some men who could point out Scottish militants to the English officers. On 26 June Janie Allan advised the Chairman of the Prison Commission that the burning of Whitekirk was a reprisal for the forcible feeding of Ethel Moorhead, and that Scottish suffragettes would take strong action if it proved that this was being inflicted on Arabella Scott and Frances Gordon in Perth: 'in view of the Royal visit to Scotland which would of course present many opportunities for protests of a memorable and disastrous nature, it seems doubly a pity to enter upon a course calculated to entail such serious consequences.' She wrote a similar letter to Dr James Devon: 'There are many women who, 6 months ago, were not prepared to do anything violently militant, but who to day would not hesitate.' Protests during the Royal visit would be regrettable, but 'to those who know how high feeling runs against forcible feeding, such incidents would cause no surprise.'[33]

The Chairman of the Prison Commission sent a copy of her letter to the Under Secretary for Scotland. He hoped the CID were watching known militants who might come to Scotland. 'As you know', he wrote, 'both these women referred to by Miss Allan are being fed and in a day or two at latest those outside will know that this must be so or else they would have been liberated.' The Scottish Office questioned whether proceedings could be taken against Janie Allan in view of her veiled threats, but the Director of Public Prosecutions advised not.[34]

According to Helen Crawfurd's memoirs, Janie Allan attempted to bargain with the Lord Provost of Glasgow: if he would arrange that the women in Perth prison would not be forcibly fed, 'she would guarantee that there would be no act of militancy during the Royal visit', whereupon Janie Allan was sacked by the Pankhursts. Helen Crawfurd wrote that the indignant Glasgow members sent her and Dr Mabel Jones as a deputation to London to speak to the Pankhursts, and were told, 'We cannot bargain with the enemy. If Scottish women are prepared to bargain on any other terms [than the vote], then English women are not.'[35]

It is difficult to know what to make of this story. Although the Lord Provost of Glasgow later wrote to the Scottish Office about Arabella Scott, Janie Allan can hardly have believed that he could prevent forcible feeding. There is no other evidence for the dismissal of Janie Allan as organiser. She could not have stopped (and the Lord Provost would have known she could not stop) all militant activity in Scotland even if she wanted to. Helen Crawfurd's autobiography is riddled with wrong dates and wrong names, which makes her a less than reliable witness. She records speaking to both Christabel and Mrs Pankhurst in London on this occasion ('Chrystabel's [sic] legal reasoning did not convince; it was Mrs Pankhurst's plain commonsense presentation'), but of course Christabel was in Paris at that time. It was perhaps in character for Janie Allan to attempt such a bargain and for the Pankhursts to react dogmatically, but the story still seems unlikely.

On 26 June Dr Ferguson Watson reported to the prison governor that Frances Gordon was 'of a highly neurotic and hysterical temperament. There has been more or less nervous prostration since I told her that I had orders to feed her.' Even during her sleep she 'talked much about tubes and feeding.' She had a very narrow pharynx and nasal passage and had 'great difficulty breathing after the tube is passed.' She vomited up so much that he decided also to feed her rectally, and from 30 June she was given nutrient enemas as well as food through the tube. Initially he was satisfied with the results, but on 3 July he reported: 'Prisoner's condition now begins to cause anxiety.' Her temperature fell to 96.4°F and her pulse could sometimes barely be felt. He thought 'this case' had not been suitable for forcible feeding, 'but I was unable to give that information before a careful trial had been given.'[36]

Dr Ferguson Watson was stunned by the furore provoked when his 'treatment' of Frances Gordon was revealed. A typical response was that of H.T. Gillespie, who wrote from London to the Scottish Office about his horror and disgust, 'feelings which must be shared by all Scotchmen who are aware of the facts': 'When forcible feeding is coupled with abominable obscenities...I, and many others, feel a sense of personal degradation, that such a thing can be done by the instructions of those who represent us in Parliament.'[37]

When Frances Gordon was released on 3 July she was taken to Glasgow, where Dr Mabel Jones described her as:

> Like a famine victim – the skin brown, her face bones standing out, her eyes half shut, her voice a whisper, her hands quite cold, her pulse a thread, her wrist joints were slightly swollen, stiff and painful – this not from rough handling but from poisoning. The breath was most offensive unlike anything I have smelt before and the contents of the bowel over which she had no control, smelt the same.[38]

Dr Ferguson Watson indignantly denied many of the allegations in the report. Lord Hugh Cecil advised the Scottish Office that he intended to ask a question in the House of Commons about Miss Gordon's treatment.

The prison commissioners and medical officer had by this time convinced themselves that the reason she had retained so little food was because she was drugged before admission to prison. Dr Ferguson Watson claimed to have suspected this from the first, but his daily reports of her prison stay mentioned no such suspicion.[39]

From 3 July the WSPU staged a constant picket around Perth prison. One of the women who took part (Mrs S.C. Wilson, of Glasgow) wrote

> By bringing our prisoners to Perth and forcibly feeding them, the Government have placed a living, human question before the people of that city. The authorities would have kept it hidden from the people that there were in their midst three women fighting for their faith. But the prison has been picketed day and night, and all people have seen and heard that three women fighting for their cause with their lives lay within. Hundreds have learnt more about the cause of the Suffragettes in looking at this demonstration of solidarity and loyalty.[40]

The third woman – admitted to Perth prison on the day (3 July) that Frances Gordon was released – was Maude Edwards, who had slashed the picture of the King in the Royal Scottish Academy. The report of her trial at Edinburgh Sheriff Court was headlined 'STORMY COURT SCENES' in the *Edinburgh Evening Dispatch* (3 July). At the beginning of the trial she shouted to the Sheriff, Lord Maconachie, 'I will not be tried. I am not going to listen to you or anyone whatever.' The Sheriff took this as a plea of not guilty. When suffragettes applauded he ordered the court to be cleared. 'This was an operation attended with some difficulty and no little amusement', reported the *Evening Dispatch*. Many women resisted the efforts of the policemen to eject them, especially Dr Grace Cadell who 'required three officers to remove her.' From the dock Maude Edwards kept up a running fire of commentary, making so much noise that some witnesses had to cross the court to give evidence where the jury could hear them. She was sentenced to three months' imprisonment.

Dr Ferguson Watson examined Maude Edwards on 4 July. She was in a somewhat hysterical state; the medical officer reported that 'she did not behave like a sane person.' One reason why she braved such a public act which she knew must result in her arrest and imprisonment, in spite of English precedents for forcible feeding, was because she had armed herself with a medical certificate stating that she had a cardiac condition and could not be forcibly fed without mortal risk.[41]

From remarks which she made to Dr Ferguson Watson at the outset she clearly felt safe from forcible feeding, but although he did not consider her 'a very good case for feeding' he saw no reason why he should not try. He placed little credence in the medical certificate 'because it was written by a *lady doctor* [his emphasis] who is not now able to judge whether forcible feeding will do any harm.' In his daily reports on Maude Edwards's condition he admitted that if she struggled or fought there would be very real danger to her, but as she always remained passive during the operation – clearly terrified of the effects of doing anything else – he continued the regime. She suffered a great deal of sickness and vomiting, and on 8 July he reported: 'She is not a very good case for feeding as there is much congestion of the stomach owing to cardiac dilation...but I am satisfied I can detain her quite as long as Frances Gordon without doing any further harm to her diseased condition.'

On 10 July Maude Edwards applied to the prison commissioners to be liberated under licence and undertook 'to refrain from militancy in the future.' ('My special reason for making such an offer', she added, 'is the fact that the medical officer of the prison tells me that excitement is injurious to my heart.'). She was liberated on 14 July. Maude Edwards was not amongst those willing to die for the cause.

While she was in prison the Royal visit to Scotland took place, and though there were no serious incidents, the suffragettes certainly made their presence felt. The King and Queen arrived in Edinburgh on 6 July and made the city their base for a week while they toured the cities and industrial centres of the Lowlands. An incident on the evening of their arrival was the first of many. Two women were on a balcony at the east end of Rutland Street, facing the entrance to the railway station. A detective remembered ejecting one of them (said to be from Dundee) from a public meeting and therefore kept an eye on them. When the Royal carriage passed the balcony the woman stood up; she was seized by the detective but managed to throw a package and pamphlets which did not, however, reach the carriage. The package contained a small rubber ball with a label attached to it with the words 'To remind HM King George V that women are being tortured in prison'. The women were taken to the police station, but no charges were pressed against them.[42]

The following day, when the royal procession took place in Glasgow, banners were displayed in Argyle Street, Old Dumbarton Road, Bank Street, Great Western Road, and Sauchiehall Street, with the words 'We implore Your Majesty to stop forcible feeding in Perth Prison.' The same words were spoken through a megaphone in various streets, and petitions were thrown at the Royal couple in the grounds of the Western Infirmary and at the university. Banners were also displayed and petitions thrown in other towns, such as Dalmuir and Dumbarton, and when the King visited the Clyde shipyards a woman with a megaphone appealed to him to stop forcible feeding.[43]

In Dundee the WSPU organiser, Olive Walton, climbed to the roof of the office in the Nethergate, but the police had been watching this obvious vantage point, and she was forced to climb down. However, she found a spot along the route of the procession and flung what was first thought to be a bomb, but which turned out to be another rubber ball with a petition attached, into the Royal carriage. Olive Walton also managed to throw a rubber ball with a petition attached into the Queen's lap while Her Majesty was leaving St Giles' Cathedral in Edinburgh by coach on the Sunday.[44]

The likeliest city for suffragette incidents was, of course, Perth, where a young woman dressed in black dashed out from the crowd, placed her foot on the step of the Royal car, and struck at the window of the car before being dragged off by the police. (She gave her name as Rhoda Fleming and the WSPU address in Glasgow.) The *Suffragette* and the *Forward* insisted that no animosity was shown to any of the women protesting to the King and Queen; the Scottish press on the other hand depicted great hostility, so much so that police protection alone prevented the women from being injured by the angry crowds. The impression one gets from Scottish newspapers – several of which carried special photographic supplements – is of almost hysterical adulation over the Royal visit, which makes the latter reaction the more convincing one.[45]

Helen Crawfurd was supposed to be on picket duty in Perth the day of the Royal visit, but she was keen to see the procession, so another woman took her place. The police spotted her among the onlookers; they had left her alone when she was making speeches but obviously thought she had designs on the King and Queen, and she was rearrested under the Cat and Mouse Act. She, too, was consigned to Perth prison but was not forcibly fed, and after five days of hunger striking she was released. She claimed in her memoirs that this was because the authorities were afraid of trouble, but the prison files reveal that it was because her original conviction was for such a minor offence (breaking two windows) and because she willingly drank potash water; in other words she was not worth the bother.[46]

Before, during and after the Royal visit other protests also occurred in Perth. One evening Muriel Scott addressed a large crowd at the High Street Port. 'In the course of a pathetic appeal on behalf of her sister', reported the *Dundee Advertiser* (8 July), 'Miss Muriel [sic] became so affected that she was compelled to resume her seat for a time, while many of her audience were also visibly affected.' Subsequently she invited her audience to follow her to the prison where she would attempt to see her sister. By the time she reached the Edinburgh Road the crowd numbered nearly 2,000. On her call 'three cheers were raised, while a couple of verses of "Scots Wha Hae" were sung.' (But her attempt to see her sister was unsuccessful.)

Prayers for the prisoners were interjected by suffragettes into services at Perth churches most Sundays in July. Even cinema performances were interrupted with appeals. In London the Secretary for Scotland was attacked with a dog whip by two suffragettes who called themselves Wallace and Bertha Watson. One of them yelled, 'You Scotch pig. If you don't stop forcible feeding we shall smash you up, and you can't say you have not been thrashed by a woman.' In court they demanded that the case should be adjourned for the attendance of Mackinnon Wood. The magistrate said this was unnecessary, and when the women were sentenced to 14 days' imprisonment they refused to leave the court and had to be carried out, kicking and shrieking.[47]

More insidious was the pressure put on the staff of Perth prison by the constant picket at the gates. On 8 July the there was a tip-off that the suffragettes intended to damage property that night; the governor posted six officers outside the boundary wall until 2.30 am but 'nothing unusual occurred'. On the evening of the 11th a warden saw a man and two women measuring the ground to the north of the boundary wall 'in rather a suspicious manner.' The governor informed the police and 'took precautions by sending a number of the staff to patrol the outside boundary wall, which was kept up until daylight.' The only thing that happened that night was that a woman shouted a message of support through a megaphone. The governor added: 'The officers whose houses are facing the Edinburgh Road inform me that they cannot get sleep at night with the noise caused by the suffragette picket and their followers.' On the 12th he noted that the suffragettes and their followers had created a disturbance by singing hymns at night until they were moved on by the police. On the 20th he recorded a suffragette meeting at the prison gates with about 2,000–3,000 people present.[48]

Although Arabella Scott was the last prisoner released, another woman was also forcibly fed at Perth prison. Fanny Parker has been absent from this book for quite a while. She ceased to be the Dundee WSPU organiser some time in 1913; in view of the fact that she was now caught attempting to destroy a Scottish national monument it may be conjectured that in the preceding months she had been similarly employed. The house which she and another woman hoped to blow up was Burns's Cottage, the birthplace of the poet at Alloway, near Ayr. Not surprisingly, this enraged the press.[49] Yet some papers related that at court she calmed a distraught woman who had been sentenced to pay a fine or go to prison for 10 days for receiving stolen goods, eventually paying the woman's fine so that she went free, an action at odds with the usual press caricature of a hysterical suffragette virago.[50]

The attempt on Burns's Cottage was foiled by a watchman, who had been employed for more than a year against such an eventuality. At 2.30 am he discovered two women on the premises and grabbed one of them while the other escaped; subsequently two 'bomb-like objects' were

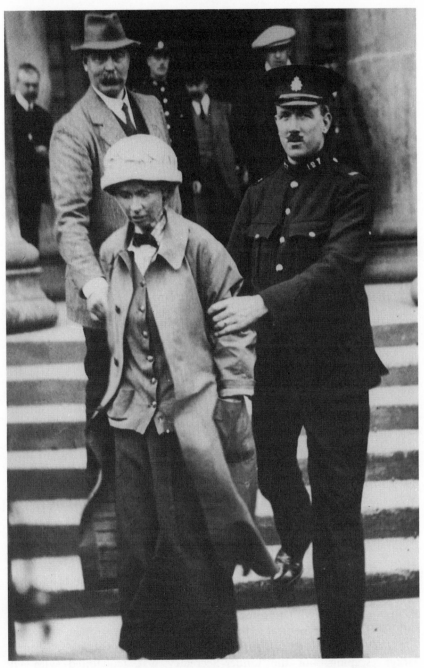

25 Fanny Parker as Janet Arthur escorted from Ayr Sheriff Court. Reproduced
by permission of the Keeper of the Records of Scotland (HH16/43)

found.[51] The captured woman said her name was Janet Arthur, and it was a while before she was identified as Fanny Parker.

As an untried prisoner on hunger strike she posed a dilemma to the Scottish Office. Neither bail nor release under the Cat and Mouse Act seemed a realistic option. Dr Dunlop examined her and reported that she would have to be liberated in a few days if she continued hunger striking. The preferred option was a 'house arrest' in a nursing home in Ayr, and Janie Allan tried to persuade her to go there, but she refused to go anywhere except to a house of her own choice in Prestwick (presumably Janie Allan's house). The Prison Commission would have allowed that, but the police would not undertake to watch the house even at Scottish Office expense; the Procurator Fiscal urged her removal to Perth, and on 13 July she was transferred there. She had been without food or drink since the 9th and was forcibly fed from the 13th until her release on the 16th. In spite of the furore over Frances Gordon, feeding by tube was again supplemented by rectal feeding.[52]

This is the only known Scottish case where family influence was brought to bear on behalf of a suffragette prisoner. She was a niece of Lord Kitchener and when her brother, Captain Parker, intervened, the Under Secretary for Scotland, the Chairman of the Prison Commission, and the medical prison commissioner, James Devon, all agreed to see him. The fact that he declared 'no sympathy with his sister's views' was another point in his favour. His main request, apart from her release, was that a second doctor be allowed to examine her. After long discussions Fanny Parker was released to be taken by her brother to a nursing home in Edinburgh, and to be examined by a doctor of his choice, Dr Chalmers Watson.

The prison medical officer, Dr Ferguson Watson, had fears about Fanny Parker's condition during the first day or two of forcible feeding, but by the 16th when she was liberated he considered it to be very satisfactory. However, Dr Chalmers Watson found her to be 'a very thin woman in a state of pronounced collapse' who would take several weeks to regain anything like her usual health. She complained of pain in the genital region, and the medical examination revealed swelling and rawness, which Dr Chalmers Watson attributed this to 'rough and faulty introduction of instruments'; Fanny Parker referred not only to rectal feeding but to 'a grosser and more indecent outrage'. Dr Chalmers Watson expressed his distaste for the whole business with the words 'I sincerely hope that I will have no more medical experience of forcibly fed women.'

The Scottish Office was still jittery about the possibility of Fanny Parker escaping, but the Under-Secretary was acquainted with Dr Chalmers Watson and did not think that he would 'lend himself to any tricks.' On 28 July Dr Chalmers Watson informed the police that between

5 and 6 pm on the previous evening Fanny Parker had 'walked out of the Chalmers Street Nursing Home unobserved by anybody.'

Unlike the women who had horrific but short experiences of forcibly feeding, Arabella Scott endured five weeks of it. Although there were at one time four suffragettes in Perth prison, they were kept isolated. They were allowed no letters and no visitors and were not even permitted to sit up as this produced vomiting. The only faces that Arabella Scott saw for five weeks were those of prison staff, who watched her night and day. The medical officer's daily reports – in which he constantly reiterated that her condition was 'satisfactory' and that she was 'fit for further treatment' – reveal wide fluctuations of mood on her part.[53]

In the early hours of 2 July, for example, after being awakened by thunder and lightning 'she became very depressed and expressed the hope that she would be struck by the lightning.' On the 5th she 'was excited for the greater part of the day yesterday and required three wardresses to restrain her.' On 7 July he wrote: 'As she has threatened "to do something that will cause her release" very special precautions are being taken...lest she make some impulsive attempt on her own life.' On the night of 18 July her sister called through a megaphone 'Arabella, Arabella, fight on, you are bound to win'.

In early reports Dr Ferguson Watson emphasised the lack of resistance on Arabella Scott's part, but on the 14th he confessed that she had 'on two separate occasions which I forgot to record, stated in front of several wardresses and myself that she would shoot me when she got out.' (He also confessed that within a few days of her arrival she had bitten his left forefinger which became septic.)

On 23 July the Chairman of the Prison Commissioner wrote to the Scottish Office that he felt bound to recommend Arabella Scott's liberation soon on licence. He did not doubt that she could be kept longer but only 'at a tremendous strain and cost, and as we cannot keep her for anything like her whole sentence and have shewn her and her friends that we can keep her for a good while at a time, I think we may just as well liberate her now.' He went on to say more about the strain imposed on the prison system: six extra wardresses brought in, holidays stopped and working overtime, extra men posted day and night at the outer gates. 'The governor was on point of resignation, the Medical officer did resign. The Matron and female staff much strained and all nervous and irritable.'

Arabella Scott was released under licence on 26 July, and a press report gloated that she was in 'good bodily health'. In a letter published in the *Glasgow Herald* she stated that the only effect of her experience was 'to strengthen my principles.'[54]

Throughout July both the *Suffragette* and the suffrage column of the *Forward* commented on the effect that the suffragette pickets and speakers

were having on the citizens of Perth. At a special meeting of Perth Trades
Council on 21 July members resolved to protest against forcible feeding of
suffragettes in Perth prison and to petition members of Parliament on the
subject. This was entirely on their own initiative. The secretary of the
Council, Mr J.M. Rae, who had called the meeting, said

> The militant section had carried the war into their midst, and in doing so
> they had taught them much that they had been ignorant of. Twelve months
> ago a militant could not receive a hearing, and was hooted and bawled at as
> if she were a fanatic. Now, large crowds nightly assembled to hear and
> express sympathy with them. No one could stand and listen to the recital of
> the sufferings of those confined in their prison unmoved.[55]

It is difficult to imagine what might have happened if the Great War had
not broken out. Non-militant campaigning would have continued, but
the violent militant campaign in Scotland would certainly have gone on
and presumably nullified constitutional efforts. Arabella Scott had at one
time given an undertaking to her school board to commit no further acts
of militancy and had kept her pledge, but this had not stopped her being
forcibly fed for weeks, so that one can hardly be surprised that, at the time
of her release, she felt 'more militant than ever'; Dr Ferguson Watson
opined that she was 'about to do something desperate'.[56] The prison
experiences of Ethel Moorhead and Fanny Parker can only have hardened
their militancy. The Scottish Office really had no way of keeping such
women in prison, yet the government was as determined as ever not to
give in to 'terrorism'.

As it happened, within a week of Arabella Scott's release all this became
irrelevant. The assassination of Archduke Franz Ferdinand in Sarajevo on
28 June received plenty of coverage in the Scottish press but not as
something that directly affected Britain. Eunice Murray wrote in her
diary: 'The Austrian heir has been murdered in Serbia. The papers are
making much of this, but surely nothing very serious could result from
it.'[57] During July it dropped out of the news, and fears of civil war in
Ireland claimed more attention. It was not until the end of the month that
the British public realised the implications of what was happening on the
Continent. When Belgium was threatened Britain sent an ultimatum to
Germany, and when it was ignored – on 4 August – war was declared.

The WSPU immediately announced a truce on militancy and the
leadership threw its support behind the war effort. Following the lead of
the Home Office, the Secretary for Scotland announced on 10 August the
mitigation of all sentences on suffragettes passed in Scottish courts (and
Fanny Parker was not to be tried). Women did not yet have the vote, but
militancy was at an end.

The War Years and After

In August 1914 Emmeline and Christabel Pankhurst did not merely suspend militancy; they dropped all suffrage work entirely and threw themselves into the war effort. Eunice Murray of the Women's Freedom League recorded in her diary: 'The WSPU has dissolved & left all their organisers unpaid, several applied to me for help to get them to their various homes.'[1] The Pankhurst telescope vision, which for so many years beheld no other goal besides votes for women, now alighted upon the 'Hun' as an enemy more heinous than the Liberal Government, and they redirected their energies to rousing the fighting spirit of the nation. The *Suffragette* became *Britannia*, and white feathers were handed out. How many women – either Scottish or English – followed such an extreme example is not known, but Jean Lambie of the Edinburgh WSPU became organising secretary of a breakaway organisation, 'The Suffragettes of the W.S.P.U.', who aimed to 'entirely disassociate themselves from the line Mrs Pankhurst has taken up since the outbreak of war'.[2]

While the Pankhurst jingoism represented one end of the spectrum, women peace campaigners represented the other. The NUWSS executive committee was bitterly divided. The president, Millicent Garrett Fawcett, adopted a pro-war stance, as did some other central executive committee members like Lady Frances Balfour, but in 1915 many of the executive committee resigned and devoted themselves to organisations working for peace. Amongst them was Chrystal Macmillan, who became Secretary of the International Committee of Women for Permanent Peace, in Amsterdam.[3]

Sylvia Pankhurst had remained true to the socialist principles long since abandoned by her mother and Christabel, and in 1913 when she was expelled from the WSPU she formed the East London Federation of Suffragettes (later Workers' Suffrage Federation), which had had its own journal, the *Woman's Dreadnought* (later *Workers' Dreadnought*). This organisation, both before and during the war, was a focal point for socialist suffragettes. At least two Scottish women, Mary Phillips and

Jessie Stephen, were employed as organisers. (However, Sylvia Pankhurst, of necessity, spent far more time and energy attempting to mitigate the effects of the war on working-class women than in campaigning for peace.) Within Scotland, the socialist newspaper, the *Forward*, was anti-war, and on 10 June 1916 the Women's Peace Crusade was launched in Glasgow, with Helen Crawfurd as one of the initiators and a speaker at the first major demonstration, at Glasgow Green on 23 July.[4]

Chrystal Macmillan and Helen Crawfurd are the only Scottish suffrage campaigners known to have worked actively for peace. There may have been others whose activities were less prominent, but although the Women's Peace Crusade was launched in Glasgow, it does seem that English women outnumbered Scots in peace campaigns.

The rights and wrongs of the war were not the major preoccupations of most suffragists/suffragettes. With the main breadwinner of the family going off to fight, women and children needed help and relief. In August 1914 societies affiliated to the Scottish Federation followed the line set by the executive committee and suspended 'all political activity', throwing themselves into various schemes to ease life for the women and children left behind. But the fact that they stuck together in their tightly-organised societies meant that when women's suffrage returned to the political agenda they could take concerted action.

At the outbreak of the war, the Dundee Women's Suffrage Society offered its entire organisation – office, staff, and the services of its members – to the city of Dundee, to aid in any municipal schemes for the relief of distress caused by the war. The offer was publicly accepted by the Lord Provost; his wife, Lady Urquhart, became convener of the Dundee Women's War Relief Committee, while the honorary secretary of the Dundee Women's Suffrage Society, Mary Henderson, became honorary secretary. They mobilised women of all shades of opinion (including anti-suffragists) and soon spread beyond their original headquarters to form branch depots in each of the eleven municipal wards.[5]

The Edinburgh National Society for Women's Suffrage undertook the visiting and care of the wives and dependants of fighting men in Leith, and other forms of relief work. Members of the Inverness Women's Suffrage Society were on all the relief committees and qualified as Red Cross nurses. The Glasgow and West of Scotland Association opened an Exchange for Voluntary Workers and engaged in various fund-raising activities. The minutes of the Association for the war years convey a sense of vigorous, purposeful activity, suggesting that members found such practical work far more fulfilling than their earlier fruitless campaigning for the vote; not least because they now received praise and tangible support for their efforts.[6]

The most important Scottish Federation initiative was the Scottish Women's Hospitals. It was the idea of Dr Elsie Inglis to set up special units of female doctors, nurses and ambulance drivers to work on the Front. Initially the War Office refused to have anything to do with it, so money had to be raised from private sources. The NUWSS was willing to adopt the scheme but wanted the hospital to be called the NUWSS Scottish Federation Hospital; the Scottish Federation was determined to call it the Scottish Women's Hospital for Foreign Service.[7]

Elsie Inglis wrote to the NUWSS president, Mrs Fawcett, to explain the Scottish Federation's stance. The original scheme was growing into something 'much bigger than anything we had thought of at the beginning.' A hospital with a neutral name would attract wide support from men and women. Dr Inglis reassured Mrs Fawcett that 'NUWSS' would appear at the head of all appeals, press notices and papers.

> But – if you could reverse the position, – & imagine for a moment that the Anti-suffrage Society had thought of organising all these skilled women for Service – you can see that many more neutrals, & a great many more suffragists would have been ready to help if they sent their subscriptions to the 'Scottish Women's Hospital for Foreign Service', than if they had to send it to the Anti-Suffrage League Hospital.[8]

The NUWSS assented, and by the end of October enough money had come in for Dr Inglis to form a unit ('Our hospital is secure, and it is to go to Serbia'); by mid-November a second unit had been raised, to go to France. Raising funds for the Scottish Women's Hospitals was an important activity for Scottish societies. And when the Scottish Women's Hospitals proved their worth – a story well documented elsewhere – the credit and pride was shared by the Scottish suffrage movement.[9]

At the beginning of the war – before they were called to work in munitions factories and to replace the men swallowed up by the war – many women were thrown out of work, and their plight was a major concern of Women's Freedom League branches. A Women's Suffrage National Aid Corps was formed (Eunice Murray was on the executive committee), with branches in Edinburgh and Glasgow. Both these branches turned their WFL shops into workrooms for girls who had lost their employment, to make garments for Belgian refugees.[10]

In 1915 the WFL started a new department based in London, the WFL National Service Organisation; its purpose was to 'bring women workers in touch with employers and find the right work for the right women.' The honorary organiser was Miss Frances M. Parker ('who has had long

experience in the Woman Suffrage Movement'), with the assistance of
Miss Ethel Moorhead. This says a lot about the respect maintained
between the WSPU and the WFL, and the choice of these Scottish WSPU
members to initiate a national scheme says something about the high
regard in which they were held. (After a visit by Miss Parker to the
Glasgow branch of the WFL, a branch of the National Service Organisation was also started there.)[11]

But though the Women's Freedom League undertook relief work,
unlike the NUWSS it did not suspend political activity. Martin Pugh
noted that the WFL took advantage of the 'slackened efforts of their rivals
to make up their membership figures.' While the Glasgow and West of
Scotland Association was apologising to all and sundry that it could no
longer provide speakers on women's suffrage as promised, the WFL had
Ada Broughton addressing the Renfrew Co-operative Women's Guild
and many other suffrage speakers operating in Scotland.[12]

The WFL had a particular cause to rally round when curfews and other
discriminatory measures were passed against soldiers' wives; in January
1915 demonstrations were organised in London and Edinburgh. Two
months later the WFL asked the Prime Minister to receive a deputation to
press for an emergency measure granting votes to women in view of their
major contribution to the war effort. Eunice Murray also approached the
Secretary for Scotland along the same lines (on the grounds that the WFL
was particularly strong in Scotland). Both requests were refused.[13]

In January 1916 Eunice Murray 'in an eloquent and impassioned speech'
urged the Dundee branch of the WFL to go on demanding the vote, since
when the war ended 'many pressing problems will have to be faced, not
the least of these being the struggle which is certain to take place between
Capital and Labour and woman's place in the labour market. Without the
protection of the vote women will be in danger of being thrown
overboard.' A few months later she wrote a stirring piece about the effect
of wartime independence on the attitudes toward the vote of women
previously in domestic service and other subservient positions.[14]

Rather surprisingly, the other organisation that continued to campaign
was the Northern Men's Federation for Women's Suffrage. Just after the
outbreak of the war Maud Arncliffe-Sennett asked Janie Allan if she
would take over its organisation. She declined, partly because she had a
low opinion of men who needed a woman to prod them into action,
partly because she was exhausted and had 'orders to rest', and partly
because she thought that 'we must all work to relieve distress arising from
the war & this will I expect tax all our energies for many months to
come.'[15] (Janie Allan subsequently offered to accommodate a convales-
cent soldier. She was also on a committee, which included Helen
Crawfurd – initiated by Margaret Irwin of the Scottish Council for

Women's Trades – to help women who had lost their jobs.[16]) So Maud Arncliffe-Sennett continued as president of the Northern Men's Federation.

The *Edinburgh Evening Dispatch* (3 May 1915) gave the headline 'WOMEN'S WAR WORK – "PROVING THEIR RIGHT TO THE VOTE"' to its report of the Federation's first open-air meeting of 1915. It was held in Edinburgh, in the Meadows, with J. Wilson McLaren presiding 'over a large audience'. A much bigger demonstration was held there on 18 July, to celebrate the second anniversary of the deputation of men to Asquith on 18 July 1913. Maud Arncliffe-Sennett came up for the meeting, and Elizabeth Finlayson Gauld was the other female speaker. Many members, including Councillors Crawford and Cameron, were serving with the army, but there were enough men left for three platforms to be set up. The *Evening Dispatch* gave the event sympathetic coverage, though the reporter thought that one platform would have been better, as it was a fine sunny day, and the crowd of about a thousand drifted between platforms rather than stand and listen to speeches from beginning to end. At a Northern Men's Federation meeting in August 1916 J. Wilson McLaren 'expressed warm appreciation of the fair and impartial manner in which the meeting and deputations of the Federation had been reported in the Edinburgh Press.'[17]

It is ironic that women's suffrage returned to the political agenda at a time when there was little agitation for it – though without the pre-war pressure it would not have happened. The annual revision of the electoral register had been suspended in 1914, and during the war very few men would be found at the addresses where they had been previously registered. Moreover, for a man to qualify as a householder he had to occupy a dwelling for at least a year preceding an election, so if a new register were compiled on the basis of the old qualifications most of the men away fighting would be ineligible. In order to accommodate soldiers and sailors the franchise would have to be widened, which required legislation. In the spring of 1916 the NUWSS president, Millicent Fawcett, wrote to Asquith to stress that, in view of women's important role in the war effort, a women's suffrage clause must be included in any new bill. Asquith replied that no legislation was then contemplated, but that he fully appreciated the magnificent contribution by women and promised that the points made in her letter would be fully considered.[18]

By this time the press was full of praise for all the work women were doing. Eunice Murray wrote a Women's Freedom League pamphlet about this, entitled *Woman – The New Discovery*, which was more than a little cynical about men's sudden realisation of women's capabilities. While anti-suffrage arguments by no means ceased, it did become harder to credit women for everything from their dangerous work in munitions factories to running essential services yet claim that they were unfit to vote.

There was now a coalition government, so party lines no longer ruled in the same way. And the suspension of militancy meant that a government passing a women's suffrage measure at this time could not be accused of giving in to terrorism. Martin Pugh commented that Christabel 'quickly perceived that war provided the chance to withdraw without loss of face from an untenable position', and the same could be said for many anti-suffragists. Lord Balfour of Burleigh thought that 'the War gave a very good excuse to a large number of excellent people, who had up to that time been on the wrong side, to change their minds.'[19]

In August 1916 Asquith himself gave up his opposition to women's enfranchisement, and in due course an all-party conference of Members of both Houses, presided over by the Speaker of the House of Commons, was appointed to draft proposals on the franchise and registration. While the conference was deliberating, the situation in Parliament improved still further for the women's cause, for in December 1916 Asquith was superseded as Prime Minister of the Coalition Government by Lloyd George, who had never opposed the principle of women's suffrage.

There was still the question of how wide a franchise might be granted to women. A demonstration in Glasgow on 25 June 1916 called for the vote to be given to every man and woman over 21, and many socialists continued to press for full adult suffrage.[20] However, MPs were scared because women outnumbered men – and would do so to an even greater extent after the war – and because female voters were an unknown factor. Seeking to limit the effect, the conference at the end of January 1917 proposed restricting the vote to female householders and the wives of householders, over a certain age – 30 or 35.

The NUWSS and WFL were unwilling to accept an age limit of 35 but agreed to 30, and that was the age limit that appeared in the Representation of the People Bill. The Bill passed its Second Reading. Before the crucial day (19 June) when the House was to debate the women's suffrage clause the NUWSS mobilised its societies to write to MPs and to ask local councils and other influential bodies to send resolutions to MPs.[21] In Edinburgh the WFL got together with the NUWSS, the Scottish Churches League for Woman Suffrage, and the Conservative and Unionist Women's Franchise Association for a 'tremendously successful' mass meeting at the Mound in support of the inclusion of women in the Bill.[22] When the division came 385 MPs voted in favour of the clause and only 55 against it.

All but the most fervent adult suffragists were thrilled by this result. Even the *Forward* commented that 'compared with the slow entrance of the male, prolonged over half a century, the promised extension to women is, for them, as favourable a sample of the British practice of compromise as history warranted us to expect.' The idea persists that the vote was conferred on women as some kind of reward though, as Martin Pugh commented, 'it would not then have been consistent to refuse to enfranchise the younger women who were largely engaged in munitions factories.' At the time the *Edinburgh Evening Dispatch* refused to 'belittle women's influence and the new power which is about to be placed in their hands' by claiming that the franchise was a reward for their work in the war: 'Such an assertion is not creditable either to the nation that confers the boon or the women who receive it.'[23]

However, the Bill still had to go to the House of Lords. The NUWSS organised a memorial to the Lords from women war workers, and the Union's societies wrote to appropriate women in their district asking them to sign it.[24] In December 1917 the Bill was debated in the Lords, and Brian Harrison has commented that the high quality of the debate 'suggests that the conclusion there was not yet foregone'. The former Marchioness of Tullibardine, now Duchess of Atholl, remained as anti-suffrage as ever for she believed that 'the arguments advanced in pre-war days by Anti-Suffragists apply with more force than ever to-day.'[25] However, the tide had irrevocably turned, and on 10 January 1918 the women's suffrage clause passed the Lords; the Representation of the People Act received Royal Assent on 6 February 1918.

In the final edition of the *Anti-Suffrage Review* Lady Griselda Cheape wrote, 'We were anti-suffragist, and we are so, as God made man to rule; but the vote has been thrust on us, and we must use it, but let us use it prayerfully, carefully and trying to love our neighbour as ourself.' At the other end of the political spectrum, Sylvia Pankhurst was very dissatisfied with such a limited measure. And women who were over thirty but did not fall into specific categories were also angry. Jean Morrison related that her step-sister, Margaret Robertson, was unmarried and lived at home with her mother and therefore did not qualify for the vote. However, the statute did give the vote to lodgers renting unfurnished rooms for which they provided the furniture, so by buying a piece of furniture from her mother Miss Robertson got the vote. Ellen Wilkinson later remarked in the Commons: 'a woman has to have a husband or some other furniture to vote'.[26]

The NUWSS held a public meeting in London to celebrate the passing of the Act, while in Scotland the Freedom League and the Glasgow and West of Scotland Association had a 'Joint Local Celebration'.[27] After 1918 the NUWSS became the National Union of Women for Equal Citizenship, and the Edinburgh Society became the Edinburgh National Society for Equal Citizenship, with Frances Simson (late of the Scottish Universities Women's Suffrage Union) as president and Rosaline Masson, late of the Conservative and Unionist Women's Franchise Association, as honorary press secretary. However, for the most part, suffrage societies quietly disbanded.

Many members of disbanded suffrage societies joined newly-created Women Citizens Associations. The secretary of the Women Citizens Association in Edinburgh in 1920 was Agnes MacDonald, who before the war was secretary of the Edinburgh branch of the WSPU. Two former Glasgow WSPU activists, Margaret McPhun and Mrs S.C. Wilson, were on the executive committee of the Glasgow Women Citizens Association, and the president was Frances Melville, late of the Scottish Universities Women's Suffrage Union. Mrs Mill, a leading Liberal 'suffrage before party' activist, was the president of the Dundee Women Citizens Association, and Agnes Husband (president of the Dundee branch of the Women's Freedom League) was on the executive committee.[28]

Not only were women 30 and over given the vote in 1918, a bill was also rushed through enabling them to stand for Parliament – something which they had always publicly claimed they did not crave. These rights were first exercised at the 1919 General Election, which resulted in another Coalition Government, with Lloyd George as Prime Minister. Christabel Pankhurst stood as a candidate but was defeated. It is ironic that the only woman mentioned in this book who went on to become a Member of Parliament was the Duchess of Atholl who, as Marchioness of Tullibardine, had been one of Scotland's leading anti-suffragists.[29] Helen Fraser stood as a Liberal candidate three times without success before resigning from the Party.[30]

During the 1920s the WFL continued to press for a wider franchise.[31] That was a very different era, with none of the drama of the Edwardian struggle. When all women over the age of 21 were given the vote in 1928 this had less to do with feminist agitation and more to do with the realisation that all the dire predictions of the effects of women voting had proved unfounded.

What of the women who devoted so much energy to the cause of women's suffrage? Anna Munro became a magistrate in England and Lila Clunas of the Women's Freedom League was a member of Dundee Town Council for some years; other Scottish suffragists probably found similar niches in local government.[32] Few of the leading activists can be traced in later years. In the 1920s Ethel Moorhead was in Paris co-editing an English-language review of art and literature. Catherine Blair established the first Scottish Women's Rural Institute in 1917 and in 1919 founded the Mak'Merry pottery studio. Nannie Brown and Elizabeth Finlayson Gauld were also involved in the Scottish Women's Rural Institutes. The Edinburgh home of Sarah Elizabeth Siddons Mair remained a centre for all kinds of activity connected with women's issues until her death in

1941.[33] Eunice Murray's book *Scottish Women of Bygone Days* was published in 1930, and another book, *A Gallery of Scottish Women* in 1931.

Those women looked forward. Others looked back on the suffrage years with nostalgia for an unrepeatable intensity of experience and comraderie. A decade or so after the war such women formed the Suffragette Fellowship to keep the memories alive. Reading the correspondence (particularly letters querying a particular woman's eligibility which hinged on whether she had *really* been in Holloway) one cannot help finding this obsession with that part of their lives somewhat morbid. Some Scottish women, like Amy Sanderson and the McPhun sisters, provided information about themselves, but when Janie Allan was asked about her suffrage activities and imprisonment, she replied (on 13 January 1931), 'I don't really think the details you ask for would be of the slightest interest to anyone!'. This may not have been true, but it does seem healthier. When former suffragettes were invited to the unveiling of Emmeline Pankhurst's statue in 1930, Elizabeth Finlayson Gauld wrote a pathetic appeal to be included; she had been an invalid for many years and her part in the women's suffrage movement had been forgotten.[34]

But, then, that is true of nearly all the Scottish women who devoted themselves to the cause. They have been almost forgotten: yet never has any other cause mobilised so many women the length and breadth of Scotland in the way that 'Votes for Women' did before World War I.

Conclusion

This book began with the question 'why study the women's suffrage movement in Scotland?'. There is a plethora of books on the subject of women's struggle for the parliamentary franchise, but with very few exceptions (most notably, *One Hand Tied Behind Us* by Jill Liddington and Jill Norris and, more recently, *The Life and Death of Emily Wilding Davison* by Ann Morley with Liz Stanley), they have looked at the national leadership or events at Westminster. That emphasis has seriously distorted the picture of a movement that was truly national.

The concentration on the Pankhursts has fostered the belief that the Women's Social and Political Union was a centralised and autocratic organisation whose members had little choice but to obey the dictates of their leaders. This view has recently been challenged by Morley and Stanley, and what has been seen of the activities of WSPU members in Scotland demonstrates a high degree of independence and autonomy. Probably a study of English regions – or of Wales – would reveal a similar story.

What a study of English regions might not reveal is the part played by the Women's Freedom League, since its membership was so unevenly spread in the country. Dismissed by historians as weak and ineffectual, the WFL's continuing presence in Scottish cities shows its hidden strength; it could cooperate with both militants and non-militants, and it continued its feminist campaigning long after the vote was won.

The National Union of Women's Suffrage Societies has received insufficient attention by historians, although this neglect will be ameliorated by David Rubinstein's biography of Millicent Garrett Fawcett. His study must, of necessity, look at the NUWSS at national level, as have all other historians apart from Liddington and Norris. My own account has tried to redress the balance by presenting the activities of local societies, which underpinned the women's suffrage movement across Britain.

Until now the relationship between the different suffrage organisations has been little explored. This is understandable since at national level they worked independently; only at local level can one see the cooperation and shifts of allegiance between them. The details of suffrage campaigning at local level are not all that has been lost by an preoccupation with national events and figures; key individuals who did not happen to live in London (or leave published memoirs) have been forgotten. How can one appreciate the composition and strength of the movement without knowing something of the individuals – not just the national leaders – who fuelled it?

All this is as true of England as of Scotland, yet we have also seen the 'Scottishness' of the Scottish movement. The situation in Scotland was quite different from that in Ireland, where the independence issue fostered a separate women's suffrage movement. Scottish suffragists were proud to be part of Britain and part of the British movement, without ever losing their parallel sense of being Scottish. In what Christopher Smout has called 'concentric loyalty', they could as easily back up their arguments with examples of women voting in England under Queen Elizabeth as with defiant women martyred in the Covenanting period or William Wallace fighting for Scottish liberties (the popularity of the song 'Scots Wha Hae' amongst Scottish suffragettes has been noted more than once).

The class composition of the movement in Scotland has been revealed as similar to that in England, i.e. largely middle class. There were socialist suffragettes in Glasgow and Dundee, as in the east end of London. Correspondence columns in the Scottish press show as wide a range of views as has been noted by historians of the movement in England. Given the dearth of regional studies, it is impossible to say whether Scottish suffragettes were more or less militant than their English or Welsh counterparts. What was most distinctive in Scotland, as shown in this study, was that unique organisation, the Northern Men's Federation for Women's Suffrage. Male involvement in England has been played down in most histories of the movement, but there certainly was no comparable group of town councillors and magistrates fighting determinedly for the women's cause in the closing years of the struggle.

This previously unknown story of women's struggle for the vote in Scotland adds a new dimension both to the history of women's suffrage in Britain and to the history of modern Scotland.

Notes

Prologue, pp.5 to 10

1 William Ferguson, *Scotland 1689 to the Present* (Edinburgh and London 1968), pp.288-90.
2 *Edinburgh Review* Vol.57 (1833), p.1.
3 Barbara Taylor, *Eve and the New Jerusalem* (London 1983), p.122.
4 Ibid., 276.
5 Dorothy Thompson, *The Chartists* (London 1984), c.7 and 'Women and Nineteenth Century Radical Politics: A Lost Dimension' in Juliet Mitchell and Ann Oakley eds. *The Rights and Wrongs of Women* (Harmondsworth 1976). David Jones, 'Women and Chartism', *History* 68 (1983).
6 L.G. Wright, *Scottish Chartism* (Edinburgh 1953), pp.43 and 105. Alexander Wilson, *The Chartist Movement in Scotland* (Manchester 1970), pp.51, 74, 123, 133, 151, 169-70. There are also many examples of Scottish women's involvement mentioned in the sources cited in Note 5.
7 Thompson, 'Women and Nineteenth-Century Radical Politics', 123. The letter appeared in the *Northern Star* 23 June 1838.
8 James D. Young, *Women and Popular Struggles: A History of Scottish and English Working Class Women, 1500-1984* (Edinburgh 1985), p.70.
9 'The People's Charter familiarly illustrated', *Chartist Circular*, 2 January 1841.
10 *True Scotsman* 10 November 1838.
11 Ibid, 24 November 1838.
12 Dorothy Thompson considered the Chartist movement entirely working class; she writes of the enormous gulf that separated the classes as the reason why so few middle-class men joined. Thompson, *Chartists*, 254-5. L.G. Wright, on the other hand, included a whole chapter on middle-class Chartism in Scotland and wrote of the understanding that existed between the classes. Wright, *Scottish Chartism*, 163-7 and 179. If this is true it is harder to understand why Scottish Chartism did not feed into the women's movement, although there was, of course, a gap in time between the two movements.
13 Robert LeBaron Bingham, 'The Glasgow Emancipation Society 1833-76' (unpublished M.Litt. thesis, Glasgow 1973), pp.125-6.
14 Louis Billington and Rosamund Billington, '"A Burning Zeal for Righteousness": Women in the British Anti-Slavery Movement, 1820-1860', in Jane Rendall ed. *Equal or Different: Women's Politics 1800-1914* (Oxford 1987), p.96.
15 Ibid, p.97. Bingham, 'Glasgow Emancipation Society', 155. C. Duncan Rice, *The Scots Abolitionists 1833-1861* (Baton Rouge 1981), p.42.

16 C. Duncan Rice, *Scots Abolitionists*, 42-3. In *Faces of Feminism* (Oxford 1981), pp.20-5, Olive Banks discusses women in the anti-slavery movement and also the significance of the Quaker sect as a source of feminism, but though she uses the word 'Britain' her evidence appears to be entirely English.

17 Ibid, 44 and 158. Ferguson, *Scotland 1689 to the Present*, 306.

18 Billington and Billington, 'A Burning Zeal', 98-9. The Anti-Corn Law League is claimed by many historians of the women's movement in England to have been the most important catalyst in politicising women. The League certainly existed in Scotland, but I have not found any material to show that it performed a similar function there.

19 Ibid, 111.

20 Foreword to the Edinburgh 1988 edition of *A Plea for Woman* (originally published Edinburgh 1843), pp.vi-vii.

21 John Dunlop, *Autobiography* Dunlop Papers, [V.1] (London 1932), pp.276-7.

22 Forward to 1988 edition of *A Plea for Woman*, v.

23 Like many future promoters of the enfranchisement of her sex, she did not argue for the enfranchisement of all women but merely for the vote to be given to them on the same basis as it was granted to men. However, *unlike* many future promoters of women's suffrage, she made it clear that she could not herself see why a propertyless man should not be able to vote for his representative in Parliament and that she asked for a limited franchise for women simply because she did not wish to suggest that all women should possess a privilege which only some men enjoyed.

24 *A Plea for Woman*, 8-9.

25 *Edinburgh Review* Vol.73 (April 1841), p.209.

26 See Lettice Milne Rae ed., *Ladies in Debate: Being a History of the Ladies' Edinburgh Debating Society 1865-1935* (Edinburgh 1936).

Chapter 1, pp.11 to 31

1 James D. Young, *Women and Popular Struggles: A History of Scottish and English Working Class Women, 1500-1984* (Edinburgh 1985), p.71.

2 Constance Rover, *Women's Suffrage and Party Politics in Britain 1866-1914* (London 1967), p.1.

3 There were four sisters, but the name of the fourth does not appear in any of the sources I looked at. A contemporary, who knew them well, after describing Flora as 'the ablest' and Louisa as 'also a clever woman' went on: 'Another sister was artistic and did much for the Kyrle Society ... while the last was housekeeper and kept all the domestic wheels running smoothly.' E.S. Haldane, *From One Century to Another* (London 1937). See also *Recollections of the Public Work and Home Life of Louisa and Flora Stevenson* (privately printed, Edinburgh n.d.).

4 Jenni Calder, 'Heroes and Hero-makers: Women in Nineteenth-Century Scottish Fiction' in D. Gifford, ed. *The History of Scottish Literature Vol.3* (Aberdeen 1988), p.263.

5 J.B Mackie, *Life and Work of Duncan McLaren* (London 1888), pp.102-3.

6 Letter from Clementina Taylor to Lydia Becker 8 August 1867, Manchester City Library archives, M50/1/2/27.

7 Manchester City Library archives, M50/1/9/1. *Englishwoman's Review* January 1869. Elspeth King, *The Scottish Women's Suffrage Movement* (Glasgow 1978), p.10.

8 *Englishwoman's Review* October 1868.

9 *Cases Decided in the Court of Session*, Third Series, Vol.VII, M.281.

10 Both these articles were found in Manchester City Library archives, M50/1/9/1.

11   Nigel Shepley, *Women of Independent Mind. St George's School, Edinburgh and the Campaign for Women's Education 1888-1988* (Edinburgh 1988), p.6.

12   Rosalind Marshall, *Virgins and Viragos* (London 1983), p.259.

13   Shepley, *Women of Independent Mind*, 6. For a summary of the situation in Glasgow see King, *Scottish Women's Suffrage Movement*, 11-12.

14   For an explanation of the differences see Katherine Burton, ed. *A Memoir of Mrs Crudelius* (Edinburgh 1897), pp.47-8 and 53-5.

15   Rosamund Billington, 'The women's education and suffrage movements, 1850-1914: innovation and institutionalisation' (unpublished Ph.D. thesis, Hull 1976), p.332. Her opinion of the ultra-conservative nature of medical faculties is borne out by Brian Harrison, 'Women's Health and the Women's Movement in Britain: 1840-1940' in Charles Webster ed. *Biology, Medicine and Society* (Brighton 1981).

16   See, for example, Enid H.C.M. Bell, *Storming the Citadel: The Rise of the Woman Doctor* (London 1953).

17   Burton, *Memoir of Mrs Crudelius*, 27.

18   Shepley, *Women of Independent Mind*, 5-6. Lettice Milne Rae ed., *Ladies in Debate: Being a History of the Ladies' Edinburgh Debating Society 1865-1935* (Edinburgh 1936), p.33.

19   *The Attempt*, Vol.V, pp.265-72.

20   Millicent Garrett Fawcett, *What I Remember* (London 1924), p.122.

21   Haldane, *From One Century to Another*, 54.

22   I am indebted to Maureen Lochrie, Paisley Museum, for this information on Jane Arthur.

23   *Women's Suffrage Journal* 1 March 1870.

24   Manchester City Library archive, M50/1/9/1.

25   I am grateful to Alison Gray at Strathyclyde Regional Archives who brought this to my attention.

26   *Paisley and Renfrewshire Gazette* 12 March 1870. I owe this reference and information about Robert Cochrane to Maureen Lochrie, Paisley Museum.

27   *Women's Suffrage Journal* 2 May 1870.

28   Dorothy Thompson, *The Chartists* (London 1984), p.252.

29   *Women's Suffrage Journal* 2 January 1871.

30   Mackie, *Life of Duncan McLaren*, 104. According to Mackie it was Mill's high regard for Duncan McLaren that induced him to come to Edinburgh.

31   *Women's Suffrage Journal* 1 February 1871.

32   Ibid. 1 May 1871.

33   Ibid. 1 August 1871.

34   Ibid. 1 November and 1 December 1871. *Orkney Herald* 11 and 18 October 1871. I am grateful to the archivist at Orkney archive who located and sent me copies of these press reports.

35   *Women's Suffrage Journal* 1 January 1872. On 14 December she delivered a lecture in the Glasgow Athenaeum on 'Illustrations of Womanly Character, derived from the writings of Sir Walter Scott'. Another important English figure, who would become the leader of the non-militant movement in the Edwardian period – Millicent Garrett Fawcett – also spoke on women's suffrage in Scotland at this time. And Lydia Becker returned to Scotland on later occasions. (See *Women's Suffrage Journal* 1 March 1876 and 1 November 1877.)

36   Rae, *Ladies in Debate*, 34.

37   *Women's Suffrage Journal* 1 May 1872. Billington, 'The Women's Education and Suffrage Movements', 461. Marian Ramelson, *The Petticoat Rebellion* (London 1967), p.92 (fn).

38   *Women's Suffrage Journal* 1 January 1873.
39   Ibid. 1 March 1873.
40   Ibid. 1 October and 1 November 1873.
41   Billington, 'The Women's Education and Suffrage Movements', 443.
42   In the summer of 1873 Jane Taylour was presented with a testimonial consisting of a piece of jewellery and 150 guineas for her work. At that time she had delivered 152 lectures in Scotland. *Women's Suffrage Journal* 1 July 1873.
43   Ibid. 1 February and 2 August 1875.
44   Ibid. 1 July 1876.
45   Ibid. 1 March 1876.
46   *The Ladies' Edinburgh Magazine*, Vol.II (1876), pp.97-102.
47   *Women's Suffrage Journal* 2 July 1877.
48   Ibid. 1 April 1878.
49   Ibid. 2 September 1878.
50   *The Ladies' Edinburgh Magazine*, Vol.VI (1880), pp.106-7. The article was signed E.S. which must have been Eliza Stevenson. The Society stopped publishing a magazine after that year.
51   The 1881 statute extended only to Royal and Parliamentary burghs. This was extended to police burghs (endowed with powers of local self- government under the General Police and Improvement Act) by further legislation in the spring of 1882. *Women's Suffrage Journal* 1 August 1882.
52   Ibid. 1 September 1882.
53   Ibid. 1 May 1882. *Englishwoman's Review* 15 January 1883.
54   *Women's Suffrage Journal* 2 October and 1 November 1882. A summary of the number of women who voted for the first time in local elections was given in *Englishwoman's Review* 15 November 1882 and *Women's Suffrage Journal* 1 December 1882.
55   *Glasgow Herald* 4 November 1882. *Englishwoman's Review* 15 November 1882. *Women's Suffrage Journal* 1 December 1882.
56   *Women's Suffrage Journal* 1 April 1884. *Englishwoman's Review* 15 April 1884.
57   *Scotsman* 25 March 1884.
58   Ibid. 24, 25, and 26 March 1884.
59   Teresa Billington-Greig, *The Militant Suffrage Movement* (London n.d. [c.1911]), pp.150-51.
60   Rae, *Ladies in Debate*, 33.

Chapter 2, pp.32 to 39

1   David Rubinstein, *Before the Suffragettes* (Brighton 1986), p.138.
2   *Women's Suffrage Journal* 1 January 1887.
3   Ibid. 1 April and 2 May 1887. *Englishwoman's Review* 14 May 1887.
4   Marian Ramelson, *The Petticoat Rebellion* (London 1967), pp.91-8.
5   Lady Frances Balfour, *Ne Obliviscaris Dinna Forget* (London 1930), pp.114, 127.
6   *The Bailie* 19 October 1904.
7   *Englishwoman's Review* 15 January 1891 and 15 January 1893.
8   Letter from Margaret Smith to her mother 7 December 1891, Strathclyde Regional Archives TD1/950. She added: 'Another good reason is that this vote which would be almost entirely for law and order would just make the difference of keeping it safe that law and order should prevail.'
9   Linda Walker, 'Party Political Women: A Comparative Study of Liberal Women and the Primrose League, 1890-1914' in Jane Rendall ed. *Equal or Different: Women's*

Politics 1800-1914 (Oxford 1987), pp.172, 184. After the Home Rule schism in the Liberal party in the 1880s there was also a Women's Liberal Unionist Association, but I have not found anything on its activities in Scotland.

10 Balfour, *Ne Obliviscaris*, 114-5.

11 Helen Blackburn, *Women's Suffrage: a record of the women's suffrage movement in the British Isles* (London & Oxford 1902), p.172.

12 *Women's Suffrage Journal* 1 January 1887.

13 Walker, 'Party Political Women', 184. Rubinstein, *Before the Suffragettes*, 152.

14 *Englishwoman's Review* 15 January 1982.

15 Walker, 'Party Political Women', 185-8.

16 Scottish Women's Liberal Federation (SWLF) executive committee minutes, Edinburgh University Library, 25 April 1893.

17 English historians writing about the political organisations of the period appear to be totally ignorant of the existence of the Scottish Women's Liberal Federation.

18 SWLF minutes 24 June and 24 September 1895.

19 Rubinstein, *Before the Suffragettes*, 148-9. A. Buchan, *History of the Scottish Co-operative Women's Guild 1892-1913* (Glasgow 1913), pp.1, 68.

20 *Report of the Twenty-Fifth Annual Meeting of the Edinburgh National Society for Women's Suffrage* 5 April 1893.

21 The Edinburgh National Society for Women's Suffrage was represented on the Central Committee by Louisa Stevenson. NUWSS Collection Box 85 Part 1, Fawcett Library, City of London Polytechnic.

22 Scottish Record Office GD433/2/318. This series contains copies of family letters (or parts of letters) made by Lady Betty Balfour at an unknown later date. I am grateful to Lord Balfour for permission to quote from the letter.

23 National Society for Women's Suffrage *Occasional Paper* 4 March 1897, pp.18-19. Rubinstein, *Before the Suffragettes*, 146.

24 SWLF minutes 14 April 1897.

25 Ibid. 21 September 1900. On the same date the executive committee considered a letter from the Male Elector's League for Women's Suffrage, which asked the committee's help in urging candidates favourable to women's suffrage to introduce the subject in their election addresses. I have not seen this League mentioned anywhere else.

26 *The Lady's Review of Reviews* may be seen in the Glasgow Room, Mitchell Library, Glasgow.

27 Elspeth Janet Boog Watson, *Edinburgh Association for the University Education of Women 1867-1967* (Edinburgh n.d.). William N. Boog Watson, 'The First Eight Ladies', *University of Edinburgh Journal* (XXIII No.3 spring 1968). H.B. Charlton, *Portrait of a University 1851-1951*, Appendix pp.153-62. I am grateful to Alan Ferns, Information Officer, Manchester University, for sending me a copy of this. I owe the information on Oxford and Cambridge to Rosalind Mitchison.

28 M. Laurence, *Shadow of Swords, a biography of Elsie Inglis* (London 1971), pp.80-81. According to the author, Elsie Inglis threw herself into building up the women's suffrage movement in Scotland from 1900 onwards, but the list of committee members in the Edinburgh National Society for Women's Suffrage annual report of 1903 does not include her name, nor is she listed amongst those present at the annual meeting.

29 The story of the women's suffrage movement in Lancashire is the subject of Jill Liddington and Jill Norris, *One Hand Tied Behind Us: The Rise of the Women's Suffrage Movement* (London 1978).

30 Manchester City Library Archive M50/1/2/79-85.

31 The executive committee minutes of the Glasgow and West of Scotland Association for Women's Suffrage are in the Department of Rare Books and Manuscripts, Mitchell Library, Glasgow.

32 Glasgow Association minutes 7 July-13 October 1902. SWLF minutes 14 November 1902. Annual Report of Scottish Co-operative Women's Guild, Strathclyde Regional Archives CWS1/39/6/11.

33 Glasgow Association minutes.

34 Ibid. 23 December 1903 and *Women's Suffrage Record* June 1903 and 1904.

35 *Women's Suffrage Record* June 1904. Glasgow Association minutes 15 September 1904 and 17 January 1905. NUWSS executive committee minutes, Fawcett Library, City of London Polytechnic, 4 February 1904 and 16 February 1905.

Chapter 3, pp.40 to 55

1 The history of the WSPU has been well told in Andrew Rosen, *Rise Up Women! The Militant Campaign of the Women's Social and Political Union 1903-14* (London 1974). For a more personal history see E. Sylvia Pankhurst, *The Suffragette Movement: An Intimate Account of Persons and Ideals* (London 1931).

2 E. Sylvia Pankhurst, *The Suffragette* (London 1911), pp.50-51.

3 Glasgow and West of Scotland Association for Women's Suffrage executive committee minutes, Department of Rare Books and Manuscripts, Mitchell Library, Glasgow, 8 May 1906.

4 *Dundee Advertiser* 11 December 1907. This was an article headed 'WHY WOMEN SUFFRAGISTS DISTURB MEETINGS – A JUSTIFICATION' by Bella D. Brand MA. A rejoinder to this piece was published on 12 December, Bella Brand's response to the rejoinder on 14 December and a further rejoinder on 17 December, as well as correspondence on the subject.

5 *Glasgow Herald* 1 May 1906. Supportive letters from men also appeared; see, for example, 4 May.

6 Graham Moffat, *Join Me in Remembering – The Life and Reminiscences of the Author of 'Bunty Pulls the Strings'* (privately printed 1955), p.51.

7 Lady Frances Balfour, *Ne Obliviscaris Dinna Forget* (London 1930), p.140. Scottish Women's Liberal Federation (SWLF) executive committee minutes, Edinburgh University Library, 11 May and 2 June 1906.

8 See *Englishwoman's Review* 16 April 1906, J. Chrystal MacMillan, 'The Scottish Women Graduates' Lawsuit', *Votes for Women* December 1907 and Leah Leneman, 'When Women Were Not "Persons" – The Scottish Graduates' Case 1906-8', *Juridical Review* (1991 Part 1).

9 Copy OPINION of Lord Salvesen in Action at the instance of *Margaret Nairn and Others (Women Graduates of Edinburgh University)* v. *the Universities of St Andrews and Edinburgh*, St Andrews University Court Records 16 July 1906.

10 Brian Harrison interview with Helen Fraser Moyes 19 August 1975, Harrison Tapes Collection, Fawcett Library, City of London Polytechnic.

11 Glasgow Association minutes 17 October 1906.

12 Pankhurst, *The Suffragette Movement*, 261.

13 Glasgow Association minutes 29 November and 11 December 1906.

14 SWLF minutes 11 January and 21 February 1907.

15 Helen Corr, 'The Schoolgirls' Curriculum and the Ideology of the Home, 1870-1914' in Glasgow Women's Studies Group, *Uncharted Lives: Extracts from Scottish Women's Experiences, 1850-1932 (Glasgow 1983)*, p.78 and 'Home-Rule' in Scotland: The

Teaching of Housework in Schools 1872-1914' in J. Fevell and F. Paterson eds. *Girls in their Prime: Scottish Education Revisited* (Edinburgh forthcoming), p.17.

16   Lindy Moore, 'The women's suffrage campaign in the 1907 Aberdeen by- election' in *Northern Scotland* Vol.5, No.2, 1983, pp.155-78. I would refer anyone interested in reading about the campaign in depth to this article. She also wrote about it from a different angle in 'Feminists and Femininity: A Case Study of WSPU Propaganda and Local Response at a Scottish Bye-Election' in *Women's Studies International Forum* Vol.5, No.6, 1982.

17   Harrison interview with Helen Fraser Moyes.

18   Caroline Phillips's collection of correspondence and papers relating to her period as Aberdeen WSPU secretary was passed down through her family and was deposited at the Aberdeen Art Gallery and Museum by a surviving relative, Miss Rosemary Watt. For access to the collection contact the Keeper, Applied Art. It will hereafter be cited as the Watt Collection.

19   Draft letter (undated), Watt Collection.

20   *Edinburgh Evening Dispatch* 9 January 1907.

21   Glasgow Association minutes 29 February 1907.

22   *Edinburgh Evening Dispatch* 25 March 1907. *Women and Progress* 29 March 1907. (This journal was edited by Lady Frances Balfour but survived only a short time.)

23   *Women and Progress* 3 May 1907.

24   Harrison interview with Helen Fraser Moyes. *Women and Progress* 1 March 1907. Moffat, *Join Me in Remembering*, 52.

25   Thomas Johnston, *The Case for Women's Suffrage and Objections Answered. (Glasgow n.d. [1907]).*

26   *Forward* 12 and 26 January 1907. On 2 February a letter from Emmeline Pankhurst expressed the 'admiration, respect and esteem which every member of the W.S.P.U. has for Mr Hardie as a man and a politician.'

27   Ibid. 19 January and 2 February 1907.

28   Ibid. 9 and 23 February, 2 March, 11, 18 and 25 May 1907.

29   Moffat, *Join Me in Remembering*, 52. See also Graham Moffat's letter to a strong advocate of Scottish Home Rule, Roland E. Muirhead (8 May 1907) in which he tried to persuade the latter that a women's suffrage bill could be passed very easily, whereas the Home Rule issue would require a General Election. National Library of Scotland Acc.3721, Box 148(2).

30   *Edinburgh Evening Dispatch* 14 May 1907. For Aberdeen there are letters from Emmeline Pankhurst to Caroline Phillips dated 13, 15 and 17 April 1907 (Watt Collection). For accounts of a meeting in Dumbarton see *Forward* 18 May 1907 and Moffat, *Join Me in Remembering*, 53.

31   *Forward* 23 June 1907.

32   *Women's Franchise* 25 July, 1 and 8 August 1907. *Forward* 27 July and 3 August 1907.

33   *Women's Franchise* 22 August and 26 September 1907. Glasgow Association minutes 3 July 1907. SWLF minutes 13 September 1907. *Forward* 21 September 1907. Letter from Mrs Elizabeth Bell, Comely Bank, Edinburgh (secretary responsible for the overall running of the procession) to Caroline Phillips, 26 September 1907 (Watt Collection). *Edinburgh Evening Dispatch* 2 October 1907.

34   Mary Phillips in *Forward* 12 October 1907.

35   *Women's Franchise* 10 October 1907.

36   Glasgow Association minutes 17 October and 6 November 1907.

37   *Votes for Women* 18 June 1908.

38   Watt Collection. The letter is undated but she was on holiday in Derbyshire and referred to being there until 29 August.

39   Moore, 'The women's suffrage campaign in the 1907 Aberdeen by-election', 165. In her bitter notes at the time of the schism, entitled 'POINTS OF PERSONAL ATTACK' (London Museum Suffragette Fellowship Collection. Group D. Vol.3 Z6070), Teresa Billington-Greig also began with the Aberdeen by- election. She went on to list problems within one or more of the other Scottish branches, including complaints about Helen Fraser, but the notes are too cryptic to make much sense of, and the facts were never made public. Helen Fraser also thought the Pankhursts jealous of Teresa Billington-Greig. Harrison interview with Helen Fraser Moyes.

40   The Women's Freedom League continued to report its activities in *Women's Franchise* while the Pankhursts, along with Emmeline and Frederick Pethick Lawrence, started their own journal, *Votes for Women* (but for some months after *Votes for Women* was started Helen Fraser still reported on Scottish WSPU activities in *Women's Franchise*).

41   Andro Linklater, *An Unhusbanded Life* (London 1980), pp.25-6 and 145.

42   *Forward* 28 September and 26 October 1907.

43   Ibid. 2 and 23 November, 24 December 1907.

44   Linklater, *An Unhusbanded Life*, 167. The book has no footnote references.

45   Les Garner, *Stepping Stones to Women's Liberty* (London 1984), p.29.

46   *Votes for Women* December 1907.

47   SWLF minutes 8 and 30 November 1907. At the latter meeting the committee also considered a request from the Glasgow and West of Scotland Association that the Federation affiliate but decided it would violate their constitution to do so.

48   *Women's Franchise* 7 and 14 November 1907.

49   Ibid. 28 November 1907.

50   *Votes for Women* April 1908.

51   *Forward* 7 December 1907. An account of the first suffragette interruption of a political meeting in Dundee appeared in the same issue. The WSPU later held a meeting to explain 'Why we heckled Captain Sinclair' which was packed out and responsive. Ibid. 28 December 1907.

52   For correspondence with Caroline Phillips before the meetings – showing the disquiet that local Liberal women felt at the prospect of interrup ting Asquith's meeting – see Watt Collection.

53   This account has been culled from *Votes for Women* January 1908 (which included lengthy extracts from local press reports); *Forward* 28 December 1907 and 4 January 1908; and Pankhurst, *The Suffragette*, 180.

55   *Votes for Women* January 1908. Letter from Christabel Pankhurst to Caroline Phillips 28 December 1907, Watt Collection.

Chapter 4, pp.56 to 70

1   Collection of suffrage material donated by Miss Rosemary Watt to Aberdeen Art Gallery and Museum (Watt Collection).

2   Scottish Women's Liberal Federation (SWLF) executive committee minutes, Edinburgh University Library, 10 January 1908.

3   Watt Collection. The letter is dated 11 January 1908.

4   My tape-recorded interview with Elizabeth Somerville 28 November 1989.

5   E. Sylvia Pankhurst, *The Suffragette Movement: An Intimate Account of Persons and Ideals* (London 1931), p.221.

6   Watt Collection. An Aberdeen suffragist later wrote that Christabel 'did not impress me in the least. She came to Aberdeen, scolded us and bored me.' Louisa Innes Lumsden, *Yellow Leaves – Memories of a Long Life (Edinburgh and London 1933),* p.171. And a Scottish Women's Freedom League member found 'the redoubtable

Christabel' to be 'aggressive and disagreeable'. Eunice Murray's diary May 1908.
(This diary is in the possession of her nephew who has kindly allowed me to quote
from it.)

7   *Scottish Record Office* (SRO) GD433/2/337. I am grateful to Lord Balfour for
     permission to quote from this letter.

8   *Forward* 8 February 1908.

9   *Women's Franchise* 9 and 23 January and 20 February 1908.

10   *Forward* 8 February 1908.

11   Lady Frances' letter is in SRO GD433/2/337. I am grateful to Lord Balfour for
     permission to quote from this letter. Tom Johnston wrote of Mary Phillips'
     imprisonment in *Forward* 22 February 1908; she herself described the incident and her
     experiences in Holloway in *Forward* 28 March and 4 April 1908. Amy Sanderson was
     among the 69 women imprisoned in Holloway at this time.

12   Roy Jenkins, *Asquith* (London 1967 edition), pp.60, 276. Lady Frances Balfour, *Ne
     Obliviscaris Dinna Forget* (London 1930), pp.158-9.

13   *Women's Franchise* 9 and 23 April 1908.

14   Ibid. 30 April 1908.

15   Ibid. (same date).

16   Eunice Murray's diary May 1908. *Dundee Advertiser* 5 May 1908.

17   *Women's Franchise* and *Votes for Women* 7 and 14 May 1908.

18   *Forward* 16 May 1908.

19   *Women's Franchise* 14 May 1908.

20   Ibid. (same date).

21   *Votes for Women* 21 May 1908. The *Dundee Courier*'s correct account of the incident
     was quoted, and mention was made of the distorted accounts given by the London
     press. For the story in a London paper see the *Daily Express* 13 May 1908.

22   *Votes for Women* 21 May 1908. Christabel Pankhurst, *Unshackled* (London 1959), p.91.

23   *Votes for Women* 21 May 1908. *Women's Franchise* 28 May 1908.

24   The definitive book on suffrage processions in London is Lisa Tickner's *The Spectacle
     of Women: Imagery of the Suffragette Campaign 1907-14* (London 1988). She did not
     write about Scottish processions.

25   Glasgow and West of Scotland Association for Women's Suffrage executive com-
     mittee minutes, Department of Rare Books and Manuscripts, Mitchell Library,
     Glasgow, 10 April, 20 May and 27 June 1908.

26   *Votes for Women* 4 and 18 June 1908.

27   Ibid. 23 July 1908.

28   Brian Harrison interview with Helen Fraser Moyes 19 August 1975 (my transcrip-
     tion), Harrison Tapes Collection, Fawcett Library, City of London Polytechnic.

29   Suffragette Fellowship Collection, Museum of London, Group 3. Vol.2 Z6072.

30   Watt Collection.

31   Suffragette Fellowship Collection, Museum of London, 75/16/18.

32   *Aberdeen Daily Journal* 6 May 1914.

33   Lumsden, *Yellow Leaves*, 170.

34   She originally had the caravan built to transport her sick dog from Aberdeen to
     Edinburgh by road instead of by train and found travelling in it so delightful that she
     and her friends did much more of it later. Ibid., 145-6.

35   Glasgow Association minutes 4 September 1908.

36   *Women's Franchise* 9 July 1908.

37   Ibid. 23 and 30 July, 27 August and 3 September 1908. See also Teresa Billington-
     Greig, 'Scotland and the Women's Suffrage Movement' in *The Queen* 12 September
     1908.

38 *Votes for Women* 17 and 24 September 1908.
39 Letter dated 18 September 1908, Watt Collection.
40 See *Daily Mirror* and *Daily Graphic* 19 September 1908.
41 *Forward* 26 September 1908.
42 R.D. Anderson, *The Student Community at Aberdeen 1860-1939* (Aberdeen 1988), pp.79-80.
43 These journals are all in the Department of Special Collections, Aberdeen University Library.
44 SRO GD433/2/337. I am grateful to Lord Balfour for permission to quote from this letter.
45 Letter from Christabel Pankhurst to Caroline Phillips 18 September 1908, Watt Collection.
46 *Votes for Women* 22 October 1908.
47 Letter from Chrystal MacMillan to Sylvia Murray 18 November 1908, Autograph Collection, Fawcett Library, City of London Polytechnic.
48 A complete transcript of the hearing and judgment appeared in *Women's Franchise* 19 and 26 November, 3 and 17 December 1908. *Votes for Women* summed up the arguments 19 November and 17 December 1908. For a fuller discussion of this case see Leah Leneman, 'When Women Were Not "Persons" – The Scottish Women Graduates' Case 1906-8', *Juridical Review* (1991 Part 1).
49 Letter from Chrystal MacMillan to Eunice Murray 19 November 1908, and press cuttings. Autograph Collection, Fawcett Library, City of London Polytechnic.
50 SWLF minutes 13 November 1908.
51 *Votes for Women* 17 December 1908.
52 Brian Harrison, *Separate Spheres: The Opposition to Women's Suffrage in Britain* (London 1978), pp.137, 152-3.
53 A file on Mrs Parker Smith and her article is in Strathclyde Regional Archives TD1/541.
54 Harrison, *Separate Spheres*, 81-2.
55 Mrs Parker Smith was never mentioned in the *Anti-Suffrage Review* as an active member of the Anti-Suffrage League, but she clearly remained a supporter, for a letter of 14 October 1912 from the Glasgow branch of the League asked her if she was willing to provide accommodation for supporters coming to attend a large anti-suffrage demonstration in Glasgow. Strathclyde Regional Archives TD1/434.
56 Eunice Murray's diary June 1908.

Chapter 5, pp.71 to 90

1 *Votes for Women* 14 and 28 January and 4 February 1909.
2 Collection of suffrage material donated by Miss Rosemary Watt to Aberdeen Art Gallery and Museum (Watt Collection). The letter was from Anne McRobie, dated 22 January.
3 Ibid. Undated draft letter.
4 Fourth Annual Conference Report, WFL Collection, Fawcett Library, City of London Polytechnic.
5 *Votes for Women* 12 March 1909 mentioned a particularly inspirational meeting addressed by Mrs Pankhurst in the Synod Hall, Edinburgh; it seems likely that this was the meeting attended by Lilias Mitchell and her mother.
6 Lilias Mitchell, 'Suffrage Days'. This unpublished memoir is in the hands of her family, to whom I am greatly indebted for allowing me access.

7   Brian Harrison interview with Helen Fraser Moyes 19 August 1975, Harrison Tapes
     Collection, Fawcett Library, City of London Polytechnic. Script of Anna Munro's
     BBC broadcast talk, read by herself, in Ibid. *Votes for Women* 5 April 1912.
8   Memories of Miss I. Carrie compiled by S. Cubbage, History Department, Glasgow
     University December 1976. Dundee Archive and Record Centre GD/X53.
9   *Women's Franchise* 18 February 1909.
10   Glasgow and West of Scotland Association for Women's Suffrage executive com-
     mittee minutes (Department of Rare Books and Manuscripts, Mitchell Library,
     Glasgow), 10 March, 28 April and 19 May 1909.
11   *Forward* 13 March 1909. Christabel Pankhurst, *Unshackled* (London 1959), p.124.
12   E. Sylvia Pankhurst, *The Suffragette Movement: An Intimate Account of Persons and Ideals*
     (London 1931), p.377.
13   *Votes for Women* 4 June 1909. *Common Cause* 24 June and 1 July 1909.
14   John W. Gulland conceived a great respect for Helen Fraser, as evidenced by letters he
     wrote to her at that time and later in the same year. Suffragette Fellowship Collection,
     London Museum, 75/16/9-15.
15   *Common Cause* 22 and 29 July 1909. *Votes for Women* 23 July 1909.
16   *Votes for Women* 23 July 1909.
17   *Common Cause* 12, 19 and 26 August.
18   *Common Cause* 19 and 26 August, 2, 9, 16 and 23 September 1909. Helen Fraser's
     descriptions of their experiences in various towns they visited are highly entertaining.
19   Caravan touring did not suit all temperaments. Eunice Murray tried it once: 'Washing
     arrangements nil, sleeping ones bad – sanitary nil — caravan plastered with Votes for
     Women continual crowd by day & noisy people around me & by night of lowing
     cattle.' She gave up after two nights and stayed in hotels. Eunice Murray's diary June
     1912. (The diary is in the possession of her nephew who has kindly given me
     permission to quote from it.)
20   Ibid. August 1908.
21   She added, 'Even yet I have a horrid pang at the remembrance of it'. Mitchell,
     'Suffrage Days'.
22   *Women's Franchise* 2 September 1909.
23   Ibid., 29 July and 12 August 1909. Mitchell, 'Suffrage Days'.
24   Lady Frances Balfour to Millicent Garrett Fawcett 29 June 1909. Millicent Garrett
     Fawcett Collection, Fawcett Library, City of London Polytechnic.
25   *Dundee Advertiser* 1 September 1909.
26   E. Sylvia Pankhurst, *The Suffragette* (London 1911), pp.416-7. Pankhurst, *Unshackled*,
     136. *Votes for Women* 27 August (including extracts from press reports) and 3
     September 1909. An eye-witness account by Thomas A. Kerr in *Votes for Women* also
     appeared in *Forward* 28 August 1909.
27   *Dundee Advertiser* 14 September 1909. But on the same date the paper carried a jolly
     interview with Miss Kelly and pictures of the suffragettes, which must have inspired
     many young women to join the WSPU. The *Dundee Courier* told the story without
     editorial comment.
28   *Dundee Courier* 15 September 1909.
29   Scottish Record Office (SRO) HH16/36.
30   *Dundee Advertiser* 15 September 1909.
31   Ibid. 18 and 20 September 1909. *Dundee Courier* 17 and 20 September 1909. *Votes for
     Women* 24 September 1909.
32   My tape-recorded interview with Elizabeth Somerville, 28 November 1989. She
     remembered some older girl pipers who had taken part. But her most vivid memory
     was of a meeting held by Christabel Pankhurst some weeks later at the King's Theatre

when she presented everyone who had taken part in the pageant with a brooch. In the 1980s Mrs Somerville sent her treasured brooch to the first woman Prime Minister, Margaret Thatcher.

33 *Common Cause* 30 September, 7, 14 and 21 October 1909.

34 *Common Cause* 30 September 1909. According to Chrystal MacMillan the Shetland Women's Suffrage Society was already in existence when she arrived in September, but the minutes date the first meeting as 23 October; presumably it was an informal group before then. I am grateful to Tristram Clarke for telling me about these minutes and to Brian Smith for supplying me with a copy and for information on Christina Jamieson.

35 Glasgow Association minutes 28 June, 1 and 23 September, and 3 November 1909.

36 *Dundee Courier* 9 October 1909. The paper also published the correspondence between the WFL secretary, Lila Clunas, and Churchill's agents, which bore this out.

37 *Dundee Courier* and *Dundee Advertiser* 19 October 1909. Pankhurst, *The Suffragette*, 452-3. Sylvia Pankhurst contrasted his remarks on this occasion with his statements at the time of the Manchester and Dundee by- elections, when he had claimed that there was a great popular demand for women's enfranchisement and that he would do what he could to help, calling this change of tune a 'flagrant example of political dishonesty'.

38 *Dundee Advertiser* and *Dundee Courier* 18 October 1909. Pankhurst, *The Suffragette*, 450-52. The police constable's report is in SRO.HH55/323.

39 However, residents of Abernethy, both male and female, protested strongly at the treatment the suffragettes had received. *Dundee Courier* 22 and 23 October 1909.

40 *Dundee Advertiser, Dundee Courier* and *Scotsman* 20 October 1909. Pankhurst, *The Suffragette*, 453. Miss MacGregor owned the estate of Abbeythune; the prisoners stayed with her after their release.

41 SRO.HH16/37 and HH55/323.

42 *Scotsman, Dundee Advertiser* and *Edinburgh Evening Dispatch* 25 October 1909. SRO.HH55/323.

43 *Anti-Suffrage Review* November 1909.

44 *Votes for Women* 26 November 1909.

45 Ibid. November and December 1909.

46 *Common Cause* 4 November 1909.

47 Autograph Collection, Fawcett Library, City of London Polytechnic.

48 *Common Cause* 2 December 1909.

49 Ibid. 25 November 1909.

50 Ibid. 16 December 1909.

51 Shetland Women's Suffrage Society executive committee minutes, Shetland archive, 3 and 16 December 1909 and Secretary's report of the work of the Society during the year 1909-10.

52 Scottish Women's Liberal Federation executive committee minutes, Edinburgh University Library 12 November 1909.

53 *The Vote* 9 December 1909.

Chapter 6, pp.91 to 108

1 Report of Fifth Annual Conference, WFL Collection, Fawcett Library, City of London Polytechnic.

2 *Votes for Women* 18 February 1910.

3 My tape-recorded interview with Elizabeth Somerville 28 November 1989.

4 *Votes for Women* 4 March and 1 April 1910.

5   *Glasgow Herald* 29 April 1910. *Votes for Women* 6 May 1910.
6   *The Vote* 16 April 1910.
7   Glasgow and West of Scotland Association for Women's Suffrage executive committee minutes (Department of Rare Books and Manuscripts, Mitchell Library, Glasgow), 31 March and 27 April 1910. The Glasgow Association had additional cause for complaint as the National Union was apparently convinced that the Scottish Federation had been Edinburgh's idea. N.B. One of Elsie Inglis's biographers incorrectly states that the Scottish Federation was formed in 1906. M. Laurence, *Shadow of Swords, a biography of Elsie Inglis* (London 1971), p.81.
8   *Common Cause* 27 January, 10, 17 and 24 March 1910.
9   *Shetland Times* 22 and 29 January 1910. I am grateful to Brian Smith for bringing these articles to my attention.
10 *Common Cause* 5 May 1910. Siân Reynolds, *Britannica's Typesetters. Women Compositors in Edwardian Edinburgh* (Edinburgh 1989), p.140.
11 Olive Banks, *Becoming a Feminist − The Social Origins of 'First Wave' Feminism* (Brighton 1986), p.11. Jill Liddington and Jill Norris, *One Hand Tied Behind Us: The Rise of the Women's Suffrage Movement* (London 1978). Geoffrey Mitchell, ed., *The Hard Way Up. The Autobiography of Hannah Mitchell, Suffragette and Rebel* (London 1968).
12 Brian Harrison interview with Jessie Stephen 1 July 1977, Harrison Tapes Collection, Fawcett Library, City of London Polytechnic. My interview with Elizabeth Somerville 28 November 1989. *Dunfermline Press* 2 March 1968. I am grateful to Eric Simpson for a copy of this cutting.
13 R.S. Neale, 'Working-class women and women's suffrage' in his *Class and Ideology in the Nineteenth Century* (London and Boston 1972), pp.158-9. A. Buchan, *History of the Scottish Co-operative Women's Guild 1892-1913* (Glasgow 1913), p.68.
14 *Anti-Suffrage Review* May and June 1910.
15 *Common Cause* 9, 21, and 30 June, 4 and 11 August, 8 September 1910. Helen Fraser gave up working for some months then because of illness and exhaustion. (Afterwards she worked in England as the chief organiser for by-elections.) *The Vote* 23 July and 3 September 1910.
16 *Votes for Women* 15 July 1910. *The Vote* 16 and 23 July 1910. *Scotsman* 25 July 1910.
17 *Edinburgh Evening Dispatch* 25 July 1910. The paper also reported sympathetically on the Hyde Park demonstration, perceiving a change from the 1908 one when there had been laughter and hostility; on this occasion there was 'an entire absence of a counter-demonstration.'
18 Ibid. and *Scotsman* 12 July 1910. The latter also carried a leader on the debate the following day but no new points of note were made in it.
19 *Votes for Women* 9, 16, and 23 September 1910.
20 *Common Cause* 15, 22 and 29 September, 13 October, 3 November 1910. *The Vote* 19 November 1910. In October the WFL had held joint meetings with the WSPU in Glasgow and Edinburgh. Ibid. 29 October 1910.
21 Minutes of the Corporation of Glasgow 18 August 1910, Strathcylde Regional Archives. *Common Cause* 1 September 1910. Councillor Pratt was the speaker at a WFL At Home in Glasgow on 28 September. *The Vote* 8 October 1910.
22 Edinburgh Town Council Minutes 4 October 1910, Edinburgh archives. *Common Cause* 27 October 1910. Kirkwall Town Council Minutes 19 October 1910. I am grateful to Orkney archives for sending me a copy of the minutes.
23 Glasgow Association minutes 5 September and 26 October 1910. Scottish Women's Liberal Federation (SWLF) executive committee minutes, Edinburgh University Library, 9 September and 11 November 1910.

24   *Forward* 5, 12 and 19 November 1910. He also thought that married women would demand wages for their work in the home.

25   *The Vote* 10 December 1910. The report of the interview with the constitutionalists appeared in *Common Cause* 8 December 1910.

26   *Votes for Women* 16 December 1910. The men who heckled Churchill at meetings to which women were not admitted were thanked by the author. Churchill's majority was reduced by 2,640.

27   Glasgow Association minutes 15 December 1910.

28   *The Vote* 17 December 1910.

29   *Common Cause* 15 December 1910.

30   *The Vote* 10 December 1910 and 7 January 1911. *Edinburgh Evening Dispatch* 20 December 1910.

31   SWLF minutes 13 January 1911.

32   *The Vote* 4 and 11 February 1911.

33   Teresa Billington-Greig, *The Militant Suffrage Movement* (London n.d. [1911]), p.13.

34   Ibid., 90-98.

35   Brian Harrison, *Prudent Revolutionaries – Portraits of British Feminists between the Wars* (Oxford 1987), p.64.

36   *Votes for Women* 17 March and 28 April 1911.

37   Edinburgh Town Council Minutes 2 May 1911. Resolutions in favour of the Conciliation Bill were later passed by the town councils of Bonnyrigg, Dumfries, Kirriemuir and Wick. *Votes for Women* 16 June 1911.

38   *Anti-Suffrage-Review* February, April and May 1911.

39   Lady Frances Balfour, *Ne Obliviscaris Dinna Forget* (London 1930), pp.166- 7.

40   Brian Harrison, *Separate Spheres: The Opposition to Women's Suffrage in Britain* (London 1978), p.137.

41   *Dundee Courier* 1 and 3 April 1911. *Edinburgh Evening Dispatch* and *Scotsman* 3 April 1911.

42   Executive committee minutes, WFL Collection, Fawcett Library, City of London Polytechnic, 24-5 March and 24-5 April 1911. She was called 'Miss Halley' there, but her daughter, who wrote to me in response to my letter in the *Courier & Advertiser*, knew of no other Halleys in Dundee. Letters from Joyce Halley November 1989.

43   Shetland Women's Suffrage Society committee minutes, Shetland archive, 6 April and 8 June 1911. Glasgow Association minutes 20 April and 31 May 1911.

44   Scottish Record Office (SRO) GD433/2/342. No addressee is given at the top of this copy of an extract from the letter, but it was Lady Betty Balfour who made the copies and it was clearly addressed to her. I am grateful to Lord Balfour for permission to quote from it.

45   *Common Cause* 15 and 29 June 1911.

46   Ibid. (same dates).

47   *Votes for Women* 16 June 1911. My interview with Elizabeth Somerville 28 November 1989. Shetland Society minutes 8 June 1911. *The Vote* 1 July 1911.

48   Minutes of the Corporation of Glasgow 8 May, 1 and 15 June 1911.

49   *The Vote* 22 and 29 July, 5 August 1911.

50   *Votes for Women* 25 August and 15 September 1911.

51   *The Vote* 23 September 1911. *Votes for Women* 15, 22 and 29 September 1911. *Common Cause* 28 and 28 September, 5 October 1911.

52   *Common Cause* 12 October, 16 and 23 November 1911.

53   Shetland Society minutes 26 October 1911. Christina Jamieson's pamphlet has survived, and I am grateful to Brian Smith for sending me a copy. It is mainly a historical account of the movement and is disappointingly general, employing none

234

of the arguments relating specifically to Shetland which she used so effectively at other times.

54 *Anti-Suffrage Review* November 1910 (and many other issues).
55 *The Standard* 11 October 1911.
56 Ibid. 20 October 1911.
57 Information supplied by Hugh Cheape.
58 Harrison interview with Jessie Stephen (my transcription).
59 Lilias Mitchell, 'Suffrage Days' (unpublished memoir in the possession of her family).
60 *Votes for Women* 3 November 1911. *The Vote* 2 December 1911.
61 Shetland Society minutes 7 December 1911.
62 SRO.GD433/2/343. I am grateful to Lord Balfour for permission to quote from this letter.

Chapter 7, pp.109 to 130

1 A.J.R., ed. *The Suffrage Annual and Women's Who's Who* (London 1913). (In prison records her name is given as Greig.)
2 Andrew Rosen, *Rise Up Women! The Militant Campaign of the Women's Social and Political Union 1903-14* (London 1974), p.243.
3 *Glasgow Evening Times* 23 February 1912.
4 Scottish Record Office (SRO) HH16/39.
5 Roger Fulford, *Votes for Women - The Story of a Struggle* (London 1957), p.249.
6 Lilias Mitchell, 'Suffrage Days' (unpublished memoir in the possession of her family to whom I am grateful for allowing me access).
7 *Votes for Women* 15 April 1912.
8 Helen Crawfurd, Unpublished Autobiography, Marx Memorial Library, London. This was written long after the event and is unreliable on facts but nevertheless useful as a first-hand account. A copy of the manuscript is held in the William Gallagher Library, Glasgow, and I am grateful to George Hunter for obtaining a copy of the copy for me. My thanks to the Marx Memorial Library for permission to quote from the manuscript.
9 Brian Harrison interview with Dr Barclay Barrowman 2 March 1976, Harrison Tapes Collection, Fawcett Library, City of London Polytechnic.
10 I am very grateful to Libby Scott for giving me a copy of this letter of her great-aunt's. It is dated 'Monday evening April 1912.'
11 Sylvia Pankhurst had executed the illuminated address with great care and was distressed when it was reproduced by lithography as in the re-drawing it had become almost unrecognisable. E. Sylvia Pankhurst, *The Suffragette Movement: An Intimate Account of Persons and Ideals* (London 1931), p.218. An illuminated address inscribed to Agnes MacDonald is in the Edinburgh Room, Central Public Library, Edinburgh; Janet Barrowman's is in the People's Palace Museum, Glasgow; Lilias Mitchell's is in the possession of her family.
12 He wrote another letter to her the following day about the conspiracy charges they were bringing against the WSPU leadership and reiterated, 'The harm done to the prospects of the Bill is immense.' As those letters were for private consumption they persuade me that Haldane's support for the Conciliation Bill was sincere. National Library of Scotland Haldane Papers Ms.6011, ff.191-4.
13 *Forward* 16 March 1912. However, Tom Johnston gave space to an anti-suffragist (C.H. Norman) on 4 and 11 May. Lucy Burns refuted his arguments on 18 May. From 25 May through 20 July *Forward* carried articles by Sylvia Pankhurst.
14 *The Standard* and *Glasgow Herald* 13 March 1912.
15 *Glasgow Herald* 12 March 1912.
16 *Common Cause* 4 and 11 April 1912.

17 *Votes for Women* 22 March 1912. *The Vote* 23 March 1912.
18 Charlotte Despard's biographer naturally discusses this at length. Andro Linklater, *An Unhusbanded Life* (London 1980).
19 Report of the Special Conference 27 and 28 April 1912, WFL Collection, Fawcett Library, City of London Polytechnic. *The Vote* 4 and 11 May 1912.
20 *The Vote* 15 June, 6 and 20 July 1912. *Edinburgh Evening Dispatch* 10 July 1912.
21 *Common Cause* 6 June and 15 August 1912.
22 *The Vote* 29 June 1912.
23 Ibid. 22 September 1912. National Executive Committee minutes 20-21 September 1912, WFL Collection, Fawcett Library, City of London Polytechnic.
24 *Votes for Women* 13 September 1912. *Glasgow Herald* 9 September 1912. Fulford, *Votes for Women*, 271.
25 *Votes for Women* 5 April 1912.
26 Brian Harrison, *Separate Spheres: The Opposition to Women's Suffrage in Britain* (London 1978), p.162.
27 *Votes for Women* 20 September 1912.
28 SRO.HH16/40.
29 Mary Richardson, *Laugh a Defiance* (London 1953).
30 NUWSS executive committee minutes 12 September 1912, NUWSS Collection, Fawcett Library, City of London Polytechnic.
31 *Common Cause* 5 September 1912. The by-election was also covered on 29 August and 12 September.
32 Sandra Stanley Holton, *Feminism and Democracy* (Cambridge 1986), p.83.
33 *Common Cause* 26 September 1912.
34 *Votes for Women* 11 October 1912. *Edinburgh Evening Dispatch* 5 October 1912.
35 *Edinburgh Evening Dispatch* 7 and 9 October 1912.
36 *Edinburgh Evening Dispatch* 2 November 1912. *Votes for Women* 8 November 1912.
37 *Dundee Advertiser* 4 November 1912.
38 *The Vote* 16 November 1912. Ethel Moorhead's Bill of Suspension before the High Court of Justiciary (27 December 1912) may be seen in the Edinburgh Room of the Central Public Library, Edinburgh.
39 WFL National Executive Committee minutes 20-21 September 1912, Fawcett Library, City of London Polytechnic.
40 L.S.W.S. Collection, Edinburgh-London march, Fawcett Library, City of London Polytechnic.
41 *Edinburgh Evening Dispatch, Scotsman, Dundee Advertiser* 14 October 1912. *The Vote* 19 October 1912. *The Suffragette* 25 October 1912.
42 *The Vote* 2 November and 21 December 1912.
43 This delightful ephemera (along with Nannie Brown's silver badge) was found among the effects of Nannie Brown's last surviving relative. The executor kept it in the hope that it might someday prove of interest. I am grateful to Mr Macdonald for responding to my letter in the *Scotsman* and for supplying me with a copy of the text of the speech.
44 *Dundee Advertiser* 18 and 30 October 1912.
45 Ibid. and *Evening Telegraph and Post* 30 October 1912. An unsuccessful attempt at window smashing took place in Aberdeen the same night.
46 *The Suffragette* 8 November 1912. SRO.HH16/42.
47 *Anti-Suffrage Review* December 1912.
48 *Glasgow Herald* 5 November 1912. Harrison, *Separate Spheres*, 113. A recent biography is S.J. Hetherington, *Katharine Atholl 1874-1960: Against the Tide* (Aberdeen 1989).
49 Glasgow and West of Scotland Association for Women's Suffrage executive com-

mittee minutes (Department of Rare Books and Manuscripts, Mitchell Library,
Glasgow), 8 November and 16 December 1912. *Glasgow Herald* 10 December 1912.
Shetland Society sent the Scottish Federation five guineas for the occasion. Shetland
Women's Suffrage Society committee minutes 3 December 1912.

50   *Common Cause* 8 November, 6 and 13 December 1912.
51   *Aberdeen Free Press* 30 November 1912.
52   *Dundee Courier* 2 December 1912. The *Aberdeen Free Press* 4 December 1912 carried a
     complete transcript of the proceedings, which makes fascinating reading.
53   SRO.HH16/41. The governor advised the prison commissioners that 'the whole staff,
     male and female, behaved with commendable patience, dexterity, and gentleness.' Cer-
     tainly when the women were released it was the unfairness of their trial, not their treat-
     ment in prison, which they complained about. *Votes for Women* 13 December 1912.
54   *Scotsman* 12 and 16 December 1912. SRO.HH16/41. 'Mary Humphreys' subse-
     quently raised the question of being refused bail and being forced to spend the night
     in a police 'drunk' cell so successfully that the Secretary for Scotland had to answer a
     question about this in Parliament.
55   Arnclife-Sennett Collection, British Library, Vol.26. The letter on which this
     comment appears is dated 18 January 1915.
56   C.f. 'It is sometimes assumed that the constitutionalists and militants were very
     different from each other, but in fact the comparison made here shows them to have
     been in many respects very similar.' Olive Banks, *Becoming a Feminist – The Social
     Origins of 'First Wave' Feminism* (Brighton 1987), p.67.
57   Ibid., 39.
58   Letter from Dr Mary Tod (in response to mine in the *Scotsman*), 2 November 1989.
     My interview with Dr Elizabeth Baxendine 25 January 1990.
59   *Glasgow Herald* 6 December 1912. The *Suffragette* 13 December 1912.
60   *Edinburgh Evening Dispatch* 6 December 1912. One young man was arrested for
     pasting sheets of paper bearing the words 'Votes for Women' over the opening of
     letter-boxes. He said that he did it to show his complete approval of militant tactics.
     Glasgow Herald 19 and 28 December 1912.

Chapter 8, pp.131 to 147

1   *Dundee Advertiser* 23 January 1913. *Edinburgh Evening Dispatch* 21 January 1913.
2   *Dundee Courier* 28 January 1913.
3   *Scotsman* 24 January 1913. But David Rubinstein has pointed out to me that many
    moderate women's suffrage supporters believed it was deliberate; that various issues
    of *The Times*, including those of 26 November and 9 December 1912, had warned
    that the women's suffrage amendments might have this effect; and that Asquith was
    delighted at the ruling.
4   *Glasgow Herald* 28 January 1913. *Forward* 1 February 1913.
5   E. Sylvia Pankhurst, *The Suffragette Movement: An Intimate Account of Persons and Ideals*
    (London 1931), pp.401-2. In the *Forward* of 15 February 1913 she urged the need for
    militancy.
6   Brian Harrison interview with Jessie Stephen 1 July 1977, Harrison Tapes Collection,
    Fawcett Library, City of London Polytechnic. Jessie Stephen also talked about her
    pillar-box activities in an interview published in *Spare Rib* February 1975.
7   Ibid. and my interview with Dr Elizabeth Baxendine 25 January 1990.
8   *Suffragette* and *Votes for Women* 7 February 1913. *Edinburgh Evening Dispatch* 31
    January 1913.
9   *Votes for Women* 7 February 1913. *Dundee Courier* 30 January 1913. The *Courier*
    continued, 'Humorous interjections were made, but the women always had a smart
    retort.'

10 *Edinburgh Evening Dispatch* 30 January 1913. *Suffragette* and *Votes for Women* 7 February 1913. Scottish Record Office (SRO) HH16/40.

11 SRO. HH16/40. The prison governor suppressed a letter she wrote to Arabella Scott on 3 February because it contained 'indecorous and improper matter'. In that letter she wrote that she was being treated like a convicted criminal, not an untried prisoner, but that 'having to fight nearly all the time keeps me from being dull.' She went on, 'there is a plot hatching – was visited today by a blurry-eyed doctor (I thought smelling of whiskey) and with an affectionate manner!'

12 *Edinburgh Evening Dispatch* 5 February 1913.

13 *Dundee Advertiser* and *Dundee Courier* 5 February 1913. *Suffragette* 7 February 1913. The *Advertiser* discovered on 8 February that Margaret Morrison was Ethel Moorhead, 'who is not unknown to Suffragette fame in Dundee and beyond its bounds'.

14 *Common Cause* 7 February 1913.

15 Examples of the reporting of non-militant meetings at this time may be found in *Edinburgh Evening Dispatch* and *Scotsman* 22 February 1913, *Dundee Advertiser* 18, 22 and 24 February 1913, *Dundee Courier* 24 February 1913, *Glasgow Herald* 4 March 1913.

16 SRO.HH16/40.

17 *Dundee Advertiser* 24 February 1913. There were many more letters on the subject in the correspondence columns of this paper at that time.

18 *Votes for Women* 7 March 1913.

19 *Common Cause* 14 March 1913. Scottish Churches League for Woman Suffrage Report of the Executive Committee Meeting for Year Ending 1913, National Library of Scotland Miscellaneous Suffrage Material X.222.d.1. This collection also contains Edinburgh University Women's Suffrage Society's journal of 1913, *The Only Way*.

20 Shetland Women's Suffrage Society committee minutes, Shetland Archive.

21 Answers from the NUWSS, Manchester City Library archive M50/2/5/4. The societies were: Aberdeen, Abernethy, Alloa, Alva, Ardrossan, Saltcoats and Stevenston, Berwickshire, Blairmore, Crieff, Cupar, Dingwall, Dollar, Dunbar, Dundee, Dunfermline, Edinburgh, Falkirk, Fortrose, Glasgow, Glenfarg, Gourock, Greenock, Haddington, Hawick, Innerleithen, Inverness, John O'Groats, Kelso, Kilmarnock, Kincardineshire, Kirkcaldy, Kirkwall (Orkney), Largs, Lenzie, Leven, Melrose, Montrose, Nairn, Oban, Paisley, Peebles, Perth, Bridge of Earn and Scone, Port Glasgow, St Andrews, Selkirk, Shetland, Stirlingshire, Tain, Tayside.

22 *Votes for Women* 21 March 1913. *Dundee Advertiser* 15 and 25 March 1913.

23 *Dundee Courier* 4 April 1913.

24 *Glasgow Herald* and *Edinburgh Evening Dispatch* 14 March 1913. *Forward* 23 March 1913. Harrison interview with Jessie Stephen.

25 *Glasgow Herald* 18, 20, 22 and 25 March 1913. See also L. Leneman, 'The Scottish Churches and Votes for Women', *Records of the Scottish Church History Society* (forthcoming).

26 *Edinburgh Evening Dispatch* 11, 12, 13 and 15 March 1913.

27 *Glasgow Herald* (and other Scottish newspapers) 7 April 1913.

28 My tape-recorded interview with Elizabeth Somerville, 28 November 1989.

29 Andrew Rosen, *Rise Up Women! The Militant Campaign of the Women's Social and Political Union 1903-14* (London 1914), p.243.

30 *Suffragette* 23 May 1913. James Logan, 'The East of Scotland Suffragist/Suffragette Movement 1900-1914' (unpublished Open University essay 1977), p.17.

31 *Edinburgh Evening Dispatch* 15 April 1913.

32 *Edinburgh Evening Dispatch*, *Dundee Courier*, and *Dundee Advertiser* 29 April 1913. The *Advertiser's* reporter interviewed the women and – perhaps unwittingly — presented

them sympathetically. According to the *Courier* of 30 April the Dundee suffragettes were expected back the following night, and a mob of several hundreds congregated at the High Street Port 'in the expectation of participating in another raid on Suffragettes', but they were disappointed (as, clearly, was the reporter), for 'no militants appeared'.

33 Scottish Women's Liberal Federation (SWLF) executive committee minutes, Edinburgh University Library, 9 May 1913. For a view of events from the government side see David Morgan, *Suffragists and Liberals* (Oxford 1975) and Brian Harrison, 'Women's Suffrage at Westminster 1866-1928' in Michael Bentley and John Stevenson eds. *High and Low Politics in Modern Britain: Ten Studies* (Oxford 1983).

34 *Forward* 2 May 1913. From this date until the war there was a weekly feature entitled 'Our Suffrage Columns' edited (except when she was in prison) by Janie Allan.

35 SWLF minutes 9 May 1913. NUWSS executive committee minutes, 15 May 1913, NUWSS collection, Fawcett Library, City of London Polytechnic. *The Vote* 9 May 1913.

36 *Dundee Advertiser* 12 May 1913.

37 *Edinburgh Evening Dispatch* 12 May 1913. *Dundee Advertiser* 25 May 1913. The two women in Broughty Ferry were May Grant and Lila Clunas (a surprising combination as May Grant was a WSPU member and Lila Clunas was secretary of the Dundee branch of the Women's Freedom League).

38 *The Scotsman* 20 May 1913 carried a report of the trial.

39 *Forward* 31 May 1913.

40 SRO.HH16/44.

41 *Edinburgh Evening Dispatch* 24 May 1913.

42 Ibid. 27 May 1913.

43 M. Laurence, *Shadow of Swords, a biography of Elsie Inglis* (London 1971), pp.53-5, 84.

44 *Edinburgh Evening Dispatch* and *Scotsman* 10 June 1913.

45 SRO.HH16/44. The *Edinburgh Evening Dispatch* (13 June) noted that when she was rearrested Arabella Scott was with 'the well-known Edinburgh suffragette, Miss Moorhead', and that neither of them made any fuss.

46 *Dundee Courier* and *Edinburgh Evening Dispatch* 4 June 1913. The *Courier* said snidely that Miss Christie 'did not risk another journey to the Fair City'. Fanny Parker wrote to the editor (5 June) to say that Miss Christie had been very anxious to go, but as she was a working woman and would have had to get a midnight train back to Dundee in order to be at her work in the morning she had been persuaded not to go.

47 *Edinburgh Evening Dispatch* 10 June 1913.

48 Ibid. and *Scotsman* 17 June 1913.

49 *Edinburgh Evening Dispatch* 20 June 1913. Harrison interview with Jessie Stephen.

50 *Glasgow Herald* 23 June 1913. Letter from T.G. Jarrett to me, 25 October 1989 in response to mine in the *Dundee Courier and Advertiser*.

51 St Andrews University Library archive McIntosh Album 6.

52 See Ann Morley with Liz Stanley, *The Life and Death of Emily Wilding Davison* (London 1989).

53 SRO.GD 433/2/345. I am grateful to Lord Balfour for permission to quote from this letter.

54 *Dundee Advertiser* 12 June 1913. *The Vote* 20 June 1913.

55 *Votes for Women* 25 July 1913.

Chapter 9, pp.148 to 168

1 Maud Arncliffe-Sennett left a 26-volume collection of press cuttings, letters and other suffrage memorabilia, with her own added comments. The collection is in the British Library.

2 *Votes for Women* 25 July 1913. Alexander Orr invented and patented a successful carpet beating machine (his obituary appeared in the *Edinburgh Evening News* 1 October 1919).

3 Arncliffe-Sennett Collection Vol.25.

4 *Votes for Women* 25 July 1913.

5 *Forward* 26 July 1913.

6 *Dundee Advertiser* 21 July 1913. Further letters on the deputation and the question of women's suffrage appeared on 22 and 23 July, and the latter date saw another leader on the subject. There was also correspondence after the deputation in the *Glasgow Herald*.

7 *The Vote* 25 July 1913.

8 Arncliffe-Sennett Collection Vol.25.

9 *Dundee Advertiser* 28 July 1913. May Grant responded (29 July) by recalling a similarly impressive demonstration (the Coronation procession) in which she had taken part but which had got them no further in obtaining the vote: 'I admit the value of the silent forces of time and weather in breaking down the rock of granite; but, sir, gunpowder is more rapid in its effect, and if the rock is imprisoning women and children, some of us think the more rapid its demolition the better.'

10 Louisa Innes Lumsden, *Yellow Leaves – Memories of a Long Life* (Edinburgh and London 1933), p.180.

11 Letter from J.D. Allan Gray in response to mine in the *Scotsman*, 1 November 1989. A letter protesting about the closure of Holyrood Palace appeared in the *Edinburgh Evening Dispatch* 7 July 1913.

12 *The Vote* 18 and 25 July, 1 and 15 August 1913.

13 Scottish Record Office (SRO) HH16/40. 'Margaret Morrison' asked the prison commissioners to instruct the governor 'that it is not his duty to endeavour to tame the suffragettes and quite a hopeless task to undertake during their stay in HM prisons.' The press somehow found out what happened inside Duke Street prison, for the *Dundee Advertiser* of 30 July described their treatment and behaviour there.

14 SRO.HH16/40.

15 *Edinburgh Evening Dispatch* 8, 21, 25 August 1913.

16 *Dundee Advertiser* 15, 19, 22 August 1913.

17 SRO.HH/16/44.

18 *Edinburgh Evening Dispatch*, *Dundee Advertiser*, and *Aberdeen Daily Journal* 29 August 1913.

19 *Aberdeen Daily Journal* 30 August and 2 September 1913.

20 *Dundee Advertiser* 30 August, 2 and 6 September 1913.

21 Arncliffe-Sennett Collection Vol.25. *Forward* 20, 27 September, 4 October 1913. *The Vote* 29 August, 19, 26 September, 3, 17 October 1913.

22 Glasgow and West of Scotland Association for Women's Suffrage executive committee minutes, Department of Rare Books and Manuscripts, Mitchell Library, Glasgow, 27 September, 1 and 24 November 1913.

23 *The Vote* 17, 24, 31 October 1913.

24 *Common Cause* 17 October and 14 November 1913.

25 Shetland Women's Suffrage Society executive committee minutes, Shetland archive, 1 October 1913.

26 *Scotsman* and *Glasgow Herald* 16 October 1913. *Suffragette* 24 October 1913. *Forward* 25 October 1913. See also SRO. JC13/130 and JC26/1551. The latter contains the two postcards found on the scene. One has written on it 'To British Tyrants Asquith and Co. Beware! The destruction of property is but the beginning' and the other, 'A protest against Mrs Pankhurst's re- arrest.'

27 *Suffragette* 24 October 1913. *Scotsman* and *Glasgow Herald* 16 October 1913.

28 SRO.HH16/40.

29 Ibid. The Prison Commission and Scottish Office wanted the police to enter the house and arrest her, but the chief constable did not believe that the Cat and Mouse Act gave police such powers. It transpired that it could be done if a warrant was obtained, but the chief constable advised the prison commissioners that application had been made to the procurators fiscal for police and sheriff courts and that 'both Procurators have declined to move for Warrants.' A similar situation occurred in England.

30 Ibid. and *Daily Record and Mail* 20 November 1913. The chief constable confirmed that the press report was substantially correct.

31 Olive Banks, *Becoming a Feminist: The Social Origins of "First Wave" Feminism* (Brighton 1987), p.39. *Glasgow Herald* 30 April 1985.

32 Letter from Ina Deuchars 26 February 1990.

33 *Dundee Advertiser* 3 November 1913. *Votes for Women* 7 November 1913. According to the *Edinburgh Evening Dispatch*'s version of the story (3 November) the women 'joined hands and thus formed a barrier across the road.'

34 *Votes for Women* 7 November 1913. *Scotsman* 4 November 1913.

35 My tape-recorded interview with Elizabeth Somerville 28 November 1989.

36 *Dundee Advertiser* 10 October 1913. May Grant was one of the interrupters.

37 Ibid. 15, 16, and 27 October 1913. It must have been on this occasion that Isabella Carrie (see Chapter 5) was ejected and joined the WSPU.

38 *Glasgow Herald* 5, 7 and 8 November 1913.

39 *Aberdeen Daily Journal* and *Aberdeen Free Press* 12 November 1913. *Dundee Advertiser* 13 November 1913.

40 *Dundee Courier* 15 November 1913.

41 *Dundee Advertiser* 18 November 1913.

42 *Dundee Courier* 22 and 24 November 1913. *Aberdeen Daily Journal* and *Aberdeen Free Press* 21 November 1913.

43 *Aberdeen Free Press* 22 November 1913. *Dundee Advertiser* 25 November 1913. This was a period when intense debate on the suffrage question was carried out in the correspondence columns of the *Advertiser*.

44 *Edinburgh Evening Dispatch* 15, 17 and 20 November 1913.

45 *The Vote* 21 and 28 November 1913.

46 *Dundee Advertiser* 25 and 26 December 1913.

47 Arncliffe-Sennett Collection Vol.25.

48 *Dundee Advertiser* 4 and 5 December 1913. Harcourt Davidson responded to May Grant's letter (6 December), saying that he firmly believed his views were held by the majority of the nation, both men and women. Her reply to that letter was published on 10 December.

49 National Library of Scotland Acc.4498. The letter is dated 19 December 1913. Versions of it appeared in various newspapers, including the *Dundee Advertiser*, provoking a response from May Grant (29 December) and further correspondence.

50 *Edinburgh Evening Dispatch* 20 October 1913. *Suffragette* 24 October 1913.

51 NUWSS executive committee minutes 20 November 1913, NUWSS Collection, Fawcett Library, City of London Polytechnic.

52 *Common Cause* 14, 21 and 28 November 1913. The WFL also campaigned and its report echoed both the difficulties (the size and layout of the constituency and the dreadful weather) and the almost unanimous agreement with all they said. *The Vote* 12 December 1913.

53 *Common Cause*, 12 December 1913. *Forward* 19 November, 6 and 13 December 1913.

54 James D. Young, *Women and Popular Struggles: A History of Scottish and English Working Class Women, 1500-1984* (Edinburgh 1985), pp.104 and 116.

55 *Edinburgh Evening Dispatch* 12 and 14 November 1913. *The Vote* 21 November 1913.
56 Edinburgh Town Council minutes, Edinburgh archive, 18 November and 2 December 1913. *Scotsman* 2 and 6 December 1913. *Forward* 18 December 1913.
57 Glasgow Town Council minutes, Strathclyde Regional Archive, 27 November, 11 and 23 December 1913.
58 *The Vote* 21 November 1913.

Chapter 10, pp.169 to 187

1 *Edinburgh Evening Dispatch, Scotsman*, and *Glasgow Herald* 8 January 1914. *Forward* 17 January 1914. *The Vote* 23 January 1914.
2 *Scotsman* 8 January 1914. The editor thought that the Church should steer well clear of the subject, but if it did take sides 'it ought, in fidelity to the Scriptural law which it interprets, to range itself against the advocates of women's suffrage.'
3 Ibid. 9 January 1914.
4 *Forward* 17 January 1914. *The Vote* 23 January 1914.
5 See L. Leneman, 'The Scottish Churches and "Votes for Women"', *Trans actions of the Scottish Church History Society* (forthcoming).
6 Edinburgh Town Council minutes, Edinburgh archive, 13 January 1914. *Edinburgh Evening Dispatch* 14 January 1914.
7 *Suffragette* 13 and 27 February 1914.
8 Ibid. 30 January 1914. *Glasgow Herald* 10 February 1914.
9 *Scotsman* and *Edinburgh Evening Dispatch* 23 February 1914. *Suffragette* 27 February 1914.
10 *Edinburgh Evening Dispatch* and *Glasgow Herald* 26 January 1914. *Suffragette* 30 January 1914.
11 Letter from Miss W.K. Bowie to me 22 January 1990.
12 *Dundee Courier* 5 February 1914.
13 Ibid., and *Suffragette* 13 February 1914.
14 Letter from Mrs Isobel Cartwright 10 November 1989.
15 *Glasgow Herald* 6 February 1914.
16 Scottish Record Office (SRO) HH16/39. *Dundee Advertiser* 13 and 14 February, and 8 June 1914.
17 *Common Cause* 13 and 20 February and 13 March 1914. Shetland Women's Suffrage Society committee minutes, Shetland archive, 15 January and 14 February 1914. Glasgow and West of Scotland Association for Women's Suffrage executive committee minutes, Department of Rare Books and Manuscripts, Mitchell Library, Glasgow, 6 January and 10 February 1914. Glasgow and West of Scotland Association for Women's Suffrage letter book (letters dated 12 and 14 January 1914.).
18 *Edinburgh Evening Dispatch* 12 February 1914. *Common Cause* 13 March 1914.
19 *Glasgow Herald* 17 February 1914. He continued: 'The ladies who run the movement did not forget to emphasise in their speeches the contrast between what was described as the indifference to and even frivolous treatment of the subject in England and the fine public spirit displayed by the northern party in having twice within a period of six months devoted three or four days to the great cause of convincing the South.'
20 *Edinburgh Evening Dispatch* 16 February 1914. *The Vote* 20 February 1914.
21 *Votes for Women* 13 February 1913. Maud Arncliffe-Sennett wrote on a letter from Bailie Alston that he died 22 November 1915 after a short illness 'in the Vigour of his Manhood'. Arncliffe-Sennett Collection, British Library, Vol.26.
22 *The Vote* 20 March 1914. Arncliffe-Sennett Collection Vol.26. Letter dated 14 March. Maud underlined the last few words and added her own exclamation mark.

23   Letter from Traquair Estate Office to Herbert C. Maxwell Stuart 21 February 1914. I
     am grateful to Rosalind Mitchison for telling me about this letter and to Mrs
     Maxwell Stuart for kindly sending me a copy and allowing me to quote from it.
24   Ibid. The letter describes the elaborate precautions taken to prevent suffragettes
     getting anywhere near the house. SRO.HH16/40.
25   *Dundee Advertiser* 23 February 1914. *Suffragette* 27 February 1914.
26   *Forward* 6 March 1914. In the same issue Tom Johnston too expressed horror that
     prison officials in Scotland had 'resorted to the despicable and barbarous outrage of
     forcible feeding'.
27   A.E. Metcalfe, *Woman's Effort* (Oxford 1917), p.326.
28   SRO.HH16/40. (Letter from James Devon to the Chairman of the Prison Commis-
     sion 24 February 1914) A report of the interview appeared in the *Edinburgh Evening
     News* 25 February 1914.
29   SRO.HH16/40. *Edinburgh Evening Dispatch* 26 February 1914. *Suffragette* 6 March
     1914.
30   SRO.HH16/40. Dr Graham Sutton suggests that this was a 'referred pain'. The vagus
     nerve, which innervates the stomach and oesophagus, also supplies the eardrum, so a
     trauma to the former might be felt as an intense earache.
31   *Suffragette* 27 March 1914.
32   SRO.HH16/4O.
33   Ibid.
34   Ibid. (Letter from James Devon to the Chairman of the Prison Commission 26
     February 1914) *Edinburgh Evening Dispatch* 17 March 1914.
35   James Logan, 'The East of Scotland Suffragist/Suffragette Movement 1900-1914'
     (unpublished Open University essay 1977), p.18. *Suffragette* 6 March 1914. SRO.
     HH55/336.
36   C. Blair, *Suffragettes and Sacrilege* (WSPU pamphlet, n.d.).
37   Logan, 'East of Scotland Movement', 6-7. Monica Sharon, 'Catherine Blair: Living
     her "Splendid Best"', *Scottish Home and Country* December 1987.
38   SRO.GD433/2/347. Letter dated 6 March 1914. I am grateful to Lord Balfour for
     permission to quote from this letter.
39   See Leah Leneman, 'Suffragettes and the Burning of Whitekirk Church',
     Transactions of the East Lothian Antiquarian and Field Naturalists' Society (forth-
     coming).
40   See, for example, *Edinburgh Evening Dispatch* 3, 6, 7, 11, 12, 17, 19 March 1914. There
     was also a debate in the columns over the extent to which the Northern Men's
     Federation supported militancy. The only non-suffragist paper I discovered (apart
     from the *Forward*) which carried articles sympathising with the militants was the
     Ardrossan and Saltcoats Herald, which carried a series of articles under the heading
     'SHOULD WOMEN HAVE THE VOTE?', subsequently published as a pamphlet,
     by Andrew Henry Lowe.
41   *Scotsman* 14 February 1914.
42   Glasgow Association minutes 2 March 1914.
43   Ibid. 16 March 1914.
44   Eunice Murray's diary April 1914. The diary is in the possession of her nephew who
     has kindly allowed me to quote from it.
45   Lady Frances Balfour, *Ne Obliviscaris Dinna Forget* (London 1930), p.144. E.S.
     Haldane, *From One Century to Another* (London 1937), p.266.
46   Ann Morley with Liz Stanley, *The Life and Death of Emily Wilding Davison* (London
     1989), p.153.
47   Brian Harrison, 'The Act of Militancy. Violence and the Suffragettes, 1904-1914' in
     his *Peaceable Kingdom: Stability and Change in Modern Britain* (Oxford 1982), p.42. In

this most interesting and thoughtful essay the one inaccurate statement (on p.61) is that 'militant acts needed to be focused primarily on London'.

48   Ibid., 68. Andrew Rosen, *Rise Up Women! The Militant Campaign of the Women's Social and Political Union 1903-14* (London 1974), pp.243-5.

50   SRO.HH55/336. This bulky file is concerned mainly with the arrest of Mrs Pankhurst and what followed.

51   Rosen, *Rise Up Women!*, 227.

52   Morley with Stanley, *Life and Death of Emily Wilding Davison*, 176.

53   *Forward* 14 March 1914.

54   Brian Harrison interview with Jessie Stephen 1 July 1977, Harrison Tapes Collection, Fawcett Library, City of London Polytechnic.

55   Antonia Raeburn, *The Militant Suffragettes* (London 1973), p.224. *Suffragette* and *Votes for Women* 13 March 1914. National Library of Scotland (NLS) Acc.4498 'Miss Janie Allan's Suffrage Material'. SRO.HH55/336.

56   *Edinburgh Evening Dispatch* and *Scotsman* 11 March 1914. *The Vote* 20 March 1914. The eye-witness account in that journal was provided by Eunice Murray who also wrote to the *Glasgow Herald*.

57   *Glasgow Herald* 11 and 12 March 1914 (on the 12th there were no less than 10 letters on the subject). Many more letters appeared on 13, 14, 16 and 17 March, though not all of them agreed that the police action had been wrong.

58   *Suffragette* 13 March 1914. SRO.HH55/336.

59   *Suffragette* 20 and 27 March 1914. *Scotsman* 18 March 1914. *Glasgow Herald* 20 March 1914. Metcalfe, *Woman's Effort*, 325-6. SRO.HH55/336.

60   *Suffragette* 10 April 1914. Metcalfe, *Woman's Effort*. 326-7. *Dundee Advertiser* 31 March 1914.

61   SRO.HH55/336. *Suffragette* 13 March and 10 April 1914. However, not all those galvanised by the event joined the WSPU: 72 new members were acquired by the Glasgow and West of Scotland Association in March. Glasgow Association letter book, Katherine Lindsay to Andrew Sloan 3 April 1914.

62   NLS Acc.4498. Letter dated 15 March 1914.

63   David Rubinstein does not agree with my assessment of Christabel: 'the "general", the chief strategist, who had not been present, was *bound* to think like that' (private communication).

64   Memories of Miss I. Carrie compiled by S. Cubbage, History Department, Glasgow University December 1976. Dundee Archive and Record Centre GD/X53.65 *Suffragette* 20 March 1914. SRO.HH16/45. Helen Crawfurd, Unpublished Autobiography, Marx Memorial Library, London, p.90. (A copy of this manuscript is available at the William Gallagher Library, Glasgow.) I am grateful to the Marx Memorial Library for permission to quote from the manuscript.

66   *Scotsman* 16 March 1914. *Suffragette* 20 March 1914.

67   *Aberdeen Daily Journal* and *Aberdeen Free Press* 16 March 1914.

68   *Edinburgh Evening Dispatch* 23 March, 2 and 3 April 1914. *Scotsman* and *Dundee Advertiser* 2 April 1914.

Chapter 11, pp.188 to 208

1   *Common Cause* 9 April 1914 (in the whole of the NUWSS there were 485 societies with over 52,000 members). *The Vote* 20 March 1914. *Anti-Suffrage Review* May 1914.

2   *Edinburgh Evening Dispatch* and *Dundee Courier* 4 April 1914.

3   Ibid. (same dates). E. Sylvia Pankhurst, *The Suffragette Movement: An Intimate Account of Persons and Ideals* (London 1931), p.559. *Suffragette* 10 April 1914.

4   *Forward* 11 April 1914. The tension was mainly due to the fact that Mrs Pankhurst had said she would try to come to Ladybank.

5   *Edinburgh Evening Dispatch* 13 April and 4 May 1914.

6   *Forward* 18 April 1914.

7   *Votes for Women* 17 April 1914. *Dundee Courier* 8 April 1914.

8   NUWSS executive committee minutes 7 and 21 May 1914, NUWSS Collection, Fawcett Library, City of London Polytechnic. Scottish Women's Liberal Federation executive committee minutes, Edinburgh University Library, 8 May 1914. According-ing to the NUWSS minutes the S.W.L.F. action was prompted by the National Union.

9   NUWSS minutes 21 May 1914.

10 *Votes for Women* 15 May 1914.

11 *The Vote* and *Votes for Women* 22 May 1914.

12 Ibid. and *Common Cause* 22 May 1914. *Glasgow Herald* 16 May 1914.

13 Scottish Record Office (SRO) HH16/336. A.E. Metcalfe, *Woman's Effort* (Oxford 1917), p.327. *Daily Record and Mail* 10 April 1914.

14 The Magistrates Committee suppressed this offer in its report to the Town Council, as Janie Allan later pointed out to the Town Clerk of Glasgow. Metcalfe, *Woman's Effort*, 328. *Glasgow Herald* and *Glasgow Evening Times* 24 July 1914.

15 Letter from F.T. Cooper to David Congelton, 15 May 1914. National Library of Scotland (NLS) Acc.4498 'Miss Janie Allan's Suffrage Material'.

16 Ibid. He continued: 'I will assume for the moment that it is a matter of conscience and honour with Miss Allan that she should spend some time in a prison. If she were to delay achieveing [sic] her object of being in one, she could after the Enquiry into the behaviour of the Glasgow Police, still fulfil what she believes to be her duty and be happier for the thought that she had done all she could for her cause ... speaking for myself if I wanted to get into prison, I should choose the time when I had nothing better to do.'

17 *Forward* 30 May 1914. On 3 June the *Glasgow Herald* printed a letter from Janie Allan about the behaviour of the plain-clothes policemen.

18 NLS Acc.4498. Letter from J.T. Cooper to Dr Murray 3 June 1914.

19 SRO.HH16/44. *Suffragette* 22 May 1914.

20 *Edinburgh Evening Dispatch* 9 May 1914. SRO.HH16/44.

21 SRO.HH16/44.

22 *Edinburgh Evening Dispatch* 19 May 1914. *Suffragette* 29 May 1914. The Scottish prison system would have rejoiced to see the last of Arabella Scott, but as she had been convicted in a Scottish court the chairman of the Prison Commission reluctantly informed the prison governor that the Scottish Office said she could not be imprisoned in England. SRO.HH16/44.

23 Letter dated 26 May 1914. NLS Acc.4498.

24 Cliona Murphy, *The Women's Suffrage Movement and Irish Society in the Early Twentieth Century* (Hemel Hempstead 1989), pp.77-8.

25 Glasgow and West of Scotland Association for Women's Suffrage executive committee minutes, Department of Rare Books and Manuscripts, Mitchell Library, Glasgow, 18 May 1914.

26 NUWSS executive committee minutes 7 May 1914. Scottish Federation executive committee minutes, Scottish Women's Hospitals Collection, Department of Rare Books and Manuscripts, Mitchell Library, Glasgow, 25 April 1914. This appears to be the only volume of Scottish Federation minutes still in existence, solely because it covered the period of the Scottish Women's Hospitals and was therefore kept as part of that collection.

27 NUWSS executive committee minutes 18 June 1914. Scottish Federation executive committee minutes 30 May and 25 July 1914. Glasgow Association minutes 10 February 1914. Letter from Catherine Marshall to W.C. Anderson 8 June 1914 and letter from Scottish Federation to Miss Evans 30 June 1914, Catherine Marshall papers (D/Mar/3/29), Cumbria County Record office, Carlisle. I am grateful to the archivist for sending me copies of these letters.

28 *The Vote* 5 and 12 June, 3, 17 and 31 July, 7 August 1914.

29 Shetland Women's Suffrage Society committee minutes, Shetland archive, 15 May 1914. *Glasgow Herald* 8 June 1914. *Edinburgh Evening Dispatch* 4 July 1914. Catherine Marshall papers (D/Mar/3/29), Cumbria County Record office, Carlisle. *Common Cause* 10 July 1914.

30 SRO.HH16/44.

31 *Glasgow Evening Times* 23 June 1914. (The report was reproduced in *Suffragette* 3 July 1914.) SRO.JC14/33 and JC/26/1555.

32 SRO.HH16/44 and 46. *Suffragette* 3 and 10 July 1914. Helen Crawfurd wrote in her memoirs that as a result of this agitation the women were released without being forcibly fed; her unreliable memory was never more wrong. Helen Crawfurd, Unpublished Autobiography, Marx Memorial Library, London, p.104. (A copy of this manuscript is available at the William Gallagher Library, Glasgow.) She certainly knew all about it at the time, for she was editing 'Our Suffrage Columns' for *Forward* and protested strongly about the forcible feeding that was going on in Perth prison.

33 SRO.HH55/336.

34 Ibid.

35 Crawfurd Autobiography, 110-1. I am grateful to the Marx Memorial Library for permission to quote from this manuscript.

36 SRO.HH16/46.

37 Ibid. (Letter dated 9 July 1914).

38 Ibid. *Suffragette* and *Votes for Women* 10 July 1914.

39 Ibid. Referring to the Scottish Secretary's allegation in the House of Commons that Frances Gordon had systematically drugged herself *Votes for Women* (24 July 1914) commented 'For this entirely unfounded allegation, which is emphatically denied by the prisoner and her medical attendant he did not offer the slightest evidence.'

40 *Forward* 11 July 1914.

41 SRO.HH16/47. All material on Maude Edwards is in this file.

42 *Scotsman* and *Edinburgh Evening Dispatch* 7 July 1914. According to the *Scotsman* it was the policeman's prompt seizing of the woman that caused the pamphlets and package to fall short of their target; the *Evening Dispatch* merely stated that 'the aim was faulty'.

43 *Edinburgh Evening Dispatch* 8 and 9 July 1914. *Suffragette* 17 July 1914.

44 *Dundee Advertiser, Dundee Courier* and *Edinburgh Evening Dispatch* 11 and 13 July 1914.

45 *Edinburgh Evening Dispatch, Scotsman, Dundee Advertiser, Dundee Courier* and *Glasgow Herald* 11 July 1914. *Suffragette* 17 July 1914. *Forward* 18 July 1914.

46 *Forward* 18 July 1914. Crawfurd Autobiography. SRO.HH16/43 and 45.

47 *Suffragette* 10, 24, and 31 July 1914. *Dundee Advertiser* 13 and 16 July 1914. *Scotsman* 16 July 1914. I have not been able to discover the real names of Wallace and Bertha Watson.

48 SRO.HH12/63/12 (Governor's Journal Perth Prison). At time of writing this file was closed to the public, and I am grateful to the Scottish Office for allowing me access to it and for permission to quote the extracts in the text.

49 E.g. *Dundee Advertiser* 9 July 1914. Helen Crawfurd wrote in her memoir that she was horrified by the act and that she said in her speech at Perth that 'the two women who

attempted it were not aware of the reverence that Scottish people had for Burns.'
Crawfurd Autobiography, 105. Another distorted memory, for her actual words in
the Perth speech were: 'Could he [Burns] have foreseen that the sacrifice of his house
would form a stepping-stone in the path towards freedom none would have felt so
glad and honoured as he by the offering of that sacrifice.' *Forward* 18 July 1914.

50 *Scotsman, Edinburgh Evening Dispatch* and *Glasgow Herald* 9 July 1914.
51 Ibid. Helen Crawfurd wrote that the other woman was 'an Irish woman, Mary
Moorhead the artist.' Crawfurd Autobiography, 104. *Ethel* Moorhead was at large at
this time, and it is entirely possible that she *was* the second woman, but one can hardly
cite Mrs Crawfurd's confused memories as evidence for this.
52 SRO.HH16/43. All material on Fanny Parker as Janet Arthur is in this file. Her own
statement appeared in *Votes for Women* 7 August 1914.
53 SRO.HH16/44. All material on Arabella Scott in prison is in this file.
54 *Dundee Courier* 27 July 1914. *Glasgow Herald* 28 July 1914. Arabella Scott's detailed
statement appeared in *Suffragette* 7 August 1914.
55 *Dundee Advertiser* 22 July 1914. *Suffragette* 31 July 1914.
56 SRO.HH16/44.
57 Eunice Murray's diary July 1914. The diary is in the possession of her nephew who has
kindly allowed me to quote from it.

Chapter 12, pp.209 to 217

1 Diary of Eunice Murray October 1914. This diary is in the possession of her nephew
who has kindly allowed me to quote from it.
2 Roland E. Muirhead Collection, Department of Rare Books and Manuscripts,
Mitchell Library, Glasgow. Andrew Rosen, *Rise Up Women! The Militant Campaign
of the Women's Social and Political Union 1903-14* (London 1974), p.254. There was
another breakaway organisation, the 'Independent Women's Social and Political
Union', as well.
3 Jill Liddington, 'The Women's Peace Crusade: The History of a Forgotten Campaign' in Dorothy Thompson ed., *Over Our Dead Bodies: Women Against the Bomb*
(London 1983), pp.180-88. J.V. Newbury, 'Anti-War Suffragists', *History* 62 (1977).
Ann Wiltsher, *Most Dangerous Women – Feminist Peace Campaigners of the Great War*
(London 1984), pp.58-62 and 126.
4 E. Sylvia Pankhurst, *The Suffragette Movement: An Intimate Account of Persons and Ideals*
(London 1931), pp.523 and 525. Brian Harrison interview with Jessie Stephen 1 July
1977, Harrison Tapes Collection, Fawcett Library, City of London Polytechnic.
Liddington, 'The Women's Peace Crusade', 190. Wiltsher, *Most Dangerous Women*,
148, 150-1.
5 *Common Cause* 9 October 1914.
6 *Common Cause* 4 September and 16 October 1914. Glasgow and West of Scotland
Association for Women's Suffrage, executive committee minutes, Department of
Rare Books and Manuscripts, Mitchell Library, Glasgow.
7 Scottish Federation executive committee minutes 3 October 1914, Scottish Women's
Hospital Collection, Department of Rare Books and Manuscripts, Mitchell Library,
Glasgow.
8 Letter dated 9 October 1914, Scottish Women's Hospital Collection, Fawcett Library,
City of London Polytechnic.
9 *Common Cause* 30 October and 20 November 1914. Shetland Women's Suffrage
Society committee minutes, Shetland archive, 22 December 1914. The great bulk of
M. Lawrence's biography of Elsie Inglis, *Shadow of Swords* (London 1971) is about the
years 1914-17 (Elsie Inglis died in Serbia in 1917).
10 *The Vote* 14 August, 4, 11, 18 September, and 2 October 1914.

11   Ibid. 18 and 25 June, 6 August and 10 September 1915.

12   M.D. Pugh, 'Politics and the women's vote' *History* 59 (1974), p.361. Glasgow
     Association letter book 18 August 1914. *The Vote* 18 December 1914.

13   Andro Linklater, *An Unhusbanded Life* (London 1980), pp.180-81. *The Vote* 9 April
     1915.

14   *The Vote* 21 January and 1 September 1916.

15   Letters dated 10 and 15 August 1914, Arncliffe-Sennett Collection, British Library,
     Vol.26.

16   Letter from Katherine Lindsay to Mrs Muir 17 September 1914, Glasgow Association
     letter book (see also letter from Katherine Lindsay to Mabel Jones 4 September 1914).
     Helen Crawfurd Unpublished Autobiography, Marx Memorial Library, London,
     p.15.

17   *Edinburgh Evening Dispatch* 12 and 19 July 1915. *The Vote* 11 August 1916.

18   The summary of events at national level in this and later paragraphs comes from the
     following sources which will not again be footnoted except when directly quoted:
     Ray Strachey, *The Cause: A Short History of the Women's Movement in Great Britain*
     (London 1928), pp.352-66. Pugh, 'Politics and the women's vote'. Rosen, *Rise Up
     Women!*, 256-66. Les Garner, *Stepping Stones to Women's Liberty* (London 1984),
     pp.96-7. Brian Harrison, *Separate Spheres: The Opposition to Women's Suffrage in
     Britain* (London 1978), pp.204-17.

19   Quoted in Harrison, *Separate Spheres*, 204. Pugh, 'Politics and the women's vote', 359.

20   *Workers' Dreadnought* 1 July 1916.

21   See Shetland Women's Suffrage Society committee minutes, Shetland 1 May 1917
     and Glasgow Association minutes 11 June 1917.

22   *The Vote* 1 June 1917.

23   *Forward* 30 June 1917. Pugh, 'Politics and the women's vote', 366. *Edinburgh Evening
     Dispatch* 20 June 1917.

24   Glasgow Association letter book 11-24 June 1917.

25   Harrison, *Separate Spheres*, 216. *Anti-Suffrage Review* December 1917.

26   *Anti-Suffrage Review* April 1918. *Workers' Dreadnought* 16 February 1918. My
     interview with Jean Morrison 22 November 1989. Rosalind Mitchison told me of
     Ellen Wilkinson's remark.

27   Glasgow Association minutes 1 February 1918.

28   Scottish Record Office GD1/1076/1 and 4.

29   See S.J. Hetherington, *Katharine Atholl 1874-1960: Against the Tide* (Aberdeen 1989).

30   Johanna Alberti, *Beyond Suffrage Feminists in War and Peace, 1914-28* (London 1989),
     p.159.

31   Joyce Halley sent me a draft of an article or speech of that period by her mother, Mary
     Halley, a Dundee WFL member, urging the need to extend the vote to all women.

32   Interviews by Brian Harrison with Anna Munro's son and daughter, Harrison Tapes
     Collection, Fawcett Library, City of London Polytechnic. The information on Lila
     Clunas was supplied to me by Norah Montgomerie, who remembered her well, in a
     telephone conversation 10 November 1989.

33   Denys Val Baker, *Little Reviews 1914-1943* (London 1943), p.20. Monica Sharon,
     'Catherine Blair: Living her "Splendid Best"', *Scottish Home and Country* December
     1987. Elspeth Janet Boog Watson, *Edinburgh Association for the University Education of
     Women 1867-1967* (Edinburgh n.d.).

34   The Suffragette Fellowship Collection is in the London Museum. It is symptomatic of
     the schismatic nature of the women's suffrage movement that while the bulk of
     material relating to the movement was deposited in the Fawcett Library, the
     Suffragette Fellowship insisted on its material being housed separately (information
     provided by Nichola Johnson of the London Museum).

Appendix 1

Calendar of Events at National Level

1866	First petition by women for the suffrage presented in House of Commons by John Stuart Mill
1867	
May	Mill moves an amendment to the Representation of the People Act altering word 'man' to 'person' (74 voted Aye, 194 against)
Aug-Oct	Suffrage societies started in London, Manchester and Edinburgh
1870	Jacob Bright's Bill passes Second Reading by majority of 33
1871-3	Second Reading of Jacob Bright's Bill each year fails to secure majority
1875-6	Christian Forsyth's Bill fails to pass Second Reading
1877	Same Bill is talked out
1878	Same Bill fails to pass Second Reading
1884	William Woodall's Amendment to the Reform Bill is rejected
1888	Schism in national women's suffrage organisation
1892	Second Reading of Sir Albert Rollit's Bill rejected
1897	The two national women's suffrage organisations reunite as the National Union of Women's Suffrage Societies (NUWSS) Faithfull Begg's Bill passes Second Reading by a majority of 71
1903	Emmeline Pankhurst forms Women's Social and Political Union (WSPU) in Manchester with her daughters Christabel and Sylvia, joined shortly thereafter by Annie Kenney and Teresa Billington
1905	
June	Second Reading of Bamford Slack's Bill talked out
Oct	Public meeting held by Liberals, addressed by Sir Edward Grey, in Free Trade Hall, Manchester; Annie Kenney asks about votes for women and Christabel Pankhurst unfurls banner; the question is not answered, the women make a disturbance and are arrested, refuse to pay fines and are jailed
Dec	General Election

1906

Jan | Results of General Election: an overwhelming majority for the Liberals; WSPU demands votes for women that session and promises to harass Liberals until this is achieved

March | Sir Charles Dilke's Bill talked out; Emmeline Pethick-Lawrence becomes WSPU treasurer; *Daily Mail* coins term 'suffragette' for militant suffragists

Apr | Debate on Keir Hardie's Resolution interrupted

June | Teresa Billington and Annie Kenney arrested for causing a disturbance while attempting to call on Asquith and become first suffragettes to be imprisoned in Holloway

Oct | Eleven women arrested for causing a disturbance at opening of Parliament, imprisoned in Holloway in Second Division; a fuss is made and they are transferred to First Division; on their release they are feted by the constitutionalists

1907

Feb | 3,000 people march in heavy rain from Hyde Park to Strand (organised by NUWSS); dubbed 'the Mud March'

Feb | 'Women's Parliament' in Caxton Hall presided over by Mrs Pankhurst deplores the omission of any reference to women's suffrage in the King's Speech; women march to Parliament Square where mounted police attempt to turn them back; mêlée lasts for hours, leaders are arrested

March | Women's Suffrage Bill introduced by W.H. Dickinson is talked out at Second Reading; subsequently another 'raid' on House of Commons is organised by WSPU; tussle lasts several hours, with many arrests

Oct | A group of women led by Charlotte Despard and Teresa Billington-Greig object to Pankhurst style of leadership and break away to form the Women's Freedom League

1908

Feb | Another WSPU 'Women's Parliament' in Caxton Hall; march to House of Commons; many arrests

Feb | Second Reading of Stanger Bill (identical to Dickinson's Bill of the previous year): 271 votes for, 92 against

June | 13,000 suffragists march from the Embankment to the Albert Hall, carrying colourful banners

June | WSPU organises 7 processions from different parts of London to converge on Hyde Park where a large rally is held (spectators estimated at half a million)

Oct | WSPU attempts to 'rush' the House of Commons; the leaders are arrested for incitement, conduct their own defence at trial in Bow Street police court and receive wide publicity

1909

March	Howard Bill passes Second Reading by majority of 35
Apr	Successful WSPU bazaar held in Prince's skating rink, with replica of Holloway prison cell — over £5,000 made
June	More than 100 women arrested in repeated sorties against House of Commons
July–Oct	Women's Freedom League peacefully picket outside House of Commons, waiting to present a petition to Asquith
July	A WSPU member (Marion Wallace-Dunlop) imprisoned in Holloway refuses to eat anything unless placed in First Division
July–Sept	Suffragettes are released from prison before the end of their sentences because of hunger strikes
Sept	First case of forcible feeding (at Winson Green prison, Birmingham)
Dec	General Election

1910

Jan	Result: Liberals lose 100 seats but retain power
Spring–Summer	All-party 'Conciliation Committee' drafts limited women's suffrage bill (giving the vote to householders only); WSPU and Women's Freedom League suspend militancy
	Grand suffrage procession after introduction of the Conciliation Bill in House of Commons
July	Second Reading of Conciliation Bill: 299 votes in favour, 189 against
Nov	Asquith calls General Election on House of Lords issue, which means abandonment of Conciliation Bill; suffragettes march to Parliament Square and are brutally treated by police for hours on the 18th ('Black Friday')
Winter	Asquith gives promise that Liberal Government, if returned, would give facilities for a suffrage bill
Dec	Result of election: little change in composition of House

1911

May	Second Conciliation Bill debated, with large majority (167) in favour; Cabinet says no further time could be spared that session but reiterates Prime Minister's pledge that time for a suffrage bill would be found during the life of the Parliament; truce on militancy continues
June	Grand procession by militants and constitutionalists preceding coronation of King George V
Nov	Asquith announces that the Government would introduce an adult suffrage bill next session, capable of amendments to include women; WSPU objects as it means little hope is left for the Conciliation Bill

1912

March	Shop windows around Piccadilly, Regent Street and Oxford Street, and later in Kensington, are smashed in WSPU 'raid'; more than 200 women are arrested and imprisoned

March	Police arrest WSPU leaders on conspiracy charge; Christabel flees to Paris; the rest are sentenced to 9 months' imprisonment
March	Second Reading of new Conciliation Bill (similar to 1911 version) defeated by 14 votes
July	Suffragettes throw hatchet into Asquith's open carriage in Dublin and attempt to set fire to Theatre Royal Attempt made by suffragettes in England to set fire to a Cabinet Minister's house
Aug	Emmeline and Frederick Pethick-Lawrence question the wisdom of more extreme militancy, are expelled from the WSPU which is led thereafter by Mrs Pankhurst and Christabel (from Paris)
Oct	Non-militant Edinburgh to London suffrage march

1913

Jan	Franchise and Registration Bill is debated in House of Commons, with four women's suffrage amendments; Speaker announces that if an amendment approving women's suffrage were carried it would cause such a fundamental alteration to the Bill that it would have to be withdrawn
Apr	Passage of Prisoners (Temporary Discharge) Bill, giving powers for release of hunger-striking suffragette prisoners and their re-arrest when recovered, known as the Cat and Mouse Act
May	Private Member's (Dickinson) Bill fails to pass Second Reading by 47
June	Emily Wilding Davison throws herself in front of the King's Horse at the Derby and is killed
Spring-Summer	Escalating attacks on property by militants, including bombs placed in Lloyd George's unfinished house, railway stations burned down etc
Summer	'Pilgrimage' of suffragists from various parts of the country converging on London
Summer	Sylvia Pankhurst is expelled from the WSPU for her socialist connections, forms the East London Federation of Suffragettes

1914

Jan-July	Frequent attacks of arson and homemade bombs throughout the country
May	Lord Selborne's Bill in the Lords fails to pass Second Reading by 44! The authorities raid WSPU headquarters
June	Suffragettes attempt to force their way into Buckingham Palace to petition the King
Aug	War is declared; WSPU suspends militancy and suffrage work; all suffragettes convicted of militant attacks are pardoned

1916

Oct-Dec	All-party conference, presided over by Speaker of the House of Commons, drafts proposals for new franchise legislation

1917
Dec   Electoral Reform Bill giving votes to certain women over 30 passes
                    the Commons

1918
Feb   Electoral Reform Bill receives Royal Assent
Nov   Armistice; Bill enabling women to stand for Parliament is rushed
                    through both Houses

Appendix 2

Women Active in the Movement in Scotland

These notes are compiled from a wide range of sources, a few of them very full, others very scanty, and some contradictory. It is impossible, therefore, to ensure the accuracy of anything which appears in this appendix, though naturally I have done my best to sift out the facts. For details of my sources for any individual please contact me through the Department of Scottish History, University of St Andrews. I hope someday others will be able to find out more about some of these women.

N.B. Married women are given their husband's name first and their maiden name second, as in Scottish legal custom; where a maiden name is unknown they are styled 'Mrs'.

ISHBEL, COUNTESS OF ABERDEEN – chairman of both the English and Scottish Women's Liberal Federations in the 1890s, she was a leading figure in the women's movement in the late nineteenth and early twentieth centuries. Although active on many fronts (she was president of the International Council of Women 1883-9 and the Glasgow Council for Women's Trades) she always made clear her commitment to the enfranchisement of women. She became a vice-president of the Glasgow and West of Scotland Association for Women's Suffrage when it was formed in 1902 and was a vice-president of the NUWSS until 1914.

JANIE ALLAN – the daughter and sister of owners of the Allan Shipping Line, well-known for their socialist principles, she was one of the key financial supporters of the militant suffrage movement throughout its existence. When the Glasgow and West of Scotland Association for Women's Suffrage was formed in 1902 she was on the executive committee but retired from office when the WSPU came to Scotland in 1906 and joined that organisation. When the Women's Freedom League broke away she remained with the WSPU but nevertheless helped the WFL financially until 1912. In April of that year she was sentenced to 4 months' imprisonment in Holloway for smashing windows. In 1913 she chaired Emmeline Pankhurst's meeting in Glasgow; she was charged before the Court of Session for refusing to pay inland revenue; and she began editing 'Our Suffrage Columns' for *Forward*. In 1914 she led the deputation protesting against police brutality at the time of Mrs Pankhurst's arrest, and that same year she was arrested in connection with the WSPU deputation to the King.

MARY S. ALLEN – WSPU organiser for Edinburgh 1913-14 (also Aberdeen in 1913), her English origins appear to have been the source of some local friction. When war broke out she was recruited by the Women's Freedom League as one of the first women police.

LILIAS ANDERSON or SCOTT – born in Dundee in 1874, she was the daughter of a tailor and worked as a dress-maker and tailoress. Before her marriage to George Anderson (a keen socialist) in 1911, she was a member of the Women's Freedom League in Glasgow. Afterwards she continued to be interested in both the women's movement and socialism, and was an admirer of Sylvia Pankhurst. She died in Glasgow in 1944.

HELEN ARCHDALE or RUSSELL – born c.1876. Her mother had been active in the Edinburgh women students' fight for medical education, championed by her father, Alexander Russell, editor of the *Scotsman*. A WSPU member, she was charged with breach of the peace and imprisoned in Dundee in October 1909 but released 4 days later after hunger striking. She took part in the WSPU's window smashing raid in London in 1912.

Mrs MAUD ARNCLIFFE-SENNETT – an actress before she married and became involved in her husband's business, she was at various times an executive committee member of the WSPU, WFL and Actresses' Franchise League. In 1912 she helped her sister, Mrs de Fonblanque, arrange the women's march from Edinburgh to London. She arranged the deputation of Scottish men to London in 1913, then formed, and became president of, the Northern Men's Federation for Women's Suffrage. She kept over two dozen volumes of scrapbooks on the suffrage movement which are in the British Library.

JANE ARTHUR or GLEN of Barshaw – born in 1827, she was a leading member of the women's movement in Paisley. The mother of five children, Mrs Arthur belonged to an influential family and used her influence in a variety of philanthropic ways. She was vice-president (her sister being president) of the Paisley Ladies Sanitary Association, which in 1866 initiated a public baths scheme, and treasurer of Paisley Infirmary Dorcas Society which provided clothing and blankets for people in need after they had been in Paisley Infirmary. In 1873 she stood at the first school board election and came head of the poll. She was very active in the suffrage cause and was fully supported by her husband and other male members of the family. She died in 1907.

LADY BETTY BALFOUR – her sister, Lady Constance Lytton, was a well-known figure in the WSPU, while her brother, the 2nd Earl of Lytton, was president of the Men's League for Women's Suffrage. Lady Betty channelled her own suffrage activities through the NUWSS and the Conservative and Unionist Franchise Association, becoming president of the Edinburgh and Glasgow branches.

LADY FRANCES BALFOUR – born in 1858, daughter of the 8th Duke of Argyll, she became active in the women's suffrage movement in the 1880s and during the decades that followed she spoke at meetings all over Scotland and England. She was on the NUWSS executive committee and was President of the London Society for Women's Suffrage but spent much time in Scotland and was always conscious of her Scottish roots. Lady Frances was President of the Scottish Churches League for Woman Suffrage. She died in 1931.

MARGARET SIMPSON BARNETT or MAIDEN – a keen non-militant, she regularly attended meetings of the Edinburgh National Society for Women's Suffrage, leaving her young daughter in the care of her supportive husband. She was born in 1874 and died in 1956; she acquired a teaching certificate in 1894 and was an L.L.A. of St Andrews University.

JANET BARROWMAN – a WSPU member, she was born in 1879 in Glasgow, where her father was a lime merchant. In 1912 she served two months' hard labour in Holloway for breaking a window valued at 4 shillings. She lost her job as a clerk because of this but was able to get another (where she remained until retirement) and did not commit any other militant acts.

Mrs CATHERINE BAXENDINE – active in the Edinburgh branch of the WSPU, Mrs Baxendine did not commit acts of militancy herself as she had three young children (a fourth was born in 1915). Born c.1872 she moved from the Borders to Edinburgh at the age of 18 and became a librarian with Carnegie public libraries and later at the university library.

TERESA BILLINGTON GREIG – although born (15 October 1876) in Preston, Lancs, her influence on the movement in Scotland was great. She was the first woman national organiser in the ILP in 1905 and one of the earliest members of the WSPU. In 1906 Scottish WSPU branches were formed by her; as a speaker she made a lasting impression on those who heard her. In 1907 she married Frederick Lewis Greig, an Aberdonian by birth who worked as a branch manager of a billiards firm in Glasgow. Later that year she was one of the leaders of the group who objected to the Pankhurst style of leadership and formed the Women's Freedom League. By 1911 she was also disillusioned with the WFL and attacked both societies in her book, *The Militant Suffrage Movement*, but after the war she was again active in the Freedom League.

CATHERINE BLAIR or SHIELDS – the daughter of an East Lothian farmer, she was born 8 January 1872 and married Thomas Blair in 1894, setting up home at Hoprig Mains Farm, Gladsmuir. A WSPU member, Catherine Blair had four children to bring up and therefore did not commit acts of militancy herself, but she was one of Scotland's most ardent defenders of militancy, both as a speaker and as a writer of countless letters to newspapers. She also provided a refuge for suffragette prisoners released under the Cat and Mouse Act. Her husband fully supported her, resigning his vice-presidency of the local Liberal party because of the government's treatment of the suffrage question. In 1917 Catherine Blair established the first Scottish Women's Rural Institute and in 1919 she founded the Mak'Merry pottery studio. She died in 1946; in 1990 she was still well remembered in Edinburgh.

NANNIE BROWN – a woman whose charm was frequently mentioned, she was an active member of the Women's Freedom League in Edinburgh, and in November 1912 she was one of only six women who marched the whole way from Edinburgh to London to promote the cause of women's suffrage. When the Northern Men's Federation for Women's Suffrage was formed in 1913 she became Honorary Secretary for the Edinburgh branch. From 1917 onwards she was involved in the newly-formed Scottish Women's

Rural Institutes, and she also joined the Edinburgh Women Citizens Association. Her sister, Jessie, with whom she lived, was also active in the WFL and NMF, and after the war their house became a cultural centre. Jessie Brown died in 1937 and Nannie Brown in 1944.

JANET BUNTEN – treasurer of the Scottish Council of the Women's Freedom League, she resided at 10 Polwarth Gardens, Glasgow. In 1909 she was arrested for attempting to present a petition to Asquith at Downing Street. In 1911 she was the first woman in Glasgow to refuse to pay inhabited house duty. Her refusal to pay her dog tax resulted in her being tried in Glasgow in January 1912 and when she would not pay her fine she was sentenced to ten days' imprisonment. Later that year, and again the following year, goods of hers were publicly sold for non-payment of taxes. She was imprisoned in Holloway in 1913 for obstruction while taking part in a WFL protest in Downing Street.

LUCY BURNS – an American of Irish ancestry from New York, she became caught up in the movement and joined the WSPU in London. She took part in the first militant protests in Scotland, at Glasgow and Dundee in August and September 1909, and in November of that year became organiser of the WSPU's Edinburgh branch, remaining in that position until c.1913. After her return to America she was one of the founders of the Congressional Union for Woman Suffrage, a militant organisation.

GRACE CADELL – born 25 October 1855, she was one of the first students at Sophia Jex-Blake's Edinburgh School of Medicine in 1887. She and her sister were expelled for leading a rebellion against Dr Jex-Blake and were subsequently awarded damages. She was later appointed co-equal senior consultant with Elsie Inglis at Bruntsfield Hospital. Dr Cadell was president of Leith branch of the WSPU in the summer of 1907, but after the split she adhered to the Women's Freedom League. As she was a tax resister some of her goods were sold at the Mercat Cross in 1912 and 1913. In the latter year she was also prosecuted and fined for refusing to pay National Insurance contributions for her staff. When suffragettes were imprisoned in Scotland and released under the Cat and Mouse Act she not only provided a house of refuge but also helped them to escape. At an unknown date (probably at the outbreak of the war) she adopted four children. Dr Cadell died 19 February 1918.

ISABELLA CARRIE – born in Arbroath 3 May 1878, her first few years as a schoolteacher in Dundee coincided with the heyday of the suffrage movement. Although a believer in the enfranchisement of women and an admirer of Emmeline Pankhurst as a speaker, it was only after she was brutally ejected from a meeting of Winston Churchill's that she was driven to join the WSPU. She did not play a public role in the organisation but helped with the library and provided accommodation for WSPU members who came to Dundee.

LADY GRISELDA CHEAPE – one of the most prominent anti-suffragists in Scotland, from 1909 until July 1912 she was president of St Andrews branch of the Scottish National Anti-Suffrage League. At that time she was also president there of the British Women's Temperance Association. In September 1913 she formed her own local anti-suffrage organisation, The Beehive. Before her marriage, Lady Griselda went on a course of training — and then worked – in children's hospitals. She was intensely religious and based her anti-suffrage views on biblical injunctions of woman's rightful place in relation to man. Her three children passed on memories of a highly eccentric upbringing.

LILA CLUNAS – born in Glasgow, she graduated from Moray House, Edinburgh and then worked as an elementary school teacher in Dundee. She joined the militant movement in September 1906 and was secretary of the Dundee branch of the Women's Freedom League from 1908-12. She was Dundee's first suffrage prisoner in Holloway in August 1909 for attempting to present a petition to Asquith in Downing Street. In October of that year she was one of two spokeswomen in a WFL deputation to Churchill in Dundee. From 1912 to 1914 many of her letters were published in the press, and she spoke at various public meetings. After the war she was for some years a member of Dundee Town Council with a particular interest in education. She was remembered three-quarters of a century later as a quiet, small, kindly person.

G.M. CONOLAN – she was organiser for Glasgow branch of the WSPU from 1908-9 and was arrested in London on 'Black Friday' (November 1910). Both her grandfathers had been MPs, and she worked for women's suffrage at many by-elections. In January 1913 she became Honorary Secretary of the newly-formed Federated Council of Women's Suffrage Societies.

ANNA RHODA CRAIG (sometimes given as Greig) or WALKER alias Rhoda Robinson – born at Gravesend, in 1899 she married Francis McCulloch Craig, a stevedore, and lived at Warwick Villas, Mill Road, Yoker, Glasgow. She was the first ILP member in Dunbartonshire, served a term as a member of her local School Board, and became secretary of Dumbarton branch of the WSPU. She was imprisoned for 10 days in Holloway for breaking War Office windows and later in Glasgow for smashing the window of Churchill's car. As Rhoda Robinson she was charged with fire-raising in Stirlingshire in February 1914 but was released for lack of evidence. In April of that year she was again arrested (as Rhoda Robinson) and charged with setting fire to a wood plantation in Dunbartonshire.

LILLIAS CRAIG – according to the obituaries which appeared after her death in Edinburgh in March 1883 (aged 72), she was one of the earliest and most energetic friends of women's suffrage and a valued member of the Edinburgh National Women's Suffrage Society from its commencement.

JESSIE CRAIGEN – the daughter of an Italian actress and a Scottish sailor, she addressed innumerable meetings – many of them out of doors and to working-class audiences – throughout Scotland and the north of England during the early 1870s. She had no paid employment in the movement but collected minimum expenses to keep her going.

HELEN CRAWFURD (often misspelt Crawford) or JACK – she was born 9 November 1877 in the Gorbals, Glasgow, but grew up in Ipswich. In 1898, shortly after her family's return to Glasgow, she married the Rev Alexander Montgomerie Crawfurd (a much older man, who died in 1914); they lived at 17 Sutherland Street, Hillhead. After attending suffrage meetings in Rothesay and Rutherglen she joined the WSPU in 1910. In 1912 she was arrested and imprisoned in Holloway for breaking the windows of the Liberal Minister of Education's residence. Between 1912 and 1914 she was a regular speaker at WSPU meetings in Scotland. Although brought up in a Conservative home, her involvement in the women's movement changed her outlook, and she became a socialist. In March 1914 she was imprisoned in Glasgow for breaking windows at the army recruiting office, and went on hunger strike; she was re-arrested under the Cat and Mouse Act in April and again in July and went on hunger strike each time. During the war she was one of the founders of the Women's Peace Crusade. She later joined the Communist Party and remained a committed Marxist until her death in 1954. Helen Crawfurd left behind an unpublished autobiography.

ALICE CROMPTON – born in Manchester, she was the niece of Lydia Becker and thus imbued with suffrage ideals from an early age. In 1910 she became secretary of the Dundee Women's Suffrage Society. From 1911 she was anorganiser for the Scottish Federation of the NUWSS.

MARY CRUDELIUS or MCLEAN – born 23 February 1839, she was one of the leaders in the fight for higher education for women in Scotland. In 1861 she married Rudolph Crudelius, a German businessman in Leith. In 1867 she was the founder of the Edinburgh Association for the Higher Education of Women (originally called the Edinburgh Ladies' Educational Association). Although most of her energies were channelled into that particular fight, she was a signatory of the first petition to Parliament for the enfranchisement of women and worked quietly behind the scenes to further that cause as well. She died, aged 38, on 27 July 1877.

FLORA DRUMMOND – although brought up in Arran, she lived in London where she was a leading figure in the WSPU, known as the 'General'.

MARGARET MILNE FARQUHARSON – a graduate with an M.A., in 1908 she founded the Queen Margaret College Suffrage Society and in 1909 became its president. That same year she represented the women of the four Scottish universities in the Women's Freedom League attempted deputation to Asquith in London, and was imprisoned in Holloway in consequence. Thereafter she lived, and worked for the suffrage cause, in England.

ANNIE FRASER – the younger sister of Helen Fraser; in 1907 she was one of the first Scottish women to be imprisoned in Holloway for the cause when she attempted to march from the Women's Parliament in the Caxton Hall to the House of Commons.

HELEN FRASER – from the day she heard Teresa Billington-Greig speak in Glasgow, Helen Fraser devoted herself full-time to the cause, becoming the first Scottish WSPU organiser in 1906. She was arrested in that year for attempting to enter the House of Commons, yet when the WSPU began to throw stones she resigned in protest and joined the NUWSS. She helped to form various Scottish branches though later she was mainly active in England where she was known as the 'chieftainess'. During and immediately after the war she worked for the government in the south of England. She stood as Liberal candidate for Govan in 1922; after failing to be elected in that year and the two following years she resigned from the Liberal Party. She later married and lived in Australia.

EMILY FUSSELL – she came up from Bristol to Aberdeen as Honorary Secretary of the WSPU branch there in 1911. In 1912, at the age of 28, she travelled from Aberdeen to London to take part in the window-smashing raid and was imprisoned in Holloway as a consequence. She remained in Aberdeen the following year as WSPU organiser.

Mrs ELIZABETH FINLAYSON GAULD (often misspelt Gould) – one of the most active WSPU members in Edinburgh, at her trial for window-breaking at Newington in 1912 (aged 59) she promised to refrain from future violent acts because as matron of a children's home she could not be absent for long periods of imprisonment. This did not deter her from speaking out in defence of violent militancy on every possible occasion thereafter. Between 1910 and 1912 she spoke mainly for the Women's Freedom League, and even after that, when she appears to have switched her allegiance to the WSPU, she spoke at such non-WSPU events as the beginning of the Edinburgh to London march and the Scottish bailies' deputation to Asquith in London. Immediately after the war she was involved in the newly-formed Scottish Women's Rural Institutes, but as an invalid in later years she played no further part in public life.

ELLISON GIBB – born in Glasgow (her address was given as Elliot House, Elliot Street, Hillhead), she was a descendant of William Skirving, one of the men charged with sedition in 1794 and banished to Botany Bay. An active WSPU member, in 1910 and 1911 she was imprisoned twice in Holloway and once in Aylesbury where she was forcibly fed. In 1912, when she was said to be 32, she was imprisoned again in Holloway and later in Dundee (for smashing windows). In that year she brought a successful charge of assault against a Mr E.H. Smith of Dundee who had grabbed and held her when she tried to speak to Asquith at Ladybank. In 1913 she bought Mrs Pankhurst's 'Cat and Mouse Act' licence (sold in aid of WSPU funds) for £100.

Dr MARION GILCHRIST – one of those who fought for the right of women to a medical career, she took a preliminary training in Arts at Queen Margaret College before entering on medical studies, and became the first woman to receive a medical degree in Scotland. (She was also an L.L.A. of St Andrews University.) In 1903 she joined the Glasgow and West of Scotland Association for Women's Suffrage but resigned in 1907 to join the WSPU.

BESS GLADSTONE – of Craigknowe, Biggar, she worked in an office in Glasgow and took part in the census resistance of 1911. She married a Biggar scholar, Dr Robert Harris, in 1915. She died in 1974.

FRANCES GORDON – she was arrested for house-breaking and attempted fire-raising in Glasgow in 1914, when she was described as a little woman of about 40 years of age with a pronounced English accent. She was sentenced to 12 months' imprisonment in Perth prison, where she was forcibly fed through the rectum for 10 days before being released under the Cat and Mouse Act.

LISA GORDON – an NUWSS organiser (from c.1909–c.1914) based in Edinburgh, Lisa Gordon was active in all the Scottish by-elections, including the Election Fighting Fund Labour/suffrage campaigns. Her sister, Clementina, was NUWSS organiser in Newcastle.

MAY POLLOCK GRANT (alias Marion Pollock) – the daughter of the minister of St Mark's parish church in Dundee, May Grant took part in missionary work both at home and abroad before the women's suffrage cause claimed her full-time commitment. A WSPU member, she first became known in December 1912 as one of the women imprisoned for smuggling themselves into the Music Hall, Aberdeen, with the plan of disrupting a Liberal meeting. (She was said to be 36 at that time.) Throughout 1913 and 1914 she wrote numerous letters to the press and was frequently ejected from public meetings for causing a disturbance.

EMILY GREEN or HICKSON – matron of a home for women in reduced circumstances in Glasgow, she was arrested for smashing windows in Sauchiehall Street, an action committed on her own initiative without WSPU approval. She stated at that time that she was English but a member of Glasgow branch of the WSPU.

Mrs GREIG – president for a number of years of the Glasgow Women's Liberal Association, she was the first Chairman of the Glasgow and West of Scotland Association for Women's Suffrage when it was formed in 1902.

Mrs GRIEVE – a wealthy widow, of Collesdene House, Joppa, she was described in 1913 as a prominent sympathiser with the cause who had suffered imprisonment in London. Mrs Grieve was a WSPU member and provided shelter for at least one Scottish suffragette released under the Cat and Mouse Act. In 1913 she refused to pay her taxes and some of her household effects were sold by public auction. She was remembered as a large, stately woman

Mrs MARY HALLEY – a Dundee Women's Freedom League member, she held the distinction of being the only census resister threatened with prosecution. She was born 9 August 1866, married in 1896, and died in 1959. Her father had been a skilled artisan who found difficulty in securing employment because of his trade union activities. Mary Halley once stood unsuccessfully for the Dundee Town Council.

MARY J.H. HENDERSON – the daughter of an architect, she was born in Dundee in 1874. In 1911 she was appointed organiser by the Scottish Federation of the NUWSS but had to resign a month later because of ill health. However, from 1912 to 1914 she was honorary secretary of the Dundee Women's Suffrage Society and in 1913 she was also parliamentary secretary of the Scottish Federation. In January 1914 she presided over a joint ILP/NUWSS meeting in Dundee and in March of that year she was a candidate for the Dundee School Board. During the war she was honorary secretary of the Dundee Women's War Relief Committee.

J.C. HOWDEN – she resided at The Boggs, Pencaitland and in 1911 tried to form WSPU branches in Tranent and Pencaitland. Subsequently she went over to the NUWSS and became president of the Haddington Women's Suffrage Society.

EDITH HUDSON (alias Mary Brown) – an Edinburgh hospital nurse, she was an active WSPU member. She was imprisoned for the first time in Edinburgh in 1909. In 1912 (when she was stated to be aged 40) she served a sentence in Holloway for breaking windows; she was said to have fought against being forcibly fed, knocking down six wardresses. Conversely she was later remembered by another woman, who had been a child at the time, as a very gentle person. In 1913 she was charged with attempting to set fire to Kelso racecourse stand and sentenced to 9 months imprisonment in the Calton jail, Edinburgh; after a 7-day hunger strike she was released under the Cat and Mouse Act and disappeared.

NELLIE HUNTER or GALBRAITH – born in Rutherglen, she was the daughter of James Galbraith, Sheriff Substitute of Lanarkshire. In 1886 she married James T. Hunter, a Glasgow yarn merchant, and had three children. She resided at 18 Wilson Street, Hillhead. She was secretary of the Glasgow and West of Scotland Association for Women's Suffrage from its inception in April 1902 until March 1911, when she became secretary to the National Vigilance Association of Scotland. Nellie Hunter helped to initiate the Scottish Federation of the NUWSS.

AGNES HUSBAND – before 1906 she was a member of the NUWSS but in that year she joined the militant movement, and from 1909 onwards she was president of the Dundee branch of the Women's Freedom League. She was born in Tayport, was elected a member of the Parish Council in 1900 and of Dundee School Board in 1905, and was a prominent member of the Labour Party in Dundee. Her address was given as 67 Murraygate. After the war Agnes Husband was on the executive committee of the Dundee Women Citizens Association.

Dr ELSIE INGLIS – born in India in 1864, her family moved to Edinburgh in 1878. She became a suffrage supporter while at Elizabeth Garrett Anderson's Hospital (then called the New Hospital for Women) in London where, newly qualified, she went in 1892. She returned to Edinburgh in 1894 and set up the city's first hospital for women and children. She later became an executive committee member of the NUWSS and secretary of the Scottish Federation of Women's Suffrage Societies. During the war she was the organiser and leader of the Scottish Women's Hospitals and died in Serbia in 1917.

MARGARET IRWIN – secretary of the Scottish Council for Women's Trades, she was a member of the executive committee of the Glasgow and West of Scotland Association for Women's Suffrage until 1907. From 1908 onwards she was a regular speaker at Women's Freedom League meetings in various parts of Scotland, depicting the situation of women workers in the sweated industries. After the war Margaret Irwin was on the executive committee of the Glasgow Women Citizens Association.

ALEXIA B. JACK – a teacher in Edinburgh, she was the first secretary of Edinburgh branch of the Women's Freedom League and was also honorary secretary and treasurer of the WFL's Scottish Council.

CHRISTINA JAMIESON – secretary and guiding spirit of the Shetland Women's Suffrage Society (founded in 1909 and affiliated to the NUWSS) she was born in the isolated parish of Sandness in the 1870s, the daughter of the local schoolmaster. (Her brothers went on to successful careers in academia and medicine while she remained at home.) Her involvement in the women's suffrage movement began after the family moved to Lerwick. The Shetland press published numerous letters and articles of hers on the subject. In 1916 she became a member of Lerwick School Board (probably the first woman to serve on any public body in Shetland). Christina Jamieson was very interested in local history and collaborated with the local scholar, E.S. Reid Tait, producing two books based on kirk session records, as well as writing short stories for the Scottish press and founding the Shetland Folklore Society. In 1935 she emigrated to New Zealand to live with her brother; she died there in 1942.

Mrs N.A. JOHN – a member of the WSPU contingent from Glasgow who were imprisoned in Holloway in 1912, she was a regular speaker at Glasgow WSPU meetings in the years that followed.

Dr MABEL JONES – based in Glasgow, she was medical adviser of two of the suffragettes forcibly fed in Scotland, writing damning reports of their condition on release. She was an occasional speaker at WSPU meetings in Glasgow.

ELIZA SCOTT KIRKLAND, J.P. – in the 1870s and 1880s, as secretary of the Edinburgh National Society for Women's Suffrage, she was a regular speaker throughout Scotland. She was also one of the women in charge of the Scottish National Demonstration of Women held in Edinburgh in March 1884.

JEAN LAMBIE – an Edinburgh WSPU member, her most notorious act was an assault on James Devon after he had assumed responsibility for forcible feeding of suffragettes in Scottish prisons in March 1914. The previous summer she had taken part in a WSPU caravan tour of the Borders. She did not hold an official position in the WSPU, having apparently incurred the wrath of Christabel Pankhurst. In 1916 she became organising secretary of a breakaway organisation, 'Suffragettes of the W.S.P.U.'.

KATHERINE MARY LOUDON – born in Bombay in 1869, she held a Diploma of the Edinburgh Association for the Higher Education of Women. She was honorary secretary of the Edinburgh National Society for Women's Suffrage from 1912.

ALICE MARY LOW – she was the daughter of Lord Low, Senator of the College of Justice, and Annie Mackenzie, daughter of Lord Mackenzie. Alice Low was organising secretary of the Edinburgh National Society for Women's Suffrage from 1909 onwards and was also a member of the executive committee of the Scottish Federation. From 1908 until her resignation in 1912 she was a member of Whitsome School Board.

LOUISA INNES LUMSDEN – born in Aberdeen 31 December 1840, she joined the first course of lectures by university professors in Edinburgh in 1868, then went on to Girton where, in 1873, she was one of the first three women to take the Honours Examination in Classics at Cambridge and an LL.D. degree. From 1877-1882 she was the first Headmistress of St Leonard's School for girls in St Andrews. Some 15 years later, during which time she was chairman of Rhynie School Board, she returned to St Andrews to give a start to the new residential University college. A lifelong believer in women's suffrage, Louisa Lumsden became actively involved in the constitutional movement from 1908 onwards, and was president of the Aberdeen Society and, later, a member of the executive committee of the Scottish Federation.

JANE LYNAS – a WSPU member, sister of Dorothea Chalmers Smith, she was charged at the Central Police Station, Glasgow over disturbances in the High Court in October 1913; in April 1914 she was charged with setting fire to a wood plantation but did not appear in court. Her address was given as Broompark Drive, Dennistoun, Glasgow.

FLORENCE E.M. MACAULAY – the author of the Women's Marseillaise (c.1908), she was Edinburgh WSPU organiser c.1908-9. In 1913 she addressed WSPU meetings in various parts of Scotland.

ANN MACBETH – head of the Embroidery Department at the Glasgow School of Art, she designed a banner for the great Scottish demonstration of October 1909 and a linen quilt with the embroidered names of hunger strikers for the Scottish Exhibition in April 1910.

JENNY MCCALLUM – born in Inverkeithing in 1881, her father was a stone mason engaged in the building of the Forth Railway Bridge. When she was a young girl the family came to live in Dunfermline, and she worked in the linen industry after leaving school. In October 1908 she left her factory job to take part in the Women's Freedom League deputation in London and was imprisoned in Holloway. She then returned to Dunfermline and eventually got another job. She married c.1914-15, had three children, and emigrated to South Africa where she died in 1946.

AGNES MACDONALD – an Edinburgh WSPU member, she was imprisoned in Holloway in 1912. In 1913 she was honorary secretary of the Edinburgh branch of the WSPU. After the war she held a paid position as secretary of the Edinburgh Women Citizens Association.

MARGARET MACDOUGALL or ARMOUR – her mother and grandmother, both Margaret Armours, were active in the women's suffrage movement in the nineteenth century. Married to an artist, W.B. MacDougall, she made her name as a translator of Heine and Wagner. In 1911 she wrote *Agnes of Edinburgh*, a romantic novel with a sympathetic suffragist character in it.

FLORENCE MACFARLANE – in December 1909, as matron of a private hospital in Edinburgh, a post which she had held for 13 years, she resigned rather than dismiss one of her nurses who had taken part in a militant protest. She was arrested in London on 'Black

Friday' (November 1910) and again in 1912, when she was forcibly fed in Holloway. In 1910 she became honorary secretary of the WSPU in Dundee. She continued to be very active there in 1913.

A.J. MACGREGOR – proprietrix of the estate of Abbeythune, near Arbroath, she was hostess to the first Dundee hunger strikers after their release in 1909. In 1913 an antique silver urn of hers was sold by public auction because of her refusal to pay taxes.

Dr AGNES MACLAREN – she was the daughter of Duncan MacLaren (by his second wife), at whose house the agitation for opening medical schools to women began. She was joint secretary of the Edinburgh National Society for Women's Suffrage at its formation in 1867 and continued active in the movement for over half a century. She died in 1913.

PRISCILLA MCLAREN or BRIGHT – born in Rochdale in 1815, she was the sister of anti-Corn Law campaigner John Bright, and became the third wife of the Radical Edinburgh MP Duncan McLaren in 1848. In November 1867 she became the first president of the Edinburgh National Society for Women's Suffrage (the first Scottish women's suffrage society) and remained in that position until her death in 1906. (In 1886 she had a husband, two sons, two brothers, and a nephew all sitting in the House of Commons.)

(JESSIE) CHRYSTAL MACMILLAN – born in Edinburgh in 1871, she was the only daughter in a wealthy family of eight sons. She matriculated at Edinburgh University in 1892 (the first year that women could matriculate); in 1896 she graduated B.Sc. with first-class honours in Mathematics and Natural Philosophy and in 1900 M.A. with second-class honours in Mental and Moral Philosophy. From 1906-8 she was honorary secretary and treasurer of the Women Graduates of the Scottish Universities (Parliamentary Franchise) Committee which tried to establish their claim to the vote; in 1908 she pleaded the case herself before the House of Lords. She was a member of the Scottish Universities Women's Suffrage Union, a vice-president of the Edinburgh National Society for Women's Suffrage, and a very active member of the NUWSS executive committee, representing Scottish views. She was instrumental in founding the Women's International League for Peace and Freedom in 1915 and served as secretary of the International Woman Suffrage Alliance for ten years from 1915. After the war she also practiced as a barrister. Chrystal Macmillan died in 1937.

Mrs.KATHERINE MACPHERSON – holder of an L.L.A. degree, she was a Women's Freedom League secretary and convener, residing at 3 Charlotte Street, Perth. Before her marriage to Thomas Macpherson, solicitor, member of the Town Council, and ex-bailie, she trained and worked as a teacher. She had three children. In 1913 she stated that she had always been keenly interested in the suffrage and entered into active work for the cause when the militant movement came into being.

FRANCES MARY MCPHUN – the holder of an M.A. degree and a winner of prizes at Glasgow University in Political Economy, Moral Philosophy and English Literature, she and her sister, Margaret, were amongst the most active WSPU members in Glasgow. She arranged the pageant of famous Scottish women for the Edinburgh procession in October

1909, was honorary organising secretary for the Scottish Suffrage Exhibition in 1910, and was honorary secretary of the Glasgow branch of the WSPU 1911-12. She took part in the London processions of 1908, 1910 and 1911 and served a term of imprisonment in Holloway — two months' hard labour – for her part in the window-smashing protest of March 1912. She was very active in by-election campaigns in the west of Scotland. The McPhun sisters lived at 10 Doune Terrace, Hillhead, Glasgow.

MARGARET POLLOCK MCPHUN – a keen WSPU member, she took part, along with her sister, in the London processions of 1908, 1910 and 1911 and also served two months' hard labour in Holloway for window smashing. She held an M.A. degree and was a university prizewinner in Psychology, Logic and Metaphysics; she was convener of the Glasgow branch of the Scottish Universities Women's Suffrage Union 1909-10. From 1906-8 she was honorary treasurer of the N. Kelvinside and Maryhill Liberal Association, but subsequently her political views must have moved to the left, for from 1911-13 she was a contributor to the Scottish socialist journal, *Forward*. After the war she was on the executive committee of the Glasgow Women Citizens Association.

SARAH ELIZABETH SIDDONS MAIR – the great-granddaughter of Sarah Siddons, she was the founder-president (at the age of 19) of the Ladies' Edinburgh Debating Society and remained president throughout its existence from 1865-1935. At 22 she was one of the seven founders of the Edinburgh Association for the University Education of Women. She was also involved throughout this period in the women's suffrage movement. From 1907 she was president of the Edinburgh National Society for Women's Suffrage and subsequently of the Scottish Federation as well. She became a Dame of the British Empire and an LL.D. of Edinburgh University, and until her death in 1941 her home at 5 Chester Street, Edinburgh, was the centre of all kinds of activity connected with the welfare of women.

Mrs LOUISA MALCOLM – she was a prominent member of the Women's Liberal Association and a member of the School Board and Parish Council in Dollar. Not only was she the first woman councillor in Scotland, in 1913 she was unanimously elected by Dollar Town Council as Scotland's first woman provost. Mrs Malcolm was a keen supporter of women's suffrage and often addressed meetings on the subject.

ROSALINE MASSON – daughter of Professor Masson, she was the author of several books on life in Scotland as well as a school textbook on 'The Use and Abuse of English'. In 1912-13 she featured as a speaker at NUWSS meetings. In 1913 she became honorary secretary of the Edinburgh branch of the Conservative and Unionist Women's Franchise Association. After the war she was honorary press secretary of the Edinburgh National Society for Equal Citizenship.

FRANCES H. MELVILLE – born in 1873, she was the first Scottish woman Bachelor of Divinity (St Andrews); her other degrees included an M.A. at Edinburgh University and LL.D. at Glasgow. She was warden of the Women's Hall of Residence at St Andrews and subsequently Mistress of Queen Margaret College, Glasgow. Frances Melville was one of the initiators of the Scottish university graduates' lawsuit and a member of the Scottish

Universities Women's Suffrage Union. After the war she was honorary president of the Glasgow Women Citizens Association. She died in 1962.

J.C. METHVEN – from the 1890s until the arrival of militancy she was secretary of the Edinburgh National Society for Women's Suffrage; in 1897 she was one of two representatives from that society on the NUWSS Parliamentary Committee. Feeling that non-militant methods were futile, in 1906 she joined the WSPU in Edinburgh and was a keen member right up to the outbreak of war.

LILIAS MITCHELL – born into a middle-class Edinburgh family (her father ran a flourishing timber business), she joined the WSPU at 23. She was first imprisoned in Holloway in 1909 for taking part in a procession to Downing Street. In 1911 she was appointed WSPU organiser for Aberdeen. The following year she was involved in the WSPU's window-smashing campaign in London; when charged at Newington she said she 'would afterwards be proud that she had taken part in militant tactics'. She was sentenced to 4 months' imprisonment in Holloway and there underwent her first experience of forcible feeding. After that she returned to Aberdeen, during which time she tied flags with the WSPU colours on the royal golf course at Balmoral. From 1913 to 1914 she was at various times WSPU organiser at Newcastle, Birmingham and Belfast. While in Birmingham she was charged with making inciting speeches and was again imprisoned and forcibly fed. After the war she worked as a secretary with the YWCA and wrote articles for the *Scotsman*. She died of a heart condition in Edinburgh 24 September 1940.

Mrs MAGGIE MOFFAT (sometimes misspelt Moffatt) – the wife of actor and playwright Graham Moffat, herself an actress and the mother of a young girl, she travelled from Glasgow to London in 1907 to take part in the militant demonstration, thereby becoming one of the first Scots to be arrested and imprisoned for the cause. After the split she became treasurer of the Scottish Council of the Women's Freedom League, while her husband was instrumental in forming Scottish branches of the Men's League for Women's Suffrage. In the years that followed, the Moffats were too busy touring with their successful company to devote much time to the cause, but they always made their views clear when interviewed by the press.

DUCHESS OF MONTROSE – founder and president of the Scottish Women's National Anti-Suffrage League from April 1910, the Duchess was also president or vice-president of various charitable organisations, including the Scottish Council of the British Red Cross. The honorary degree of LL.D. was awarded to her by Glasgow University.

ETHEL MOORHEAD (alias Edith Johnston, Mary Humphreys, Margaret Morrison) – inaccurately called the leader of the suffragettes in Scotland by the press, she was without doubt its most turbulent character. Ethel Moorhead was brought up in India where her father was an army surgeon; the family returned to Dundee in about 1905. She made her maiden speech at a Dundee WSPU meeting in March 1910; in December of that year she threw an egg at Winston Churchill when he held a meeting there. In January 1911 she was Dundee's first tax resister; later that year, after her father's death, she moved to Edinburgh where she was known as an artist. In March 1912 she was arrested in London for damaging two windows but was discharged for lack of evidence. In September she smashed the glass at the Wallace Monument; when she was arrested she gave her name as Edith Johnston. She served a 7-day sentence in Perth prison for that offence. In October, after being ejected from a meeting in Edinburgh's Synod Hall, she marched into the classroom of the male teacher who had been responsible and attacked him with a dog whip. She was arrested in her own name and convicted at Edinburgh police court; her fine of £1 was paid in court so she did not go to prison. In December she was arrested in Aberdeen for causing a disturbance and gave her name as Mary Humphreys; she went on hunger strike but was released on payment of part of her fine after serving four days of her 10-day sentence. At the end of January 1913 she was involved in a disturbance at a meeting in Leven where she threw cayenne pepper into the eyes of a police constable and was arrested as Margaret Morrison. She caused havoc in Cupar police cells and was then sentenced to 30 days' imprisonment in Perth but was released after serving only two days because she had been hunger striking since her arrest. In July 1913 – as Margaret Morrison – she was held in Duke Street prison, Glasgow, for attempted fire-raising. She was sentenced to 8 months' imprisonment but was released under the Cat and Mouse Act after a five-day hunger strike. In 1914 she was re-arrested and was forcibly fed in Calton jail, Edinburgh, but was released after contracting pneumonia. During the war she helped to run the Women's Freedom League National Service Organisation. In the 1920s she lived in Paris and co-edited an English-language review of art and literature.

ANNA MUNRO – a woman of particular charm and beauty, she formed a branch of the WSPU in Dunfermline. After the split she was one of the most active members of the Women's Freedom League in Scotland and became Teresa Billington-Greig's private secretary in December 1907. In January 1908 she was one of three WFL members who tried to see Haldane in London and was arrested and imprisoned in Holloway. She was appointed Organising Secretary by the WFL Scottish Council in February 1908 but c.1912 she moved down to England. In 1913 she married Sidney Ashman (they adopted name Munro-Ashman), who had admired her speaking at an open-air suffrage meeting in Berkshire; shortly thereafter she was again imprisoned in Holloway. After the war she became a magistrate.

EUNICE G. MURRAY – the secretary for 'scattered members' in Scotland of the Women's Freedom League from its inception, she was born in 1877, the third child and youngest daughter of an eminent Glasgow lawyer. Eunice Murray was a lively speaker and writer of letters to the press. By 1913 she was Scottish president of the WFL and had written a number of pamphlets, the most popular one being *Liberal Cant*. In later years she was the author of *Scottish Women of Bygone Days* (Glasgow 1930) and *A Gallery of Scottish Women* (London 1935). She lived at Moorpark, Cardross, Dunbartonshire.

MARGARET NAIRN – youngest of the first eight Edinburgh University women Arts graduates (awarded an M.A. in 1893), her name was first amongst those who raised the action in the Court of Session for women graduates' right to the franchise. Her father was a Glasgow merchant who retired early and came to live in Edinburgh. She was one of the early female cyclists in the city, and she travelled widely on her own in Europe, often on church work.

HELEN OGSTON – the daughter of a professor at Aberdeen University, she held a BSc. from St Andrews University. She was a WSPU speaker 1908-9 and achieved notoriety when, after interrupting Lloyd George at a meeting in the Albert Hall, she held off the stewards with a dog whip.

ADELA PANKHURST – the youngest Pankhurst daughter, she was the only one to work as a paid organiser for the WSPU and was involved in the earliest acts of militancy and hunger striking in Scotland, in Glasgow and Dundee in 1909. Her left-wing views were not agreeable to Christabel or her mother, and she was sent to Australia to work for the women's movement there.

FANNY (FRANCES MARY) PARKER (alias Janet Arthur) – a niece of Lord Kitchener and graduate of Newnham College, Cambridge, she was arrested for the first time in 1908 and spent six weeks in Holloway. In 1909 she was a speaker for the Scottish Universities Women's Suffrage Union; in 1910 she organised their caravan tour; in 1911 she was secretary and also the Union's delegate to the International Suffrage Convention at Stockholm. In October and December of that year she campaigned in the Kilmarnock Burghs and Ayrshire North by-elections. In January 1912 she was WSPU organiser for Glasgow and the west of Scotland. In March she took part in the WSPU's window-smashing raid and was sentenced to four months in Holloway; she went on hunger strike and was forcibly fed. In October 1912 she became WSPU organiser in Dundee where she was arrested (in November) for breaking a window; she was released from prison after a three-day hunger strike. In December she was one of the women who smuggled themselves into the Music Hall, Aberdeen, with the intention of causing a disturbance at Lloyd George's meeting; this time she was on hunger strike for five days before release. In July 1914 she was caught trying to blow up Burns Cottage in Alloway, and as she immediately went on hunger strike she was sent to Perth prison and forcibly fed. In 1914 the Women's Freedom League appointed her honorary organiser of their National Service Organisation.

GRACE PATERSON – born in 1843, the daughter of a Glasgow merchant, she participated in the struggle to achieve women's admission to Glasgow University. She was principal of the Glasgow School of Cookery, founded in 1875, and one of the first two women elected on to Glasgow School Board in 1875. In 1902 she was a founding member of the Glasgow and West of Scotland Association for Women's Suffrage but resigned in sympathy with militancy in 1907. She was joint honorary secretary of the Scottish WSPU in that year, but there is no record of any later involvement. Grace Paterson died in 1925.

ALICE PAUL – an American student at the London School of Economics, she got caught up in the suffrage movement and was active with the WSPU in 1908-9, being twice imprisoned in Holloway. In September 1909 she was imprisoned in Dundee but released after a 3-day hunger strike. She helped to organise the Edinburgh suffrage procession that October and was active in the East Fife by-election. She was also arrested in Glasgow and Berwick (but not imprisoned) for her part in militant suffrage demonstrations. After her return to America she was one of the founders of the Congressional Union for Woman Suffrage, a militant organisation.

CAROLINE PHILLIPS – born 13 December 1870, the daughter of a schoolmaster, she was a journalist with the *Aberdeen Daily Journal* when militancy came to Scotland. From 1907-9 she was honorary secretary of Aberdeen branch of the WSPU in spite of the disapproval of her employer. Local infighting drove her away, and there is no record of any later involvement in the movement.

MARY E. PHILLIPS – born in 1880, for three years prior to 1907 she was organising secretary of the Glasgow and West of Scotland Association for Women's Suffrage as well as local secretary for Largs committee, but on 17 October of that year she resigned and joined the WSPU. She was imprisoned in Holloway in February and July 1908; on her release in September she was given a 'Highland welcome' as the suffragette who had served the longest prison term. From 1907-9 she was an active campaigner in Scotland and wrote the woman's column for *Forward*. After that she went to England; in 1913-14 she was with Sylvia Pankhurst's East London Federation. During the 1950s she wrote a pamphlet, *The Militant Suffrage Campaign in Perspective*.

Mrs W. RENNY – in October 1909 she was a member of the Women's Freedom League deputation to Churchill in Dundee. In 1912 she took part in the WSPU's window-smashing raid in London and was imprisoned in Holloway. Thereafter she spoke at various WSPU meetings in Scotland. She resided at Craigie Barns, Dundee.

ANNOT E. ROBINSON or WILKIE – first secretary of the WSPU in Dundee in 1907, she had previously been a teacher. She was imprisoned in Holloway for taking part in a London demonstration in 1908. In that year she married Sam Robinson and moved to England (in 1910 she was a delegate for central Manchester at the Women's Labour League annual conference). At some point she switched her allegiance to the NUWSS, who sent her back up to Scotland to fight E.F.F. campaigns in support of Labour candidates. In 1918 she became organiser of Manchester branch of the Women's International League for Peace and Freedom.

AMY SANDERSON or REID – she joined the WSPU at Forfar, but after the split she adhered to the Women's Freedom League and was a member of the WFL executive committee for three years after its formation. In February 1908 she took part in the protest at the House of Commons and was imprisoned in Holloway. Amy Sanderson was an active speaker in Scotland thereafter; in 1909 alone she reckoned that she addressed 97 meetings.

ARABELLA CHARLOTTE SCOTT – born at Dunoon 7 May 1886, she was the daughter of an officer in the Indian army. She graduated M.A. from Edinburgh University, lived with her sister, Muriel at 88 Marchmont Road, and worked as a teacher in Leith. She was very keen on open-air propaganda and spoke at open-air meetings in various parts of Scotland. In 1908-9 she spoke under the auspices of the Women's Freedom League, and as a WFL member she took a petition to Downing Street in July 1909, was charged with obstruction of the police and sentenced to 21 days in Holloway. She continued to speak at open-air meetings, but after 1912 she clearly decided that the WFL's tactics were unlikely to be effective, for in April 1913 she was convicted of attempting to set fire to Kelso racecourse stand. In June she served five days of her 9-month sentence before being released as a hunger striker under the Cat and Mouse Act; in August she was imprisoned a second time and again released under the same Act. During the following months she worked as a WSPU organiser under an assumed name in the south of England. She was re-arrested in May 1914 and again released after hunger striking, and arrested once again in June when she was sent to Perth prison to be forcibly fed for five weeks.

MURIEL ELEANOR SCOTT – born 18 June 1888 in India, she also graduated M.A. from Edinburgh University, and she lived with her sister Arabella in Edinburgh. She too was arrested and imprisoned in Holloway in 1909. She addressed numerous open-air meetings throughout the south of Scotland between 1908 and 1914. As a result of her 'spirited heckling' of Keir Hardie in Edinburgh in February 1913 she was invited to take part in a debate, 'The Case for the Militants Against the Labour Party'.

BESSIE STEWART SEMPLE – a Glasgow schoolteacher, she was the first honorary treasurer of the WSPU in Glasgow but at the split became honorary secretary of Glasgow branch of the Women's Freedom League (1907-8 and 1910-11). She was imprisoned in Holloway in July 1909 for attempting to present a petition to Asquith in Downing Street. Her left-wing political views are clear from the fact that in October 1909 she presided over a Glasgow Clarion Scouts meeting. She was active in the WFL thereafter and was a member of the Scottish Council. In 1915 she was appointed Captain of the WFL's Woman's Suffrage National Aid Corps in Glasgow.

MARGUERITE ANNE SIDLEY – although English, she was actively involved in the Women's Freedom League campaign in Scotland. She was born in 1886 and worked as a shorthand typist before joining the WSPU and being employed in the office in London. Her health suffered from working indoors, so she left her employment there to become a speaker. She then broke with the WSPU and joined the WFL. In 1909 and 1910 she was involved in the WFL's summer Clyde campaign as well as working as an organiser for Glasgow and district; in 1911 she organised the census resistance in Edinburgh.

FRANCES HELEN SIMSON M.A. – born in Edinburgh in April 1854, the daughter of the Secretary of the Bank of Scotland, she was one of the first eight women graduates of Scottish universities in April 1893. She acted as junior counsel to Chrystal Macmillan in the Scottish Graduates' appeal to the House of Lords in 1908. Frances Simson was president of the Scottish Universities Women's Suffrage Union and a vice-president of the Edinburgh National Society for Women's Suffrage; after the war she was president of the Edinburgh National Society for Equal Citizenship. She was Warden of Masson Hall of Residence for Women Students in Edinburgh for over 20 years from 1897. Edinburgh University conferred the honorary degree of LL.D. on her in 1933; she died five years later.

(ELIZABETH) DOROTHEA CHALMERS SMITH or LYNAS – she was one of the first women graduates in medicine from Glasgow University in 1984 at the age of 22 and eventually joined the staff of Glasgow's Royal Samaritan Hospital for Women. At 27 she married the Rev William Chalmers Smith, minister of Calton Church, Glasgow, and had six children. She became involved in the militant suffrage movement in 1912, and in 1913 she was caught trying to set fire to a Glasgow mansion-house. She was sentenced to 8 months' imprisonment at Duke Street prison in July but was released under the Cat and Mouse Act after a 5-day hunger strike; she was returned to prison in October and again released after five days. Her husband believed that a woman's place was in the home, and she eventually left him, taking her three daughters with her (she was not allowed to see her sons again). Dr Chalmers Smith died in 1944 and was still remembered as a wonderful doctor and remarkable woman in 1990.

M.A. FRASER SMITH – active in Dundee from 1909 to 1912, she was WSPU organiser there in 1911. In 1912 she was charged with breaking a window in the Dundee post office; she conducted her own defence, and the verdict was Not Proven.

LADY STEEL – between 1904 and 1906 she was on the executive committee and the Women's Franchise and Local Government committee of the Scottish Women's Liberal Federation. The widow of an Edinburgh Lord Provost, Lady Steel was the first woman to seek election to Edinburgh Town Council (in 1907). In 1907 and 1909 some of her goods were sold for non-payment of taxes. She was a member of the Edinburgh National Society for Women's Suffrage.

JESSIE STEPHEN – the eldest of eleven children in a closely-knit Glasgow family, she is virtually the only Scottish working-class WSPU member about whom anything is known. She wanted to become a teacher, but when her father's trade as a tailor was poor she needed to help out and she went into domestic service. Her father had joined the ILP at its formation in 1893, and at 16 Jessie joined both the ILP and the WSPU and was active in both. She was one of the undetected band of militants who placed acid in Glasgow letter-boxes, and she took part in the working women's delegation to London. At about that time she also organised a Domestic Workers' Union in Glasgow. She then got a job in the south of England and joined up with Sylvia Pankhurst's organisation, eventually working for it full-time. Jessie Stephen remained a committed socialist, pacifist and Trade Unionist throughout her life.

ELIZA STEVENSON – one of three Edinburgh sisters who were among the most active campaigners in the Victorian women's movement. She was one of the earliest members of the Edinburgh National Society for Women's Suffrage and devoted her energies to that cause.

FLORA STEVENSON – born in 1839, sister to Eliza and Louisa, she was an inspiration for many in the Scottish women's movement. She was elected to the first Edinburgh School Board in 1873 and was continuously re-elected for 33 years until her death. She later became chairman of the school board, in which capacity she overcame much male prejudice over women's ability for such functions. She was an active member of many committees and associations, including the Edinburgh National Society for Women's Suffrage, and had an honorary LL.D. conferred on her by Edinburgh University in 1903. In 1905 she was presented with the Freedom of the City of Edinburgh; she died later that same year.

LOUISA STEVENSON – born in 1835, sister of Eliza and Flora, her priority was the fight to obtain medical education for women, but she was also active on many other fronts. She was one of the first two women to be elected to the Parochial Board in Edinburgh; was re-elected six times to the Board of Managers of Edinburgh Royal Infirmary; and she was one of the founders of the Edinburgh School of Cookery and Domestic Economy. She took a keen interest in women's suffrage from the beginning of the campaign until the end of her life and during the 1890s was on the executive committee of the NUWSS. Edinburgh University conferred the honorary degree of LL.D. on Louisa Stevenson in 1906, two years before her death.

JANE E. TAYLOUR – of Belmont, Stranraer, secretary of Galloway branch of the National Society for Women's Suffrage, from 1870 until the summer of 1873 (when she went to England) she was an extraordinarily active speaker, travelling as far north as Orkney and Shetland to spread the suffrage message. Before she left Scotland she was presented with a testimonial for her work.

AGNES COLQUHOUN THOMSON – a WSPU member, in 1911 she was sentenced to 5 days' imprisonment in Holloway. In 1913, at the age of 67, she was charged with attempting to set fire to Kelso racecourse stand, but the verdict was Not Proven. Her address was given as 15 Hartington Place, Edinburgh.

ELIZABETH THOMSON – sister to Agnes, she was also imprisoned for 5 days in Holloway in 1911; in May 1912 she served a further term in Holloway. At the age of 65, in 1913, she was indicted for attempting to set fire to Kelso racecourse stand and sentenced to three months' imprisonment, but she was released after a 5-day hunger strike.

MARCHIONESS OF TULLIBARDINE – a key speaker at the most important Scottish anti-suffrage demonstration, in 1912, she became joint vice-president of Dundee branch of the Anti-Suffrage League in 1913. In later years, as Duchess of Atholl, she was one of the first women elected to Parliament.

HELEN WADDEL – one of the founding members of the Glasgow and West of Scotland Association for Women's Suffrage in 1902, her real commitment was to working for the cause of women's suffrage within the Liberal party. She was on the executive committee of the Scottish Women's Liberal Federation from the 1890s onwards, and from 1904–10 was also a member of the Federation's Women's Franchise and Local Government section. In 1908 she was the author of a leaflet entitled 'Liberal Women and the Parliamentary Vote'. In May 1914 she became convener of the Suffrage Committee of the SWLF.

OLIVE WALTON – an Englishwoman who was WSPU organiser for Dundee from November 1913 until the outbreak of war, she created disturbances during the Royal visits to Dundee and Edinburgh in 1914.

ELIZA WIGHAM – born in Edinburgh in 1820 to a Quaker family who had come from the north of England to Scotland in the 1790s, she was actively involved in the anti-slavery campaign. She was joint secretary of the Edinburgh National Society for Women's Suffrage at its beginning in 1867 and was one of the leaders of the Victorian Scottish women's suffrage movement. She joined the Scottish Women's Liberal Federation shortly after its formation and was a member of the executive committee. Eliza Wigham died at her sister's home in Dublin on 3 November 1899.

HELEN WILKIE – a graduate with an M.A. degree, she was the sister of Annot (Robinson). She took part in the Women's Freedom League deputation to Churchill in Dundee in 1909 and in 1912 she was appointed secretary for Dundee branch of the WFL.

Mrs S.C. WILSON – in 1909 she was president of the 'Western Branch' of the Women's Freedom League and chaired various meetings. In 1912 she was a member of the group of Glasgow women who participated in the WSPU's window-smashing raid in London and was imprisoned in Holloway. In 1914 she took part in WSPU picketing outside prisons where suffragettes were hunger-striking or being forcibly fed and wrote suffrage articles for the *Forward*. Her address was given as Hardhill, Cambuslang. After the war she was on the executive committee of the Glasgow Women Citizens Association.

BARBARA WYLIE – WSPU organiser for Edinburgh in 1910, she was sentenced to seven days' imprisonment in 1911; she also took part in the WSPU's window-smashing raid in London in March 1912 but was released from Holloway, along with her sister, because of her mother's illness and after promising to commit no more illegal acts. She justified her stone-throwing by referring to the appalling housing conditions she had encountered during her two years' work in Glasgow. On 20 September 1912 she sailed for Canada where her brother was a member of the Saskatchewan Provincial Parliament. During her stay in Canada Barbara Wylie continued to work for the suffrage cause and reported regularly to the WSPU. By March 1914 she was back in Britain and spoke at both Glasgow and Edinburgh after Mrs Pankhurst's arrest. On 2 July she was charged in London with incitement to violence, and as she refused to refrain from militancy or violence she was sent to Holloway; she was released under the Cat and Mouse Act on 22 July.

EMMA WYLIE – sister to Barbara, she was also imprisoned in Holloway in 1911 and 1912. She was active in by-election work and as a speaker at Scottish WSPU meetings.

TABLE 2
ATTACKS ON PROPERTY ATTRIBUTED TO SUFFRAGETTES IN SCOTLAND

(compiled mainly from the Scotsman (S), Glasgow Herald (GH), Dundee Advertiser (DA), Dundee Courier (DC), Edinburgh Evening Dispatch (ED), and The Suffragette with some additional material from other sources)

DATE IN PRESS	NATURE OF ATTACK	ESTIMATED DAMAGE	ARRESTS if any
1912			
18 Mar	6 windows smashed in Sauchiehall St, Glasgow	£100	Emily Green
7 Sep	Glass broken of case containing Wallace Sword at Wallace Monument, Stirling	Not stated	'Edith Johnston'
30 Oct	Window smashed in Dundee & attempt made on another	Not stated	Ellison Gibb Fanny Parker
18 Nov	Bottles of brown fluid poured into Edinburgh pillar-boxes	All letters deliverable	
28 Nov	Corrosive fluid poured into Aberdeen letter-boxes	Not stated	
2 Dec	Inflammable fluid poured in Edinburgh, Leith & Kirkcaldy pillar-boxes	'A number of' letters amaged	
6 Dec	Inflammable fluid poured into 2 Glasgow pillar-boxes	'Many letters damaged'	
1913			
3 Feb	Edinburgh pillar-boxes tampered with	Not stated	
6 Feb	Glasgow & Dundee pillar-boxes tampered with	Not stated	
10 Feb	Telegraph & telephone wires cut in west of Scotland	Suspension of services	
14 Feb	Damage to plate-glass case in Royal Scottish Museum	Not stated	
20 Feb	Over a score of Edinburgh and Leith pillar-boxes tampered with	Over 1000 letters damaged	

TABLE 2   275

DATE IN PRESS	NATURE OF ATTACK	ESTIMATED DAMAGE	ARRESTS if any
21 Feb	2 further Edinburgh letter-boxes tampered with	Not stated	
24 Feb	Edinburgh pillar-box tampered with	Not stated	
25 Feb	Letter-boxes in Kirklees district of Glasgow tampered with	Not stated	
3 Mar	Pillar-box attacks in Aberdeen and Edinburgh	Not stated	
8 Mar	Telegraph wires cut between Glasgow and Kilmarnock	Not stated	
8 Mar	Edinburgh pillar-boxes tampered with	Not stated	
7 Apr	Attempt to set fire to Kelso racecourse stand	None	Arabella Scott, Agnes & Elizabeth Thomson, Edith Hudson
7 Apr	Ayr racecourse stand Destroyed by fire	£2000 (DC) £3500 (GH)	
7 Apr	10 windows of a branch of Labour Exchange in Glasgow broken	Not stated	
7 Apr	Attempt to set fire to Dundee lawn tennis pavilion	None	
7 Apr	Glasgow pillar-box attack	Not stated	
9 Apr	Edinburgh and Glasgow pillar-box attacks	Not stated	
10 Apr	Dye poured into Dundee letter-box	c.30 letters damaged	
12 Apr	Glasgow pillar-box attacks	Not stated	
15 Apr	Glasgow Bellahouston bowling green cut up	Not stated	
16 Apr	Motor car sent by train to Montrose had screen smashed, horn indented and one tyre punctured	Not stated	

DATE IN PRESS	NATURE OF ATTACK	ESTIMATED DAMAGE	ARRESTS if any
28 Apr	Perthshire cricket club, Perth, destroyed by fire	£1250	
2 May	Bomb discovered in Dundee billiard room	None	
3 May	Ashley Road school, Aberdeen, set on fire	£1500 (ED) £500 (S)	
7 May	Edinburgh pillar-boxes attacked	Not state	
11 May	Farington Hall, Dundee, burnt down	£10,000 (DC,S) £15-17,000 (DA)	
16 May	Home-made bomb found in Duke of Buccleuch's private chapel, Dalkeith	None	
21 May	Black oily liquid dropped in Edinburgh pillar-box	8 letters damaged	
22 May	Bomb exploded in Royal Observatory, Blackford Hill, Edinburgh	£100	
2 Jun	Fire at Shields Road Railway Station, Glasgow	None	
10 Jun	Glasgow pillar-box attacks	Not stated	
13 Jun	Stair Park House, Tranent burned	Not stated	
14 Jun	Corrosive fluid poured into 5 Edinburgh pillar-boxes	Not stated	
23 Jun	East wing of Gatty Marine Laboratory, University of St Andrews, destroyed by fire	£500	
27 Jun	Extensive attack on Dundee pillar-boxes	Not stated	
1 Jul	Leuchars railway station destroyed by fire	£2000 (DC,S0) £1500 (DA)	
1 Jul	Ballikinrain Castle, Killearn, destroyed by fire	£70,000 (S) £100,000 (DA)	
25 Jul	Attempt to set fire to Glasgow house	None	'Margaret Morrison', Dorothea Chalmers Smith

TABLE 2 277

DATE IN PRESS	NATURE OF ATTACK	ESTIMATED DAMAGE	ARRESTS if any
22 Aug	Fire at Moreland House, Grange Loan, Edinburgh	£250	
23 Aug	Fire at Fettes College, Edinburgh	Not stated	
20 Sep	40 holes dug in Airthly Bowling Green, Bridge of Allan	Not stated	
27 Sep	3 greens on Kilspindie golf links damaged by large circular holes cut in turf	Not stated	
6 Dec	Mansion-house of Kelly on Firth of Clyde destroyed by fire	£30,000	
1914			
23 Jan	Cushions destroyed by corrosive fluid in an Edinburgh local train	Not stated	
26 Jan	Bomb at Kibble Palace, Botanic Gardens, Glasgow	Slight	
30 Jan	Bonnington House, Lanark, complete gutted	Originally valued £18,000	
5 Feb	House of Ross, Perthshire, destroyed by fire	Not stated	
5 Feb	Allt-an-Phionn mansion, St Fillans, Perthshire, destroyed by fire	£3000-£4000	'Rhoda Robinson'
5 Feb	Aberuchill Castle, Perthshire, destroyed by fire	Not stated	
27 Feb	Whitekirk church destroyed by fire	£8000-£10,000	
13 Mar	Two plate-glass windows broken at military re-cruiting office, Glasgow	£20	Helen Crawfurd
13 Mar	Mansion-house of Robertland, Ayrshire, extensively damaged by fire	£1600	

DATE IN PRESS	NATURE OF ATTACK	ESTIMATED DAMAGE	ARRESTS if any
4 Apr	Attempt to set fire to mansion-house of Springhall, Rutherglen	None	Frances Gordon
4 Apr	Attempt made to blow up Belmont parish church, Glasgow	None	
23 May	Hospital for Women, Dundee, destroyed by fire	Not stated	
25 May	Attempt to blow up Glasgow water main pipe from Loch Katrine	None	
25 May	Portrait of King slashed at Royal Academy	Not stated	Maude Edwards
6 Jun	Attempt to bomb Dudhope Castle, Dundee	None	
8 Jun	Wood plantation on Tombuie set on fire	Not stated	'Rhoda Robinson' Jane Lynas
9 Jul	Attempt to blow up Burns Cottage, Alloway	None	'Janet Arthur'
10 Jul	Chemical poured into 5 Dundee letter-boxes	Not stated	
14 Jul	Bomb exploded in Rosslyn Chapel, damaged window	Slight	
15 Jul	Attempt to burn new school at Lanark	Slight	

Bibliography

Primary Source Material

MISCELLANEOUS
Aberdeen rectorial election publications 1908 (*The Premier, Alma Mater, The Suffragette*), Department of Special Collections, Aberdeen University Library.
Janie Allan collection, National Library of Scotland.
Arncliffe-Sennett collection, British Library.
Autograph Letter collection (and other miscellaneous letters), Fawcett Library, City of London Polytechnic.
Balfour collection, Scottish Record Office.
Memories of Miss I. Carrie, Dundee Archive and Record Centre.
The Chartist Circular, Glasgow, 1840–42.
Helen Crawfurd's unpublished autobiography, Marx Memorial Library, London (copy available at Gallagher Library, STUC Headquarters, Glasgow).
Edinburgh National Society for Women's Suffrage annual reports (1876, 1879, 1892, 1893, 1903), Fawcett Library, City of London Polytechnic, National Library of Scotland, Manchester City Library.
Edinburgh Review, Vols. 57 and 73 (1833 and 1841).
Glasgow High Court records, Scottish Record Office.
Glasgow and West of Scotland Association for Women's Suffrage minute books 1902–18, letter books 1913–18, Department of Rare Books and Manuscripts, Mitchell Library, Glasgow.
Haldane papers, National Library of Scotland.
Letters to me from individuals as cited in text.
L.S.W.S. collection (Edinburgh to London march), Fawcett Library, City of London Polytechnic.
McIntosh Album 6, St Andrews University Library archive department.
Catherine Marshall papers, Cumbria Record Office, Carlise.
Miscellaneous suffrage material, Manchester City Library.
Miscellaneous suffrage material, National Library of Scotland.
Lilias Mitchell, 'Suffrage Days' (in private hands).
Roland E. Muirhead collection, Department of Rare Books and Manuscripts, Mitchell Library, Glasgow.

Roland E. Muirhead papers, National Library of Scotland.

Eunice Murray's diary 1908-14 (in private hands).

N.U.W.S.S. National Executive committee minutes, Fawcett Library, City of London Polytechnic.

Scottish Co-operative Women's Guild annual reports, Strathclyde Regional Archive.

Scottish Federation executive committee minutes 1913-14, Scottish Women's Hospitals Collection, Department of Rare Books and Manuscripts, Mitchell Library, Glasgow.

Scottish Office miscellaneous files (Dundee Suffragettes and Arrest of Mrs Pankhurst), Scottish Record Office.

Scottish Office Prison Commission files, Scottish Record Office.

Scottish Women's Liberal Federation minute books 1893-1914, Department of Rare Books and Manuscripts, Edinburgh University Library.

Shetland Suffrage Society minutes, Shetland archive.

Smiths of Jordanhill papers, Strathclyde Regional Archive.

Suffragette Fellowship collection, Museum of London.

Town Council minutes: Edinburgh 1910-14, City of Edinburgh Archive. Glasgow 1910-14, Strathclyde Regional Archive. Kirkwall, 1910-14, Orkney Archive.

The True Scotsman, Edinburgh 1838-9.

Suffrage Material donated by Miss R. Watt, Aberdeen Art Gallery and Museum.

Women's Freedom League National Executive Committee minutes and annual conference reports, Fawcett Library, City of London Polytechnic.

ORAL HISTORY

Tape-recorded interview with Elizabeth Somerville 28 November 1989.

Brian Harrison interview with Helen Fraser Moyes 19 August 1975, Harrison tapes collection, Fawcett Library, City of London Polytechnic.

Brian Harrison interview with Jessie Stephen 1 July 1977, Harrison tapes collection, Fawcett Library, City of London Polytechnic.

Brian Harrison interviews concerning Anna Munro, Harrison tapes collection, Fawcett Library, City of London Polytechnic.

Miscellaneous brief interviews as cited in text.

PAMPHLETS

Hardie, Keir. *The Citizenship of Women. A Plea for Women's Suffrage* (London 1906).

Jamieson, Christina. *Sketch of Votes for Women Movement* (privately printed, n.d. — available at Shetland archive).

Johnston, Thomas. *The Case for Women's Suffrage and Objections Answered.* (Glasgow n.d. c.1907).

Murray, Eunice. *Prejudices Old and New* (Scottish Council of Women's Freedom League, Edinburgh and Glasgow n.d.)

Murray, Eunice. *Liberal Cant* (Women's Freedom League, London n.d.)

Murray, Eunice. *Woman The New Discovery* (Women's Freedom League, London n.d.)

GENERAL PRESS

Aberdeen Daily Journal 1907-14.

Aberdeen Free Press 1907-14.

Dundee Advertiser 1909-14.*Dundee Courier* 1909-14.

Edinburgh Evening Dispatch 1907-17.
Forward 1906-14.
Glasgow Herald miscellaneous 19th century dates and 1907-14.
Orkney Herald miscellaneous 19th century dates and 1912-14.
The Scotsman 1907-14.
Miscellaneous individual issues of other journals as cited in text.

WOMEN'S JOURNALS
The Anti-Suffrage Review 1909-17.
The Attempt 1865-74.
The Common Cause 1909-15.
The Englishwoman's Review 1866-9 and 1880-1910.
The Ladies' Edinburgh Magazine 1875-80.
The Lady's Review of Reviews 1901.
The Suffragette 1912-14.
The Vote 1909-15.
Votes for Women 1907-14.
Woman's/Worker's Dreadnought 1914-18.
Women's Franchise 1907-9.
Women's Progress 1907.
Women's Suffrage Journal 1870-90.
Women's Suffrage Record 1903-6.

Secondary Source Marterial (including autobiographies of individuals involved in the movement)

Alberti, Johanna. *Beyond Suffrage. Feminists in War and Peace, 1914-28.* (London 1989).
Anderson, R.D. *The Student Community at Aberdeen 1860-1939* (Aberdeen 1988).
Balfour, Lady Frances. *Ne Obliviscaris Dinna Forget* (London 1930).
Banks, Olive. *Faces of Feminism* (Oxford 1981).
Banks, Olive. *The Biographical Dictionary of British Feminists Vol.1 1800-1930* (Brighton 1987).
Banks, Olive. *Becoming a Feminist: The Social Origins of "First Wave" Feminism* (Brighton 1987).
Bell, Enid H.C.M. *Storming the Citadel: The Rise of the Woman Doctor* (London 1953).
Billington, Rosamund. 'The women's education and suffrage movements, 1850-1914: innovation and institutionalisation' (unpublished Ph.D. thesis, Hull 1976).
Billington, Rosamund. 'Women, Politics and Local Liberalism: from "Female Suffrage" to "Votes for Women",' *Journal of Regional and Local Studies* Vol.5, No.1, spring 1985.
Billington-Greig, Teresa. *The Militant Suffrage Movement* (London n.d. c.1911]).
Bingham, Robert LeBaron. 'The Glasgow Emancipation Society 1833-76' (unpublished M.Litt. thesis, Glasgow 1973).

Blackburn, Helen. *Women's Suffrage: a record of the women's suffrage movement in the British Isles* (London & Oxford 1902).

Buchan, A. *History of the Scottish Co-Operative Women's Guild 1892-1913* (Glasgow 1913).

Burton, Katherine, ed. *A Memoir of Mrs Crudelius* (Edinburgh 1897).

Calder, Jenni. 'Heroes and Hero-makers: Women in Nineteenth-Century Scottish Fiction' in D. Gifford, ed. *The History of Scottish Literature Vol.3* (Aberdeen 1988).

Corr, Helen. 'The Schoolgirls' Curriculum and the Ideology of the Home, 1870-1914' in Glasgow Women's Studies Group, *Uncharted Lives: Extracts from Scottish Women's Experiences, 1850-1932* (Glasgow 1983).

Corr, Helen. 'The gender division of labour in the Scottish teaching profession 1872-1914, with particular reference to elementary school teaching' (unpublished Ph.D. thesis, Edinburgh 1984).

Corr, Helen.''Home-Rule' in Scotland: The Teaching of Housework in Schools 1872-1914' in J. Fevell and F. Paterson eds. *Girls in their Prime: Scottish Education Revisited* (Edinburgh forthcoming).

Dangerfield, George. *The Strange Death of Liberal England* (London 1966 edition).

Dunlop, John. *Autobiography* Dunlop Papers, [V.1] (London 1932).

Fawcett, Millicent Garrett. *What I Remember* (London 1924).

Ferguson, William. *Scotland 1689 to the Present* (Edinburgh and London 1968).

Fulford, Roger. *Votes for Women — The Story of a Struggle* (London 1957).

Garner, Les. *Stepping Stones to Women's Liberty* (London 1984).

Haldane, E.S. *From One Century to Another* (London 1937).

Hamilton, Sheila. 'The First Generations of University Women 1869-1930' in Gordon Donaldson ed. *Four Centuries — Edinburgh University Life* (Edinburgh 1983).

Harrison, Brian. *Separate Spheres: The Opposition to Women's Suffrage in Britain* (London 1978).

Harrison, Brian. 'Women's Health and the Women's Movement in Britain: 1840-1940' in Charles Webster ed. *Biology, Medicine and Society* (Brighton 1981).

Harrison, Brian. 'The Act of Militancy. Violence and the Suffragettes, 1904-1914' in his *Peaceable Kingdom: Stability and Change in Modern Britain* (Oxford 1982).

Harrison, Brian. 'Women's Suffrage at Westminster 1866-1928' in Michael Bentley and John Stevenson eds. *High and Low Politics in Modern Britain: Ten Studies* (Oxford 1983).

Harrison, Brian. *Prudent Revolutionaries — Portraits of British Feminists between the Wars* (Oxford 1987).

Holton, Sandra Stanley. *Feminism and Democracy* (Cambridge 1986).

Hume, Leslie Parker. *The National Union of Women's Suffrage Societies 1897-1914.* (New York 1982).

Jalland, Pat. *Women, Marriage and Politics, 1860-1914* (Oxford 1986).

Jenkins, Roy. *Asquith* (London 1967 edition).

Jones, David. 'Women and Chartism', *History* 68 (1983).

Kent, Susan Kingsley. *Sex and Suffragism in Britain 1860-1914* (Princeton 1987).

King, Elspeth. *The Scottish Women's Suffrage Movement* (Glasgow 1978).

Knox, William ed. *Scottish Labour Leaders 1918-1939* (Edinburgh 1984).

Laurence, M. *Shadow of Swords, a biography of Elsie Inglis* (London 1971).

Leggett, Jane. *Local Heroines: a woman's history gazeteer to England, Scotland and Wales* (London 1988).

Liddington, Jill. 'The Women's Peace Crusade: The History of a Forgotten Campaign' in Dorothy Thompson ed., *Over Our Dead Bodies: Women Against the Bomb* (London 1983).

Liddington, Jill and Norris, Jill. *One Hand Tied Behind Us: The Rise of the Women's Suffrage Movement* (London 1978).

Linklater, Andro. *An Unhusbanded Life* (London 1980).

Logan, James. 'The East of Scotland Suffragist/Suffragette Movement 1900-1914' (unpublished Open University essay 1977).

Lumsden, Louisa Innes. *Yellow Leaves — Memories of a Long Life* (Edinburgh and London 1933).

Mackenzie, Midge. *Shoulder to Shoulder: A Documentary* (London 1975).

Mackie, J.B. *Life and Work of Duncan McLaren* (London 1888).

Marshall, Rosalind. *Virgins and Viragos* (London 1983).

Metcalfe, A.E. *Woman's Effort* (Oxford 1917).

Mitchell, David J. *The Fighting Pankhursts: A Study in Tenacity* (London 1967).

Mitchell, David J. *Queen Christabel* (London 1977).

Mitchell, Geoffrey, ed. *The Hard Way Up. The Autobiography of Hannah Mitchell, Suffragette and Rebel* (London 1968).

Moffat, Graham. *Join Me in Remembering — The Life and Reminiscences of the Author of "Bunty Pulls the Strings"* (privately printed 1955).

Moore, Lindy. 'Feminists and Femininity: A Case Study of WSPU Propaganda and Local Response at a Scottish Bye-Election' in *Women's Studies International Forum* Vol.5, No.6 (1982).

Moore, Lindy. 'The women's suffrage campaign in the 1907 Aberdeen by-election' in *Northern Scotland* Vol.5, No.2 (1983).

Morgan, David. *Suffragists and Liberals* (Oxford 1975).

Morgan, K.O. *Keir Hardie: Radical and Socialist* (London 1975).

Morley, Ann with Stanley, Liz. *The Life and Death of Emily Wilding Davison* (London 1989).

Morrow, Bob. 'We Want the Vote' in *Scots Magazine* June 1988.

Murphy, Cliona. *The Women's Suffrage Movement and Irish Society in the Early Twentieth Century* (Hemel Hempstead 1989).

Neale, R.S. 'Working-class women and women's suffrage' in his *Class and Ideology in the Nineteenth Century* (London and Boston 1972).

Newbury, J.V. 'Anti-War Suffragists', *History* 62 (1977).

Newsome, Sandra. *The Women's Freedom League 1907-1957.* (London 1958).

Owens, Rosemary Cullen. *Smashing Times. A History of the Irish Women's Suffrage Movement 1889-1922* (Dublin 1984).

Pankhurst, Christabel. *Unshackled* (London 1959).

Pankhurst, E. Sylvia. *The Suffragette* (London 1911).

Pankhurst, E. Sylvia. *The Suffragette Movement: An Intimate Account of Persons and Ideals* (London 1931).

Pentland, Marjorie. *A Bonnie Fechter. Life of the Marchioness of Aberdeen* (London 1952).

Phillips, Mary. *The Militant Suffrage Campaign in Perspective* (London 1956).

Pugh, M.D. 'Politics and the women's vote' *History* 59 (1974).

Pugh, M.D. *Women's Suffrage in Britain 1867-1928* (London 1980).

R., A.J. ed. *The Suffrage Annual and Women's Who's Who* (London 1913).

Rae, Lettice Milne ed. *Ladies in Debate: Being a History of the Ladies' Edinburgh Debating Society 1865-1935* (Edinburgh 1936).

Raeburn, Antonia. *The Militant Suffragettes* (London 1973).

Raeburn, Antonia. *The Suffragette View* (Newton Abbot 1976).

Ramelson, Marian. *The Petticoat Rebellion* (London 1967).

Recollections of the Public Work and Home Life of Louisa and Flora Stevenson (privately printed, Edinburgh n.d.).

Reid, Marion. *A Plea for Woman* (Edinburgh 1988 edition).

Rendall, Jane. *The Origins of Modern Feminism* (London 1985).

Rendall, Jane ed. *Equal or Different: Women's Politics 1800-1914* (Oxford 1987).

Rendel, Margherita. 'The Contribution of the Woman's Labour League to the Winning of the Franchise' in Lucy Middleton, ed. *Women in the Labour Movement: The British Experience* (London 1977).

Reynolds, Siân. *Britannica's Typesetters. Women Compositors in Edwardian Edinburgh* (Edinburgh 1989).

Rice, C. Duncan. *The Scots Abolitionists 1833-1861* (Baton Rouge 1981).)

Richardson, Mary. *Laugh a Defiance* (London 1953).

Rosen, Andrew. *Rise Up Women! The Militant Campaign of the Women's Social and Political Union 1903-14* (London 1974).

Rover, Constance. *Women's Suffrage and Party Politics in Britain 1866-1914* (London 1967).

Rowbotham, Sheila. *Hidden from History* (London 1973).

Rubinstein, David. *Before the Suffragettes* (Brighton 1986).

Shepley, Nigel. *Women of Independent Mind. St George's School, Edinburgh and the Campaign for Women's Education 1888-1988* (Edinburgh 1988).

Strachey, Ray. *The Cause: A Short History of the Women's Movement in Great Britain* (London 1928).

Strauss, Sylvia. *"Traitors to the Masculine Cause" The Men's Campaigns for Women's Rights* (Westport, Conn. 1982).

Taylor, Barbara. *Eve and the New Jerusalem* (London 1983).

Thompson, Dorothy. 'Women and Nineteenth Century Radical Politics: A Lost Dimension' in Juliet Mitchell and Ann Oakley eds. *The Rights and Wrongs of Women* (Harmondsworth 1976).

Thompson, Dorothy. *The Chartists* (London 1984).

Tickner, Lisa. *The Spectacle of Women: Imagery of the Suffragette Campaign 1907-14* (London 1988).

Vicinus, Martha. 'Male Space and Women's Bodies: The Suffragette Movement' in her *Independent Women: Work and Community for Single Women, 1850-1920* (Chicago 1985).

Watson, Elspeth Janet Boog. *Edinburgh Association for the University Education of Women 1867-1967* (Edinburgh n.d.).

Watson, William N. Boog. 'The First Eight Ladies', *University of Edinburgh Journal* (XXIII No.3 spring 1968).

Welsh, B.V. *After the Dawn: A Record of the Pioneer Work in Edinburgh for the Higher Education of Women* (London 1933).

Wilson, Alexander. *The Chartist Movement in Scotland* (Manchester 1970).

Wiltsher, Ann. *Most Dangerous Women — Feminist Peace Campaigners of the Great War* (London 1984).

Wright, L.G. *Scottish Chartism* (Edinburgh 1953).

Young, James D. *Women and Popular Struggles: A History of Scottish and English Working Class Women, 1500-1984* (Edinburgh 1985).

Index